Fifty Year~
Big Secrets an

There is much ado about polygamy these days. Media coverage, HBO's *Big Love*, TLC's *Sister Wives*, the revolting acts committed by polygamous cult leader Warren Jeffs who still directs his followers from his prison cell—all of these keep a slew of polygamy-related issues at the forefront of society. But none can depict the ongoing, daily atrocities and heartaches hidden in these closed societies, behind closed doors, within the hearts and souls of thousands of subdued but smiling faces.

Kristyn Decker's memoir recounts the harsh realities of being born and raised in the second largest polygamist sect in America—the Apostolic United Brethren, or the AUB (Allred Group). For five decades, Kristyn (then Sophia Allred) was caught up in a cult of plural marriage . . . and lived it until she thought she would truly suffocate. When she finally had the courage to leave, she knew she had to share her story and help others escape.

This uncensored version of *Fifty Years in Polygamy: Big Secrets and Little White Lies*, even more than her first book describes the religious submission, lies, secrets, poverty, abuses, jealousies, depression, and loneliness. The gripping, detailed events in this book will shock you, but will also inspire compassion, understanding, and perhaps even the courage to change your own life.

Reviews of *Fifty Years in Polygamy*

"Incredible! No other words to describe this book but incredible. Very well-written account of a life of extreme abuse, emotional anguish, and mental torture. The strength it must have taken to break away from this lifestyle is inspiring. May it be a guideline and a shining star for everyone who wants insight into polygamy and for those who seek an avenue outside of the 'crick.'" —Badbob52 on Amazon.com

"Love it! I love to read, and this book opened my eyes to a world that I have never been a part of. It's sad to see the suffering of the woman in the book, but it is so well written." —Cheryl Mcendree on Amazon.com

"I couldn't stop reading. I really enjoyed this book. I often had to tell myself to slow down. Once I started reading I couldn't stop. It's fascinating to realize that kind of lifestyle is still being lived. I could truly feel the hurt and jealousy this woman felt and that she was torn by what she thought was the right thing to do. What an amazing story and what an amazing woman! She tells it like it is, and she is really involved helping people." —CSW on Amazon.com

"An amazing read! It's always amazing to me to read about the lives of polygamists. This one did not disappoint! It took me just a short time to get through this book. It was well written, and I felt like I was right there experiencing the horror of their lifestyle." —Yaker and Baller on Amazon.com

"Real polygamy. I thoroughly enjoyed this true-life story about an admirable woman growing up in polygamy. Her poignant story had me sitting on the edge of my seat, and I had a hard time putting the book down. This book contains many nuggets of wisdom and exposes many of the effects of being raised in an unrealistic, perfectionistic lifestyle. If you are looking for social/historical data or just wish to read a really good story, this book is a win." —Clairvina on Amazon.com

"Recommended. I loved this book! The story was the raw truth about the dysfunction of life for everyone in the grips of a polygamous lifestyle. Kristyn did a great job of telling it like it really is: painful; destructive, and mind twisting." —KB on Amazon.com

Fifty Years in
POLYGAMY

Big Secrets and Little White Lies

UNCENSORED EDITION

KRISTYN DECKER

Best wishes for genuine love, light + happiness always.
Namaste,
Kristyn Decker

Synergy Books Publishing
USA

Synergy Books Publishing
P .O. Box 911232
St. George, Utah 84791
www.synergy-books.com

Author photos by Tolga Katas
Cover design by Christine Katas

ISBN: 978-1-936434-52-7

Printed in the United States of America

Contents

Acknowledgments   ix

Foreword   xi

Preface   xiii

Chapter 1: Curtains Wide Open—The Beginning   1

Chapter 2: Mom's Devils   6

Chapter 3: Like a Piece of Dirty Garbage   14

Chapter 4: The Drill   24

Chapter 5: Plygville   36

Chapter 6: My Salvation   52

Chapter 7: Bad and Stupid Sophia   64

Chapter 8: Our Catastrophes   74

Chapter 9: Foes and Shame   79

Chapter 10: New Friends, Mother, and Siblings   84

Chapter 11: Modesty and Vanity on "The Outside"   93

Chapter 12: Men, Boys, and Confusion   98

Chapter 13: Featherweight and Cougar Speed   105

Chapter 14: "Independents" and My First Love   115

Chapter 15: High School Angst   124

Chapter 16: Legally and Religiously Married   136

Chapter 17: A Meal Fit for a Queen   149

Chapter 18: Birth Control and Girls' Camp Anxiety   161

Chapter 19: Evil Ervil   168

Chapter 20: Plural Wives and Death in Childbirth   172

Chapter 21: Guns and Murder   183

Chapter 22: Courtship and a Sister-Wife   193

Chapter 23: Nothing Sacred in This   203

Chapter 24: Poverty and Dumpster Diving   215

Chapter 25: Temple Ordinances and Blessings   221

Chapter 26: Cremation or Burial   227

Chapter 27: Infidelity in Polygamy   234
Chapter 28: Guilt and Punishment   247
Chapter 29: A Friendship from God   256
Chapter 30: Births, Death, and Suicide   266
Chapter 31: Forbidden Friendships   276
Chapter 32: Demoted to Nothingness   286
Chapter 33: Courage to Heal or Die   294
Chapter 34: Reconciliation   307
Chapter 35: Our Honeymoon and Questions for God   318
Chapter 36: Work, College, and Mom's Confessions   331
Chapter 37: Religious Perpetrators   340
Chapter 38: Life and Runaway Karleen   345
Chapter 39: Court-Appointed Recovery   357
Chapter 40: Test Angst and College   363
Chapter 41: Following My Dreams   369
Chapter 42: Cedar City and My Mother's Death   380
Chapter 43: Calling It Quits   391
Chapter 44: Leaving My Sanctuary   400
Chapter 45: Burning Bridges   414
Chapter 46: For Better or For Worse   419
Chapter 47: Places in Hell   427
Chapter 48: Enough Is Enough   438
Chapter 49: What Happened Next   451

Afterword   461

About the Author   467

Fifty Years in
POLYGAMY

Big Secrets and Little White Lies

UNCENSORED EDITION

Acknowledgments

My first and foremost acknowledgment is to my wonderful husband LeRoy, who after six incredible years together never ceases to amaze me with his devotion, love, and encouragement. He supports my every endeavor, whether it is writing or reading; spending time with our children, grandchildren, and friends; advocating for those who are leaving and have left polygamy; as director of the Sound Choices Coalition; or anything else. LeRoy was the backbone that held me securely together while I wrote of the heartaches of my past life in my first book, *Fifty Years in Polygamy*. While preparing for this book to be published, whenever I've doubted my capabilities, felt overwhelmed with life's lessons, been too emotional while trying to help rescue children and help free those who are busy fighting for the legalization or decriminalization of the bondage of polygamy, my sweetheart man has cheered me onward. Even more amazing to me is that my precious husband cherishes the immense love and adoration I have for him.

Once again, I get to express my immense gratitude for Linda Prince! Without her belief in me, this edition would also be lacking or nonexistent. Since Linda found me at the Apple Fest in 2010 and encouraged and helped me to get my first book published, she's also spent hours on end doing the first edit of this full-length book as well.

There are no words to adequately thank my dear friend Marion and others who've also left polygamy. They've contributed first-hand knowledge that gave more substance to the reality of my own life stories and of those who are still inside. They helped with dates, places, input, and advice for this uncensored version of my book.

I'm extremely grateful for the front-cover photography provided by Voices for Dignity (www.voicesfordignity.com) and renowned photographer Tolga Katas.

As always and forever, much love, appreciation, and honor goes to all of my family and loved ones, whether by blood or by heart. My experiences were both lessons and joys in this lifetime that would never have been the same without you.

Lastly, to all of my dear friends, acquaintances, and supporters whose names are not listed here only because it would consume many pages to do so: from the bottom of my heart, a tremendous amount of thanks for your constant inspiration and interest in my first book and now the rest of my life stories.

Thank you so much for reading and for caring.

Foreword

What courage it took for Kristyn Decker to write about her experiences in polygamy. Only those who have been trapped in this lifestyle can relate to the mental anguish she and countless others have endured.

After five, and seven, generations of brainwashing, we both were lulled into a religious coma, becoming paralyzed by the psychological threats of destruction from birth. Therefore we learned to remain sweet and silent. We dared not speak out for fear we would "betray the brethren." The leaders uttered the edicts threatening hell and damnation if we did not adhere to strict obedience, so we learned to comply with their religious demands.

Kristyn and I were both pawns in the scheme of polygamy. Unless you have stomached this experience, you can never understand the heartaches, disappointment, and oppression of being spiritually blackmailed into sharing your husband with other women.

I praise the book *FIFTY YEARS in POLYGAMY: Big Secrets and Little White Lies* for revealing the manipulation and hopelessness polygamist wives and children are subjected to. Thank you, Kristyn—for being a voice in the wilderness, for helping women in polygamy realize their freedom has been withheld, and they really can be free to make their own sound choices.

Through the efforts of this amazing woman, and others who dare speak the truth, anyone who has believed polygamy is really a choice can learn the difference, so they can also help thousands of religiously oppressed women and children become educated and gain respect for themselves. In this, we hope they'll become fearless and free—discovering their own worth so they will no longer be held physically, mentally and spiritually captive.

I join Kristyn as we raise our voices high, aim to be beacons of light, and campaign for the freedom of all women and children who have been and are still being abused.

–Irene Spencer, *New York Times* bestselling author of
Shattered Dreams: My Life as a Polygamist's Wife
(www.irenespencerbooks.com)

Preface

Between 1830 and 1844, Joseph Smith Jr. (founder of The Church of Jesus Christ of Latter-day Saints) taught that plural marriage was ordained of God. He also practiced plural marriage, but did so discreetly because he was concerned about repercussions from outsiders and the general public. His death was partly due to the fact that his sexual practices were discovered. Some of the men whose daughters were approached by Joseph Smith were incensed.

He first wrote of the revelation on plural marriage on July 12, 1843, and taught the principle more frequently until his death less than a year later. In 1852, LDS Apostle Orson Pratt was asked by Brigham Young to publicly declare that plural marriages were part of the new and everlasting covenant of God (see Doctrine and Covenants [Salt Lake City, Utah: The Church of Jesus Christ of Latter-day Saints], Section 132.) Joseph Smith's controversial revelation on polygamy drew contempt and hatred toward the LDS Church from around the world.

After Joseph Smith's assassination in June 1844, Mormons—including my great-great-grandfather—found solace and strength in the influential leadership of Brigham Young. Between 1847 and Young's death in 1877, Mormons in Utah were somewhat successful at evading the United States Government's attempts to abolish polygamy.

On September 24, 1890, under continued pressure from his followers and the government, the president of the LDS Church, Wilford Woodruff, published a statement in the *Deseret News* (see Doctrine and Covenants, Official Declaration 1). President Woodruff claimed he had received a revelation from God and stated that anyone who entered into plural marriage after that date would be excommunicated from the Church for "disharmony." This statement was known as the Manifesto.

For quite some time, many LDS Church members were in limbo because of the philosophical conflicts between Joseph Smith's revelation about the principle of plural marriage, and Wilford Woodruff's 1890 Manifesto forbidding Church members to practice it. Many members of the Church wouldn't uphold the Manifesto and continued to practice plural marriage and to teach and advocate its necessity here on earth.

Most Fundamentalists supported John W. Woolley (1918–1928), Lorin C. Woolley (1928–1934), J. Leslie Broadbent (1934–1935), John Y. Barlow (1935–1949), and Joseph W. Musser (1949–1954) as their priesthood leaders. These men commenced to gather a congregation of like believers and began calling themselves the Council of Friends.

Following the division in the Council of Friends (set in motion sometime between 1948 and 1951 and explained later in this book), my family continued to uphold Joseph Musser. After Musser's death in 1954, my uncle, Rulon C. Allred, became the president of those who were identified as the Allred Group. Years later, the congregation began referring to themselves as The Priesthood, or The Work, and subsequently assumed their current title, the Apostolic United Brethren (AUB).

After Rulon C. Allred was murdered in 1977, my father, Owen Arthur Allred, Rulon's first counselor, became the priesthood leader of the Allred Group until his death in 2005. LaMoine Jensen is the current president of the AUB.

As the Council of Friends came to a close, and after John Y. Barlow's death, Charles Zitting (1954), Leroy S. Johnson (1954–1986), and Rulon T. Jeffs (1986–2002) led the Short Creek Group. Years before, and after Rulon Jeffs' death, his son Warren Jeffs assumed the title of "Godhead" with his current adherents, who called themselves Fundamentalist Latter-day Saints, and now the United Order.

Since the LDS Church's Manifesto, hundreds of converts have joined self-proclaimed demi-gods and polygamist factions, while hundreds have left the polygamist groups. Obviously, those whose families have practiced polygamy for generations, and who have had it programmed into their brains, are more stalwart in their belief in polygamy.

Currently, the three largest polygamist sects are:

- The Apostolic United Brethren or AUB (formerly the Allred Group) in Salt Lake County, Harvest Haven, Eagle Mountain, Mayfield, Cedar City, Rocky Ridge, Mount Pleasant, and the Granite Ranch (beyond Delta), in Utah; Pinesdale, Montana; and Ozumba, Mexico: approximately 7,500 members.
- The Short Creek Group, the Fundamentalist Church of Jesus Christ of Latter-day Saints or FLDS (and now the United Order), in Hildale, Utah; Colorado City, Arizona; Pringle, South Dakota; Wyoming; Nevada; Texas, and Canada; as well as break-off groups in Bountiful, Canada; and Centennial Park (The Work), Arizona: approximately 12,450 members.
- Independent polygamists scattered across the Salt Lake Valley and elsewhere: approximately15,000 members.

Smaller polygamist groups comprise:
- The LeBarons (the Church of the Lamb of God): approximately 500 members.
- The Kingstons (the Latter Day Church of Christ, or Davis County Cooperative): approximately 2,000 members.
- The Missouri Community: approximately 500 members.
- The Nielsens/Naylors: approximately 300 members.
- The Petersons (Righteous Branch of Jesus Christ of Latter-day Saints): approximately 200 members.
- James Harmston/TLC (True and Living Church of Jesus Christ of Saints of the Last Days): approximately 150 members.

The above numbers come from reports in the (Utah State) Safety Net's Primer in April 2011. However, the TOTAL of 40,500 polygamists is an extremely inaccurate figure. My father had close to 200 grandchildren when he died. If all 200 of those grandchildren remained Fundamentalists and on a low average had only seven children each, that would give Dad 1,400 great grandchildren. Those figures don't include the great-grandchildren my nephews have fathered with other wives. But I'm grateful to say, many have not stayed in polygamy. Therefore, assuming only one-half of those great-grandchildren have stayed, or will stay, Dad's polygamist posterity today would total around 700. Keep in mind this figure comes from only one-half of Dad's posterity. Multiply 700 by only 100 polygamist men of my father's generation, many of which had much larger families than his, for a total of at least 70,000 members of the AUB sect, let alone all the rest of the polygamist population across the county.

CHAPTER 1

Curtains Wide Open—
The Beginning

On our front porch, which also served as our laundry room, I climbed out of Mom's galvanized tin tub, which was half full of cold, murky bathwater and ringed with lye soap residue. The stiff yellow towel that had hung on our clothesline for a whole day felt scratchy around my five-year-old chubby body.

Inside our three-bedroom basement house, photos and memorabilia concealed most of Mom's pastel-blue tricot bedspread. I wanted to sprawl out on the silky softness, but instead I carefully sat on the corner of the bed. As I stared at a five-by-seven picture of a younger version of her, I thought my heart would burst with pride.

"Mom, you look so pretty in this picture!" I said.

She quickly wiped tears from her cheeks and nose.

"What's the matter, Mom?"

"Nothing."

"Then why are you crying?"

"Oh, I don't know. It seems like I'm always crying . . ."

To me, she was beautiful, no matter what her age or whether her eyes glistened with tears of sadness or sparkled with joy.

In her younger years, my mother, Vera Cooke, was a vivacious, slender, blue-eyed blond. She loved to hang out with her friends, attend LDS Church activities, swim, dance, and roller-skate. But most of all she loved to hike.

Listening to her reminisce made me happy. I pictured her wonderful adventures as if they would someday be mine.

"The twelve-mile hike up the steep hill to the Black Canyon Dam was as easy as pie!" Mom told me years later. "I used to pick apples, sell magazine subscriptions, and watch children to earn spending money." Then Mom blushed as she brought her voice to a whisper, maybe so dad couldn't hear. "It was summer, and I was nineteen years old when I fell for Leslie Fenton. He was tall and handsome!" She giggled. "We'd been going together for quite some time when a real pretty girl came up and asked me if I was in love with him. You know what I told her? I was thinking, *Well, I guess I am, in a way*, but the words that suddenly shot right out of my mouth surprised me. 'No, I guess not, so you can have him.'"

Mother sighed. "I wonder who he married and where he's living now. Sometimes I wonder how different my life would be if I had stayed with him in the LDS Church, and not lived plural marriage with your father." After a long pause she said, "Well, you know what, Sophia? I really believe the Lord must have put those words in my mouth to keep me from marrying the wrong man."

In Mom's junior year of high school, her family moved from Emmett, Idaho; to Saint Anthony, Idaho; so they could be near relatives. Mom didn't want to leave her school and friends, so her parents gave her permission to move back to Emmett. There, she worked for her room and board and finished her senior year of high school.

One Sunday, my mother attended church with her aunt and her sister Alice. It just happened to be the LDS meetinghouse where her future husband was teaching the adult Sunday school class.

"When I saw your mom across the room, my heart stopped. I fell head over heels in love with the most beautiful woman on earth," dad often recounted years later.

And each time he would boast about his gorgeous wife, Mom would pipe in, "And Owen Allred was the most handsome young man

I'd ever laid eyes on." Then they'd snuggle and laugh.

A few weeks after my parents' mating dance began, Dad had to leave town to finish a logging contract. The three months he was gone seemed like an eternity to him. His only thoughts were to get back to Emmett where he could be near Vera, who was now his fiancée.

What Mom didn't know about my Dad and his family would change the course of our lives forever. Before long, he took her to meet most of his father's large polygamous family. My paternal grandmother, Mary Evelyn Clark, had been sealed to Byron Harvey Allred "for time and all eternity" as his second plural wife. The sealing was performed by LDS Apostle Anthony W. Ivins. This wedding ceremony took place in Colonia Juarez,, Chihuahua, Mexico, on June 15, 1903, thirteen years after the LDS Church's 1890 Manifesto (see Allred, Byron Harvey Jr. diary, page 68.).

A highly respected man, Byron Harvey Allred was known for his skills, wisdom, and integrity. My grandfather held many important positions in Idaho during his lifetime. Beginning at age twenty-two, he served two years as a state legislator. He was a member of Idaho's Council of Defense during World War I, and a state director of the U.S. Boys' Working Reserve. Grandpa served as Speaker of the Idaho House of Representatives in 1916, and state director of the Family Market in 1917. He aspired to run for U.S. Congress in 1918, but his LDS stake president urged him not to, saying Byron's religious pursuits would not be an exemplary representation of the LDS Church's views.

In one of Mom's recollections, she told me, "Your grandfather Allred encouraged each one of his children to fast and pray to gain their own testimonies as to whether they should remain in the LDS Church, or whether they should live plural marriage. When we were first dating, your father wasn't sure of his own testimony, so he was quite reluctant to talk to me about his parents' religious beliefs and the lifestyle his father and some of his brothers and sisters were secretly living."

My mother said, after she met Owen's parents, his brother Rulon and his three wives, and some of the other siblings, she came to love and trust them. She felt they were honorable, faithful people. All of them accepted her as well. She said they immediately started treating her as if she was already a member of the family. "And you know, Sophia," Mom continued, "nothing about their polygamous lifestyle was repulsive or offensive to me. From the very beginning, I had no prejudices to overcome. I felt like I finally belonged."

As months went by, Rulon and Byron spent many long hours preaching the importance of living polygamy. They answered questions from any and all prospective candidates—including my parents—and influenced many potential converts with their powerful personal testimonies. They also delivered compelling sermons about an alleged eight-hour meeting, which became the theological basis for many Fundamentalists to continue living polygamy after the Manifesto.

Concerning this supposed meeting, Grandpa Allred recorded in his book *A Leaf in Review*: "LDS President John Taylor disclosed to fourteen men and women who were present, the Lord and Joseph Smith had visited him the previous night and directed him concerning his priesthood duties. During the meeting, Taylor ordained and set apart five men to perpetuate the fulness of the gospel (polygamy) outside of the mainstream LDS Church" (ibid, 185–89).

My father proposed to my mother just after her twenty-first birthday in February 1935. Their marriage was solemnized in the LDS temple in Logan, Utah. Luckily for them, their local Church leaders didn't question them about their adherence to the laws prohibiting polygamy. My parents were extremely grateful to fully participate in the LDS temple ceremonies. Afterward, they bought a wedding ring and spent the night at the Eccles Hotel in Logan.

"While we were honeymooning," Mom told me, "your dad's brothers moved our things into a tiny shed they'd fixed up as a bedroom close to Grandmother Allred's house. The first night we got back, just after we had turned out the lights, Dad's coworkers from the sawmill started making a terrible racket outside. They began yelling and rattling tin cans. Minutes later, they crashed through the door and kitchen window. 'Get dressed and come out peaceably or we'll take you to the top of Freeze Out Mountain and make you walk home barefoot,' they yelled.

"Back then all the folks in Emmett gathered in town on Saturday evenings to dance and visit with one another. When someone got married, they would shivaree them. They'd try to separate the bride from the groom as a prank. So that night, right there in front of everyone, the guys unloaded a wheelbarrow, lifted me into it, and told Owen to push it to the end of town and back. He pushed it all right." Mom chuckled. "Your dad ran so fast no one could keep up with him! He kept on going until he ran the two of us right back home."

Mother said she felt supremely happy to be caring for her beloved husband while their testimonies of plural marriage continued to grow. But most of all she looked forward to the birth of her first child.

CHAPTER 2

Mom's Devils
1937–1946

Grandfather Allred died in January 1937, fifteen years before my birth. My parents were in St. Anthony visiting my mother's parents when they received a letter from Grandpa, asking them to rush back to Emmett so he could see them and his six-month-old grandson one last time. They were heartbroken when they found out they were too late.

The day before Grandpa died, he told my grandmother, Mary Evelyn, "I will be going home in a few days—I am going to die."

"Whatever do you mean, Harvey?" Grandma laughed nervously. "You're feeling better now than you have in a long while."

"Can't you understand, Evelyn? It's time for me to go. My father is coming for me tonight." Then Grandpa gamely chased Grandma around the kitchen, pretending to swat her with his rolled-up newspaper. Grandpa died peacefully in the middle of the night.

The same month Grandpa Allred died, my mother lost her two-and-a-half-year-old sister, Ruthie. She had a high fever and was convulsing. Mom's parents searched all day to find a doctor in one of the small towns around Emmett, but were unable to find one. Ruthie died in my Grandmother Cooke's arms.

To add to Mom's stress, she miscarried a few months later. When the doctor gave her morphine for the pain, she had a bad reaction to it. Before she fell asleep, her body began to shake and quiver. Mom's aunt knew something was wrong when she couldn't wake her nearly six hours later. She pounded on my mother's chest and poured water on her face, trying to revive her. Mom finally regained consciousness. Her first horrific reaction to morphine was passed off by the country doctor as "bad luck."

After those three ordeals, Mom was extremely grateful to regain her health and take her first trip from Idaho to Salt Lake City with her mother-in-law, Mary Evelyn. As a lasting testimony to her children, my mother delivered the rundown in her journal:

> *For nearly a week, I had a wonderful time renewing old acquaintances, meeting new converts, and attending religious meetings with them. We toured Temple Square and enjoyed an organ recital in the Tabernacle.*

> *Another one of the highlights of my trip was when Owen's sister, Beth, her husband, and his other two wives took Mother Mary Evelyn and me to see Joseph Musser. That day he related to us his personal testimony of the Eight-Hour Meeting.*

> *The next day when we went back to see Brother Musser again, he gave each of us a patriarchal blessing. When he laid his hands on my head to give me the blessing, I could feel the Spirit of the Lord permeate my whole being. Brother Musser told me of things that would happen in the future. He said God expected much of me, and I should live the "law of Sarah" by giving Owen wives as Sarah in the Bible had given Hagar to her husband for the purpose of bearing children. Brother Musser told me to support my husband in righteousness, and though I may go through many trials and tribulations, God would not give me more trials than I could endure.*

7

Brother Musser said, if I would live up to these things,
I'd have grand blessings and rewards in heaven. As he
spoke, I knew Joseph Musser had been inspired and was
a true prophet of God.

The following April, when Mom was in labor with my sister Lucinda, another doctor gave her a dose of morphine. This time, she nearly died. It was decided she was allergic to the drug, and if it were ever administered to her again, she would not survive.

❦

From approximately 1938 through 1941, polygamist meetings were held in various homes throughout Idaho, the Salt Lake Valley, and in the squalor of Short Creek, Arizona, now known as Colorado City. My parents wanted to move to Salt Lake so they could be closer to their loved ones and a larger community of believers.

Early one morning in January 1942, Mom decided to ask God for direction concerning their dreams of moving. Mother told me, she poured her heart out to God, and He gave her a clear answer: "You will move to Salt Lake City, where you will get to see your sister Alice again." By the end of March, my parents and their three children—Don, Lucinda, and Francine—had moved from Emmett, Idaho, to Salt Lake City, Utah, where they set up camp on the back lawn of Uncle Rulon's large tract of property.

Mom recalled, "Owen commenced to revamp Rulon's huge granary into a nice, big three-bedroom home for us. Meanwhile, I washed all our clothing outside and enjoyed living in the tent, but only on good-weather days." She added, "There were two ponds, two flowing artesian wells, and an outside privy on the property. I was so happy to be there I would sing and dance. But it was near winter before we were able to move into our new house."

During this time, Dad fell in love with one of Mom's closest and dearest friends. Because Mom had gained a testimony that plural marriage was necessary for a person to attain the celestial kingdom in the afterlife, she was eager to follow those religious dictates and encouraged Dad to court her friend Alice.

Alice spent days at a time with my mother, reading, sewing, cooking, and laughing. While the three of them waited for Alice to get a little older, Mom tried to emotionally prepare herself to enter into celestial marriage.

My dad was also courting a young woman named Eleanor. She and Alice had also become very good friends. Since Eleanor was older than Alice, it was decided she would be Dad's second wife, while Alice would plan her wedding for the following June.

Just one month before my brother Luke was born, mother's desire to live the law of Sarah came to fruition. In May 1943, my thirty-year-old mother placed nineteen-year-old Eleanor's right hand into her husband's right hand to symbolize her willingness to give him another wife.

When I asked Mom what happened to Alice—why she never married Dad—Mom said sadly, "Alice came to help me when Luke was born, and we spent a few more hours together, but for some crazy reason, she just up and disappeared."

"The first year after your dad married Eleanor, things went quite well," Mom told me. "Oh, some things were unfair." She tensed up. "But the next few years became my trials from hell!"

By then, Dad had nearly completed the remodeling of the granary into a three-bedroom home. Mom's four children slept in a small bedroom adjacent to her larger one. At the opposite end was Eleanor's room. While Dad took a turn sleeping with his young wife, Mom often found herself in turmoil as the sounds carried through the thin walls.

As my father turned his attentions from his first love, my mother, to Eleanor, his young, dark-haired beauty, he began to demonstrate a marked inability to calm and soothe Mom's anguish. In addition, Mom believed the devil and his imps (on whom she blamed her suppressed jealousy, as well as her feelings of inadequacy and depression) were attacking her soul, and they would surely be the cause of her demise.

Aunt Eleanor, on the other hand, was a light in the dark to Dad. She was happy, attractive, energetic, and strong-willed. Her concern was not for mother or mother's children. After all, she felt they had enjoyed my father's undivided time and attention for seven years, and now it was her turn. She was busy plotting how to gain all of Dad's love and attention for herself, and manipulating him into believing her objectives were for the greater good of the entire family.

Other women living on Uncle Rulon's property became concerned as they observed the unfair situation. They advised Mom to stick up for herself. They told her that to let Eleanor have her way all the time wasn't good for Eleanor's salvation, either.

It was never a part of my mother's nature to manipulate or coerce others. Neither did she have the appropriate skills to assertively defend herself. Therefore, her attempts to make things equal and fair ultimately failed. In fact, the more she tried to express her needs and desires, the more defensive Eleanor became—and the more determined she was to have her own way.

Despite similar trials among other families living plural marriage, the Allred commune was thriving and expanding. Large homes were built on Uncle Rulon's property, or older homes refurbished for more close relatives. Over the next few months, Dad, Mom, Eleanor, and their children painted their house, planted a garden, installed appliances, and added an indoor bathroom.

❧

In the spring of 1944, my grandmother Evelyn moved into Uncle Rulon's big house to be closer to her sons and grandchildren. Uncle Marvin's, Uncle Rulon's, and Dad's families were enjoying each other's company with a sense of peace, good fortune, and unity, with no idea their little dream world would soon be turned upside down.

On March 7, 1944, there was a widespread raid on polygamists' homes across the Salt Lake Valley and in Short Creek, Arizona. (These days, I call them "attempted rescues" as government officials knew there were underage marriages, abuses, and other crimes taking place.) Around 8:30 in the morning, one of my uncle's wives rushed over to Dad's house to tell him the police had broken into Rulon's home and confiscated everything: personal property, books, papers, diaries, records, and anything else they wanted.

The first day, Uncle Rulon and two of his wives were arrested. The following day, officers returned to arrest three more of his wives. Fifteen men from across town, one of whom would become my father-in-law, were also jailed. In early May, the men were indicted and sent to prison for unlawful cohabitation; the women were sent home to raise their children. Much of the correspondence between family members was in code, with changed names, dates, and addresses, to cover information that would surely implicate them further.

Articles expounding on constitutional rights and religious freedom hit a few major magazines. Several happy, contented-looking polygamous families appeared in full-page photos, along with stories and testimonies of Fundamentalist believers. According to my parents and relatives, stinging criticism came primarily from outside of Utah by non-Mormons who felt LDS Church leaders and members had turned their backs on the very people who were faithfully living the laws their prophet Joseph Smith had originated.

On April 7, 1944, the cover of *International Events* magazine— "The World's News in Pictures"—highlighted my future father-in-law with his five wives gathered around a piano. The photo caption read, "Mate and Five Wives in Close Harmony." Little did the world know of the real events and unrest in that "united" family.

Uncle Rulon described his prison experiences in his journal:

The warden told Joseph Musser that Church leaders and authorities were anxious to make concessions that would end this national and state issue. As parole dates were to

11

be set, Musser counseled his brethren to comply with the state's request, asking them to sign a document renouncing their beliefs and pledge to refrain from living with their plural wives. Joseph asked them to do and say whatever was necessary to get them back with their wives and children again.

With their fervent beliefs God's laws were foremost and above the laws of the land, most of the men refused to follow Joseph's advised concessions and sign a decree that seemed contradictory to their beliefs. They did not want to make an agreement "with death and hell," as they considered this "new" Manifesto to be.

Uncle Rulon told us that Joseph Musser instructed his brethren to fast and pray about their misgivings. That evening he and Joseph Musser said they had similar dreams in which the Lord instructed them to sign the document. They believed God would not hold them accountable for this kind of deceit; rather, He had opened the way for them to return to their wives, children, and religion. They were certain that to sign a document that required them to lie about their beliefs and future intentions was no more binding to them than the Manifesto had been. It would be "nothing more than a political agreement with the world."

My future father-in-law and five other men refused to sign the agreement and chose to carry out their prison terms. It was later rumored that these men accused Uncle Rulon, and the other eight men who accepted early releases, of making as damnable of a choice as Wilford Woodruff had done in signing the Manifesto. After that ordeal, many things would never again be the same among the Council of Friends.

Neighbors, merchants, LDS Church leaders, and government officials in Utah hoped polygamous activity would eventually dissolve and go away. But it was not that simple. The arrests of the fifteen men led Fundamentalists to become even more tenacious in their convictions, beliefs, and secrecy. Then and now, hardships and trials are viewed as God's test of His choice people, to see if they will remain faithful and endure to the end. Whenever polygamy was publicized, Allred Fundamentalists noted an influx of converts—proof, they felt, God was in fact upholding His cause. Those cases served to encourage Fundamentalist Mormons to "shoulder up" to their responsibility to keep building the kingdom of God, no matter the tribulations.

Of the fifteen men who were arrested, sent to prison, and released; all eventually returned to their wives to live in polygamy. With high birthrates among polygamists, the population continued to swell at an astounding rate. And the kettle was still boiling.

CHAPTER 3

Like a Piece of Dirty Garbage
1947–1952

Eleanor's second child and Mom's sixth were born in July 1947 as Uncle Rulon's family quietly disappeared. Everyone knew better than to ask questions. One rule of thumb was "If you don't know the answers, you won't have to lie when you're asked."

Some weeks later, Dad informed his families he planned to move them to Dayer LeBaron's ranch in Los Porcelas, Mexico. The LeBaron brothers had offered a place of refuge to polygamists on the run, and that's where Uncle Rulon had moved most of his wives and children. My dad felt certain the ranch would be a haven for his family, and Mexico would be a warm and welcome retreat from his painful bouts with rheumatic fever and rheumatoid arthritis.

In anticipation of the long trip, Dad borrowed an old milk truck from Eleanor's father and fashioned a makeshift bed behind the driver's seat. He installed two wooden seats that ran the length of the truck on each side, and a popover canvas to cover the whole bed of the truck.

On August 8, Dad departed Salt Lake City with Mom, Aunt Eleanor, their eight children, and one of Uncle Rulon's wives with her five little ones. For six long, hot days they were packed in the truck "like sardines in a can." Arriving in Old Mexico, they found there were only two types of weather: torrential rains and blistering winds.

Uncle Rulon had already begun building adobe homes for his families. Tents were set up for Aunt Eleanor and Mom. Their babies were allowed to sleep in Maude LeBaron's home to protect them from thousands of nagging flies.

Within weeks, several more families arrived in the barren, dusty parcel of desert that quickly became known as Tent City, a refuge from perceived persecution.

By November, Mom, Eleanor, and their children once again shared a home—this one made of adobe. The best part of their house, Mom once told me with a smirk, was the crisscross broom-straw designs they swept across the hard earth floors. "You can imagine how long those entertaining designs lasted," she jeered. On each side of the tiny family room, which also served as a kitchen, was an eight-by-eight-foot bedroom. In each of these was a two-by-two-foot window that couldn't be opened, but let in a few rays of light. The rest of the family's scanty belongings stole every inch of their meager space. Food was prepared in the tiny kitchen and served outside in the dusty, fly-infested yard.

As more and more refugees arrived, food and other commodities became scarce. When Mom could no longer breastfeed Shane, Annie LeBaron, who lived a mile or so up the road, offered Mom some of their cow's milk for his bottle. Over time Mom and Annie became close friends. At that time, neither of them imagined Annie's young daughter, Maryann would become my father's third wife.

One hot and arid day, Dad and several other men on the Dayer Ranch cleared a tract of land, overgrown with mesquite. After heaping the wood into three huge piles, Dad lit a match and watched the timber go up in flames. Others who had wandered over to see the bonfire soon found themselves in a festive mood. Before long, food seemed to appear from nowhere. Families offered whatever they could spare. And throughout the night, members of Tent City and the Dayer community sang and danced on the hard-crusted earth until the wee hours of the morning. By then, the reflection of the glowing embers glistened on the brightly colored ponchos covering the children who'd fallen asleep on a huge tarp a safe distance from the fire.

Thanksgiving and Christmas Day celebrations were much like the bonfire day and night—full of joy, laughter, and praise.

To earn a living, my father set to work building furniture. He volunteered to build new benches for the students at the Galeana schoolhouse, which was packed to the rafters with polygamous children. He also pitched in to help teach some of the classes; which didn't pan out very well. Even with his good intentions and his fourth-grade education, his obvious lack of training in the teaching profession and his inappropriate sense of humor got him ousted.

Laundry days proved to be a nightmare. Thirty-seven women had to share the only well on the property during the six laundry days before the Sabbath. Water was boiled in huge tubs over bonfires. Using homemade lye soap, the women scrubbed each piece of clothing up and down on rippled sheets of metal in wooden frames. Finally, the clothes were rinsed in vats of cold water and hung over long ropes tied between trees. On rare occasions—really lucky days—the women's laundry dried and was retrieved before it became caked with mud from the dust and rainstorms.

As February neared, Dad decided to return to Utah to find work. Just before he had to leave, Shane came down with a serious case of pneumonia. Mother told Dad, she desperately wanted to return with him. Most importantly, she could get Shane to a hospital. She also hoped to spend some time feeling like his only wife and his only love, at least for a while. But Dad betrayed my mother again. To avoid his guilt for giving in to El's pleadings and demands, and to avoid Mom's tears of anger and desperation, he waited until Mom was nearly packed and ready to go before he gave her the devastating news.

Mom thought she'd never speak to Eleanor again. It was bad enough she felt Eleanor had already stolen her husband and her soul, as well as most of her time; now she wouldn't even consider Shane's need for quality medical attention in the States. None of that mattered to El! She'd already made arrangements for herself, my dad, and her children to stay in Murray, Utah, in a comfortable apartment above her father's garage.

Things were getting crazy between some of the LeBaron men and those who had fled to Mexico. Joel LeBaron began to demand praise and adoration, claiming to be "The One Mighty and Strong"—and everyone's new priesthood leader.

In Utah, Joseph Musser decided, although Fundamentalists were still not safe in the States, moving back would be better than the poverty in Mexico and the conflicts there between the LeBarons and other brethren. Joseph directed my parents and other families to return home and count on the Lord for protection.

Mom and her children had been in Mexico for nine months before Dad brought them back to the States in May 1948. He settled them in his sister's basement in Farmington, Utah, while they waited for a house two miles down the street to become available. Mom thanked God every night their primitive standard of living had been short lived. Yet even during the most difficult experiences in Mexico, she was grateful she'd had time to read her scriptures and form a few lasting friendships.

In the fall, Dad moved Eleanor and her children into the top floor of Mom's rental home in Farmington. While they waited for a furnace to be installed in the new home my father was building for Eleanor in Murray, the LDS visiting teachers became suspicious of the living arrangements. My parents were quickly summoned to visit with the local stake's high council. The council questioned them about their beliefs in plural marriage and asked them to deny any affiliation with anyone living polygamy. Mom and Dad had no choice. They passionately defended their convictions and were subsequently excommunicated from their much-loved Church of Jesus Christ of Latter-day Saints.

Mom told me, "I cried off and on for months after that day. From the time I was a little girl, the LDS Church was an integral part of my life. When they excommunicated us, I felt like they'd punctured my heart and discarded me like a piece of dirty garbage!"

In the spring of 1950, Dad rented an old farmhouse in Draper, Utah, about eighteen miles south of Salt Lake City. Mom, Dad, and their kids loved it there.

Being typical boys, my brothers Luke and Darryl managed to burn the chicken coop down with some matches they found. A short time later, Luke and his new buddies got in trouble for chasing the neighbor's chickens and breaking their eggs. It was there in Draper, my older siblings got to know Mom's mother, Myrtle Cooke a little more. Whenever possible, she left her FLDS community in Short Creek, Arizona, to visit and give Mom a hand.

My mother's life-long friends, Cleveland and Annie LeBaron and their children, also moved back from Old Mexico. On one of their visits, shortly after Cleveland brought his daughter, Maryann, to Utah from Mexico, she'd run away and married an abusive man. Now she was left with a four-year-old son to look after. Cleveland told my parents, when they lived in Los Porcelas, Maryann "thought the world" of Dad's family. The bottom line: he wanted Dad to consider taking twenty-one-year-old Maryann as his third wife.

In general, Fundamentalists deem it a priesthood bearer's duty to prayerfully consider marrying his brother's widow or any other woman who asked for his hand in marriage. My dad once told me, "If the prospective husband says no, he'd better have a darn good reason."

One paragraph in Mom's journal about her sister-wife says:

> *January 1951*
> *Maryann and Owen were married today, after which we stopped at Brother Pollard's store to buy groceries. Brother Pollard says to Owen, "You look like you just came from a wedding." Owen didn't reply with words, only a smile.*

For nearly two years, turmoil had been brewing among the men of the Council of Friends. It was rumored, ever since Joseph Musser encouraged Uncle Rulon and several others to secure an early release from prison, those who chose to carry out their prison terms became critical of their priesthood leader's decisions. Some felt Musser had misguided his followers. And over time, Musser suspected, many of his high priest council members had commandeered unrighteous dominion over their cohorts. Musser claimed many of his council members in Colorado City and other places had been trading young daughters and sisters in marriage. Sometimes girls as young as twelve and thirteen were coerced into marrying older men—men they didn't know or love.

Mother said, "When Joseph Musser advised these men to stop their abominable behaviors, they responded with criticisms such as, 'Joseph doesn't know what he's doing—he's just a senile old man.'"

John Y. Barlow passed away in the latter part of December 1949. Joseph Musser continued to plead with his council members, whom he felt were insubordinate. He begged them to repent and support his decisions, or he would have no choice but to bypass them and call a new council. He eventually did. There was a tremendous amount of opposition when he called Uncle Rulon to be his first counselor. Those who had upheld Barlow until his death began to claim LeRoy S. Johnson as their new prophet.

My family's version of what both Fundamentalist groups called "the Split" was told over and over during my years in polygamy. The Allred, Johnson, LeBaron, Kingston, and Independent polygamous clans all had opinions of how, who, where, and why. No matter whom we followed, who we were, or where we stood, everyone claimed to have the real "truth" and the most accurate documents and information as proof.

Regardless of exactly how it happened, the Split created the Allred (later known as the Apostolic United Brethren, or simply "The Group," to its members) and the Short Creek Group, still the two largest Fundamentalist polygamous factions in the United States. The division brought heartache, torment, and disaffection between families and friends. Some men and women within these groups continued to interact with each other by simply agreeing to disagree, while others became bitter and non-communicative. Many men in the Short Creek Group forbade their wives and children to have any contact with those "dreadful Allredites." Grieving brothers, sisters, parents, and friends, strove with all their might to persuade their loved ones to change their hearts and minds. "If only you would fast and pray—longer, harder— you will know who the 'right' and 'true' priesthood leader is," they would plead.

It all made more sense to my mother, when she found out several years later why her good friend Alice quit coming around and didn't marry my father. Mother sadly reminisced, "Her father had lost re- spect for Owen, Uncle Rulon, and Brother Musser before and after the Split, so he forced Alice to marry another man."

Alice told a dear friend, who told the story to Mom. One morning Alice was awakened and told to get into her wedding dress and come downstairs. (Since many young girls didn't know when they would be called to marry—sometimes at a moment's notice—they already had a wedding dress in the closet awaiting their wedding day.) Like most Short Creek (FLDS) girls, Alice had no idea who her husband would be until the last minute. She screamed and wept in protest, telling her father she was in love with Owen Allred and still wanted to marry him. Completely disregarding Alice's desires, her father locked her in her room and told her to fast and pray until she got the "right" testimony. Then she could come out to stay. Ultimately, Alice must have received the testimony her father wanted her to get.

My thirteen-year-old sister Lucinda wanted to stay in close contact with the friends she'd made in Short Creek before the Split. My par- ents trusted my mother's parents, the Cooke family, to keep her safe while she spent a good portion of the summer in Short Creek. During her summer vacation, Lucinda fell for Wayne, a handsome—and already-married—twenty-one-year-old man. When she confided her girlish infatuation to her grandparents and friends in Short Creek, they encouraged her to get married right away, claiming her parents would never give their permission for her to marry into the (then called) Barlow Group; so she must do it now. Wayne, her grandparents and friends all told her she couldn't let anything or anyone prevent her from carrying out God's will.

Back at home, Lucinda set about asking Dad for permission to marry. Though Dad wanted her to finish high school first, she continued to beg, argue, and persuade. Finally, Dad said if she still wanted to get married after she turned sixteen, he would give his consent.

My mother told me, sometime in January 1952 (the year I was born); Wayne called to ask Dad if Lucinda could go down to stay with Grandpa and Grandma Cooke again. He said it would also allow Lucinda more time with his family, so they could get to know each other better. Wayne promised Dad, as a brother in the gospel, he would take proper care of his daughter while she was away.

Even after many years, Mom looked faint as she told me, "But the next time Lucinda returned home from Short Creek, she told us she and Wayne had gotten married and had consummated their marriage, which had been sanctioned by their prophet, Leroy Johnson." I don't think my sister ever told Mom who actually performed her underage polygamous marriage. (Then, the legal age in Utah was fourteen.) My parents were distraught and angry. Even with the recent conflict between the two groups, they couldn't fathom the idea, men they once loved and revered would stoop so low as to steal their innocent young daughter and marry her off without their knowledge or permission.

They asked Uncle Rulon if they should have Lucinda's marriage annulled, but when they approached her with their plan, she stood firm, emphatically warning them not to try to keep her away from Wayne or they'd never see her again.

꧂

Mom's "devils" were driving her mad. It seemed her family was being blown to smithereens. Eleanor's self-involved behaviors, Dad's inability to be fair, the anguish Mom felt from her daughter's childhood marriage, and Mom's confusion as to which man on this earth held the keys to the priesthood—all these threatened her values and her salvation.

Mom prayed, fasted, read the scriptures, and prayed some more. With renewed strength and conviction, she recalled the promises Joseph Musser had made in her patriarchal blessing, and after quite some time, the Spirit of the Lord returned to her. The Spirit's much needed survival message would carry her forward. "Your basement house will soon be finished and paid for. Your baby will be a girl. Your family will have the food and clothing they need, and, dear Vera, your daughter Lucinda will go through much tribulation, but she is married to the right man to receive her posterity."

❧

On March 30, 1952, my dad moved my pregnant mother from Draper into Maryann's cramped four-room bungalow. Dad needed to use the rent money from the Draper home to help build Mom's new basement house, which would be just down the street from Maryann's and Eleanor's homes.

Soon, nine children and two wives were packed into Maryann's tiny home. Dad's overnight stays were quite infrequent but joyous. His kids gathered around him to eat popcorn and listen to his jokes, songs, and adventure stories. The days ended with family prayer. Dad said he didn't need any blankets since his horde of children wrapped him with their arms and legs, and poked their knees into his ribs. They kept him warm, wide awake, and smiling.

Soon, Dad poured the concrete foundation for Mom's house. While her home was under construction, Dad's sons and brothers also built a bridge over our five-foot-wide creek, graveled our long driveway, dug a cesspool and lined it with rocks, and drilled a well. By the first week in September, Mom's three-bedroom basement home was completed enough for her and her seven children to move into.

As always, Mother considered it her "righteous duty" and sole purpose in life to share, serve, and give to everyone. She would never allow herself to consider her own needs or desires before anyone else's, especially her husband's. Therefore, it came as no surprise to anyone when she consented to Dad's latest request. She would share her new home with Maryann and her two sons.

"I really was happy to be in our new home," Mom assured me later. "When we moved in, I began to sink my roots and feel like we'd at last be safe here in Murray. But more than anything in the world, I looked forward to having you, Sophia, my darling baby girl." She smiled at me tenderly. "Oh, how truly blessed we were."

CHAPTER 4

The Drill
1952–1957

$\mathbf{M}$y thirty-seven-year-old mother didn't have any idea I would be her last child. It wasn't her choice to quit after having eight. Because of her Mormon upbringing, she believed she should have as many children as the Lord would give her. Not only is this a strong Fundamentalist conviction, but if women obey this edict, God will provide for their large families as they grow. Even more promising, Fundamentalists believe the more children a woman has, the more glorified she will be in heaven. Mom said she never did feel she'd fully completed her duty to God and her husband's posterity. She tried for many years to have more children. She conceived twice but miscarried both babies. She thought it was her unrighteousness that influenced her procreative inabilities.

Between labor pains the day I was born, my mother and her mother tried to visit with my father's sister, Beth, and her husband, Lyman. Their home, just across the street from Mom's, was always like Grand Central Station—a constant gathering place for every polygamist in our neighborhood. Mom squeezed her mother's hand as the contractions grew closer together and more intense. "I hate to end our visit," my timid mother told Aunt Beth, "but I'd better get myself up to Eleanor's before I don't make it at all." Between each labor pain,

Mother supported herself on Grandma's arm as they hastened along toward Aunt Eleanor's.

"You weren't going to wait one minute longer!" Mom told me years later, "I thought you might be born right there on the street in front of the whole world, but I pled with God to make you wait until we got to Eleanor's house."

"I still hate waiting!" I reminded Mom as we tenderly looked into each other's eyes.

"Well, God answered my prayers." Mom sighed. "Right then your Uncle Marvin showed up. He helped me into his car and rushed us up the street. Eleanor had no sooner helped me get settled onto her bed when you flew out. If she hadn't been there to catch you, I don't know . . ."

"Wow!" I chuckled. "No wonder I have so many dreams of flying." Mom and I laughed together.

"Your Uncle Rulon got there just in time to check on you and make sure all of your parts were put together properly," Mom said proudly. "Everyone was in awe of my baby girl, since I had four sons in a row!

꧁

On July 26, 1953, when I was seven months old, all of Dad's family except Mom and I had joined the rest of The Group in American Fork Canyon for Sunday school and sacrament meeting. There, in God's gorgeous array of nature and sunshine, the Allredites felt they could openly worship Him to their heart's content, free from the eyes of supposed do-gooders who might report their suspicious activities.

As Mom entered the kitchen holding me across her arm, she heard a shocking news flash from her RCA Victor radio. The reporter announced another "raid"—an ongoing, in-depth plan to rescue underage brides and polygamist children—this time in Short Creek, Arizona. Mom said the raid (that was really an attempted rescue) was called Operation Seagull. At approximately 3:00 that morning, Utah and Arizona state troopers crept into the desert city, hoping to find everyone asleep and docile. As the long procession of law enforcement reached the crossroads, they saw fireworks flash across the sky. This was the community's way of warning citizens of encroaching enemies. Rather than finding an unassertive clan of polygamists, troopers found the city of Fundamentalists huddled in a huge circle, singing hymns and praising their Lord.

Thirty-one men were taken into custody. Over a period of 10 days, 263 women and children were taken in buses to shelters in Arizona where they were allowed to stay together.

For a week, my father called the Arizona authorities every day, trying to find his daughter Lucinda. He wanted them to give him custody of her and his forthcoming grandchild. Finally, Dad got the call. Obviously not realizing my parents were also breaking the polygamy law, Social Services told my parents they could come get their daughter if they promised to keep her away from "those horrible polygamists" and never let her return to Short Creek.

Before long, Utah and Arizona authorities conceded to public pressure and to the high cost of housing, feeding, and clothing so many polygamous families. Within a few years, most of those families were back home and reunited.

My sister's baby was born eleven days after my first birthday. Lucille and her daughter stayed in Murray with our family until the spring of 1955. While at home, she completed eighth grade and helped watch James and me while Mom did shift work at Murray Laundry, and cooked at the Salt Lake County Infirmary (hospital).

❧

Early one morning just after I turned four, I woke up when I realized Mom's hand was pressed softly over my mouth. "Shh," she whispered while kneeling close to my face. "Be real quiet."

Feeling no fear, only curiosity, I did exactly as Mom told me. She wrapped a blanket around me and carried me to the car, where four of my brothers were waiting. She placed me gently into the arms of a brother sitting in the back seat, then climbed in the front of the car and quietly shut the door. Dad drove slowly down our gravel drive-way, up the next few roads, north on State Street, and out of the Salt Lake Valley.

An informant had warned polygamous families of another possible midnight raid. This time, it was to be across Salt Lake and Utah counties. Dad drove through the night. When the lull of our 1947 Hudson came to a halt, my brothers and I woke up and rubbed our sleepy eyes. "We're finally here." Mom sighed.

For most of my early years before we fled, and after Mom's and Maryann's kids returned to Murray, our basement home was full of the fun-duh-mental-ly insane. Six of my brothers haggled over the space in the small north bedroom. The middle bedroom was packed to the hilt with me, my sister Francine (before she too ran away to get married at the age of fourteen), Maryann's two daughters, and one of Dad's wives—depending on which one wasn't sleeping with him every third night in the south bedroom.

Even though living inside was quite dismal, our home was nestled in the midst of acres and acres of clover fields, grasslands, cow pastures, and swampy wetlands—a child's paradise! Along the east side of our dead-end unpaved road, eight or nine more homes overflowed with Fundamentalist friends and loved ones. Our childhood wonderlands were called Plygville.

Just before kindergarten, Dad drove me to the Allred Group's alternative doctor, a "nonbeliever." Apparently, Uncle Rulon was in hiding again somewhere—delivering another baby, with his huge family, or counseling one of his hundreds of followers.

"It's just a checkup," Dad said when we arrived at the doctor's office. "The doctor is going to see if you're healthy enough to go to kindergarten."

In the large waiting room, couches lined the bare, white walls. A few of my dad's friends smiled at me warmly. When the doctor called me, Dad gently nudged me in his direction.

"Go ahead, honey. I'll be right here waiting for you."

The doctor took my hand and led me into a cluttered examination room with the overwhelming smell of cleaning solution. As soon as we were in the room, he let go of my hand, locked the door behind us, and told me to take my clothes off and climb on the table.

In a petrified stance, I stared back at him. "My dad didn't tell me I have to take my clothes off!"

"I said, take your clothes off and climb on the table like I told you to!" the doctor ordered. "I'm not going to hurt you. I have to see if everything is normal down there."

I couldn't move. Tears began to stream down my cheeks. The doctor stared at me angrily, then grabbed me and plopped me down on the cold table. He hurriedly and roughly removed my dress and panties and told me to lie down on my back. When I still couldn't move, he pushed me back onto the table.

"Just relax now," he snapped while he spread my legs apart. But I squeezed them tightly together and began to whimper. When he forced them apart again, my chubby white legs began to tremble. The doctor traced my labia up and down, over and over again. Through foggy eyes, I saw him lick his fingers and leave them wet with spittle. While I tried to squirm my way into a sitting position, I sobbed and begged him to leave me alone.

"Stop it now! Hold still!" he commanded again. He pushed me back against the table. Holding me down, he put his face right next to mine. "Do not make one more sound, little girl!" he said slowly, emphasizing every word. "If you do, you will bother everyone out there, and that will make them really mad at you!"

Totally petrified, I tried hard to hold still and not make a sound, but I couldn't help it. When I continued to whimper, I feared he might hit me. It seemed forever. I stared at the ceiling squares and quivered in terror while his fingers pressed and manipulated just inside my vagina.

Suddenly I felt something large and cold start to push farther inside me. It hurt so much I couldn't help but scream. I sat up and tried to push him away. The doctor abruptly backed up and looked at the door behind him. Then he demanded in a guttural voice, "Get dressed now, naughty little girl!" At last, he unlocked the back door and disappeared.

All alone, I could hardly catch my breath or move. I slowly sat up on the end of the vinyl-covered table. Hot tears poured onto my chest and bare legs. I slid down to the footstool a little at a time, and then carefully stepped down to the linoleum floor. I found my underwear on a wooden chair and pressed them between my legs, hoping the burning pain would stop. Then, I slipped them up over my legs and my dress over my head as fast as I could, before the doctor could come back in.

As I shuffled into the waiting room, I looked at Dad through hazy eyes. He was oblivious and still talking to his friends. I wondered if I'd explode inside and out—all over.

Why did my dad leave me alone with the mean doctor? Why did the doctor do that to me? What if the doctor comes out here and tells Dad I was a naughty girl and misbehaved? Dad might make me go back in there and behave myself.

Next to my father, I leaned way back and pushed myself as hard as I could against the couch. I forced away my tears so he wouldn't ask me what was wrong. I wished I could become invisible. He won't believe me, my thoughts repeated. So I forced myself into perfect compliance.

On the way home, for a second or two I thought I ought to ask or tell Dad something. He smiled and spoke to me as if nothing in the world was wrong. A million things were going through my young mind. *I'm supposed to respect my elders and do as they say. Guess the doctor had to, to see if I am okay, just like Dad said. What if Mom gets angry because I let the doctor touch me "down there"? The doctor called it "down there," too. I must be a bad girl for not holding still. Maybe if I had, it wouldn't have hurt and made me feel sick all over. I won't ever tell anyone. I'm sure they'll be really mad at me.*

In our dreary, dark basement, just before I started kindergarten, I heard Mother's excited voice. I paced back and forth down our hallway so I could stay close enough to hear her. When she hung up the phone, she knelt on the linoleum floor in front of me and gave me a huge squeeze.

"I get to go to school, to become a nurse!" she said. "I'll be able to help other people get well and make some money to help your papa support our family." She smiled. "I'll still have to work in the kitchen at St. Mark's Hospital some of the time, so I won't get to see you very much, but Aunt Maryann will look after you and your brothers while I'm away."

Seeing my mother happy made me feel like giggling all day long. Whenever I asked her why she was crying, she would always say, "Oh, nothing. I'm okay. I'll be all right." Now I hoped her wishes would come true. She would at last be all right and happy.

In September, I attended kindergarten at McMillan Elementary School, just a few blocks from home. I thought the first day was the best day of my whole life. "Kindergarten must be what heaven is like," I told Mom. I was so happy to be in Mrs. Holiday's class! I woke up every morning eager to go to school. I wasn't afraid of her, and I was sure she loved me.

I loved my friend Mac. He was so much bigger than all the other kids, and he was also in my class. Mac held my hand, pushed me on the swings, and talked to me whenever he could. Every time the bell rang, he'd save a place in front of the line for me. If I charged up to the door and ended up behind anyone else, Mac would give me a piggyback ride to the front of the line, where Mrs. Holiday would make him put me down. We smiled at each other throughout the day and talked about being best friends forever.

Near the end of my kindergarten year, while Tia and I were playing house, I asked her how many moms she had. When she told me she only had one, I bragged, I had three. She was pretty excited for me. "Why do you get to have three moms and I don't?"

"I don't know," I told her.

The next day Tia said her mom told her my dad was a "pig-a-mess and a very bad man, cuz he don't follow God's rules." She added with a smirk, "And my mom told me I shouldn't play with you anymore cuz you're a pig-a-mess too."

"My dad is not a pig-a-mess!" I protested. "He does too keep God's rules! And my dad does too keep all of his things nice and neat. He's not ever messy. Sometimes my mom says my brothers' room gets messy like a pigsty, so maybe . . . I guess they are pig-a-messes, but my dad isn't a pig-a-mess!"

The other kids looked at both of us in wonder. Then Tia said, "Well, your dad is a pig-a-mess, cuz my mom said he is! So maybe he should keep his room clean—then he won't be a pig-a-mess anymore."

As young as five and six years old, my public school peers chanted tauntingly, "Sophia is a pig-a-mess! Sophia is a pig-a-mess!"

I hid in the toy closet behind the shelves and cried until my teacher gently pulled me out by the hand. She held me in her arms and reminded the other children to be nice to everyone.

They were nice to me after that—at least for a few more years.

In the summer before I attended first grade, a big white station wagon pulled up at our house. The homely male driver leaned toward the passenger window and said to my mom, "Good afternoon, Sister Vera. We're going for an ice cream cone and want to know if Sophia can go with us."

Mom smiled and prodded my shoulder, as she assumed I'd like to go with Gregory Maynard and my second cousin, his wife.

"No!" I blurted out. I didn't know why, but that man terrified me and made me feel sick inside. I didn't want to be in his car or near him—ever.

Mom, who always wanted to please others, seemed embarrassed by my behavior. But the more she tried to coax me into going along with Gregory and his wife, the more anxious I felt she'd make me go.

I clung tightly to her legs and cried until she finally said, "I'm sorry, Brother Gregory. I don't understand why Sophia's behaving like this, but thank you for the offer anyway. Maybe another time."

After they left, Mom, in her trusting naivety and her desire to be gracious and hospitable, scolded me for my behavior, telling me I'd been ungrateful and rude. Neither Mom nor I knew the reason for my intense feelings, and it would be many more years before we would.

※

I was a pretty good student in the first grade. I didn't like my teacher as much as Mrs. Holiday, my kindergarten teacher, but I was happy Mac was in my class again. He sat right behind me so he could play with my wavy hair, which nearly reached my tailbone. My flowing, platinum blond tresses were my pride and joy. But my tender head was my curse.

On yet another day, Mom was in a hurry and in one of her terrible moods. While she tried to untangle my hair, she took it out on my head. For all I knew, she could have been angry or jealous about Dad, Aunt Eleanor, Aunt Maryann, life, work, or school, or all of the above, or something else I had no clue about. While she yanked at my hair, I shrieked and begged her to stop, but the more I squirmed and cried, the more impatient she became. When I held on to the base of my hair with my fists so it wouldn't hurt so much, Mom smacked my hands with the back of the wooden brush and yelled, "Move your damn hands, Sophia, and stop screaming!" By then, Mom was crying too. Her face was bright red and she'd gone totally berserk.

"I've told you a million times, if you won't take care of your own hair, you don't deserve to have it!" Mom screamed at me. Horrified, I watched her head toward our beautiful sideboard and get her scissors from the top drawer.

"Please, please don't cut my hair!" I begged. "Please, Mom. I promise I'll take care of it! I won't cry anymore! I'll brush it, I promise. Please . . . please!" But all I could do was watch piles of wavy locks fall down my back and chest, and drift like feathers across the kitchen floor.

In the mirror, I could barely see through my puffy white eyelids. My now uneven, shoulder-length hair and my freakish, bulbous red face startled me. *I won't go to school today or ever again!* I swore to myself. I hid under my brother's bed until Mom left for work. Somehow I managed to stay out of sight and skip school for the next couple of days. Then Aunt Maryann discovered me asleep on a blanket in our storage room under the stairs. When I told her of my woes, she walked me over to Aunt Beth's house. Aunt Beth fixed my hair as best as she could until it was cropped above my shoulders. Then she held me while I cried some more.

At school the next day, Mac was so upset and sad because my long blond hair was gone, he told me he'd never speak to me again.

"But my mom cut it when she was really, really mad!" I cried out. "It's not my fault it's all gone."

Tears filled his eyes as he yelled back, "I don't care! I loved your hair. Now it's all gone."

I closed my eyes so tightly I got a headache, but I wouldn't let myself cry in front of the other kids. The second I was outside after school, I cried enough to fill a puddle. It wasn't me Mac loved—it was my hair. For the rest of his school years in Murray, he kept his word and never spoke to me again.

※

Nearly every family home evening, Dad would drill his kids about the safety rules. "Remember," he would say, "I could go to prison and all of you could be stolen away from your mothers if you're not careful. You've got to practice and remember exactly what you should say." He'd dart out the questions as if he was the bogeyman, policeman, or the bad guy, and we would reply in unison.

"Who is the lady who lives with your mother?" Dad would ask.

"She's my dad's sister," we'd say.

"What's her name?"

"Aunt Maryann."

"Where is your dad, little kid?"

"I don't know." We'd shrug our shoulders.

"Sure you do, kid. Where is he?"

"I don't know," we'd say.

"Who are all those kids living with you?"

"They're our cousins."

"Good!" Dad would say. "Why is that woman living with you?"

"Dad helps take care of his sister and her kids."

Our father smiled in approval. "You plyg kids are getting good at this."

My siblings would laugh, but my stomach hurt. Even though I knew the drill, I was only seven and feared I'd mess up. When my dad would see my tears, I'd tell him I'd try hard to remember.

This time, as usual, he put his arm around me and pulled me next to him. "I'm sure you'll remember, my precious," he said. "Don't worry, you'll do just fine."

After we practiced every possible "what if" scenario, as well as listening to Dad tell us all the things we shouldn't say, he leaned forward on the couch and said emphatically, "One day you will be called at a moment's notice to run and get in the car. You must jump up immediately and do exactly as you are told! There will be no time for you to stop and ask why, or to wait for anything or anyone. The last days are upon us. It won't be long before the earth will be destroyed with earthquakes and fires. The wrath of God will fall upon the wicked. Yet He will call His people out of darkness and into the light. We are His chosen handful who, if we continue to obey His commandments, will be saved. This, my children, is why it is so important for you to always be exactly where you say you will be. This is why you must come immediately without question, whenever you are called."

"You know," Dad went on, "we will all be tested to see if we will hold fast to the iron rod—the teachings of God—and follow His direction in all things. God will test us to the degree we may feel we can no longer bear to hold on to our beliefs and our convictions. Like Job of the Bible, we may cry in agony. We will be horrified because of the carnage and abominations of evil men and women. We will be devastated by the terrible destructions that will take place on this earth. Even still, my dear ones, if you will hold to the gospel of Jesus Christ and God's truth, you will be saved."

I was so scared. I wanted to yell at my dad, "Stop talking right now! Stop it, Daddy!"

"And always remember, my loved ones," he continued, "God's laws are much higher than the laws of the land. Therefore, there is nothing wrong with the little white lies you are required to tell to protect your family and others. We are living God's higher laws and commandments, and there are evil people on the outside who would rather we weren't in the graces of God. They will do anything to thwart our righteous endeavors. They will stop at nothing to destroy us!"

By then I was sobbing, and Dad stopped his lecture to console me again. He pulled me onto his lap and asked, "What's wrong, my little darling? Are you still worried?"

"Yes, Daddy," I said between sniffles. "You are scaring me."

"I'm sorry, little Sophia. You will be okay, I promise you. We'll all be okay because we love God and Jesus Christ. And because God and Jesus love us, they will protect us."

"Okay, Daddy," I said in a strong, loud voice. "I will try to be a good girl, and brave."

CHAPTER 5

Plygville
1957–1959

My stepbrother Rick acted like my best friend, at least most of the time. He played all kinds of games with me: Cowboys and Indians, No Bears Are Out Tonight, and Tag. Sometimes he'd hold my hand and stick up for me when some of my cousins called me snot-nose, chubby, or fatso. My brothers, on the other hand, couldn't stand him most of the time. Having to share a room with Rick often felt like a curse to them, since they considered him a spoiled-rotten brat. They were often angry with Aunt Maryann, because no matter how irritating or tormenting Rick was, she always took his side. To try to get her to defend them or listen to the truth was hopeless. So they'd fight instead. Maryann would clobber them with her fists or whatever object she could find.

During those battles, my heart would pound so hard and fast I thought it might pop through the top of my head. "Stop hitting Luke! Stop it!" I'd scream at her over and over again. Sometimes I wrapped myself around her legs, clinging to her thick polyester-knit pants. I'd smack her legs and bottom, wherever my arms could reach, to stop her from forcing my brothers out the door. But to her, I was nothing more than an irritation to slap off her legs like a pesky fly.

I never knew when or if my brothers would return home again, and Maryann seemed to be proud of the fact she won every encounter.

Her harshness toward my brothers, and her random kindness to me made me feel guilty and responsible for their heartaches—a soreness I could never resolve.

James would hug me and say, "Don't worry, Sophia. She hates you too. She just pretends to like us so Mom and Dad will be happy, but we both know by the way she treats us, she doesn't like us at all."

$\approx$

Aunt Maryann left her kids, James, and me home with Rick quite often. On one of those forsaken days, while the other kids were off somewhere playing or sleeping, Rick coaxed me into the bathroom.

"We're going to play a game where you have to be real quiet. You can't make one sound," he told me. "If you do, we'll get in big trouble."

Rick told me I had to pull my dress up over my head so I couldn't see where he was. Then I should lie down on the floor by the tub and hold real still.

"I don't like this game. Let's play another game!" I pled.

My soul knew none of that felt right, but I feared he wouldn't love me or be my friend anymore if I didn't concede. Still, I begged him, "Please, Rick. Let's play something else."

"Come on, Sophia. This will be fun! Just keep your eyes shut. Be quiet and you'll see. You're my very best friend, and I'm your best friend—forever, remember?"

Soon, Rick's body was on top of me. I wiggled and pushed on his chest to get out from under him. "Come on, Sophia, hold still and be real quiet!" he'd say. "This is a quiet game." I felt him push something long and sticky between my thighs. With his legs on the outside of mine, he pushed mine together so hard I could feel his nasty thing press against my pubic bone. Again I tried to push him away from me.

"Sophia, be a good girl and let me do this! I'll be really nice to you, if you'll be nice to me. I'll even buy you a candy bar the next time I go to the store."

I held still. Rick made his body go up and down on top of me and started breathing really hard. I got so scared I started to cry, but he didn't stop. A few minutes later I heard him growl like a bear, and then his whole body weight sank on mine. I couldn't breathe. When he finally climbed off me, I opened my eyes. Through the thin skirt over my head, I saw him pull his jeans up over his naked bum.

"Okay, Sophia." I heard his zipper roll up. "You were a really good girl. You can open your eyes after I go out and shut the door." Then he stopped abruptly. "You'd better not tell anyone about our game, or we'll both get in big trouble."

When I stood up to pull my dress down, a whole lot of sticky, gooey stuff ran down my legs. Trying to wash it off my legs made me nauseous, and I wondered how and why Rick put snot all over me.

⁂

Mom was nearly a licensed practical nurse, but she never dared get a driver's license. During her working and school days, my siblings and I got to ride with Dad to take or retrieve her. When we went to pick her up, Dad would stop the car in the parking lot. James, Shane, and I would stare at the door to the school or the hospital, hoping to be the first one to see our mother. "There she is!" we'd scream.

Those, it seemed, were the only times we got to see her. In the car, Mom would smile, give us big hugs, and tell us she was sorry she was so busy at work and with her studies she couldn't be with us more. And then she'd ask the horrible question: "Are you being good kids?" I'd get quiet, keep my eyes dry, and never answer out loud. *Am I?* I'd ask myself. *It doesn't feel like it anymore.*

Rick offered to tend me more and more. Maryann would dress up and head out. Sometimes she'd take her girls, Jolie and Melanie, with her. I tried to hide or get away, but Rick always found me. To cheer me, he'd bribe me with more money or candy. Then he'd make me go into the bathroom with him again.

After a while, Rick started making me take my panties off and watch while he stood above me going up and down on his penis. Even when he saw tears well up in my eyes, he wouldn't stop. As with all self-seeking perpetrators, his gratification was more important than I was.

"I'll try not to hurt you, Sophia. I'll be real careful because I love you," he'd whisper. Then he'd be on top of me again. I learned real fast, fighting or begging him to quit only infuriated him.

"Stop fighting, Sophia! You know you are in on this too! If you ever tell anyone and get me in trouble, I will hate you. I'll have to beat you up and hurt you really bad." Then he'd calm down. "I don't want to have to hurt you, Sophia, because I love you. You know I do; don't you?"

Like a petrified log, I wouldn't move. When he'd finish and shut the door behind him, I'd pull myself up next to the toilet and vomit. Tears would stream down my face as I washed myself over and over again. Sometimes I'd stay in the bathroom for a long time, staring at my pathetic face in the mirror and wishing I could disappear.

After several months, Rick and I hardly ever saw each other outside of the bathroom. His plans no longer included me, unless it was to serve one purpose. I couldn't look at him anymore, no matter where he was. I hated his guts.

However, my wishes in front of the bathroom mirror came to my rescue. Whenever Rick molested me, I imagined I was as high as the tallest trees, on top of my tall, lanky father's shoulders. He'd charge around the yard like a prancing horse. I'd raise my shimmering purple wand toward the sky and shout, "Now I'm a princess! Take me to my beautiful white castle in the sky!" And then Dad would turn into a magnificent white unicorn and we would fly into the white fluffy clouds. "I am more brave and strong than any girl in the world," I'd proclaim. "In my castle way up here in heaven, no one can call me names or touch me. Up here I am in charge and safe, not in our bathroom."

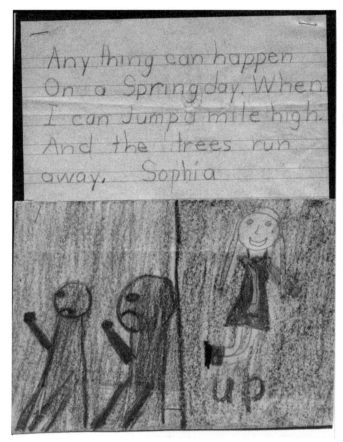

***My own description of wanting
to fly away! (Age 7)***

My mother's words reverberated in my head. She was always reminding us to be good kids so God would "protect us and keep us from harm and danger." For as long as I can remember, our daily prayers included those words. "Always do what's right and be obedient," Mother would say. "If you're not good, God won't protect you. Harm and evil will befall you."

Every day, I questioned why God had concluded, I, Sophia Allred, was such a bad person I deserved to be punished. Maybe, I suspected, was why He wouldn't let Francine come and take me home with her.

More often than not, I assumed I was a dreadful little girl.

In the quiet, dark lonely nights, when I'd hide under my covers from the devil's imps and the bogeymen that were always after me, someone deep inside of me would lull me to sleep. "That's not true, Sophia. You're not a dreadful child. It never was true!" I'd hear the soft, kind voice repeat. "You are a good girl, and God loves you."

On other nights Jolie, Melanie, and I would sneak huge scoops of peanut butter from the kitchen and lick the delectable stuff like a lollypop. We'd hide the spoons under our double bed and ditch them in the mornings. We'd jump on the bed until our heads scraped the ceiling and laugh until our guts ached. During those times together, it crossed my mind to tell Jolie about Rick's so-called horrible game. *No! What a stupid, stupid thought!* I'd tell myself. *I'm a bad girl, and if she knew, she might tell her mother. For sure I'd get punished.*

There were no more cookies left after we ransacked the jar. There were never enough cookies! I piled on the pounds, while Jolie and Melanie stayed as skinny as sticks. All I wanted to do was eat, eat, and eat. In the kitchen I'd open the cupboards and the fridge, searching for something to relieve my restlessness. *Since Rick is Jolie's brother, she wouldn't believe me anyway,* I'd remind myself every time I got tempted to tell her the deep, dark secret. I wished there had been a whole lot more food for me to eat. I'd have felt a whole lot better.

❦

I loved summers: running, jumping, climbing trees, riding my brother's bike, playing in the ditch, and following my brother James whenever he'd let me. Those were glorious days.

Then one day, I no longer had to fear Rick. My brother Shane's early years of polio had curled his toes under so much he was still having a hard time walking. After the surgeon had done more repair work on his feet, he got to recover in the living room on a hospital bed, where he could always see the bathroom door. I pictured being able to run up to Shane's bed, jump up on his chest, and tell him how much I loved him. I'd have begged him to stay there forever, even after his toes healed. "You could make this your bedroom forever!" I'd have pled with him. I wanted so much to tell him he was my guardian and savior. But Shane could never know.

The best part of the summer before second grade was Mom and Dad let James and me stay in Duchesne with Francine for a few months.

I was still terrified of the dark. The evil spirits and ghosts continued to hide and wait to grab me from behind. They'd follow close behind every time I was alone. If I wanted to get up at night, I'd have to stand up on the bed, get balanced, then leap as far away from the bed or couch as I could possibly get so they wouldn't grab me and drag me under. There was definitely no way in heaven or hell I dared head outside alone to Francine's privy during the night. By morning, I'd be in total agony.

One of those mornings, when my bladder felt as if it would burst all over the house, Francine asked why I was doubled over in pain and crying. Ashamed to tell her why I avoided the dreaded trip to their outhouse, I tried to make other excuses.

Without a word, my perceptive, ingenious sister saved my dignity and freed me from further terror and discomfort. She located a large metal mop bucket and an old rickety toilet seat. Then she told my brother, all her kids, and me, "From now on, everyone has to use this during the night, and I'll empty it in the morning."

While James and I were in Duchesne, we went with Francine's family to Brother Jon Thomas's house. Francine said the Thomas family had been in The Group for a long time. All day long the brood of Thomas kids, Francine's kids, and James and I discovered childhood treasures and trinkets as we frolicked around the Thomas's slice of land near the top of a volcanic cliff bank. While the adults visited for hours, we navigated and explored our surroundings like pirates on a new island.

With the major exception of Mr. Thomas, I liked everyone in his family. At mealtime, whenever he looked at me, I felt lifeless and un-responsive—as if his venomous eyes and hands had ravaged my body. The rest of the evening was totally destroyed. I ached to get away from him. I couldn't eat, talk, or play anymore. With Mr. Thomas's eyes on me, I wanted to become invisible again. On the road back home, I told Francine I never wanted to be around that stinky man ever again. Later in our lives, the reasons for my feelings became clear.

Every time James and I went to stay with Francine, it was a new adventure. Her husband was always moving her sister-wife (who is Aunt Eleanor's daughter, Hannah) and their kids somewhere different. It seemed they relocated two or three times a year, but it never mattered to us where they lived. I loved staying with my sister so much, going home was a miserable occasion. Each time before the dreaded trip back to Murray, I'd call Mom and beg her to let me live with my sister forever—well, at least a year. And when Mom said no to that too, I begged for just a few more months, or even another week. But she always made me go back home.

One summer when James and I returned to Murray after staying with Francine, we saw a new home in our yard. Dad had built another house on top of the basement. I walked through the new rooms like a child in a mystical land, totally in awe of all the space and beauty. Dad, I thought, must be the richest man in the world. To me, he became the greatest king on earth when I found out the new house was for our mother.

A few months later when the house was completed, Mom moved upstairs. Aunt Maryann moved into Aunt Eleanor's newly painted little green house I was born in. Aunt Eleanor and Dad repaired, painted, and carpeted her new basement before she moved in downstairs.

Our kindhearted mother was famous for letting everyone live with us. Her friend Marlene stayed in one of our three bedrooms while she went to nursing school with Mom. My five brothers shared the second room, and Mom let me sleep with her in her bed. "Mom's night" with Dad meant it was time for me to crash on the couch again.

Some time before I was born, one of my older, more affluent cousins began to rent the large, drab Murray Recreation Hall for the Allred Group dances. The monthly dances were for everyone twelve years of age and older, unless it was Christmastime. Then everyone, including Santa Claus, was invited to attend the festivities.

Our enormously fat, white-bearded Santa always plopped himself down in a huge easy chair right in the center of the stage and patiently listened to the wishes of at least a million polygamous children. While I waited in the long line, my wishes kept changing or getting totally shamed into nonexistence. I thought of the Christmases I could remember and realized this one wouldn't be any better than the last five.

"Are we bad kids?" I had asked Mom at the end of Christmas Day the previous year. "Why doesn't Santa bring us anything? Doesn't he like us?"

"You should be grateful you have a house and a roof over your head and you're not starving," she responded.

"I am grateful! I just don't understand why Aunt Eleanor's kids and Aunt Maryann's kids and all of my cousins in our neighborhood get beautiful dolls, doll clothes, toys, and hair ribbons. Their brothers get cars, trains, and a lot of other stuff—"

"I don't know," Mom interrupted impatiently. "Santa isn't always able to be fair, and we just can't afford to make up for the things he doesn't bring. I have to give your dad all of my money so he can pay the bills and give the mothers grocery money. We can barely get by, let alone have any money for gifts."

Mom blinked back her tears. "I'm sorry you don't have any toys or new clothes, Sophia, but we must be grateful for everything we have, and glad for those who do have things. We shouldn't be selfish. Wanting things for ourselves will distract us from keeping the Spirit of the Lord with us." Then her voice perked up. "You know what we do have to be grateful for? We have each other!"

A quick hug and a kiss on the cheek and Mom was back to reading, while I quietly stepped into the bathroom to hide my jealous, shameful tears.

So, it was just as well I had a long wait in a long line before I could talk to Santa, to change my *stupid* mind. What good would it have done to ask for a *stupid* new pair of tennis shoes, or a *stupid* used bike? I determined I would ask Santa for the most important thing in the whole world. And since God hadn't helped much in that matter, maybe Santa would.

After all the children got to speak to Santa and he left, our parents would come alive. While they'd dance, laugh, and visit, the children would get going on a good run across the massive tiles by the stage, and then slide as far as the hard soles of our Oxford shoes would take us. It was never far enough for me, so I'd try again and again to beat my last mark, as well as the mark of every child who would dare to compete with me.

After sliding until we were worn out, we'd sit and watch the adults, until it was our turn to dance the Bunny Hop, Pop Goes the Weasel, or a vigorous, heart-pumping polka. I never got to dance to my heart's content.

Pretty soon Mom made me stop dancing and come sit next to her. She had that look on her face—the one that always made me wonder what was going on in her mind. *What did I do, or not do this time? I thought I had it figured out. I've been too rambunctious again . . . I just about plowed over a few smaller tykes while I was leaping across the dance floor to the beat of John Paul Jones.* "I'm sorry, Mom," I quickly said. "I'll slow down and try to be—"

She smiled, leaned toward me, and whispered, "Someone told me what you asked Santa to bring this year. It made me cry."

"I'm sorry, Mom. I didn't mean to hurt your—"

"It's all right, my precious," she cut in. "These are not sad tears, but happy tears."

I felt a little bit embarrassed, but she pulled me close to her. "My good friend said you told Santa, since God wasn't helping much in this matter, maybe he could. He said you promised Santa you wouldn't ask him for anything ever again, if he'd promise to bring your mother the gift of happiness. Oh, my darling little Sophia, you are my gift of happiness! Don't you know how much I love you? San—I mean my friend—said you told him your mom is sad or mad all the time, and all you want is for her to be happy."

Crying, Mom pulled me onto her lap. I felt her warm breath on my cheek. While she whispered in my ear, she wiped away her tears with her hand. "I am so, so sorry, Sophia. I've been a mean, ornery, grouchy, depressed mom! I've treated you kids awful! That's not the kind of mother I wanted to be. I've let all of my stresses and worries make me behave really badly. I promise I'll make myself be happy. I'll smile more. I have so much to be grateful for."

Long before the festivities would've normally ended, the music abruptly stopped, and everyone was asked to gather in a close circle to hear an announcement. A priesthood bearer began to pray for safety, protection, and guidance for all of us. Someone said there were more threats against polygamous families.

In the parking lot, faces carried fretful smiles. Folks all around us spoke in quiet voices as they quickly exchanged hugs and encouragement, as if they were being scrutinized and in danger.

"Godspeed," I'd hear.

Another voice would ask, "Where is Uncle Rulon? Anyone know?"

"Don't worry, brother. God is watching over us. We're in His hands."

Our splendid Christmas celebration ended in gloom that year.

Once we were in Dad's car, Mom promised she'd always love me, no matter what happened to her or to Dad. She said if anything were to happen—if they ever had to go away without me—I would go live with my sister Francine. Was I ever excited! I hoped Mom and Dad would have to go away together for a while. All I ever wanted, it seemed, was to go live with Francine, and if Mom would go away with Dad, I thought, it would make her so happy. They might get to spend a lot of time together, hug and kiss, and love and talk some more. I hardly ever saw them smooch, but when they did, my whole insides would jump for joy.

After school one afternoon, I sat next to my mother and enjoyed the pictures as she turned the pages of her photo album. She said she couldn't find more than five or six pictures of me.

"I remember when Lucinda took this picture!" Mom smiled.

In the small, black-and-white photograph, Lucinda's baby and I were sitting in a wagon just outside of the basement house. Holding her tiny hand out toward her mother, my niece looked like a princess. I looked unhappy and ready to jump.

I told Mother, "I felt like a princess when I could stand on the car seat next to Dad. I'd put my left arm around his neck as he drove. I also remember when I was learning to walk I'd parade back and forth in our hallway to get applause and cheers from everyone. I think I would have been close to a year old when I was standing in my crib, drinking the milk from my baby bottle as fast as I possibly could so I could get to the syrup from the bottom. Oh, and I remember when I heard Aunt Eleanor tell someone my sister was going to have a baby, and you got mad at me when I was telling everyone." (My sister, Hannah was William's second wife, which was why no one was supposed to have evidence of yet another plural marriage. Pregnancies were kept secret for eons; especially in underage cases.)

Girls "disappeared" during pregnancy for many reasons. We were not supposed to tell people if someone was pregnant.

"Another great memory," I told her, "was when an older woman handed me a baby doll, then lifted me onto her lap. She rocked back and forth, with her arms wrapped around my tummy. I felt like I'd melted into a huge soft pillow. I wanted to stay there forever."

"I'm sure you're remembering grandma Balmforth. She was one of my dad's wives, and was really good to you kids," Mom said. Then in a solemn voice she told me, "I'm glad you have such a good memory of her, because she died when you were only four years old. Your dad's mother died several years before you were born, and my mother died when you were barely two, so you didn't get to know any of them."

I always wished for a wonderful grandmother to love and care for me, but those memories of Grandma Balmforth started the ball rolling, and my mother wanted to hear more. So I told her.

"I guess I was close to two years old. I woke up in our dark basement and looked all over to find someone, but no one was home. I was so scared, and my bottom hurt so bad I could hardly walk. I cried until snot and tears dripped into my mouth. Then Francine came home. She gathered me in her arms, changed my diaper, powdered my blistered bottom, and dressed me in dry, warm clothes. After she got me some food, we walked all over the house and yard. Then she snuggled right next to me on the piano bench and let me bang out noises on Maryann's piano." Again, I told Mom how much I loved Francine, and how much I wished she'd come home and live with us all the time, since Mom wouldn't let me go live with her.

More tears welled up in Mom's eyes. "No wonder you love her so much. She did love and care for you, didn't she?" Then, Mom shouted angrily, "Why in the world wasn't Maryann looking after you? She was supposed to be taking care of you kids while I was gone!"

Many years later, Francine told Mom it was always the same. It was common for her to find us kids screaming, hurting, hungry, and disheveled. Francine often talked Maryann into letting her skip school to take care of James and me. Maryann was grateful for Francine's offer. It freed her of her supposed commitments so she could be about her own daily agenda with her friends and her own children.

My new friend, Mary, didn't know I was a plyg kid like most of the other kids did, so she invited me to her birthday party with the other girls in my second-grade class. I was super excited, but I didn't have a penny to my name, so I had no way to buy a gift. I doubt I ever asked my parents for anything. I'd already come to realize asking for anything was relatively pointless.

The summer before, when I was hanging upside down on the monkey bars, my knees slipped and I landed on top of my head. I heard my skull crack against the blacktop. Though I was sick and dizzy with headaches the whole summer, I still didn't tell my parents or ask for help. But this time, I wanted to go to the party, and I'd have to take a gift.

Mom's friend Marlene was nice to us from the day she moved in. She watched over us now and then, if she had a different schedule than Mom. So I decided she'd be a safe person to ask for help.

On Saturday, she took me to get a gift and then delivered me to Mary's parents' home. As soon as I stepped inside the enormous house, I realized our home, which I thought was so magnificent, was bare and ugly in comparison. Until then, I had no idea the interiors of those attractive, massive homes all around us were so beautiful.

As my peers laughed and played, I felt ugly, awkward, and out of place. The whole time I was there, I wasn't sure what to do or how to act. This was my very first experience with children away from elementary school, outside of our culture, and in such an elegant environment.

After the party, just before Marlene picked me up, I told Mary thanks for inviting me, and then I invited her to my birthday party the following Saturday. All the way home, I wondered, what made that big fat lie shoot right out of my mouth? And even worse, I didn't have a clue how I was going to get out of such a mess. What, with another fib? Then I figured it all out. The next day at school, I'd tell Mary that my mother said I couldn't have the birthday party. My foolish predicament would be all done and over with.

The following Saturday afternoon, when I walked in the door after a day of play, Marlene glared at me. "Your little friend Mary and her mother came by today with a gift for your birthday party. What on earth was that all about, Sophia? It isn't your birthday for months. I don't think there were any party plans either."

I had forgotten to tell Mary another lie to cover up the first one. Full of shame, I confessed my stupidity to Marlene. She forgave me but said it was Mary I should apologize to. She told me I had to ask Mary for forgiveness. But I was way too embarrassed and self-conscious. I had no idea what to tell her about my mistake. Mary and I never talked again, and for years I was full of remorse and shame. It wasn't until I joined a twelve-step program many years later I learned to forgive my childlike mistakes. I was only a little girl begging for love and acceptance. In another insecure, vulnerable moment, I sought for approval that was never meant to be.

❧

I think Mom and her kids were the last in our neighborhood to get a black-and-white television. No matter we were only supposed to watch "approved" programs—we were more grateful than buzzards on a dead carcass to finally have a TV. I watched it sporadically. I was way too antsy to hold still long enough to finish anything.

One afternoon James, Shane, and I were watching Bugs Bunny narrowly escape being cooked for dinner by Witch Hazel while he was trying to save Hansel and Gretel. We heard the kitchen cupboard doors slam shut, and our mother yelling angrily. Soon, she was sobbing.

"Why can't anyone clean up after themselves?" she screamed. "At least put this stinking food away! How can anyone stand to live in this pigsty?" Her anger increased by the second. I edged closer to the kitchen entryway. I really wanted to give her a hug and tell her I was sorry I hadn't done the work, and I'd do it now if she wanted me to. But I knew if I went in the kitchen right then, I might get hit or screamed at. I'm sure my brothers felt the same way, but they inched their way in and told her they were sorry. "What can we do to help you?" they asked.

"If you really wanted to help, you would have long before I had to turn into a raging maniac!" Mom's bloodshot eyes and runny nose intensified her miserable, enraged appearance. The glass plate she slammed into the sink shattered into pieces, slicing the palm of her hand open.

By then, tears were sliding down my cheeks. I felt ashamed of myself for not cleaning the kitchen, and sad for my mother. *When I'm older*, I decided, *I'll do all of the work for her. Then she'll never have to be sad or angry again.*

CHAPTER 6

My Salvation
1960

About thirty-five miles from Murray, near Tooele, a caravan of seven or eight cars pulled off Highway 80, traveled a half mile or so down a dirt road, and parked near a water hole approximately six feet in circumference and about four feet deep.

On a bitter cold Saturday in the spring, I stepped out of Dad's car wearing only a pair of white socks and my long, white cotton slip, with a large blue towel wrapped around me. There was a brother eleven months older than me, a brother six months younger than me, several of our cousins, and a few more kids who were just over the age of eight who were going to be baptized.

For those who would become members of the LDS Church, baptisms were then (and still are) customarily done in a baptismal font in an LDS chapel. For fundamentalist Mormons, this ordinance is performed wherever possible—usually in a swimming pool, a pond, or a mud hole.

This ritual served to wash away our sins, grant us membership into God's church, and prepare us to be confirmed with the gift of the Holy Ghost. In Sunday school we learned, "having the gift of the Holy Ghost, would let us know right from wrong, if we listened."

In the middle of the pond, clothed in white, Jon Thomas held both of his arms above his head, with both hands facing forward away from him, and began to pray. "Our Father in Heaven, by the power of the holy Melchizedek Priesthood, I dedicate this pool of water for the purpose of baptism. I ask Thee at this time to cleanse these waters from earthly elements that might be harmful to the human body. I ask Thy Spirit to be with us at this time; and I say these things in the name of Jesus Christ, amen."

We watched Jon baptize two of his children. He called my name and reached in my direction as if to take hold of my shivering hand. Mom directed me toward him, but his haunting eyes forced me backwards, away from him.

"I won't go in the water with him," I told my mother. "I don't like Jon! I want Uncle Marvin to baptize me."

This time, Mom didn't try to persuade me into compliance. She respected my childhood intuitions. Holding my little hand, she smiled.

While Jon Thomas performed baptisms for several more children, I wondered if something was terribly wrong with me. *Why do other children and adults seem to trust and like a man my little soul is so repulsed by?*

Uncle Marvin's white shirt and white slacks clung to his long old-fashioned undergarments as he baptized his son and a daughter. "Um, you ready now, Sophia?" he asked. He stretched out his large, comforting hand and helped me slide into the muddy pond. He grasped my hands snugly and showed me how to hold my nose closed while he ducked me under. "Are you ready now, honey?" he asked.

I nodded.

He said, "Sophia Allred, having been commissioned of Jesus Christ, I baptize you in the name of the Father, and of the Son, and of the Holy Ghost. Amen." Then Uncle Marvin pushed me backwards under the water. An assigned witness made sure every single part of my body had been immersed.

I got dressed in the car, my privacy protected only by the towel Mom held in front of the window nearest the crowd.

I'd been taught the baptismal lessons several times. Still there were things I didn't understand. Dad said God is perfect, and He also created nothing but perfection. His babies and our souls all come to this earth perfect and innocent, without sin or blemish. Yet by the time we are eight years old, we must have committed so many sins they have to be washed away. I was still uncertain about the sins I'd apparently committed. I also wanted to know what bad things all the other kids had done. If I only knew, I could determine if they measured up to the bad things I'd supposedly done.

No one was quite sure how to satisfy all of my never-ending questions. "It's okay," they'd tell me. "Sometimes we don't understand all there is to know. But now you have the gift of the Holy Ghost, to discern right from wrong. It's all in God's plan of salvation. Surely you want to be part of his kingdom, don't you?"

With all my heart I wanted to be part of salvation, whatever it was. I certainly didn't want God to take all of my family to heaven except me. Yet I was quite sure He would do exactly that. After all, I got the impression everyone in our neighborhood knew me as the naughty, abandoned kid with a dirty face and unkempt clothing— the matted-hair orphan for whom God and most of the adults had no special regard.

❦

Our huge upstairs front room served a dual purpose. In my heart, I knew there had to be another reason why Dad built such a massive room and kept it so empty. My brother Darrell would set up a row of folding chairs so Uncle Rulon and his priesthood council—my father, Uncle Marvin, Eslie Jenson (father of the current prophet of The Allred Group or Apostolic United Brethren), and Jon Thomas—could face their small but rapidly growing congregation. Here, each of the men would take turns conducting Sunday school, Sunday sacrament meetings, and Wednesday-night priesthood meetings.

I still felt sick to my stomach around Jon, so I always tried to sit as far away from him as possible, which was never far enough.

My cousins, siblings, and the few non-relatives in the Allred Group looked proud when they were asked to stand and bear their testimonies. It really shouldn't be hard, I often thought to myself, especially since I'd heard the same exact words repeated over and over again since I was an infant. Still, I just about slid off my chair when Daddy asked me to come up and bear my testimony. I was sure my heart was going to pound right out of my chest and bounce across the floor.

I let go of Mom's hand, and sauntered to the front, where everyone in the room stared at me in contemplation. Of course, all my know-it-all thoughts escaped me in holy terror and got stuck somewhere between my brains and mouth. I couldn't get one word out.

After what seemed forever, Daddy—who was directly behind me—gently held onto my arm. "It's okay, little Sophia. You can say a few words, can't you? You don't have to be so scared. Just tell us what you are thankful for."

I shook in fear, with what seemed like five hundred people gawking at me, expecting me to come through. At last, I attempted a few familiar words I'd heard from the older kids so many times before.

"Uh . . . uh, I'm thankful for uh, uh, my mom and my dad, and uh . . . uh, I'm thankful for God and for Jesus . . ." With those few words finally out, I was able to pick up speed and start feeling pretty good about myself. "And I'm grateful He died on the cross for me and you, to pay for our sins . . ."

What sins? I still wondered. Sidetracked, I stopped cold. What sins did all of us commit? For a minute or so I panicked. Would everyone know what I was thinking? They must not have, because their kind eyes and gentle smiles urged me on. *Okay, I can do this*, I told myself.

"And uh, I'm thankful for my brothers and my sisters and . . . for my cousins and . . . for all of my relatives." Then I blurted out the most important part: "I know the gospel of Jesus Christ is true."

My eight-year-old convictions had just gone on a replication rampage, but inside my heart, it didn't feel real. *Did I just lie again?* I questioned myself. *I'm not sure if I know the gospel is true or what the gospel really is. All the other kids say they know. Why don't I know? I shouldn't have said I did, when I don't.*

Flustered again and scared I may have been caught in a lie, I felt my face turn red and my eyes start to water. I had to finish and get back to my chair as fast as I could.

"In the name of Jesus Christ, amen," I said really quickly

Dad squeezed my arm. "Good honey," he whispered.

A few of the adults giggled appreciatively as I made my way to the far end of the front row. Once I was in my seat, a few more smiling relatives gazed in my direction.

Mom put her arm around my back and kissed my forehead. "Very good, my darling!"

I'd passed my performance with flying colors.

✣

One day, Dad asked me if I wanted to walk up to Aunt Maryann's house with him. Of course I did. He held my hand, and we walked so slowly it was driving me nuts.

"Dad can't you walk any faster?" I asked.

"Sure." He picked up his pace.

"Come on, Daddy, can't we run?"

"Guess so, if you're sure you want to be left behind." He looked at me questioningly.

"Of course I'm sure. Let's race to Aunt Maryann's front door."

"I'll be leaving you in the dust." Dad smiled.

I smiled back and said, "One, two, three, go!"

I waited on the front porch for Dad. "What took you so long?" I teased. It felt so good to shout those familiar words my brothers used whenever they won a race.

"I had no idea you could run so fast, Sophia," he said as he picked me up and gave me a huge bear hug. I kissed his neck, and so he wouldn't feel bad, I told my forty-six-year-old father, "It's not because you're slow, Daddy. It's because you're getting so old."

Dad laughed. "No. For your young age you are quite speedy!"

For weeks after our daddy-daughter competition, I overheard him brag about my incredible speed.

Running was exhilarating, and it was as close as I could come to flying. I stretched every leap and stride to the maximum. I'd dream the wind would swoop me up and carry me high above the trees, where I'd be in control of my speed and zenith. Once I was completely exhausted and couldn't sprint a minute longer, I would drift down to earth and catch my breath again.

Now I had a reason to run even faster. I wanted my dad to be more proud of me than he already was. I ran faster and longer every day. I begged everyone to race with me. Dad's praise of my speed gave me a short-lived sense of purpose, and for the first time, I felt I had an individual identity among his huge family.

⁂

In our Sunday school class, the seven- and eight-year-olds would sit on the edge of the two beds in my brothers' room while one of our older cousins gave the lesson.

One conflicting subject was faith. Our teacher told us, in Mathew 17:20 Jesus says, "If ye have faith as a grain of mustard seed, ye shall say unto this mountain, remove hence to yonder place: and it shall remove; and nothing shall be impossible unto you." And in Luke 17:6, He says, "And the Lord said if ye have faith as a grain of mustard seed, ye might say unto this sycamore tree, be thou plucked up by the root, and be thou planted in the sea, and it should obey you." But even more, my cousin ardently told us, if we had no doubt or fear, and faith as strong as Jesus' faith, we too could walk on the water, even as He did.

After her profound lesson, I knew I had strong enough faith to walk on water as well. I didn't know one iota about swimming and was terrified of water even up to my chin, but at Uncle Rulon's pool I boldly stepped toward the deep end to prove to myself and to Jesus, I too had far more faith than just a grain of a mustard seed.

I waited for a good clearing between the guys who were diving off the board and coming up in the shallow end. *I am not afraid. I have faith!* I told myself again. And without a shadow of a doubt, I knew I could walk on top of the water clear to the other side. My faith was strong. I could hear my teacher's reassuring voice, "If ye have faith, even as a grain of a mustard seed . . ."

It seemed I'd taken two or three steps before my terrifying descent to the bottom of the pool. Panicked and devastated, I thought I was going to die. Later, Mom heard me tell God, I didn't like or trust Him anymore, especially this time, because He always made promises He didn't keep.

"He did respond," Mom exclaimed. "He didn't let you drown. He made sure Shane would jump in for you and pull you to safety, didn't He?"

"But what about the faith I had? What about those promises from God, you, Dad, my Sunday school teachers, and the scriptures? All of you keep promising me protection, and again, it didn't happen!" I cried. No matter how hard Mom tried to explain God's reasons for letting me down another time, I was heartbroken and in turmoil. Either God hated me and felt I had to be punished, or He didn't care about me enough to protect me. There had already been way too many unkept agreements.

Aunt Beth's three youngest daughters were all close to my age. I loved to hang out with them, but they were girls—girls who wanted to play house or dolls most of the time. I always preferred playing tough boys' games, but Plygville, to me, bore the signs of entitled male egos and chauvinistic, patriarchal mentality. Because I was a girl, I was banned from basketball, football, and soccer games with the guys, no matter how many times I begged. I had to pacify myself by playing house with my female cousins. My role, I always insisted, was of the storekeeper, the nurse, and mailman—anything but one of the moms, kids, or wives. Aunt Beth's girls portrayed their female rolls to perfection. Just like their mother, they were humorous, exuberant, and full of pizzazz.

Because of the stroke Uncle Lyman had when I was two years old, I never could understand what he said. His half-leaning shuffle, saggy bloodshot eye, and drooping mouth always scared me, but I felt sorry for him. One afternoon, while playing house in the barn, deeply immersed in our laughter and child's play, we heard his loud voice coming from an open door. He sounded irritated and angry. Apparently, his daughters already knew how to evade his temper. Without a second's hesitation, they quickly darted around him and disappeared, leaving me trapped and scared senseless. Uncle Lyman shook his doubled-up fist near my face while he ranted on and on. Not one of his angry words made a bit of sense to me.

"Wh–why are . . . are you . . . ma–ma–mad?" I tried to ask. I squeezed past him, aiming for the narrow doorway, but not swiftly enough to escape his fury. Powered by his pent-up frustration, Uncle Lyman's functioning arm swept way back before he landed his doubled-up fist in the middle of my back.

In the bathroom, I often stared at the baseball-size, hideously colorful bruise between my shoulder blades to remind me why my back hurt so much. From then on, I avoided Uncle Lyman. He always scared me, and after that unwarranted incident, I didn't like him either.

One beautiful summer day, a cousin who was close to my age asked, "Why did you pick all of the tulips and daffodils from my mother's flower garden?"

I told her I didn't, but she insisted I did. Trying to convince her or anyone else of my innocence was totally futile. She said someone saw me do it, so it was a fact. She said, "Everyone knows you did it, Sophia! So you're a big, fat liar."

Tormented by her accusations, I felt the whole Plygville nation had thrashed me with a belt and condemned me to hell. I was chock-full of sadness and injustice, feeling insignificant in our community, in heaven, and at home, school, or anywhere else I would wander. At home, deep under the covers of Mom's bed, I'd cry myself to sleep and wondered why I was on earth in the first place. Why did I exist?

A few weeks after the flowers were stolen; another cousin told me they'd been discovered in a large paper bag in the backyard where my accuser had tried to hide them. Remnants of leaves and petals were left in a tin can.

❧

Still, in my opinion, neither God nor Santa came through for my mother. Either she was gone, crying, angry, sleeping, working, or reading. She, I believed, had become proficient at escaping unpleasant life situations. Whenever she was through with her work, she read. She read at home, on the bus, in the car, in the bathroom, and in bed. When we'd talk to her, she answered, "Uh-huh, uh-huh," as if she was listening. Our method paid off when we wanted to go somewhere or do something she would otherwise have answered no. In the realms of her religious books, Mother could avoid her conflicting feelings and emotions. She would stay in her soothing, peaceful solitude and gather a million more righteous reasons to sojourn there even longer.

Even so, Mom tried with all her might to keep her promise to be a better, happier parent. In order to spend more time with James and me, she took us, one at a time, with her to Linton's Rest Home where she worked graveyard shifts. My paper sack held a coloring book, some crayons, a jacks set, and a book—things for me to do between the times I watched or helped with her geriatric patients. Occasionally, Mom had something significant to talk about besides the gospel of Jesus Christ and how I should always be a good girl. Otherwise, more often than not I felt ignored.

No matter what did or didn't happen, I was sure she loved me. Late at night when most of her patients were asleep and I was dozing off next to her, she would cuddle close to me, kiss my forehead and cheeks, and tuck the loose strands of hair behind my ears over and over again.

Lincoln was a twenty-seven-year-old amputee for whom Mom had been caring at the rest home. She felt so sorry for him she invited him to come live with us since Marlene was married as a second wife, and gone. Besides, helping Lincoln meant Mom could earn a little extra money.

I was fascinated by the way he could maneuver his whole body through the house without his wheelchair. He moved swiftly by swinging his torso and the five-inch stumps of his legs back and forth using his large, muscular arms and hands as legs and feet.

Lincoln was really kind, and always wanted me to hang around to visit or play games, so he wouldn't be so bored and lonely. Yet right from the start, something about him gave me the creeps. To sit with him very long made me feel crazy, but I felt so sorry for him, and every now and then Mom reminded me to be nice to him. So I'd make myself sit long enough to listen to another one of his gruesome war stories.

On one of those annoying occasions, Link said I should check out how terrible his scars looked. He took my hand and put it on his thick, grotesque scars where his legs had been cut off. I cringed.

"Now feel this," he said as he moved my hand onto his swelling penis. I gasped, pulled away and ran for the door.

"Stop, Sophia, please stop," he yelled.

Because of my stupid, childish worry for him, I froze. I was sorely tempted by his bribe of five dollars if I promised not to tell anyone. That would be twenty-five bucks nowadays, but for me, back then, like having a hundred. I walked out of the room without saying a word to him. All I could think about for the next little while was what I could have bought with *five whole dollars.*

In spite of everything, a tiny part of my heart felt bad for ratting on him. Until Lincoln had another place to go, Mom forbade me to go near him ever again. "Stay clear away from that evil man!" she said. "I was stupid to let him stay here in the first place." Maybe I shouldn't have told Mom what happened and just stayed away from him, but Lincoln was not my brother, family, or anyone I was afraid of or believed I had to protect.

Most of the time, I had no idea to whom I was accountable or who was responsible for my well-being while Mom was gone. After school I played outside until it got dark and cold. Sometimes I'd hang out at Aunt Beth's house until she'd send me home. I'd wander down our long driveway toward home—to nothing, to no one. I'd dangle my legs over the side of the bridge and stare at torrents of white water bouncing across the boulders, dancing in my direction. They'd smash against the concrete portals on either side of the conduit and then, in one deep surge, disappear under our bridge.

Why doesn't Aunt Beth know how lonely I feel? I asked myself. If she really loved me and cared, she'd let me live with her and treat me like one of her own children. Maybe she'd adopt me, but doesn't want to hurt my mom's feelings.

Whenever I'm at Uncle Marvin's home, he always had a hug and a smile for me, but I never feel welcome by any of his wives.

Mom's words popped into my head: "Be grateful for your blessings when you feel sad. Don't ever feel sorry for yourself!"

"I am okay!" I heard my voice say out loud. The words startled me back to the reality of the entrancing ditch water. Chills ran across my arms. "I'm glad Aunt Beth lets me stay as long as she does," I said repeatedly. I smiled the rest of the way down our long driveway.

Every night in my dreams, I walked to the top end of the south field near our home. Though the ditch was wide and swift at the high point, I'd tromp into the middle of it, lie down on my back, and float peacefully all the way down and under our bridge. As I'd float under it I'd see splotches of black and green moss, along with innumerable cobwebs and spiders, covering the rock-and-concrete walls. I'd glide on the water as it wound its way between our yard and Uncle Marvin's. As I approached his bridge, I would sweat with anxiety. There was no stopping, and I knew once I floated under his bridge, I'd get stuck and drown. Until I could wake myself up, it felt like I was really dying.

Over and over again, night after night, I woke up crying from those dreams. I didn't dare play in the ditch during the day, nor did I want to fall asleep at night. One night when I could no longer resist sleep, I decided I'd let myself drown under the bridge. No one would miss me anyway. My lungs hurt like there'd be no tomorrow, but the nightmares never returned again.

Near the end of that long, hot summer, I stood in our enormous yard full of dirt and rocks, spun around three times, and wished summer would hurry and end. I wanted to be in third grade.

CHAPTER 7

Bad and Stupid Sophia
1961–1962

Every summer my brother James and I, and sometimes other siblings, would take the long, hot trek with Mom and Dad to Short Creek, Arizona—today the FLDS community is called Colorado City/Hildale. We never got to know my sister Lucinda. Our occasional, brief trips couldn't reconcile the umpteen years we'd missed together after the groups split. For many years after she went back to her husband, mom said she wasn't allowed to come two-hundred-fifty miles to Murray to see us, but we were invited to go down there.

We would see hundreds of Barlow and Cooke nieces, nephews, and cousins, plus our grandmothers—Grandpa Cooke's wives—and Grandpa Cooke himself. Other than those once-or-twice-a year trips down south, those relatives hardly existed in our lives.

My brothers and I made sure we stayed as far away from Grandpa Cooke as possible. None of my siblings liked him. Every time we visited him, he would lecture, rant, and swear at us. By this time I was nearly nine years old and James was eleven. We weren't about to let him hit us again—ever.

On the other hand, our mother believed, to "honor" her father meant she was obliged to sit and let him verbally abuse her. She called it "visiting." Grandpa would tell her she should make her children come sit down and listen to his sermons so we wouldn't go to hell with her and Dad. But as soon as he'd start his preaching, we were out of there.

He lectured Mom on everything. It was either those evil Allred men who were acting on behalf of the devil, or what a terrible, dishonorable daughter she was to not be following the "true" prophet, Leroy Johnson.

"How can ya follow Rulon Allred?" Grandpa Cooke would yell. "He has an evil spirit ta be doin' what he's doin', and what he's done!"

If Mom tried to defend herself or her opinions, Grandpa's belligerent voice just got louder. Soon he'd be swearing at her. Finally, when she couldn't take any more of his madness, she'd storm out of the room in tears. But each year, she'd go back for more of his "honorable" cruelty.

On Grandpa's front lawn we played the same games we played at home. Many aunts and uncles at Grandpa's house were close to my age or younger, and all of them seemed to have a cute southern drawl I'd subconsciously mimic, as if to guarantee I was "fer sure thar genu-ine next of kin."

When Mom's younger sisters and I tried to bathe at night, Grandpa Cooke would tell us we couldn't shut the door, even when we dressed and undressed. Aunt Maggie, Mom's sister who was four years my senior, told me he'd always had that rule. He just wants to "make sure we aren't gonna do things we shouldn't be doin'," she'd say.

"Alright then," I told her, "I won't be taking a bath at all!"

As I went back upstairs to the girls' bedroom, Grandpa hollered, "Sophia, git yer arss back in that thar bathroom and take yer bath right now befur I have ta come after ya!"

But he was too old to come after me. "Just try, Grandpa," I'd say under my breath while I kept climbing the stairs as if I hadn't heard him.

The next morning when I tiptoed barefoot down the stairs to get to the bathroom, I was startled to see Grandpa sitting on the sofa, wide-awake.

"Sophia!" he barked just as I saw his face. "Git back up them stairs and cover yer damn ankles!"

He was the only living grandparent we had, and he treated us like trash.

Even when I was only nine years old, it irked me, all of the women and girls in Colorado City looked like clones, with their hair all done up in buns or braids with the same identical and distinct "Short Creek waves" swooped up and down, then draped across the sides of their foreheads.

When we stayed over at Lucinda's house, I asked my nieces and their half-sisters why every girl in town wore the exact same hairstyle every single day.

One of the older girls explained, "A long, long time ago, before I was born, one of our priesthood leaders told all the women they should dress and look like Sister . . . uh, I don't know her name. Anyway, he told everyone, she kept her hair done up nicely and looked very becoming, so all of us should exemplify her."

"So all of you have to wear your hair exactly like hers all the time?" I asked.

The four or five young girls in the room questioned each other with their eyes. "Well, I guess so," one of them answered. "We like it like this. Our hair has been fixed like this since we were little, and we don't know how to fix it any other way."

I told them they could look "well-kept and becoming" by fixing their hair a lot of different ways, but they just plain didn't buy it. I was the weird one, the minority who felt way out of place.

My nieces had already been scrutinizing my blond hair. It was parted in the middle, and had grown near the middle of my back. "Do you ever fix your hair any other way?" my nieces wanted to know.

"I fix it different all the time," I announced, putting my big foot in my mouth.

My nieces promptly asked if they could do my hair just like theirs. "So you'll look beautiful," they told me.

I caved in. When they finished styling my hair, they stood behind me, their big smiles beaming in the mirror as I stared at myself in shock.

"Oh, Sophia, you should wear your hair like this all the time. You look so sweet!"

There was no doubt their feelings would be hurt if I let them know how I really felt about the waves above my forehead and the enormous, football-shaped bun on top of my head. I forced a smile. For their sake, I suffered through "The Look" all day long, but gave them an emphatic no the next morning when they wanted to style my hair again.

Before my brother-in-law (the town's mayor), began building onto Lucinda's and his other wives' already huge house, they had to use an outhouse like my sister Francine's. Now they had a new bathroom inside. His huge family washed their clothes in an old wringer washer and rinsed them in a galvanized tub before they hung them on the clothesline to dry, just as we had always done. It would take my sister Lucinda two or three days to finish the laundry, one day less than it took Mom and me, by the time we got it all gathered, sorted, washed, rinsed, hung on the lines, gathered in again, folded, and put away.

But winters back in Murray, Utah, were quite different. After we washed fifteen batches of clothes in our old wringer washer, Mom had no choice but to spend her precious dollars on coin-operated dryers at the local laundromat. While we'd wait for each batch of clothing to dry, Mom read to herself and munched on a chocolate candy bar, while I ate mine. When we folded what seemed like a billion pieces of clothing, towels, sheets, socks, and everything else everyone had soiled for the past two weeks, Mom talked about the "good books" she'd been reading.

"I've read the Book of Mormon at least ten times," she would proudly announce. "Every time I read it, I find new information, as if it wasn't there before. There is a promise in the beginning of the book. When you read it and pray about it, you will gain a testimony of its truth, and the truth of the gospel of Jesus Christ." Mom would tell me again and again how important it was to pray three times a day, dress modestly, and to stay virtuous so I could marry the right man—the one and only man God had in store for me so we could bring righteous children into this world. As I promised her I would try my best, I shuddered to think of how wicked I already was.

At the beginning of the year, every third-grade student was asked to write the alphabet as well as he or she could on a piece of paper. Each of us put our name on the back before our work was posted in the hallways to be reviewed by the judges who would decide the winners of the Best Handwriting Contest.

The day after my teacher took them down, she announced the third-, second- and first-place winners. I was both giddy and mortified when she called my name last. It meant I won the blue ribbon for first place. I was sure there had been a mistake. My handwriting was very nice, but I was never recognized for anything.

All of the students' eyes were on me when the teacher called my name again and made my classmates clap for me. In front of them, I felt shy and embarrassed, but after school was out I proudly marched across the playground toward home. I was anxious to show Mom the beautiful blue-and-white certificate that proclaimed in big bold letters across the image of an American flag: "This certificate is awarded to Sophia Allred, for Best Handwriting."

I was unaware that anyone was behind me, when Trevor suddenly snatched my papers from my hands. He threw all of them but my certificate on the ground, while Chad watched. Then with both hands against my back, Chad shoved me forward across the blacktop.

"You stupid girl!" Trevor scoffed as he got down on the ground in front of me and shook my certificate in my face. "You only got this because the teacher feels sorry for you!" Then he shredded it into tiny pieces and showered them over my head.

Snot and tears soaked the front of my white blouse. My shoes, socks, legs, torn jumper, and the cold, wet cloth I used to scrape tiny rocks from the lesions on my knees—all were blood red.

Why did I even think of telling Mom about this? I wondered. I didn't want to hear what she had to say! What I really wanted her to do was tell me that I am a good girl because I am a good girl—not because I'm being persecuted! I wanted her to hold me, cry with me, and stick up for me. I wanted her to lash out and want to punch those boys! She should have yelled, "Tell me who those little creeps are so I can go beat the living daylights out of them! They'd better keep their disgusting hands off my beautiful little girl or I'll—" But, of course that's not at all what she said. I could hear the same preaching words I'd heard a zillion times over again, tormenting my ears: "Blessed are the persecuted for righteousness sake. God is . . ."

"God is mean and dishonest," I wanted to scream at her. "He never keeps His promises! He didn't let me walk on water when I had the faith He promised. He made me stupid. He takes all my friends away, and He makes you sad! He lets Aunt Eleanor and her kids have everything they want! He didn't stop Maryann from pounding on my brothers, and He let the doctor and Rick . . ." But I could never go there.

I screamed out a thousand sorrows as loud as I could—all inside my head—so I couldn't hear my mother preach to me anymore.

She must've heard me wheezing and gasping for air, felt my body shaking next to hers. She saw my swollen, wretched face, but she couldn't see me.

With her arm around me, Mom thought she was comforting me as she sermonized, "And those who endure to the end for righteousness sake shall inherit the kingdom of God. You see Sophia; He loves you because you are such a good girl. He just wants to—"

I wanted to push my hand over her mouth to make her shut up.

Can't you hear me, Mom? I was pleading inside. *I don't want to hear what God wants anymore. Not now, not ever!*

Of course, I didn't touch her mouth or shout at her. I'd never do that. I never did tell her what I wanted, what I didn't want, what I needed, or who I was. And she never asked.

⁂

One day after school, while we were waiting for everyone to gather for a game of Five Step on the soccer field, my cousin told me about a girl who believed the same way we did and lived in the subdivision behind Aunt Beth's house.

The petite blond could have passed for my sister if I hadn't been so much taller than her. Ann was very nice and invited my cousin and me into her house. When she opened the front door, my cousin followed her right through the front room and into the kitchen. But I couldn't move. The door handle seemed glued to my hand. I was frozen with fear while five or six pairs of male eyes focused on my blushing face.

Ann finally came back to see what happened to me, and introduced me to several of her handsome brothers. She fixed us each a jam sandwich. Then we went downstairs to find something to do.

Ann asked her thin, dark-haired, nearly eighteen-year-old brother Mark if we could borrow his Monopoly game.

"No way!" he teased. "I don't loan my games to ugly little girls like you." Then he smiled. "Of course you can. You can use my games anytime you want."

I thought Mark was one of the nicest guys I'd ever met. Who would have known then we'd spend more than thirty-three years of our lives together?

By the middle of third grade, I discovered the extent of our polygamous notoriety. Unless the kids in our elementary, middle, and high schools were totally aloof, or brand new to the area, they knew who the plyg kids were and where we lived. There were well over a hundred of us. At least twelve families on our block practiced plural marriage. We referred to our half-brothers and half-sisters as cousins. If the children's mother wasn't the first and legal wife, most carried their mother's maiden names.

The kids outside of polygamy already knew, or were rapidly realizing from others, just which plyg kids they could tease and ridicule, whom they'd accept (or pretend to), and which ones they shouldn't mess with.

Though I couldn't wait to be in third grade the previous summer, by midyear I hated school. Still, I showed up just in time every day. My teacher demanded I pay more attention and stop daydreaming. I didn't fit in at all.

One day when I didn't know the answers again, the kids started making sarcastic comments. My teacher didn't even attempt to stop them from ridiculing me for my mistakes, my clothes, and my too-big, ugly, black, masculine-looking shoes Dad insisted "are the best shoes ever made and will last until next year, before you grow out of them."

All around me, the kids in my class taunted, "Plyg, plyg, plyg!"

I was always hungry, tired, and worried, especially at school, where I had to hold still. I felt all alone in an unsafe world. There was always one thing or another to be anxious about: Mom's unhappiness, my loneliness, self-hate, and Rick haunting me again.

I worried almost constantly my family might have to leave and go into hiding again. *Will I be ready, standing in holy places when the earth comes to an end? My whole family will probably be chosen and called to be saved, but not me. I'll be left behind.* I feared every day would be the day God (according to my parents and our ancestors) destroyed the wicked with fire and earthquakes, and only the righteous people would be saved or lifted up.

My teacher nagged me to master my addition and subtraction facts. She required everyone to recite the answers in front of the whole class. The few times I dared think I had them mastered, some fifty-four eyes stared me down, as the other students waited to harass me when

I messed up. I always did.

The reading and math charts posted around the room were proof to me and to the others of my ignorance. Sophia Allred was at the bottom of all of them. I was in the lowest reading group, and couldn't get one good grade on spelling tests. The more I tried, the more stupid I felt. The more stupid I felt, the less I tried. So, one day I decided to quit trying.

All I really wanted to do was fly away. "Please, God, please let me fly," I prayed. "At the very least, let me out of these school doors so I can run . . . run . . . and soar under the beautiful blue sky."

I'd beg and plead and beg Mom some more. "Don't make me stay overnight at Aunt Maryann's house! I can go home to sleep or stay somewhere else," I'd say. But I couldn't give her a plausible excuse, and she said there wasn't anyone else for me to stay with while she worked graveyard shifts at the Cottonwood Stake Maternity Hospital. I thought I had no choice but to stay at Aunt Maryann's two or three times a week.

Rick had begun molesting me again. These times weren't nearly as terrifying, I convinced myself. With Maryann's two girls, two boys, and me all in one tiny bedroom, he didn't dare risk going as far. He'd sneak in during the middle of the night. If I could sleep, he'd wake me up, reach under the covers, and slip my panties aside or down, then fondle me while he manipulated himself. During the day, Rick's gaze and actions were tormenting. He let me know in no uncertain terms he wielded the sword of power. *If* I didn't sleep on the outside of the bed, *if* I wriggled away from his reach, and *if* I didn't hold still…he'd lift the blade higher the next day.

CHAPTER 8

Our Catastrophes
1962

By 1962, there were so many converts to the Allred Group Dad had to install a speaker system in nearly every room in the house to accommodate the large crowd who wanted to attend any meetings. You couldn't always see who was speaking, but you could hear them.

Every Saturday, it was my job to clean the house. It was still my brother, Darrell's job to set up chairs. He'd also put two large pitchers of water, a couple loaves of Mom's homemade bread, and her best sacrament plates on a small table near the front of the room. Then he would neatly cover all of it with a beautiful, white linen cloth.

During the meeting, the young priests would kneel in front of the table and say the sacrament prayer on the bread. Then, they'd break the loaves of bread into small pieces and place them on four plates. Each one held his left arm behind his back while he offered each person in the house a small piece of bread. Since I'd been baptized I, like the other kids, could participate in this ordinance. With our right hand, we'd take one piece of the bread, which represented Jesus' body. While we chewed it, we were to contemplate the sacrifice He made for us and what we would do with our lives to be worthy of His offerings.

Then, the water was blessed in the same manner and served to each person in a glass. We were to think of the blood of Jesus and how He spilled it freely to pay for our sins.

We were told we wouldn't become ill from the germs passed from mouth to mouth on the edge of the glass because the water had been blessed. But it still concerned me to take my sip of water from the same glass others had. It especially bothered me if Jon Thomas, Gregory Maynard, or my cousin Craig, all men I couldn't tolerate—had taken their swallow from the glass before it got to me.

One Sunday morning when one of my cousins came over, I was still in bed. She wanted to know why I wasn't ready for Sunday school.

"I have morning sickness," I told her.

"No, you don't," she retorted.

"Yes, I do," I insisted.

"No, you don't, Sophia!" she yelled.

"I do too!" I screamed back at her. "It's morning, and I am sick, sick, sick! So I'm not going to Sunday school today. Okay?"

The more she laughed, the more offended I felt she didn't believe me. Finally, she explained. When a lady says she has morning sickness, it means she is pregnant and going to have a baby. The representation of my ten-year-old naivety was so embarrassing to me, I nearly cried.

Fourth grade was even worse. Whenever my teacher asked me questions, I didn't know the answers. Most of the time, I didn't even understand what she'd asked me. Everything on my mind was how hungry I felt, and when school would be out so I could run home and fix some bread and milk with honey all over it.

One day at school we heard what sounded like an explosion. Within a few seconds our desks began to vibrate in front of us. My teacher screamed, "Get under your desks!" I watched her climb under hers and heard her yell again, "Hurry, class—get under your desks!"

But my hands were frozen and wouldn't dislodge from the sides of my desk, even as it quivered back and forth. The window panels stretched across the length of our whole classroom rumbled and began to crackle. We screamed.

I was sure it was the end of the world—the catastrophes Dad and Uncle Rulon and the other brethren had prophesied. There wasn't one protective angel in that classroom to watch over me, and it had never felt like "holy ground."

The thundering sound carried on for minutes, it seemed, and the war inside my head didn't stop when the earthquake subsided. My delirium kept going. *After all, most of The Group has gathered and left this wicked city—they won't even miss me! No one will ever come after me.* "I'll starve to death," I heard myself say out loud. Several class-mates started laughing.

"Good grief, what a rush," the class comedian yelled. "Come on— let's have some more!"

The students laughed. They'd already pulled themselves back up from underneath their desks and were filing out of the room, per the teacher's orders.

"Come on, hurry up, kids. Quickly now. Line up by the door fast. Come on, kids. Move faster," she demanded. Then I felt her hands on top of mine, prying my clenched fists from my desk. She smacked my arms and shoulders. "Get up now, Sophia," she yelled. "I know you can hear me! Why in the world are you just sitting here?"

As if I'd come back to life, I noticed my heart pounding. The world hadn't come to an end after all. My thumping heart reassured me I was still well and alive. Some of the kids looked back to snicker at me, while I noticed Jeanie's eyes reflected sadness and concern.

God stopped the destruction of the earth this time, but that earth-quake must have been one of His tests and warnings I've been told about all of my life. I'll have to be a better girl from now on.

Jeanie, the new girl in our class, was a black-haired, brown-eyed beauty, as they say. I'd stare at her and wonder where she came from. On my way home another day, I saw her walk toward a big brown house at the top of our street, catty-corner from our school. When I said hello to her, she invited me in for some snacks.

When she asked me if I was going to church, I told her, "No, I don't go to church."

"Aren't you a Mormon?"

"Yes, I am."

"Then why don't you go to church?"

"I don't know," I lied.

She grinned. "Maybe you could come with me to Primary tomorrow afternoon."

"I'll ask if I can," I fibbed again, trying to act normal. I didn't have to ask anyone. There wasn't one person who would even know I was gone.

The next day, we walked up the street from Jeanie's house to the LDS meetinghouse. When I walked into the building, where most of the kids in our school attended church meetings, I was amazed. "It's huge and pretty!" I said, sorely wishing we had a church building like theirs.

In Jeanie's Primary class, the teacher started her Bible lesson about the Tower of Babel. When I correctly answered several of her questions, she asked me again who I was.

"Sophia Allred," I said.

"And where did you say you live?" she asked. "Did you say you are a Mormon, but you don't attend church? How is it you know so much about these stories?"

I told her my mom and dad were too busy to go to church, but they read to me and told me the stories in the Bible and Book of Mormon, and we had Sunday school in our house, every week. I was pretty good at this by then. Even so, I felt queasy every time I had to make up one story to cover for another one.

On the way out the door, the Primary teacher told me to be sure to come back the next week. Jeanie touched my hand and beamed, saying, "I can tell we're going to be best friends."

For nearly a week I was in my glory. After school, Jeanie and I drew pictures, watched television, and played Parcheesi. Her mother prepared the most delicious snacks I'd ever eaten and treated me royally. Feeling a little bit like a normal kid was exciting and wonderful. I was ecstatic to be going to Primary like the rest of the kids near our neighborhood.

All of my life I'd heard good things about the LDS Church. I grew up with the same scripture lessons and beliefs. I'd been taught the same Mormon values and principles as my peers on the outside had been learning. Dad said the main difference between us and the LDS Church is we believed in the "fulness of the gospel." He frequently affirmed his love and respect for the LDS Church, as well as the laws of the land—unless, of course, they violated the laws of God. He admonished us to adhere to those same ideals.

As soon as Jeanie and I entered the classroom the next week, the Primary teacher took me aside. "I am so sorry, Sophia, but I can't allow you to stay." She removed Jeanie's hand from mine and guided her to a nearby chair, then returned to me. "Our bishop said you can't come to this church anymore because of your parents. They are breaking the law and are apostates."

I didn't even know what an apostate was, but once again I knew the overwhelming feeling of being discarded.

Across the street at McMillan Elementary School, I sat on the cold concrete stairs leading down to the playground and tried not to cry. More than anything, I was angry at myself for caring, for wishing and hoping to feel normal and accepted.

Like the other short-lived friends who came and went in my life, Jeanie would never be my friend again. I was dispensable and replaceable. *Why should they care anyway? I thought. Something really is wrong with me. I am stupid, bad, ugly, and fat.*

While crying nearly all the way home, my soul again reminded me to keep going, reassuring me, I really was a good person.

CHAPTER 9

Foes and Shame
1963

Along with my maturing age came more responsibility. I made simple meals, did the dishes, cleaned the whole house, and did the laundry with Mom or alone. I helped my brother Darrell set up hundreds of chairs in our new garage, which served as The Group's church, and then I played outside as long as possible. I really didn't mind having those duties, but I knew unless someone realized I hadn't finished one of my chores, I would not be noticed or missed at all.

One long weekend break from school, I decided to prove my point. Friday morning I ran and walked twelve miles to Draper City to stay with a new friend. Once I got there, I told her mother if it was okay with her, I could stay over for two nights and then ride back home with them when their family drove to Murray for Sunday afternoon sacrament meeting.

Sunday evening, Dad asked angrily, "Why didn't you clean the house and help prepare for church today, Sophia? Where have you been all day?"

"When did you notice I was gone?" I asked.

"When we noticed the house hadn't been cleaned," he complained.

"It wasn't at all presentable for church."

"I knew, Dad," I replied, the magnitude of my disappointment reflected in my voice. "I knew I wouldn't be missed by you, Mom, or anyone else unless my jobs weren't done! I've been gone for three days, and no one even noticed or missed me until this morning."

The sadness in my dad's eyes melted my heart. He got down on one knee and said, "I am so sorry, honey. Who is supposed to be watching over you while your mother is working and sleeping?

"I don't know, Dad! I haven't known forever."

Most of the children in our community loved the pond between our home and Uncle Marvin's, with its muddy water, willows, tadpoles, and frogs. When the adults filled it with gravel and dirt to create a big parking lot for our growing congregation, the children felt betrayed and devastated. It seemed every opportunity for fun and adventure was eventually ruined by the growth of our fundamentalist community.

Toward the front of the parking-lot field, and fairly close to the main street (which was no longer a dead end), my cousin Craig and his wife Charlene built a simple three-bedroom home for their rapidly growing family.

Mom was a friend and spiritual guide to Charlene, who often confided her deepest concerns to my mother. She would hold Charlene's hands while she cried. As with most curious children, I'd often tune in to their conversations, even though some of them made me cringe.

"I'm always fertile, having one baby after another, faster than I can physically or emotionally handle," Charlene told Mom one day. "I want him to leave me alone! He won't even stay away from me when I'm pregnant."

Being nearly eleven, I had a good idea what Charlene was talking about, and I winced. Little by little, I'd figured out what "the birds and the bees" had to do with how babies came to grow inside the womb. Pregnancy didn't come about from that great big, juicy wedding kiss or the wedding ceremony like I used to think. And God didn't just make a new baby magically appear after a mother spent hours of agony in a bedroom and then suddenly emerged looking much thinner. I don't know just how I figured it out, but I learned that condition came about by the thing you do that Mom says is "evil and disgusting if you're not married, but wonderful and beautiful if you are."

So, I was puzzled. Charlene and Craig were married, so it was supposed to be wonderful and beautiful, yet Charlene told Mom that she felt plagued by her oversexed husband. Those conversations made me despise Craig more than I already did. I hated the way he looked at me and the other little girls. I hated the way I felt if he was home when I had to help at Charlene's house.

When they moved in next-door, Mom assigned me to be Charlene's personal maid and assistant. After school, on weekends, and whenever Charlene needed a housekeeper or babysitter, I was expected to be her servant. It was okay at first, but I started to resent my lack of playtime, and all of my hard work, for which I rarely received a word of appreciation.

"But she needs your help!" Mom charged whenever I'd try to ditch my responsibilities. "You know you should always place others and their needs before yourself. You are a servant of the Lord, and by serving others you are serving Him. Now put your shoes on, Sophia, and get over there now!"

I helped Charlene with housework and with her children so much that I felt like I practically raised her first two or three children, as if they were my responsibility. Now she was expecting again. Based on Mom's convictions and example, I believed it was my job to help Charlene fulfill her parental and household duties, so I tried to be sweet and happy about it.

One day, I'd finished cleaning their house, and was nearly done with the dishes, when Craig came in the kitchen door. The look in his eyes completely drained me. Then, as if he had picked up on my loathing, he made his body brush against mine as he passed by. I felt diminished and sickened. I should have just left, but my obligatory respect for adults and my codependency kicked in.

For a few seconds, I stood in the kids' room where they were watching Elmer Fudd hunt Bugs Bunny with his double-barrel shotgun. I stood by the chair Craig was sitting in and tried to find the courage to tell him I was leaving even if Charlene wasn't back yet.

Without a word, he grabbed my arm and forced me down onto his lap. He made sure my legs straddled his. I tried to get up, but he held tightly onto my forearms. At first, I thought Craig was just teasing me and he'd let me up in a second. But he didn't. Then both of his hands crawled under my blouse and up to my newly developing breasts. I was scared to death, yet I'd been told over and over to respect adults. Craig's slimy hands were on my body where they didn't belong. I hated him!

Is this love? Is he loving me? I asked myself. Maybe I should like this because he does. I didn't! I felt terrible and ashamed. While he squirmed beneath me, he held me so tight against his chest with his arms wrapped around me and his hands on my tiny breasts, that I started crying. *If I scream, his kids will turn around. If I jump up and run away, he might hurt me. If I run, that might hurt his feelings. He'll feel bad. He'll get mad at me. None of this makes any sense!* I was crying when I finally broke away from Craig and ran to the bathroom.

My vomit splashed back onto my face as it hit the water in the toilet. I could hardly breathe. *What will he do when I open the bathroom door? Will he grab me or hit me? Maybe he'll pull me back into Charlene's room and torment me some more.* It must have been ten minutes before one of his kids banged on the door. I opened it and ran home.

His assault haunted me for many years. No matter how many times I thought about telling Mom or anyone else, I couldn't. Craig was my elder whom I'd been taught to respect. If I told Charlene or Mom, they might think I was lying, and if they did believe me, Charlene's world might have fallen apart. She was already too depressed and fragile as it was. I wasn't brave enough to cause her more grief.

After that horrible episode, something inside of me became stronger. I turned into what I supposed back then, was a rebellious child. The next time Charlene or Mom wanted my help, I said, "No, I have other plans." No matter what they did or said, no one could persuade or bribe me back into that sick and subservient situation.

Never again would I stay overnight at Aunt Maryann's, either. What, for heaven's sake, took me so long to realize that Mom wouldn't know where I slept—whether I was at home, at the neighbors, in a tent, or in a field? After Craig molested me, I slept back at our house, in Mom's bed, unless Dad was sleeping with her instead of another wife. I knew no one could make me change my mind without a physical fight. No one ever tried.

My deepest dreams during those years were to be able to survive in the mountains. I would live with the animals where no one could ever treat me badly. I wouldn't have to go to school or feel stupid anymore. I fantasized a normal life—a dad, one mom, and one family—and I wished with all of my heart, that God could never hear me think wicked things like that.

CHAPTER 10

New Friends, Mother, and Siblings
1963

In Mom's bedroom, I gazed at her long, old-fashioned underwear. Like most adult members of our fundamentalist church, she wore long garments, which were as sacrosanct as life itself. Mom and Dad had started wearing them when they were married in the Logan Temple forty-seven years earlier. All of the markings on their garments had a special purpose and meaning. The thin lace tie that held the front closed; the stitched markings over each nipple; the abnormally large collar; and the gaping, crescent-shaped opening in the pelvic and buttock area—all carried significance. For my parents, dressing and undressing were ceremonial events.

Mother would ceremoniously slide her right foot in one leg, then the left foot in the other. She pulled the one-piece garment up over her body, put her right arm and then her left into the long sleeves and guided them over her shoulders, then pulled the garment around her chest and tied it shut. Before she could put her slip and dress on, she put her bra and underpants over the top of her garments. Then she would meticulously fold up the legs of the garment from her ankles to a few inches below her knees. To prevent the garment legs from sliding below the hem of her mid-calf-length dresses, she'd use tiny gold pins to hold them in place. Afterward, she'd repeat the same process with each sleeve, so they too would stay hidden under her three-quarter-sleeved dresses.

"No one should ever divulge the meaning of these symbols," Mother replied whenever I asked her to tell me what they were about. "But what I can tell you, Sophia, is garments are an extraordinary blessing to those of us who have been through the temple and have had our work done. The garments will protect us from harm and evil, and it makes me sad I can't wear them down to my ankles and wrists the way I am supposed to. I hope God will forgive me for folding them up to hide them, but if I don't, they'll be seen by those who don't understand and will criticize them. To let others ridicule or scoff at my garments would be like casting pearls before swine."

Mother sadly complained about the LDS Church doing away with most of the lengthy temple ceremonies and the long garments. "Originally, the temple ordinances took nearly two full days to complete," she said. "Now, I hear the ceremonies take just a few hours. The modern-day garments have been reduced to a short-sleeved top and pants cut off below the knees. They've also discarded some of the significant markings. It's just one more way the LDS Church keeps changing and deleting the sacred teachings of Joseph Smith."

"God's laws don't change," Mom would say again and again. "Someday Jesus and Joseph Smith will come back to this earth and set things in order. They will perform plural marriages and all of the ordinances in the temples and reinstate other tenets the LDS Church authorities have forsaken. Meanwhile, we must never forget our responsibilities to carry on God's work. Always keep in mind, Sophia, where much is given, much is expected."

I was sure I'd never be worthy to wear those garments. Even if I were worthy, I knew they would not protect me. Nothing or no one had thus far. And if, just *if* I ever qualified to wear those long, thick garments, I was sure I'd die from heat exhaustion.

I could never tell Mom how I really felt about her garments, because it would hurt her feelings. And just like everything else I'd done in my life, I'd wear garments for her sake, Dad's sake, even for God's sake—if I really had to. It was already torturous to have to wear dresses to school every day and all day long on Sundays. All I ever wanted to wear was a blouse and a pair of Levi's. Then, I could be physically free to soar.

Guilt had been plaguing me for two long days and nights, ever since I tended our neighbors' children. The parents had told me I could have all the chocolates I wanted, so I did. Those delicious morsels, right there in my face, kept begging and forcing me to eat them. "One more!" they'd call out to me. "Oh, come on, just one more. We're so delicious! Have another one." When the adults returned, the candy bowl was completely empty. Most were in my stomach, and the rest were in my coat pocket.

"The kids and I ate them while we watched a movie," I lied.

I really didn't steal them, I told myself. After all, they did say I could have all I wanted. But inside I knew such conduct wasn't polite. I'd never been so embarrassed, and I hated myself. I'd been taught and drilled on how to lie. Dishonesty had become second nature to me. I felt guilty, but I wasn't sure how to stop lying. Half the time, I couldn't keep track of all the untruths I had to tell to protect the perpetrators in my life, versus the fibs that would just pop out of my mouth. Some lies were just plain wrong! So I forbade myself to ever lie again. But at my young age, my brain and heart were not strong enough to stop my perjuring mouth. It was a given, I would someday burn in hell.

The following Friday afternoon, Carol took me to her house so she could teach me how to sew. Surely it was because she'd decided I needed a new dress. I packed my clothes, a peanut-butter sandwich, and the pocketful of candy—just in case.

I wanted to look just like Carol. She was a short, brown-eyed, petite woman. Her husband wasn't very large, but he looked huge next to her. This beautiful young couple, who were converts to the Allred Group, mesmerized me with their Southern drawl.

Carol fixed one of the most fabulous meals I'd ever tasted. My stomach was totally satisfied when I settled on her couch bed in front of a large picture window.

In my nightmare, I relived something that had happened a few weeks earlier on my way home from school. Rocks pelted my arms and back. "Plyg, plyg! Stupid little plyg girl!" the boys mocked as they chased me toward home. No matter how fast I ran my body felt as if it was barely moving across the ground. As the neighborhood bullies closed in on me, I could feel them grasp my back and neck. Just in the nick of time, I screamed myself awake.

I wiped the tears and sweat from my face with my arm, and unwrapped my pink flannel nightgown that was twisted around my legs. My bladder felt like it would burst, but I couldn't get up. It had crossed my mind earlier to ask Carol to leave a nightlight on, but my embarrassment and pride wouldn't let me, and there was no way I dared go anywhere in the dark. I was pathetically afraid of everything. Again, I chastised myself for being a ten-year-old wimp. *If Carol really knew what a pathetic little girl I was, she wouldn't have invited me over in the first place,* I thought.

The rest of the chocolates were right next to me in my sack. I scarfed down every last piece and then hid the wrappers under my things. Then, gorged but feeling miserably consoled, I fell back to sleep.

I dreamed the bathroom light was on, so I hurried in to relieve myself. I went several times, again and again, all night long. But as the sunlight started to creep through the curtains, I still had to go to the bathroom. I pulled up my nightgown and sat down on the toilet. Within seconds, I woke to a warm sensation on my thighs, around my buttocks, and drenching the sheets. I was mortified! *Now what will I do or say?*

There was no lie on this earth that could protect me from this unpleasant disgrace. I had wet the bed too many times, for too many years.

I promised myself I'd never sleep overnight anywhere until I stopped wetting the bed for good. But my vow didn't help me feel a single bit better, and I had no choice but to confess my accident to Carol. Humiliated, I tried to explain my fears and about my dream. She promised me everything was just fine.

At the fabric shop, Carol told me to choose any cotton material I wanted. The dark pink material with bright blue, green, yellow, and purple nickel-sized polka dots was beautiful. She picked out a spool of matching thread and a pattern for a size-12 A-line dress.

Carol smiled sweetly. "Sophia, you are a beautiful young girl! If you will eat better food and get more exercise, we'll buy you a size 6 or 8 pattern next time.

How could I get more exercise? I wanted to know. I already ran everywhere I went: to school, from school, up and down our stairs, and nearly every day after school.

Still, Carol was right. Even my dad let me know in his well-meaning way, "If you weren't so active, Sophia, you and our cows would be the same size by now!"

My homemade dress turned out perfect and beautiful. I was extremely grateful to Carol. But even her goodness couldn't erase my insecurities about my weight and bedwetting. Because I was so self-conscious and humiliated, I couldn't even speak to Carol after the dress was finished and she took me home. Sometimes, before or after Sunday meetings, she would smile at me from across the room, and I hoped she understood why I avoided her. After all these years, I can still see her kind, smiling face. I'm sure I didn't adequately appreciate her efforts back then, but a few years later I came to understand the importance of what she had done for me. From her, I learned how to sew. As years passed I sewed everything from denim jackets to wedding dresses.

She and her husband didn't stay in the Allred Group long; so many families came and went. Wherever Carol is in this vast, wide world, I wish I could give her a big hug and thank her for her wonderful gift to me, and for treating me with such kindness.

☙

Fourth- and fifth-grade students got to volunteer in the cafeteria. If we worked there, we could have free hot lunches. As always, I had the same old dry, whole-wheat sandwiches made with homemade cheese or peanut butter. Those lunches had become so revolting I always looked forward to my turn to help in the lunchroom.

As in previous years, I watched my peers eat or waste their lunches. Sometimes they'd devour everything on their trays. Or they'd take only one or two bites before discarding the rest. To pretend I didn't care was nearly impossible. Desperately, I wanted someone to be considerate enough to offer me his or her fruit, dessert, or yummy-looking white bread. If it were the other way around, I thought, I would have offered any extra food to them, or even shared what I had; but my peers were always in a predicament. They couldn't pay attention to me, a plyg kid—an outcast—even if they wanted to. That would have required risking their relationships with their classmates. I understood. It was much too scary for them.

The best part about "fall canning season," as my family always called it, was we got to have fresh fruit or vegetables in our lunches. During this time, all of Dad's kids, even the younger ones, became assembly-line workers for weeks on end. From the second we got home from school until late at night, we helped peel, core, and cut the produce. We'd stuff it into hundreds of pint or quart bottles. Aunt Eleanor, Maryann, or Mom would wipe the tops off, tighten the lids, and place the bottles in a huge vat of hot water on top of our coal stove. Once the food had boiled for an allotted time, the jars were removed. As the jars cooled down, each lid made loud popping sounds. To us, it was the satisfactory proof our food storage was sufficiently sealed before it would be placed on the shelves in the fruitroom space, I wanted to be mine.

Almost every day, I daydreamed of having a space of my very own; even a tiny spot would be better than nothing. I'd meander down the long flight of steps and slip into the fruitroom under the staircase. There, I'd envision what wondrous things I could do with the tiny space under a shelf. Sometimes I'd stand outside on Mom's six-by-eight-foot front porch and wish for that space. Even in our huge new garage, where meetings were now held, I longed for a corner, even a tent or a hut. If only I had a small space of my own, I would be in heaven.

҂

An older cousin, Kenneth, moved his family back to the Salt Lake City area from Pinesdale, Montana. His family had lived on the massive ranch the Allred Group had purchased in the early sixties.

Luckily for me, he relocated his second wife and her two daughters in Murray, fairly close to us. Kenneth's eldest daughter, Valerie, and I began to hang out together. She was the first true friend I'd ever had.

To me, Valerie's mother was perfect. On weekends, she took us swimming and shopping. Sometimes she'd play games and visit with us. Valerie and her little sister always had chores and piano lessons. It seemed they were the only girls with perfect mother-daughter relationships—at least until Aunt Amelia came along.

Several years earlier, Amelia and her three children had moved from the LeBaron Group in Mexico to California, and then to Salt Lake City. Prior to that, she had corresponded with my parents and planned to join our group. Before long, Amelia's oldest daughter, Amy, and I became almost inseparable.

The first time Amy came into our house, my mom was wearing her nurse's uniform and making her bed. When I first went to Amy's house, her grandmother was wearing a white pinafore apron, and dusting the living room. A short time later, we discovered each of us had assumed the other's family was wealthy enough to have a maid. We laughed and laughed at our mistake, since both of our families were poor as paupers.

One of the best days of my adolescent years was when Amy's mom brought my little sister Jolene with her, and called Amy and me down from the massive Weeping Willow tree in Aunt Maryann's front yard.

"Hey, girls, I have a great big surprise for you. I want to tell you girls; you have a new sister!" Aunt Amelia gathered her arms around Jolie and me. With a soft, kind voice she whispered, "I married your dad." Then she hugged Amy tightly. "I married my good friend, Owen. Now you have a whole bunch of sisters and brothers."

We jumped up and down and screamed in delight. I was ecstatic and crazy with joy. My new friend, Amy, who was only six months older than me, had suddenly become my sister. And I had a new mother who had already begun to treat me like gold.

CHAPTER 11

Modesty and Vanity
on "The Outside"
1964–1965

There were two reasons I seldom looked in the mirror. Other than to make sure my long blond hair looked all right and my face was clean, Mom said looking in the mirror—and taking extra time to primp—was vain and wicked. Mom's reasoning allowed me to sleep in a few minutes longer every morning.

Mom warned me at least a hundred times, "Never look at yourself and think you are pretty. God cannot abide vanity in any sense of the word. A servant of God should be totally humble with a contrite spirit. If you think of yourself first, or that you're better than you are or better than someone else, you are not serving the Lord in the proper manner. Now, hurry up, Sophia! Comb your hair, brush your teeth, and move away from the mirror."

❧

We never used the term "rite of passage," but I think most of us girls thought turning twelve meant we'd be miraculously transformed from an awkward, even homely, little girl into an attractive young woman. The highlight of turning twelve was the privilege of attending The Group's monthly dances. The closer it got to my twelfth birthday, the farther away it seemed. Between babysitting kids for free and crushing on boys, the dances were all I dreamed about. Though my twelfth birthday was only months away, it seemed like ten years.

Whenever there were special adult meetings or gatherings at our house, Dad, Mom, or Aunt Eleanor offered my services as the babysitter— particularly for new converts. I loved kids, was good at babysitting, and felt confident and appreciated by the children, who loved me back. In this, I finally felt a purpose in serving God. But whenever I wasn't needed to babysit, clean or do laundry, I'd take the bus to Aunt Amelia's house.

Her house was in Salt Lake City near everything. I loved to hang out with my new sister, Amy. To me, she had everything and was energetic and gorgeous. Her mom let us do nearly anything we wanted to do after we finished Amy's chores.

We got to listen to the "wicked" Beatles and the Beach Boys. We swung our hips and shook our bodies, dancing around the room like I'd never been allowed to dance before. Though I felt clumsy and like a total idiot, we had a wonderful time.

Quite often, Amy and I would walk several city blocks north and then up several more steep half city blocks into the Avenues. At the LDS Hospital where Aunt Amelia worked as a nurse's aide, she would buy us lunches from the cafeteria and the three of us would eat and visit on the veranda in the sunshine.

On our way uptown, we noticed a Negro girl sitting on the lawn in front of the local high school. Once we got close to her, she jumped out in front of me. "What's this white trash doing in my neighborhood?" she asked in an unfamiliar dialect. She placed her hands on my chest and shoved me backwards. "What's the matter with you, bitch?

You afraid of me?" she challenged.

I was terrified. I couldn't figure out why she was so angry at me since I hadn't done anything to her.

Amy had attended multicultural schools in Salt Lake City for several years. Some of her friends were black, so she was used to their dialect and cultural differences. Not me. Until I started visiting Amelia's family in Salt Lake, I'd never seen a colored person in my whole life. But I'd certainly heard about them many times before.

My parents didn't consider themselves hateful, bigoted people who discriminated against African-Americans. However, they intensely held on to many of the original teachings of the early LDS leaders. My whole life I was taught, all black people were descendants of Cain; therefore, they were called "Canaanites." God cursed them with dark skin and promised they would suffer and be despised, all because Cain chose to follow Lucifer and rebel against God. Cain's posterity would never have an opportunity to receive the blessings of the priesthood until every white descendant of Adam had a chance first (see Joseph Fielding Smith, *The Way to Perfection* [Salt Lake City: Bookcraft, 1931], 101–2; Brigham Young, *Journal of Discourses*, 26 vols. [Salt Lake City: Deseret Book, 1859] 7:290–91).

"Okay, okay!" Amy retorted as my heart pounded. "If you really want to fight, Sophia will fight with you! But right now we have to get uptown, so we'll meet you back here at 3:00 PM. Then my really tough friend will beat the crap out of you. So you'd better be here and ready!" Then Amy grabbed my arm and prodded me up the sidewalk.

"No! I'm not going to fight with her!" I snapped at Amy after we were at least thirty feet away. "We both know I'm really strong, but I don't want to beat—"

Amy started laughing. "I'm sure she won't be there when we get back. She knows you could beat her to a pulp if you wanted to. She was just trying to act tough!"

Before our long trek back home from the hospital, we slid down the steep hill off H Street into Memory Grove. Since we'd done this a few times before, we already knew we'd end up with several bloody

scratches. Each time we went there, I wanted to spend more time playing in the stream that wound through the magnificent grove. Our time
in the park was worth the pain from the abrasions on our arms and
legs.

We had so much fun we forgot to show up for the big fight. Amy
blew it off like a breeze. "Don't freak out, Sophia. There's no way she
showed up either. She didn't want to fight you any more than you
wanted to fight her."

My new brother, Amelia's son Ari, drove us back to our house in
Murray, for Sunday school. When we were nearly home, Aunt Amelia
turned around and smiled at me. "Sophia, you really are a beautiful
young girl. Do you know how pretty you are?"

"No," I said, feeling quite uncomfortable. I don't think I'd ever
heard anyone say that before.

"Well, you are. I wish you knew it! You poor little darling—you
don't have any self-esteem, do you?"

I slumped a little and didn't answer.

"Do you know what that means, Sophia? If a girl has self-esteem,
she feels good about herself. I bet you don't think you are valuable at
all, do you?"

My throat tightened and my face turned hot as I fought back tears.
When we reached our house, Aunt Amelia opened the back door of the
car and gently pulled me into her arms. She hugged me tighter than I'd
ever been held before. Along with her, I grieved for the young girl she
embraced.

I knew there was someone who genuinely cared for me.

❧

"Happy birthday to you, happy birthday to—" I heard as I woke
up in Amy's bed. Aunt Amelia and her kids stood there holding a large
tray with tiny, wrapped goodies surrounding a decorated birthday cake
with twelve flaming candles. It was the first birthday in my life I felt
any significance. I could finally go to The Group stomps, and my

birthday was actually being celebrated.

At that noteworthy age, I decided to get brave and ask Mom to let me buy fabric for a birthday present. The day before the dance, I followed the directions and placed all of my pattern pieces on the cornflower blue fabric, just as Carol had taught me. I cut them all out and started sewing. Friday after school, I hand-stitched white lace around the bodice and puffy sleeves, and adjusted the hem.

At The Group stomps, as we began to call them, we girls had the opportunity to come out of our shells and dance to our hearts' content. I was still uncomfortable knowing all ages of men would be on the prowl, scrutinizing us young girls as potential wives.

However, at my very first Friday-night stomp, I finally began to believe God was going to let me be really happy. Somewhere in the Book of Mormon it says, "Men are that they might have joy." I hoped God meant women also, because dancing was real joy. It seemed my life was finally there for the taking. I wouldn't allow even the miserable minutes of a round dance, where I had to dance with icky old perpetrator Craig, thwart my blissful evening.

In the fall, dad took my mother, Aunt Amelia, and their kids to The Group's ranch in Pinesdale, Montana. We had an incredible time at the Great Scott Motel, which was owned by a member of The Group. Dad reserved a room for the boys, a room for Amy and me, and one for Aunt Amelia, Mom, and himself. It was the first time in my life I got to stay in a motel.

Amy and I were ecstatic. We pretended we were older teens living a life of wealth and abundance. Our motel room was our own cozy, classy apartment. We briefly considered marrying the same man, and then quickly banished the idea. We each found our own imaginary, perfectly wonderful, handsome boyfriend and got married right away. Then we tried to find second wives for our new husbands. That lamebrain idea didn't last either. In our wondrous, make-believe situation we realized we certainly didn't want to, nor did we have to share our husbands at all.

During our trip home from the Pinesdale Ranch, we camped a few nights in Yellowstone National Park. One day, inside Dad's station wagon, we were overwhelmed with fear and exhilaration as two bear cubs crawled all over the car.

At the camping grounds, Dad decided his older kids should receive a gift from God: a father's blessing. He told us it was a patriarchal blessing, considered a special gift among Mormon believers. A *worthy* father—one who held the priesthood—can give these blessings to his children or to others who requested them. Dad instructed our mothers to record his inspired words as he dictated the blessings God had in store for each of us.

After all of God's blessings and promises had been doled out through my father's voice, I knew I remained without value in God's eyes. Clearly, He had no respect or love for me. He had a myriad of blessings and promises for Amy and my brothers. Amy was still the strong, faithful, valiant soul she had been in heaven—a perfect young lady—therefore, she was qualified to teach women the gospel and lead them back to heaven. My blessing, however, said I carried the perfect, unblemished blood of my ancestors. I was warned to keep myself pure (was I pure?) so my family line would never be tainted. Through my father, God told me I should not marry into the blood of Cain, and I should not do things to tempt evil men to do evil things (did I do that?). I should always stand in holy places (where were those?). And if I was good enough and heeded all of those warnings, God would direct me to the man I should marry—the one and only man I had made covenants with in the pre-existence.

How would I find that man or know who he was? What was the pre-existence all about for Amy and me, anyway? She must have been a much better person than I was. I wondered what terrible things I'd done to require so many warnings and tests, before I might be worthy of one man's love.

CHAPTER 12

Men, Boys, and Confusion
1965

There was nothing I could do or say to cheer my mother after she and Dad had a fight. Although I didn't hear them fight often, I always felt devastated when I did. One day in 1965, I stood outside their bedroom door as my fifty-year-old mother again implored Dad to hear and understand her.

"I'm telling you for the last time how I feel about this, Owen, and then I'm going to drop it. I want you to know Eleanor is busy conniving again! Her 'family' dinner plans are nothing but a downright dirty attempt to keep you and me from taking the trip you promised me. It's our anniversary to plan, not Eleanor's anniversary!

"Eleanor didn't plan this special dinner just to keep us from going on a trip," Dad insisted. "She just wants to celebrate with us because she loves us."

Mom yelled back, "Why are you letting *her* make arrangements for *our* twenty-seventh anniversary when she knows darn well we've already made plans?"

I'm certain Mom knew her efforts were in vain, but she gave it one last try. "Whenever you are with me, she comes upstairs in *my* house; she sits with *us* at nearly every meal. If you invite me or another one of your wives to run an errand with you, she has to go. But whenever the tables are turned she lets us know loud and clear everyone is expected to stay away. Yes, she loves us when it's our time with you, but not when it's hers."

"Oh, my darling Vera, you've got it all wrong. Eleanor doesn't want you or my other girls to stay away. She wants to be part of your lives and near all of you. I'm sure if you girls can and want to be with us when I'm with her, it would be just fine."

"Owen, you are just plain duped by her, and the rest of us have to pay for your ignorance!" Mom courageously said.

"How can you say that, Vera? You know that's not true! I do the best I can to be fair with my girls. I won't fight with you about this anymore."

When he turned the corner, he bumped into my shoulder, gave me a hostile look, (as if he assumed I was in on Mom's rare insurrection), and then tromped down the first flight of stairs and out the back door.

I moved toward Mom. Her five-foot-three-inch body slumped down on the edge of her bed. Tears rolled down onto her lap. I couldn't believe she had actually tried to stick up for herself, and had done so with such integrity. Most of her disagreements with Dad turned into raging, nonsensical mania. I was so proud of her. Everyone in our family and in Plygville seemed to know Aunt Eleanor always manipulated Dad to get her way, everyone except Owen.

I sat next to Mom and put my arm around her shoulders. "Will you go to your own anniversary dinner if Aunt Eleanor plans it and goes with Dad?"

"Of course I will!" Mom mopped more tears off her cheek with her sleeve. After a few minutes of silence she said, "Everything will be all right, Sophia. This is my fault. I was wrong! I shouldn't have said anything to your dad about my feelings. It never works anyway. He really tries to be fair."

Then Mom stood up, looked me square in the eyes, and reiterated for the millionth time her very favorite mantra: "The gospel of plural marriage is true! It's just weak people [speaking of herself] who make it look and feel wrong. Don't ever let insecure feelings sway you from your testimony. I am so sorry I behaved that way. I should keep sweet and be a better example to you."

Mom forced a smile, patted my arm, and went into the bathroom— her solitary space in our crazy-making world.

※

Learning to sew my own skirts and jumpers saved me from additional insecurity. I could adjust their length to conform to Mom's theory of modesty, which meant calf- or ankle-length dresses and skirts, and still fit in somewhat amid the "outsiders'" fad—miniskirts.

One day, I forgot to switch back into my behind-the-times, old-fashioned look. My jumper was still held high with the straps across my shoulders. So, when I sat, the hem hit midway between my thighs and crotch. When Mom saw me, she flipped out.

"That's so immodest, Sophia! Wearing skimpy clothes and showing off your body is evil! It attracts the attention of evil boys and men, and if something wicked happened to you, it could be your own fault. You've got to keep your body covered. You know your guardian angels won't look after you if you continue to dress like that."

For the first time in my life, as far as I remembered, I raised my voice at my mother, saying, "I will never fit in if I dress like you and the Crickers do! ["Crickers" is slang for Short Creek folks.] Wearing peculiar clothes draws more attention than fitting in, Mom. Don't you get it? Don't you see what total freaks we look like around everyone else?"

I pled with Dad to convince Mom I was right. Then he persuaded her to compromise her lifetime ideals concerning modesty. My dress hems could fall as high as the middle of my knees—halfway between miniskirt and calf-length.

※

Three of my brothers and I placed five or six empty soup cans in a row against a hillside covered with sagebrush and rocks. Dad turned around and walked several steps before he drew a long line in the dirt with the heel of his work boot.

Forty miles southwest of Murray, in the middle of nowhere, he marked our firing line by placing two army-green ammunition boxes on each side of his mini trench.

"Once again, and as always," Dad reminded us, "you will abide all the safety rules. You will never, and I mean never point a gun at anyone! Stand ten feet behind the person who is shooting. Hold the gun away from yourself while you load and reload, or you may kill or get killed. Is that clear?"

We nodded.

Dad looked at me. "Do you remember how to load the gun, Sophia?"

"Of course I do, Dad." I was miffed he didn't remember I already knew how. His question was for his daughter, not my two brothers—one a few months older and the other a few months younger than me.

None of that really mattered. I wouldn't miss a chance to go target practicing with my dad. I would do anything and give everything I owned to always be outside, day or night, doing guy things rather than having to do girl stuff in the house.

"All right then," Dad said to us. "Let's be safe and have some fun!"

I got to sit next to him on the way home. He bragged, "Good grief, Sophia, you've become quite the marksman—uh . . . uh-hum, I mean markswoman." We chuckled. "Every time we come out here, you get better and better. My goodness, girl! You can whip the boys at arm wrestling, win all your running races, and now you're even outshooting them!"

My heart relished every single word Dad said. His pride in my successes filled my whole being with delight, but my heart went out to my gloomy brothers. I wished he wouldn't have carried on about me in front of them. He often boasted about his tomboy Sophia's strength, stamina, drive, competitive nature, and athletic abilities. From the very start, I never wanted to let him down. In those things I felt valued, accepted, confident, and loved by him, but not when it came to liking the boys.

Something wonderful began touching my heart and my nerve centers: boys! They were everywhere. My parents told me the most important thing to remember was I'd made a previous covenant with God to marry one specific man. It was my job or opportunity (thank God) to find the "one and only," particular man out of millions. For some reason, this notion sounded ludicrous. How could I—little old me—trust myself to know who that man was? How could I trust God to not pull another vanishing act or prank on me even if I did? It was evident neither one of us had proven ourselves to each other thus far.

No matter how many times I tried to explain my quandary to my parents, Mom would say, "You'll just know, Sophia. I don't know how to tell you how, but when the right man comes along and when it's the right time, you will know."

"But how will I know?" I persisted.

"Say your prayers, be a good girl, and stay close to God, and He will direct you to the right man."

"Even if I do all of that, what will happen? What will God do or say to prove it to me so I will know that I know?"

"You will know by a burning in your bosom," Mom stated.

It still didn't click, and I was feeling more and more like a total ignoramus.

A few weeks later, I asked my sister Francine, "Will my bosoms really burn when I find the right man? Why my breasts? Why will they burn?"

She laughed so hard her eyes watered. "No, Sophia. It means you will have a real strong sense of truth—like a warm, deep feeling in your heart."

I told Francine, "Mom said confusion is from the devil. I worry all the time. I feel confused; especially if a guy I like talks to me. My heart beats fast, and I get warm all over."

The summer before I turned thirteen, Aunt Eleanor's oldest daughter, Hannah (who was also married to my sister Francine's husband as a second wife), told me she wanted me to marry their husband when I got older. I always thought he was handsome and nice, and since I loved my sister Francine so much, being in her family might not be such a bad idea.

Hannah arranged a weeklong visit to her place in the west desert so I could get to know her and Francine's husband, William. Instead of hanging out with a man fifteen years my senior, I hung out with William's nineteen-year-old nephew. He was a tall, handsome cowboy who wore western shirts, Levis, boots, and a cowboy hat. The best part was he owned horses. We rode them and visited for hours on end. I helped him repair fences and feed the animals. With others on the ranch, we bucked at least a hundred bales of hay from the field, loaded them onto a big flatbed trailer, and then stacked them in a barn.

The next thing I knew, Hannah's nephew and I were sitting under a giant oak tree in a nearby field, talking about our lives, dreams, wishes, and the future. Before and shortly after I got back home, there was so much joy and burning in my bosom I had a movie going on in my head: the two of us living on the ranch, a cowboy country wedding . . . Was he the right guy? Should I marry him? By the time he came from the west desert four weeks later to see me, I had a crush on another handsome young man. My cowboy friend was devastated. I felt empathy for him—and guilt. I had absolutely no belief I could ever find the "right" man.

A month or so later, I sensed I was in love again. For a few days, we thought our biggest problem was he belonged to the FLDS (Colorado City) group. His parents, of course, wanted him to marry whomever their prophet told him to marry—certainly not me, an "apostate Allredite." They forbade our association, and he complied. After that two-week fascination, I moved on again.

I despised myself for hurting the guys. I hated being and feeling so crazy. How could I force my feelings or heart to behave any differently than they did? I felt tormented by God. Why wouldn't our omnipotent Lord be up front, outspoken, and forward, instead of all of this brouhaha? If only He would just tell us out loud the way it is supposed to be, we'd all have a better chance. Having only one life and one chance to get things right just wasn't fair. Instead, helping God build His kingdom felt like an everlasting series of guessing games—games I would surely lose if I couldn't find the right answers.

It occurred to me, since I hated not knowing whom I'd marry beforehand, maybe our prophet, Uncle Rulon, *should* tell me whom I should marry. After all, prophets are supposed to receive "the word of the Lord," right? But knowing God, he'd set me up with an old, ugly, stinky man. And what if the man was mean? I quickly became grateful I could take my chances and decide for myself.

CHAPTER 13

Featherweight and Cougar Speed
1965–1967

In the patriarchal blessing Dad conferred upon me when I was twelve, he said I was born into a noble lineage and our ancestral blood was pure and unblemished as far back as Jesus. There was not one drop of Cain's blood to blight our eternal progress. Apparently, I wasn't the only Allred kid who'd received the same message from God.

In meetings, in the neighborhood, all around me, I heard claims of superiority. We carried "royal" Allred blood. This encouraged an attitude of supremacy, with many considering themselves "God's chosen ones." We were told we were His "handful" of righteous people who, above all others, were entitled to His love and blessings. Because we were such valiant souls in the pre-existence, we had the opportunity to be born under the covenant of plural marriage.

If women continued to prove themselves, they would be exhausted. No matter how impoverished we were, or how miserable we were because our fathers' and our husbands' time was spread between their ever-expanding families; we hoped we could go to heaven for being perfect women. We could be God's righteous ones who would be saved when He poured his wrath upon the face of the earth and destroyed the wicked.

Of all the religious principles I was taught as a child, that one was probably one of the most difficult to fathom. Why would God save only a handful of His children when His whole world was full of them?

Two of my cousins were totally infatuated with each other. They appeared to be joined at the hip, but like the rest of us, both had been educated about the consequences of inbreeding. If God's kingdom was to be built up, it required new blood, converts, and opportunities for those who should find the truth. To risk the wellbeing of our future generations by marrying relatives simply wasn't an option for The Allred Group.

"There are plenty of virtuous and honorable people out there," Dad preached. "God will simply inspire and guide the right ones to the right place."

Consequently, back then, the majority of our families wholeheartedly disagreed with the justifications Colorado City, the Kingstons, Independents, and other polygamous groups used to justify intermarriages. Often siblings as close as half-brothers and half-sisters were married; creating severe birth defects in way too many cases.

※

I'd begun to think I had a split personality. With all the controversy going on in my head and heart, I felt as if there were two souls inside of me, fighting with each other for survival. One of them felt sorry for my beautiful sixteen-year-old cousin who decided to leave The Group.

Folks around me said she'd probably go to hell when she died. At the very least, she would only make it to the telestial kingdom—the lowest glory of heaven. After all, she was one of those "valiant spirits" who'd been born and raised under the covenant but chose not to participate in the "fulness of the gospel."

The other girl inside of me was terribly envious of my cousin. She had enough courage and determination to leave The Group to find happiness outside of polygamy. The feminine soul inside of me wanted to be brave like my cousin, but knew I'd break my parents' hearts if I ran away. Living a few joyous years on earth, versus eternity without my family, just wasn't acceptable to me—or at least for the religious part of me. I just kept on plugging along, hoping and wishing I would someday make the grade, and God would forgive me for all of my sins.

My brother Rick tried to be friendly toward me on the rare occasions when we saw each other. He wanted me to act like nothing had ever happened. I thought it was because he felt so terrible about the wicked things he had done to me. Oddly enough, something inside of my young heart made me feel sorry for him. Maybe, I surmised, it was because when he died, he'd be spending his time in purgatory.

During a summer race with my brother James, Rick's comment changed my life. I was already angry for not pushing myself harder to become better, stronger, and faster. When James won our race up the street and back to our front porch, Rick happened to be standing there.

"Sophia, you could run a whole lot faster if you weren't so fat!" he jeered.

None of my dad's ongoing, well-intended harassment about Mom's weight and our bad habits had changed my eating behaviors, nor had the constant harassment from cousins and school bullies. Their comments had only intensified my feelings of inferiority and my addictive behaviors. But that day, Rick's cruel words had a significant impact on me. They inspired an inner challenge. I would do anything to be able to run faster.

At twelve years and six months of age, I carried 140 pounds on my medium-boned, five-foot-six-inch-tall frame. I went beyond all the starvation diets I'd ever heard about. I didn't eat or drink anything but water for the first week. One day while I was guzzling water from the drinking fountain at school, I blacked out for a few seconds. A male student nearby caught me before I hit the floor. He waited with me until I got my equilibrium back. After the first week, I added a variety of fruit juices from our canned goods, and by the third week, I added a few more solids to my diet. It felt so good to not eat! Oh, how I wanted to maintain that feeling and end my compulsive overeating. I desperately wanted to hold fast to my anorexic regime for the rest of my life.

Four weeks later, at 120 pounds, I delighted in my featherweight body that seemed to soar at the speed of a cougar.

※

The trip to The Crick (Colorado City) with Dad driving Mom and I, was long and tedious as usual. As with every trip we'd ever taken down there, she begged me to conform to the weird dress standards I detested.

To some degree, I'd become an assertive, rebellious teen (according to my mother), wearing medium-length (short, according to Mom) skirts and sticking up for myself a little more. My newfound strength (character flaw) made it more difficult for her to pressure me into compliance.

"It won't hurt you to wear a long dress! I don't want you to offend anyone," she would say.

Again, in the most logical way I could possibly divine, I tried to sway Mom's rationale by using the good old guilt, analogy method. "Mom, if I dress like they do just to appease them, isn't that being hypocritical? And didn't you say being deceitful is wrong?"

"I guess you're right." Mom smirked, realizing I'd gotten the best of her. "Okay, then. At least make sure you wear a modest dress."

When we arrived at Grandpa's house, Mom's half-sister Maggie (who was four years older than me) and her new baby were there. Maggie and I had a lot of catching up to do.

She informed me her husband had written her a "Dear Jane" letter and confessed to committing adultery while he was in the army. He wouldn't be coming back to Maggie. She felt sad, but said it could've been worse if they'd have had time to fall in love before their assigned marriage and his induction.

Somewhere along the line, Maggie informed me their community changed its name from Short Creek to Colorado City. I also found out her leaders didn't believe they should adulterate their "royal" blood with new converts. For quite some time, intermarrying was the norm. Rather than send missionaries into the field to preach the fulness of the gospel to the Gentiles, which they'd originally believed was God's will, their young men were asked to quit school and dedicate two years of their lives to a "work mission." They were to donate their time, without pay, to help build the kingdom of God. Many of the young men were told, completing their missions would earn them a bride or two. This free labor helped pay for homes, fences, gardens, roads, a park, a school, a church, and supporting their prophet, "Uncle" Leroy Johnson.

The townsfolk were delighted their new Colorado City High School was under construction by the young men serving their work missions. The construction was also funded with government money, granting an entire polygamous faculty to serve humongous polygamous families who all followed the dictates of their prophet.

Maggie and I both knew the rules from day one. It was unacceptable for girls and boys to talk to or to look at each other longer than necessary, lest they be tempted to fall in lust or in love. However, on a beautiful summer day, our rebellious minds and young libidos got the best of us, and we decided to pay a visit to the school construction site.

In the school bathroom, Maggie changed from her ankle-length, long-sleeved, dress into a pair of tight jeans and a form-fitting blouse. Who knows where she found them. Zap! In a flash, she was a seductive-looking teenage beauty.

Though I had no cleavage to show off, I undid the first and second buttons of my blouse (the ones Mom always fastened back up, when I supposedly forgot to) so my tantalizing collarbone could be seen. I rolled the waistband of my brown-and-black plaid skirt a few times so it would reveal my long, bare legs from three inches above my knees.

Lastly, I folded my long sleeves up to my elbows and untucked my beige Lady Manhattan blouse to hide the rolled-up waistband.

There, in the jurisdiction of archaic dress codes and philosophy, Maggie and I must have appeared like Lady Godiva, without her horse.

Our flirtatious smiles and mannerisms caused the eyes of those "wicked" young men who dared look at us, to bug right out of their heads. Those who were dedicated to "avoiding even the appearance of evil" turned away so their souls wouldn't burn in hell. A few brave, "evil" guys drew near—six or seven of the teenage boys.

Maggie and I wanted to completely ditch the rules. We joked about being able to spend hours on end in un-chaperoned conversations. Fat chance that would ever happen! The young men were quickly called back to work by a stalwart brother, who told us to "Beat it! Now!"

Before we got back to the house, some "good Samaritan" had already informed Grandpa of our vile sins.

"Ya nasty little trollops," he shouted as soon as we walked in the front door. "Ya both have committed a carnal sin taday! Yer not only responsible fer yer own evil behaviors but fer the lustful state ya musta put those young men inta. I'm sure they were unduly tempted by yer nasty, lewd getups. You two oughta be ashamed of yerselves! Now git yer nasty little arses up them stairs right now! I don't want ta see ya horrible little sinners fer the resta the day."

Maggie and I didn't mind missing supper. It gave us time to review our exciting, wild day on the town while her sisters ate and had to do the dishes. I think we both felt a little guilty. Would we be held accountable for messing with those boys' libidos, we wondered. Until her two impressionable sisters, both close to my age, came along, Maggie and I entertained ourselves in retrospection. "What if we . . ." "Did you see his eyes?" "We could have . . ." The two of us laughed until our guts hurt and our eyes watered.

Maggie's baby, her two sisters, and I sprawled across their double bed and continued our merriment, mixed with the usual girl talk, late into the evening.

Soon, all three of these attractive and charming aunts from Colorado City would be assigned to their covenant mates. Each one said she explicitly trusted their prophet's decisions, no matter what. They'd been taught since birth, God would reveal to "Uncle Leroy" when, and to whom, all eligible girls and boys should marry.

In this, my young aunts confirmed parts of the story Mom had told me not long before, about her dear friend Alice. They too would most likely not know who their husbands would be until their wedding day. At first, they might despise or be repulsed by their husbands. It would be okay though, my aunts assured me. After some time, they'd learn to love the head of their household. But more importantly, they told me, if they were sweet, obedient wives, their husbands might learn to love them as well.

Of course, I was concerned about marrying the "right" guy. But after hours and hours of talking to my teenage aunts, I told them, "I'd still rather choose my own husband, even if I married the wrong man, rather than have to marry an old man like your sister Dorothy did, or a total stranger."

The girls were heartbroken for me. If only I would stay there and be part of their group like my sister Lucinda had done nearly fifteen years earlier... "This way," they coaxed, "our prophet can make sure your future spouse is the man God wants you to marry."

Even with our differences, the four of us felt a deep bond.

We looked into each other's eyes in dismay. "Do you think we have the same God?" I asked my aunts. "How do you feel about a loving God who promises to damn everyone who doesn't follow the one and only prophet on this earth? That could be you or me. Is your prophet or mine the right one?"

Sadly enough, all four of us girls were sure *we* knew the right answer.

Sacrament meeting had already started. I rushed from our back door, across the patio. Near the door to the garage, where we held our meetings, I heard a voice coming from behind our fence.

"Sophia, Sophia! Hey, Sophia, are ya going ta get married today?"

Instantly, my stomach twisted into a huge knot. "What are you doing here?" I grumbled at Pete—the boy who'd been my worst adversary and most aggressive tormenter for years.

"I came ta see ya! Ta see if I can screw ya before ya get married off to some old man," Pete said.

"Get out of here now, or I'll get one of my brothers to make you leave," I hollered back.

"Bet your brothers do ya, don't they, don't they?" Pete taunted. "I heard all of the men trade all their wives. They get together and mix up all the house keys, and then they go screw the women who live at that house. Oh, come on, Sophia. Let me do ya before the old men get to ya, please, please."

I was mortified and hurt. If I could have climbed over our fence in my Sunday dress, I'd have tried to beat the living daylights out of Pete. No one had ever talked to me like that before, let alone made such crude remarks about the good men and women in our group.

"You're pathetic and sick! Get away from here now!" I yelled.

The ignorant jerk kept calling out obscenities even as I escaped into the safety of our sacrament meeting.

If I had told my brothers about his comments, they'd have beaten the tar out of him. It would have been all right with me, but the pestering at school would have become more unbearable than it already was. Telling wasn't an option either.

※

I met Dick during youth conference at the Pinesdale Ranch. Amy and I were surprised and nervous when we found out we had to stay at his family's house. Somehow, Aunt Eleanor had made the sleeping arrangements for us girls.

Amy and I naively flirted back and forth with Dick and his brother off and on during the weekend. Later in the summer, Dick said he was coming down to Salt Lake City, and wanted to take me out. I found out later, our date had also been prearranged. Since his mom and Aunt Eleanor were good friends, my going out a few months before I turned thirteen made it okay to break the dating-at-sixteen rule.

It was only the second time I'd been to a drive-in movie theatre. Dick sat too close to me and wouldn't keep his hands off me. When he tried to kiss my neck, I pulled away and told him to stop. He just slid closer.

"Come on, Sophia, let's have some fun," he said.

I was sickened and repulsed by how he was acting. I wanted to beat him up. But he was practically a nephew to Aunt Eleanor, so I had to be polite.

"Please stop. Don't! Stop it!" I persisted. But every attempt I made to resist his advances only seemed to entice him more.

When Dick was nearly on top of me, I went emotionally and physically numb. Without one single turned-on feeling and completely devoid of fear, I seemed to disappear, and gave in to his lack of concern for me. It wasn't until he was so crazed he was ready to rip my clothes off before I came to my senses and screamed, "Stop it! Take me home now!"

There's no way to describe the emotions I felt on the long drive home. But after that night, I discovered a new and yet simple sense of courage inside of me. It felt like I won a disgraceful contest I hadn't signed up for. I was so grateful for those powerful feelings; but I was mortified about my inability to be stronger in the first place.

Dick didn't speak all the way home. But he obviously thought I'd be speaking to my parents about him, so he beat me to the draw.

When Aunt Eleanor called me into her bedroom a few days later, she scolded and lectured me on the evils of my lascivious, smutty, aggressive behaviors. She explained how dirty, nasty and evil sex was outside of marriage. She told me I should be ashamed of myself.

"I hope you know how blessed you were! Thank the good Lord you were with an honorable young man who wouldn't take advantage of your disgraceful conduct!"

Of course, when I attempted to explain what had really happened with Dick, Aunt Eleanor didn't believe me. Things hadn't changed over the years where I was concerned. I still had no validity in my father's family. Whatever Aunt Eleanor said, was the way it was.

I knew I'd have to work very hard to prove myself.

CHAPTER 14

"Independents" and My First Love

1965–1967

Many of my teenage summer days and nights were glorious. I'd never been so comfortable in my skin, and my slim body seemed to soar. Whenever I danced, ran, hiked, swam, or sailed down the steep sand-dune hills, I was in heaven. Boys were everywhere, and I cherished every minute of their attention and admiration.

By my early teens, hundreds of families had converted to our polygamous group. Our fairly new garage in Murray was nearly overflowing with new and old members who wanted to attend Relief Society, priesthood, sacrament meetings, and Sunday school there.

Amy and I stared at two scantily dressed girls, whose parents were new converts, as they walked up our driveway. I leaned into Amy and murmured, "Look at those wicked girls! They'll probably go to hell for dressing like that!"

"I know," she replied. "We won't ever dress like that!"

"Yeah, or wear so much makeup." I said, while deep inside I feared these girls would be our rivals.

My twenty-pound weight loss seemed to give me value. I suddenly became worthy of love, attention, and a special kind of treatment I'd never known. Aunt Eleanor's oldest son, Charles, wanted to take me to one of the roller-skating parties he and some of my older siblings went to on a regular basis.

"I want to show off my beautiful little sister," he told me. "Invite Amy and Valerie to go with us if you want to."

At the party, the three of us pulled our rented roller skates over our heels, laced them up, and then tied them tightly around our ankles as Charles directed us. Then we tried to skate across the floor. Finally, we plopped ourselves down on a side bench and watched everyone else glide around the room like pros. The rink was full of young Independent polygamists. Each one skated around the center poles in the same direction, moving to the music of the fifties and sixties.

A few minutes later, we found ourselves gawking at an attractive young man who glided around the rink with a familiar-looking pretty, petite blond. They twirled in circles, skating backwards, in between and around everyone else like they'd been skating for years.

Soon the owner of the S&M Skating Rink announced everyone should clear the floor because it was guys' choice to ask a girl to skate.

When the handsome guy we'd been staring at skated toward us, I bent down, pretending I was checking my skates.

"Do you want to skate?" I heard him ask Amy or Valerie. I was too smitten or shy to look up. I waited for one of my friends to stand up and skate away. They didn't budge. I could still see his feet right in front of me. "Don't you want to skate with me?" he asked again.

Simultaneously Amy and Valerie elbowed my sides. "Sophia! He's talking to you."

I looked up. "Me?"

"Yeah, do you want to skate?"

"I don't know how to skate. I've never done it before," I answered.

"That's okay, I'll teach you." He grabbed both my hands and pulled me onto the floor.

Nervous, I lost my balance umpteen times and tried to overcome the interference of my inferiority complex. Royce asked me a million questions as we tried to skate. We laughed together when I fell and when I succeeded. He gave me hugs for support and confidence, and reassured me I was making great progress. Before the evening was over, I was on cloud nine. In one evening I had become an amateur skater, skating pretty good forward and not so bad backward.

As we were about to leave, Royce asked me if I'd go on a date with him in the near future.

"I'm not supposed to date yet." I told him.

"Yet? What do you mean 'yet'? How old do you have to be before you can date?"

"Dad wants me to wait until I'm sixteen."

"Sixteen! How old are you?"

I knew if I told Royce I'd be thirteen in a few months it would end of his interest in me. I wanted to lie through my teeth and be okay with it. But by then the truth had become more and more important to me.

"I'll be thirteen in November," I confessed.

"No way! You're kidding me! You're older than that!"

"I'm not kidding you. I'm only twelve."

"You're seventeen," Royce said. "You just don't want—"

"I wish I was seventeen!"

"Listen, Sophia, if you don't want to go out with me, just say so."

"I do want to. I'd love to go out with you, but I can't."

The next morning, after Amy, Val, and I woke up from our sleep-over, Charles found me and called me aside.

"You know what, Sophia? Royce said he thinks you are wonderful and beautiful, but he about keeled over when I told him you were only twelve. He was sure you were at least sixteen or seventeen. He wants to go out with you. Just take things slow and easy, and be careful, Sis, okay?"

I was totally confused by Charles' remarks. Royce was going to be eighteen in January. I was sure he wouldn't wait three years to go out with me.

The same afternoon, Amy, Valerie, and I found out Royce was in Dad's yard for the first time that I knew of. He was there "to pick up something from Charles," he later told us. We primped as fast as we could and made our own excuses to go outside, where we might just bump into Royce.

Despite the fact that he'd spent the whole prior evening skating with me, I was still insecure about Royce's feelings. I thought all it would take was for him to see Amy or Val up close in the daylight. Once he became acquainted with their darling personalities, he'd probably fall madly in love with one or both of them.

As luck would have it, Mom hollered out the window for me to come inside to finish my work. That was the excuse she used, but I knew her real intent was to get me away from the handsome stranger in our yard.

A few days later I about died of surprise when Royce called. He called me again the same day and didn't stop calling. In our long conversations, he claimed he couldn't keep his eyes off me, and he loved my vivacious personality and laugh. "And no, I didn't want to go out with Valerie or Amy," he exclaimed. "I wanted and still want to go out with you! You're the one I'm crazy about."

All day long and when I went to bed, my heart rejoiced. Never had I expected someone so handsome and kind to be attracted to me, and I'd certainly never seen myself as having a cute, fun personality. Each day that summer, I had another chance to talk to, listen to, and laugh with someone who really cared.

At the next Group stomp, Royce showed up with a few of his brothers and his friend Mark. Between dances, Valerie, Amy, and I hung out with these good-looking guys near the back of the dance hall.

Behind their backs, we goaded the passel of "Allredite" men who hung close by to scrutinize these "wayward Independent polygamous men." They felt it was their duty to make sure they wouldn't get out of line with any of "our" young girls.

The more I hung out with Royce at our house or his—chaperoned by my brothers who were dating his sisters—the more Dad and Mom began to fret. If I fell in love with an Independent polygamist, they worried he might convince me to leave The Group and my family. On the other hand, they thought my brothers who held the priesthood would be able to convert their Independent girlfriends to become part of our group.

Though Dad was quite concerned, he didn't forbid me to see Royce, or my sister Amy to see his brother. He didn't want his children to treat anyone badly. Nor should he totally disregard the possibility that with our kindness and good examples, some of these young men "who don't know any better" might accept the truth—there is a prophet of God still on this earth. With that heroic possibility, Amy, Val, and I were thrilled to be hanging out with new, unrelated male blood.

Not much later, the three of us became known in The Group as "those rebellious girls." We were the naughty ones who opposed the general rules. We left the dance hall premises, flirted, and hung out with "malevolent" young men who were just hanging around to steal us young girls away from The Group.

In October, my brothers took me to a Halloween party held at Mark's mother's new home in Salt Lake City. I'd just met Mark at a recent skating party and the dance, so we found ourselves visiting in the basement family room for quite a while.

Mark told me the pretty blond who was swirling around the skating rink with Royce was his little sister Ann. She was the girl who had lived behind my Aunt Beth's house a few years earlier. Mark said he remembered my hair was fixed up in pigtails, and how terrified I was of all his brothers who were hanging out in the front room.

"Do you remember when you came over with my sister Ann? I'm the guy who teased you about using my games." Then Mark chuckled. "I knew the minute I saw you, you'd be my wife some day."

I blushed, turned away from more of his teasing, and went back upstairs to join the costume party.

About one month after the Halloween party, our new crowd of

friends planned a big harvest party to be held in our three-car garage / church.

"It's really another excuse, you know," Royce said, winking at me, "for us to be able to spend more time together. We have to create as many social gatherings as we can so you and I can see each other more."

I didn't tell Royce how frustrated I was when he meandered slowly around the grocery store, choosing a bunch of junk food for the party. He had to stop at his sister's house, then the gas station. All I was eager for was the party. We had the food, but we were already late.

"Aw, don't worry," Royce told me when he sensed my annoyance. "The party will go on for hours. Besides, this way I have an excuse to keep you all to myself."

By the time we got back home, our garage was nearly full of our young friends and relatives, blasting country-western music way too loudly for my sensitive ears. After Royce and I placed the food and drinks on the table, the music was turned off and everyone stopped talking. *It must be time for the blessing on the food,* I thought.

I felt like a ditz when everyone yelled, "SURPRISE!" I had no idea who the party was for. To cover my embarrassment, I continued to arrange the food, snacks, plates, and cups on the table. A few minutes later a whole bunch of people gathered around the table and screamed "Happy birthday, Sophia!"

I looked questioningly at Royce, who was standing right next to me. "Happy thirteenth, beautiful girl!" he said as he hugged me. "This party is for you. Sorry it was a few weeks late, but we didn't want you to get suspicious."

I remembered one simple birthday cake and song for me when I was nine, as well as the morning birthday song and goodies from Aunt Amelia's family the previous year, but I never imagined anyone would ever care enough to arrange a big birthday party for me. I was so overwhelmed my legs went out from under me, and I began to cry. Royce sat next to me on the floor. He gathered me in his arms and held me until I could contain myself and join in my own party.

Royce came to our house on a regular basis to see me. We went all over the place with my brothers, other couples, and with large and small groups of friends. We spent time together at the Allred meetings, at Royce's house for Sunday school, sleigh riding, horseback riding, and on hayrides. Our favorite times were the dances and roller-skating parties, where we had an excuse to touch and hug each other. We hung out together every chance we could. Between the times we saw each other, I missed him. He treated me royally and helped bolster my developing self-esteem. I knew he was meant to be a part of my life. Royce said he wanted to marry me when I was old enough, and he promised to wait for me to make "the right decision."

As time went on, I also began to hang out with Mark and my brother Alan, who had become good friends. The three of us became nearly inseparable. More than anything, we loved our long walks. We'd walk, run, and race from Dad's house through the subdivisions where Mark used to live, and over to Wheeler Farm where Mark kept his horse. We discussed our hopes, dreams, likes, dislikes, friends, families, and heartaches for hours on end. Mark told us of his sorrows when he and his eight siblings lost their mother due to heart failure when he was only twelve years old.

Mark and I mulled over my relationship with Royce and Mark's relationship with my friend Valerie, with whom he had been going for quite some time. As much as we cared for our current sweethearts, neither of us believed we were destined to marry them.

Royce and I continuously debated the differences in our beliefs. As dear as he was to me, I felt he and his father were the epitome of chauvinism, and I knew from the onset of our falling for each other, I shouldn't marry him. It baffled me, the only spiritual guidance I received when it came to my covenant mate was, I should *not* marry the guy I loved.

As with most teens, my next few years were packed with wonderful moments, as well as craziness and heartaches. Royce and I would break up, get back together, hurt each other, disagree, and then start all over again.

121

At Wheeler Farm, in one of our favorite spots, Mark carved a big heart on a wide, mature tree that had fallen over a creek bed. When his masterpiece was complete, it said, "Sophia and Mark Forever." Then, under a huge oak tree, he pulled me close and told me he loved me.

"I know the two of us will get married someday," he said. "I've known ever since I first saw that scared, little, towheaded blond following behind my sister. I've been waiting for the right time to tell you this again."

"I love you too, Mark," I told him sadly. "But I don't think we should marry each other—we're best friends."

"Someday soon you will know it's meant to be, Sophia. Until then, I'll wait for you."

A few weeks later, on a chilly day at the farm, Mark slid across the car seat and kissed me tenderly on my lips. I'd never felt that feeling before. Finally, I realized what kissing meant to others. No wonder my brothers and their girlfriends smooched so much. Royce's many attempts to kiss me with his tongue wallowing around in my mouth were nothing but repulsive to me.

I began to wonder if the good, tickly feeling all over my body was God's message to me. Was that sensation the burning in my bosom? Did it mean Mark was my covenant mate? He was certainly sure he was.

❧

The minor headaches I'd been having nearly every day since I'd fallen on my head when I was younger got worse and worse. My supposed split personality was back in full force. Back and forth, over and over again I changed my mind. My soul knew I shouldn't marry Royce, yet I missed being with him and got terribly jealous when he dated other girls.

During all the turbulence, both Mark and Royce often made sure I found out when they dated other girls so I could feel as hurt and jealous as they did.

The guys said I was a heartbreaker because I'd lead them on and then dump them. Still, I despised myself for not knowing how to control my unreliable emotions. It appeared I'd never love a man enough to marry him. And I was absolutely sure no man would ever love me enough to stick with me forever. The problem with that was, I wanted children.

The wild child in me often daydreamed of running away to California. I would live with the hippies I saw and heard about on television. They dressed really "cool," and looked so happy and in love with life and each other. Besides all of that, I was opposed to killing, and they enthusiastically objected to the Vietnam War that was drafting relatives and brothers into combat. At my age, Haight Ashbury communities' idea of "free love" sounded perfect to me. In the big state of California I could choose an intellectual, good-looking man to father my baby; then we could go our separate ways and live happily ever after.

CHAPTER 15

High School Angst
1967–1969

I was livid when my sister Francine talked Mom into buying me some training bras.

"You can't act like a boy forever, Sophia," Francine scolded. "You're going to be a woman someday whether you like it or not."

I hated my periods, my breasts, and my slim girlish figure. The only feminine thing I liked about me was my beautiful, long, taffy-colored hair, because it was so easy to manage. My tomboy life would have been especially grand if we had been allowed to wear Levis or even slacks to school. There was absolutely nothing as confining or as tortuous as having to run to and from school in a dress.

If I was lucky, I might be offered a ride with one of my aunts or uncles who drove their kids to and from school, but I really didn't mind the walk unless the weather was extremely bad.

One cold, blustery day after school, I tucked my books inside my jacket and I hurried away from the school. As I approached the sidewalk and began running south on State Street toward home, I heard a male voice calling me.

From the front passenger side, Frank had rolled down the window. "Get in out of the rain, Sophia. We'll give you a ride home."

I leaned in the window. Valerie and her best friend from school, Ruthie, were in the back seat. Frank (Ruthie's fiancé) was in the front seat next to the driver, a guy I'd never met.

When I caught Valerie's eyes and saw the look she gave me, I knew what I should do.

"No thanks," I told Frank. "I'll walk."

"Come on, Sophia, we have room. Get in now and Jay will take you home, won't you, Jay?" Frank quickly pointed at me. "Jay, this is Sophia." Then he pointed a finger at Jay. "Sophia, this is Jay."

"Sure, I'll take ya home!" Jay said with a wide, friendly smile plastered across his face.

The nervous look in Valerie's eyes let me know I had to somehow get out of accepting this ride home. Val didn't want to deal with "incrimination by association." If her friends found out her friend Sophia lived in Plygville and was a plyg kid, they'd be suspicious of her as well.

"Thanks anyway, Frank. I love running in the rain and I need the exercise," I said as convincingly as possible.

"Ya sure as hell don't," Frank said. "Not in this weather! What ya doing, trying to be polite or something?"

Frank looked back at Val, "Tell your friend to get in the car. It's okay!" Val didn't say a word. She looked dumbfounded.

Looking back at me, Frank said, "We aren't going to kidnap ya!"

"For hell sakes, get in out of the damn rain!" Jay ordered.

If Val would've had lessons, she'd have learned how to tell tall tales that would help get her out of this kind of fix. But she had never lived in Plygville. Neither of her dad's wives lived together in the same house or even near each other. So she hadn't led much of a secret life. Fibs were designed for that very reason, to protect our families and gain a safety net of approval from neighbors and peers. This had always been a crucial aspect of our survival.

Finally Frank jumped out of the car, grabbed my books from my arms, and shoved me into the front seat next to Jay. Then Frank slid in next to me and slammed the door shut.

"There!" he snapped. "I guess we'll have to kidnap ya."

"Just take me over to Val's house," I told Jay. "You're going there anyway, aren't you?"

"Why? Why not just take ya home?" Frank asked me.

"Well, maybe Val and I can do our homework together."

Frank turned around and looked at Val. "Didn't ya say ya had piano lessons today?"

"Yeah," Val murmured, "but—"

Frank interrupted her. "See, it's okay, Sophia. We really don't mind taking ya home."

Right then I thought Val was as dumb as a doornail. I'd done everything I could think of to protect her secrets, but she wouldn't say a word. If I were her, I'd have told them, "Yeah, bring Sophia over to my house. After piano lessons we can do our Spanish homework together." Whether that really happened or not wouldn't matter. Once the boys dropped me off at her house, her mother could have taken me home, or I could have walked the extra miles.

By then we were well on our way. Jay was asking for directions. As I pointed and told him where to turn, I was still trying to figure out how to rescue Val and myself from total embarrassment. I could ask him to drop me off at a stranger's house and pretend it was mine, but what if the owner saw me and wondered who in the heck was in their yard?

Between every turn I tried to think of something. At one point I said, "Just drop me off here and I'll walk the rest of the way home." Jay thought that was a stupid idea.

I could have told him, "I've got to stop at so-and-so's house to pick up a—" A what? But I didn't have a so-and-so's house to stop at.

By the time we turned right off 5900 South onto 300 East, Frank was totally keyed up. "Ya live this close to Plygville? Holy Toledo!"

"I sure do," I said sternly. I couldn't protect Val's anonymity, and she hadn't helped a single bit. "I live right next door to them."

"Shiest!" Jay said as he slowed way down. "You *do* live right here in Plygville."

"Wow, doesn't that bother you, Sophia?" Ruthie asked.

"YES!" I wanted to screech at her. "Of course it bothers me! How do you think I've felt all of my life and right this minute, while all of you act like we are freaking monsters or something?"

Instead, I frowned and said sarcastically, "Yes, I'm scared to death they are going to kill me!"

Ruthie looked nervous. She didn't say another word as she stared fixedly out the window while I gave Jay the very last direction.

"Turn right here, down this dirt driveway on your right."

"No way, Sophia," Frank yelled. "Ya don't live down here! This is where all the big-wig polygamists live . . . where they have their meetings."

Jay drove slowly down our long driveway, then asked solemnly, "You're jiving with us aren't you, Sophia?"

"No! I'm not jiving with you. This is my 'big-wig' dad's garage where he holds all of the polygamist meetings."

Frank opened the door for me. Looking quite disconcerted, he slid out of the car. Then I got out. Other than a few uneasy goodbyes, no one said another word.

I was sorry I'd let Val down. I felt sure she knew. She figured out how to explain our connection without implicating herself, and to my surprise, her free-loving, wanna-be-hippy, friends continued to be kind to me whenever I was around them.

꒳

Gary told me he wanted to ask me something after our Thespian Club meeting was over. As other students were filing out, he sat down next to me.

"I'm sure this is a ridiculous question." He was almost as nervous as I was. "I am more than likely way too late to be asking you. As nice and as pretty as you are, I'm sure you've already been asked. But if you haven't already said yes to someone else, will you consider going to the Christmas dance with me?"

Apparently Gary didn't know yet I was a polygamous kid. Had he gone to Hillcrest Junior High with my peers, he would already have the lowdown about me. If anyone in his popular crowd had informed him, the poor guy would have known why I hadn't been asked, and he wouldn't have bothered.

To my astonishment, Dad gave Gary (an outsider) permission over the phone to take me to the Christmas dance.

During our exceptionally good time at dinner and then the dance, I allowed a sense of normalcy to touch my heart. I pretended I was accepted, even semi-popular, and could be vibrant and outgoing around the crowd of kids I'd attended school with for most of my life.

At home by the front door, Gary kissed my lips once very softly. He asked me if he could take me out again sometime soon. My very foolish elation at Gary's kindness and his desire to date me was short-lived.

Before I saw him the following Monday at school, one of his cronies handed down the necessary warnings. Gary didn't show up at the lunch table where we had planned to meet. He turned the other direction when he saw me in the hall and avoided me like the plague. For days on end I felt remorseful, and an overwhelming, self-conscious angst kept me from being fully functional. Gary never did speak to me again.

In between my dates with Mark and Royce, I went out with a couple more Mormon guys from high school—relationships that also ended in discriminatory rejection. One of James's friends told us both their LDS religion and their parents forbade them to associate with any polygamists. Things hadn't changed since I was a kid.

On the other hand, my brother James warned all guys he didn't like or trust to keep clear away from his sister or he'd pound on them. Then he introduced me to a few guys he approved of.

There was a cake-decorating contest to be held at the Valentine's Day dance. My sister Hannah helped me create the most beautiful cake I'd ever seen. We placed a Barbie doll inside of an upside-down funnel cake to create her long, flowing hoop skirt. With a variety of brilliant valentine shades of icing, we dressed her from head to toe. She had a lacy, V-neck bodice and straps across her shoulders. Her elegant dress was complete with a matching umbrella she daintily held in her hands.

If any of the girls had been required to put names on our cake entries, or if the judges had seen me with my cake, I wouldn't have had the slightest chance of winning. I asked my date, with whom James had lined me up, if we could get there early and if he would carry my cake to the table without me.

As we danced, I kept glancing toward the table where the cakes were on display. Everyone fussed and commented about my entry.

"The winner of the cake contest is number 32!" someone shouted across the gymnasium to all of the hopeful contestants. "Whoever made cake number 32, please come up now."

When the crowd saw my date and I proudly approach the tables, hardly a soul clapped. Even though it cut to my core, I understood. They couldn't applaud, to show approval and acceptance of me. However, my handsome (gay—I found out years later) date smiled and proudly hugged me in front of everyone. Apparently he knew exactly how it felt to be a misfit and an outcast.

Later in my sophomore year, James introduced me to Bryan. He wasn't a handsome guy, but shortly after we met, I realized I adored him. He was funny, kind, smart, and talented. Bryan hung in there and remained my good friend for quite a while. I couldn't understand why, until it occurred to me no one, including my brother James, had told him how notorious we were.

Every day I anxiously waited for him to abandon our friendship, as so many boys and girls had done before. Surely, someone would tell him. If not, he'd soon figure it out.

One evening while Bryan and I were sitting at Mom's kitchen table doing an art project, Dad hiked up the stairs from Aunt Eleanor's, walked over to the sink where Mom was doing dishes, and planted several goodnight kisses on her neck. Though Mom loved it and giggled, she said, "Owen, stop it—the kids are in here."

I was not one bit surprised, just angry, when Aunt Eleanor was right behind him leering over the banister. Her limitless reasons and excuses to invade my mother's space would never end. If they ever did, she'd invent some more of them. Though Dad had surely said goodnight to her before heading up to Aunt Maryann's house, she had another reason to butt into my mother's few seconds. Instead of expressing her lame reason for following him up the stairs, she saw him kissing Mom. So right in front of Bryon, Aunt Eleanor smooched on Dad's lips while she gently pinched his rear. "Just had to tell you goodbye again, my darling," she cooed.

Bryan looked shocked at "Aunt" El's display of affection and her comment to her supposed brother, while Mom and I were miffed. I wanted to slap the ignorance and callousness right out of her.

"Didn't you tell me your Aunt was your dad's sister?" Bryan asked when we were alone.

"Yeah, that's what I told you." I said in frustration.

I saw hurt and confusion creep over his face. *I need to get him out of my life now—today—*I decided. *The longer he doesn't know about us, the longer it will extend my anxiety and prolong his most certain abandonment of me. He has a right to know the truth so he won't be hurt any longer than necessary. I'll tell him and get it over with for both of us, once and for all.*

On our back patio, I interrupted the pleasant sounds of Bryan's guitar strumming. "All right, here goes, Bryan," I blurted out after working up my courage. "I've been meaning to explain something to you for quite some time now."

Poor Bryan—the sadness in his eyes touched my heart. It would have been easier to have him walk out on our friendship, like I was so accustomed to.

Bryan swore he'd never heard of polygamy before. "Maybe an insignificant word or two, somewhere in the Bible," he claimed.

I thought he was lying and playing games with me because he didn't know how else to discuss the subject.

"It started with the Mormons. The Prophet Joseph Smith started it all. Don't you know your history?" I said in a grouchy voice, disliking my insolence.

"You'll figure it out and then you'll need to dump our friendship—but that's okay Bryan; everyone else on the "outside" has, so you can too."

I was shocked when he didn't grab his guitar, shove it in the case, and take off. Instead he sat down next to me on the patio bench and said,

"Whatever it is or isn't—whatever I find out—I promise I won't abandon our friendship. I promise you, Sophia."

My heart told me he was telling the truth, at least for a while.

After sacrament meeting, Dad called me into his office, which was in Aunt Eleanor's bedroom. I sat on the edge of her bed and watched a tender smile spread across his face. He chuckled and said,

"In the past few weeks, at least a dozen men have asked me if they can court you. You're a beauty, Sophia, and they know it." Then he added solemnly, "Sometimes that worries me."

"Anyway, my darling daughter, since you are now sixteen—you are sixteen, aren't you?" I nodded. "Well, you can tell these guys no, or you can tell them yes if you want to get to know any one of them and their wives."

"I don't want to talk to them at all, Dad. Please tell them no as soon as they ask you," I said. "I'm not interested in marrying an older man."

"Okay, I'll do that for you, honey," he said, "but there are three of these men I have a lot of respect for, and I'd like you to prayerfully consider each one of them before you give them an answer. Okay?"

My answer to Dad was "Absolutely no," since I wasn't at all interested in any of them. Plus, there was no sense in praying about anyone anymore. I didn't trust I'd know today, tomorrow, next week, or ever who the "right" guy was. I began to believe I must not have a covenant mate or a predestined commitment to any man, and that's why God hadn't given me a profound answer.

Our hay riding parties were some of my most cherished times. At the riding stables in Draper City, the owner hitched up two of his horses to a flatbed trailer, piled it with straw and a bunch of deliriously happy young people, and took off. Some talked, some made out, some laughed, some sang, and some of the Independents drank. The driver drove us a couple of miles into the foothills on a narrow, bumpy, dirt road winding in and out of sagebrush and scrub oak. Then we had to head back. Our excursions were always too short and ended far too soon. Afterward, most of us would gather around the fire pit to roast hotdogs and marshmallows.

Merrill, an Independent polygamist man, who'd recently married my brother, Charles's sweet-heart, as his second wife, while he was still in Vietnam, was drunk again. As the evening passed by, he started in on another of crude tirades.

"So, there you are, miss So-ph-ia Allred--one of Rulon Allred's nieces? I'm talkin about that damn bastard who thinks he's a high and mighty God? Well, he can kiss my ass and go straight to hell as far as I give a gaw damn!"

"Shut up, Merrill!" his first wife scolded. "Stop it right now. Stop being so rude."

"Do ya think I give a damn if she hears me?" Merrill thundered back at her.

I moved closer to the fire pit and to Merrill to let him know I could hear him.

"Do ya hear me, huh, Miss So-phee-a-all-red-ite? Well, the way I figure it is, ya should know yer uncle Rulon is nothing but a good-for-nothing bastard!"

Merrill kept on with his rudeness, so I stepped in front of him and said, "Shut your mouth right now!" The more everyone told Merrill to knock it off and shut up, the more he laughed and carried on. It was evident he enjoyed offending me. I was so infuriated I wanted to literally punch his lights out. Just as I swung at him, Royce grabbed around my arms, and carried me ten or fifteen feet away.

"Put me down! Let me knock the crap out of him!" I hollered. "If my brothers were here, they would do it! Leave me alone! Put me down!"

Merrill snickered.

"Listen to me, Sophia," Royce said. "Calm down and listen. Merrill may be drunk and falling on his ass, but he can and will knock you out with one punch if you get near him. And in his state of mind, he'd think nothing of it."

"Yeah, put 'er down, Royce. Let 'er come after me. Come on, little So-phee-all-red-ite," Merrill continued to taunt. "Someone needs to kick that rotten Allred blood right outta yer head!"

Merrill staggered up from his folding chair and stumbled toward me. Royce hauled me into the parking lot. He pushed me into his car, got in, and slammed the door. I was still furious, and bawling.

"Sophia, calm down. Merrill has been like this for as long as he is shallow, and that's been forever, so don't let him get to you. Just let it go."

I stayed in the car to compose myself. My eyes were again open to the hatred and prejudices men outside of The Allred Group, carried toward my uncle's position with Joseph Musser. More than sixteen years after the Split, grudges, hate, and contempt were still raging on.

After a while, I joined some of the crowd who were farther from the fire pit. Then Mark took my hand and asked me to walk across the road and down into the gully with him.

When we sat down on the cold earth, he reminded me again of his deep love for me. He said he knew without a doubt we were meant for each other, and we made covenants in the pre-existence to be together on this earth.

I told him how sorry I was I still didn't know or feel the same way, and he needed to give up on me before I hurt him even more.

For the longest time, Mark sat still; he was heartbroken and fuming. Feeling responsible for his anguish, I sobbed. Then he suddenly jumped up, angrily grabbed my arm, and pulled me up the hill, while

I fought with him to leave me alone.

"I'm going to take you home!" he snarled at me.

"I don't want to go home now," I shouted.

No matter what I did or said, Mark insisted, he'd taken me to the party, so it was his obligation to make sure I got home, whether I liked it or not. I knew he was masking his disappointment and tears by acting outraged. I wept in anger, remorse and fear while he recklessly sped home.

⚘

During the past few years, between my breaking up and getting back with Royce, he'd taken me to my junior prom at the capitol building, to the notorious Heidelberg Restaurant, and to the elegant Hotel Utah Restaurant, all the while hoping he'd win my heart and my hand in marriage.

To others, it probably looked like I had done nothing but use his and other men's love and adoration to fill my emptiness, to find some solitude, and to have a reason for being. I felt like such a despicable person.

When I broke up with Royce for the very last and final time, he still insisted he would always love me and I was making a terrible mistake—one I'd someday regret.

Sometime that Autumn Aunt Maryann packed up and left Dad for a deejay she'd "allegedly" been carrying on with. Rick went with his mother. Dad divided his and Maryann's four other children between his three remaining wives. The space I had so longed for, and the bedroom I finally had all to myself for at least six months, I gratefully shared with my precious sister Jolie.

Soon after Aunt Maryann left, horrendous things came to the attention of Dad's three wives who had custody of Maryann's kids. At last, and way too late, they realized Rick had been sexually abusing them for years. Dad and his wives felt Rick was the reason for our youngest sister's self-exploitation and promiscuity.

So many times they had begged Rick to stop, but he never did. He'd beat them up, say he was sorry, or threaten to harm another sibling if they told. He made sure his siblings felt just as responsible as he was for his disgusting behaviors and any repercussions if "they" were ever caught. The few times any of the kids tried to tell their mother Rick was abusing them; she would vehemently deny their allegations and exonerate him.

After listening to Rick's versions, Dad chose to pass their claims off as "children's vivid imaginations" or "childhood curiosity."

When I heard just a smidgen of what had happened to my siblings, I fell into a deep depression for weeks. I was sure I was responsible and would be held accountable for their anguish. If only I had been strong and brave enough to tell my parents what was going on with him, it may have put a stop to the abuse. Three of my siblings would not have had to endure Rick's torture, and suffer the terrible wounds and memories.

As usual, while in remorse, I sank to the bottom of my bed and tried to hide my shame under the heavy, suffocating covers, as I lay in the dark. It was the closest I could get myself to purgatory's fire and brimstone. I needed to be there right then—and maybe forever.

I hoped I would never, ever see Rick's face again!

CHAPTER 16

Legally and
Religiously Married
1969–1970

The Viet Nam war was raging and the draft was in full force. Among Fundamentalist Mormons, opinions vary when it comes to participating in wars. Aunt Amelia's son Ari, had volunteered to join the army, and was reported "missing in action" in September of 1967, from near the Thu Bon River in the Quang Nam Province. My brother Luke had been drafted and served time in Vietnam, as well as my brother, Charles, who was still there. Mark and a few of his brothers chose to register as conscientious objectors. In accordance with Section 6-1 of the Military Selective Service Act, they were not subject to combat duty because of their religious beliefs. However, every conscientious objector was still required to dedicate two years of civil service to his country at a nonprofit health or safety organization.

Mark and one of his many brothers served their two years working in the laundry room at the Holy Cross Hospital in Salt Lake, City. To survive the heat (long before air conditioning) they tried to keep the nuns laughing. The brothers would tease, pull pranks, tell wild tales, and invent nun jokes. The two of them even drew and posted accurate-looking caricatures of each of their coworkers in action.

Meanwhile, Mark prayed for a better job than the one in the "laundry-room dungeon," where the workforce often discovered body parts, surgical paraphernalia, and feces wrapped in blood-covered sheets and towels.

After a few more breakups and reconciliations with Mark throughout the fall and spring, he finally won my heart and steady devotion. I treasured our friendship and his adoration of me. We'd become inseparable, and yet worried about life's upcoming challenges.

My new summer job in uptown Salt Lake City was at Almo's Dry Cleaners. It kept me tied up while Mark was serving his army time. As often as possible, he would come by for a visit or pick me up from work. We'd talk and make out on the couch in the back room until a customer drove up to the window and held the buzzer down. Having our kissing and fondling interrupted caused physical distress, but enjoying and being tempted to give in to our newly discovered pleasure was even worse. Every time Mark and I would get going, I'd hear Mom's warning in my head: "Having premarital sex is as bad as murder!" Too often our passion drew Mark and me near to this worst sin on earth. Miraculously, one of us was always strong enough to stop before it was too late.

If my guilt-ridden body hadn't already run away from Mark, he'd hug me tight and beg me not to feel guilty about such "normal, God-given" sexual urges—especially, Mark stressed, "with young adults who are so madly in love."

Still, I wasn't sure if he was right. Sometimes my guilt for making out with him became so overwhelming, if suicide was acceptable by any standard, I believed I would have ended my wicked life right then—yesterday, a month ago, or a long time ago when we first got started.

One evening, I decided to dress up more than usual. On my way out the back door with Mark, I told Mom, "Goodbye, we'll see you later."

"Where do you think you are going all dressed up?" she asked.

"We're going out to dinner—for my birthday."

I'm sure Mom didn't remember. I was used to it and no longer expected her to.

"No, you're not," she snapped. "You didn't ask me if you could go anywhere!"

"Mom, I haven't had to ask you for years and years if I could go anywhere, so I didn't think I had to ask you now," I gently complained.

"That's the whole point! You always come and go as you please. It's way past time you become accountable."

My precious mother was still trying to get it right after all those years of missing out on giving me guidance and discipline. It wasn't really me she was angry at, it was herself. It was her guilt and remorse making her overreact. I was used to her inattentiveness toward my birthday, my life, and me and I was hardly torn apart by her sporadic and nonsensical outbursts. That day was just another reminder of the authority she never really held. Undoubtedly, she'd had enough of whatever was really eating away at her, so she had to remind herself, in this case, she was in still in charge.

Mark and I quietly sat on the couch in the sparse front room and listened to the dishes clanging in the kitchen. I stared at the ugly gray-and-black pebble design in the large linoleum squares. The dingy, marred walls that hadn't been painted in forever loomed in on me. *I've got to get out of here!* I thought.

A couple of tears escaped and slid down my cheeks, and I leaned my head on Mark's shoulder. The ten or so minutes we'd hardly spoken a word to each other felt like hours. Finally he moved toward the front of the couch, turned around, and looked me straight in the eyes. "Sophia, when are you ever going to marry me?" he asked, his warm voice quivering a bit.

A million thoughts raced through my mind. It was my seventeenth birthday, and Mom had said it was about time I become accountable. She was right. I wanted and needed a space of my own. If I didn't take Mark up on his offer this time, he would surely give up on me. His proposal might be the last chance I'd ever have to get married. If I were single past age eighteen, I'd be an undesirable old maid. My thoughts rambled on. *Mark loves me. He's always been here for me— sometimes even when I didn't want him to be. We know each other's heartaches; have the same lifelong dreams and the same goals for our children. Mark surely must be the "right" man for me. He's been right in front of my face this whole time, and I was too stupid and blind to see how easy God had made it for me.*

"Soon," I answered Mark at last.

"Are you serious? Did you really say soon? Is that a yes?"

"Yes. I'm thinking sometime next summer."

We waited just under a month, until Sunday, December 7, 1969, to make sure I wasn't going to back out or change my mind again. Just before sacrament meeting, Mark asked Dad for permission to marry me. Dad made me promise to graduate from high school first, and wanted us to ask his brother, Rulon, as well.

After sacrament meeting, we asked Uncle Rulon. Though he was reluctant, we proudly spread the word of our engagement to our family and friends.

As the next few months passed, Mark and I became close in every way possible, other than marriage and its consummation. We were deliriously happy together. Both of us believed with every fiber of our being we would have five boys for sure, two girls and possibly three. We planned for our children all the things we never had and always dreamed of. We wanted their lives to be perfect, and we intended to be picture-perfect parents.

In keeping his promise, my friend Bryan tried to remain my loyal friend. He would meet with Mom; and I'd join them once in a while at our house to discuss LDS doctrines and polygamy. With all of his heart, Bryan wanted to save me from "eternal damnation." Each of them found their own "truths" and "facts" in the same LDS scriptures and recorded sermons.

After all was said and done, our dear and faithful friend Bryan had no choice but to wipe his feet clean of us and leave Mom and me to the pits of hell.

The last time we spoke, he said, "Sophia, the day you allow Mark to marry another woman is the day you and he will be damned."

What a staggering contradiction, I thought. *In the 132nd Section of "his" Doctrine and Covenants, God says I will be destroyed if I don't allow Mark to marry other women.*

Somehow, even though I didn't blame him, Bryan's goodbye felt like another desertion. And even after all of Mom's and his doctrinal battles, I still worried. What if Bryan's take on the LDS religion was right? I wished it were. I wanted it to be. I didn't want to have to share Mark with other women, then or ever.

Squelch those wicked desires to be a "normal" person, Sophia! Sixteen years of conditioning ordered. *Press forward with the will of God. You must live polygamy!*

Though I still had many doubts and worries about marrying Mark, I continued to ignore them and push our wedding date closer. We bumped it up from July to the middle of April to help maintain our oath of virtue, which was becoming nearly impossible to keep.

On the big day, Val, Amy, and I spent most of the day decorating the LDS church gymnasium Dad rented for Mark's and my reception. Mark and my brother Alan gathered the arbor, flowers, cake, punch bowls, glasses, and drinks. We barely made it back to my house in time for our wedding ceremony.

I paced all alone from Mom's bedroom, down the hallway, and into our dismal-looking front room, where our family and closest friends were waiting. I smiled in delight when I saw Mark and Alan both wore tuxedos, which they swore they'd never do. My beautiful bridesmaids stood next to them.

Mark (twenty-four and a half years old) and I (seventeen and a half) stood in front of my father. He placed my hand in Mark's to symbolize the "sacred handshake." Then he recited what he believed to be the marriage ceremony originally used in the temples. Near the end of our "priesthood" wedding ceremony, Mark took from his pocket a man's gold wedding band (he'd found it in the washing machine at the hospital) and placed it on my ring finger.

"This is just for the time being," he'd informed me earlier. "It will have to do until I can afford to get you another one."

It meant the world to me Mark cared enough to come up with a ring for our wedding. We'd talked about not having one at all. However, even when we were first engaged, I longed for a diamond engagement ring and a real wedding band for our special day. I wanted to be like the other girls at school and in The Group, who pranced around with treasured proof they were cherished, and going to be married to the love of their life. I tried so hard not to care—not to be vain or worldly. After all, none of that really mattered in the vast scheme of the gospel. But without an engagement ring, hardly a soul believed I was really engaged to a single man. Many of my classmates assumed "that poor polygamous girl will soon be married off to some old geezer who already had a bunch of wives and kids, and we'll never see her at school again."

Our honeymoon was also postponed until Mark made more than minimum wage.

After our wedding reception, we celebrated with an extravagant meal at The Hawaiian, before we went home to our tiny apartment in Sandy.

Just as before when we'd make out, I'd get easily excited. I relished our lovemaking, but whenever I became aware of any bodily fluids whatsoever, I was traumatized, nauseated, and repulsed—putting a stop to everything. Neither one of us knew why I was so disgusted with something I was told was wonderful and holy after marriage.

141

At the elementary school across the street from our tiny apartment, I sat on a child-size tire swing that snuggled my bottom tightly. My eyes were blurred with tears. Mark and I had been married five and a half weeks, and most of that time I wanted to move back home and have our marriage annulled. I felt I'd made the biggest mistake of my life. I wasn't sure about the man I was living with. He looked like my friend Mark, the man who had patiently and ardently pursued me for three and a half years. He looked like the same guy who took me out on dates, who was proud to be with me, who listened to me, and who spoke to me with love, respect, and kindness. He looked like my active, attentive fiancé who said the two of us believed and felt the same way about everything that mattered in life. But I was living with a stranger. Hardly anything about him felt the same.

Nearly every night, Mark hung out with my brother Alan and other bachelor friends. When he'd get home late at night, my husband didn't want to talk or listen. And because neither of us understood my unfavorable sexual issues, there were problems with intimacy.

Before our marriage, during the thousands of hours Mark and I spent together or were in the same vicinity, I had only witnessed him lose his temper twice. The first time was when he had a knock-down-drag-out fight with one of his brothers who broke into his bedroom and took his clothes. Though it broke my heart to see them fight, Mark's reaction seemed justified. The second time I saw him become enraged was when he forced me up the hill into his car and drove recklessly home without concern for our safety. With him now losing his temper on a regular basis, it was painfully clear I'd married a volatile man.

As much as I thought about it, while sitting on the swing, I couldn't ever go home to my parents. I was too embarrassed and ashamed; and God certainly wouldn't approve of me breaking my covenants. Instead, I'd have to save face for Mark and myself. I secretly vowed to hide my discontent and keep my marriage promises, both legal and religious, forever. I was sure things would get much better.

Mark and I argued about anything and everything. Between our fights, his temper, and my cold retreats, we kept trying to build on our commitment and the deep love we both desired. The most precious gift in the universe—even with my bouts of morning sickness—was discovering our first baby was due the following March.

❧

Mark took my left hand in his and stared at it. "This ring is not good enough for you," he said. "We need to get rid of it."

When he tried to remove it, I fussed and withdrew my hand. "Leave it alone. This ring is better than no ring at all!"

"No it isn't," he said. "It's some old guy's ring. Let me take it off."

Quickly, he had the gold band off and replaced with a beautiful gold-and-silver band. I was in ecstasy over the ring and his gesture of love. I loved and stared at it every day, but it didn't satisfy my longing.

I wanted a ring even a quarter as noteworthy as the diamonds all the other girls inside and outside our group had on their fingers. My lack of clothing, shoes, decent lunches, the fact my family could never afford to let me take dance or piano lessons, and now my ring, all felt like proof of my insignificance compared to everyone else.

Even worse, I felt like an ungrateful piece of slime for not being utterly happy and satisfied with what I had.

❧

Near the first part of July, my sister Amy and her husband asked us to rent Gregory Maynard's home with them. In fear his baby would be taken away, Gregory took her from a hospital, and moved that child's mother and her six older siblings to the Pinesdale Ranch. We were told they'd be hiding there for a couple of years, and he needed renters for his home.

None of us had ever liked or trusted Gregory. I still couldn't stand to be around him since I was a little girl and he asked Mom if he could take me to get ice cream. Though it was considered evil and unrighteous, Amy and her husband and Mark and I questioned how insane it was Gregory had been called to be on the priesthood council in the first place.

We decided to help him out, only because we felt it would benefit us as well.

It was very hard on me to live with Amy and her husband. Both she and I were pregnant, but I always ended up playing second fiddle to her. Mark seemed to be more interested in her than in me. He doted on her constantly. When she felt ill, cried, or just wanted to talk, Mark stayed up for hours with Amy while her husband slept. In the quiet darkness of our room I would swallow hard, gasp in deep breaths of air, and pull the pillow over my face to keep them from hearing me weep. I didn't want Amy to know how much her grand presence seemed to completely invalidate mine. I tried every minute to be happy and gracious about the attention she always sought and received, even from my husband.

❧

Francine was finally able to get away from her west desert home and come to Salt Lake for a while to help me. I'd had morning sickness for so long I'd lost nearly fifteen pounds. She took me to see Uncle Rulon to get some medicine he recommended, and then she spent the next few hours helping me find food my stomach could tolerate. She let me cry and carry on over the few things I was willing to talk to her about, and then I cried some more when she had to return to her home and family. I felt so alone when she left, I wanted to get in our car and follow her home. There I'd be loved and appreciated.

Amy, her husband, and Mark sounded disappointed when we were told, after four months of renting Gregory's house we had only a few weeks to move out. He wanted his house back so he could move an-

144

other one of his wives in. We'd spent hundreds of dollars and hours cleaning, scrubbing, painting, mowing, repairing, and gardening. Though I loved Amy, I was so grateful to be rescued from living with her.

Mark and I moved into his aunt (and mother) Aldora's basement, where he had lived for years just before our marriage. Other than the persistent yelling matches between Aldora and Mark's father, which were always about another wife, it was a nice place to be. They welcomed us and treated us well.

༄

As a novice expectant mother, I was amazed and obsessed with the mystical creature growing in my womb. Everywhere I went, I carried a large book Doctor Fulton had given me. It was full of detailed photos depicting an infant's developing stages. I took it with me to church, to the store, to my friends' houses, and to Mom's. It was almost as if the book had become another appendage. I was as connected to my "new Bible" as a toddler was to a binky and blanket.

Nearly every night, from the time I was about sixteen weeks along, I dreamed I drew my son out of my womb to cuddle and caress his miniature toes and fingers. I'd kiss his nose, eyes, ears, and torso and talk to him about the wonderful future I envisioned for him. Then I'd gently place him back inside so he could continue to develop.

Without the luxury of modern-day ultrasounds, I described his tiny body, face, hair, and eyes to anyone who would listen.

I also asked Mom what a "mother's blessing" was. I'd heard about it from other pregnant girlfriends in The Group. She told me they were called "washings and anointings." Mom and a few other women had been "set apart" (given authority by Uncle Rulon) to carry out this "very special spiritual blessing" for any expectant woman who asked for one.

Of course I didn't want to be left out—I needed all the blessings I could get.

We knelt in prayer to dedicate the time and space to God. My mother asked Him to guide Aunt Amelia and herself with the right words. I was embarrassed when I was asked to disrobe and wrap a large white towel around me. Then I sat on the edge of Mom's bed as she instructed me to do.

Starting at the top of my head and moving down to my toes, Aunt Amelia gently washed my naked body one part at a time with a warm washcloth. Every now and then, she rinsed the cloth in a bowl of warm water. It was very quiet; no one said a word. When it came time to wash between my legs, she handed me the washcloth.

Then the process was repeated. This time Mom used consecrated (blessed by a priesthood holder) olive oil. She dipped her hand in a small bowl of oil, and as she anointed each part of my body from head to toe, she verbalized a specific decree on them.

"We bless your eyes so you will always be able to see God's will in all things and those who are in need of your love and care . . . We bless your breasts and your nipples they will develop adequately so you will be able to nurse your infant without discomfort or pain . . ."

The same procedure took place as I anointed my own female parts. "We bless your womb so all will go accordingly when you deliver this little soul you will soon bring into this world . . . We bless your legs to be strong enough to carry you through your daily duties and walks of life . . ."

Throughout the whole process, I knew I was supposed to feel the Holy Spirit, but with every touch, prayer, and blessing, all I felt was my unworthiness. With all of my heart, I wanted to feel something different than discomfort. All over again, it seemed I was never as good as others. All the way through my "mother's blessing" I conjured up the good woman Aunt Amelia, Mom, and I wanted me to be.

By November of my senior year of high school, my pregnancy was obvious. In those days it wasn't okay even if you were married,

146

so I was asked not to attend school. Apparently my pregnancy was a bad example to the other girls whose focus should be their education.

I intended to get ahead on my credits, have my baby in March, and graduate with the Murray High School Class of 1971. But Aldora's house was near Granite High School; so I signed up for classes three nights a week and planned to graduate from the high school Mark had graduated from.

Our new meeting place, and private school building in Bluffdale, nicknamed The Brown House, was nearly complete. The huge facility–which had been built and funded by tithes and donations—fulfilled a longtime dream of having a Group school for our own children. Uncle Rulon assigned a fairly new convert and his wife, who both had teaching certificates, to be in charge of the school's rudiments. My childhood desire to be a teacher also came true when nearly all who volunteered were accepted as teachers for a hundred or so "Allredite" children.

My life was inundated with learning and teaching. To make sure our lessons were accurate; Aunt Amelia and I would study, practice, and prepare every single subject before we instructed our 15 second-grade students. After I taught school all day with Aunt Amelia four days a week, I continued my night classes and then slept like a baby.

※

While living in Aldora's basement, Mark and I were constantly inundated with guests: our friends, my brothers, his brothers, their girlfriends, and their friends. Being a social person, I enjoyed our company most of the time. The difficult and crazy times were when I was exhausted, and when all the guys, including Mark, would flirt with all of the cute, young girls.

According to my upbringing, God commanded women to accept their husbands' desire to live the law of plural marriage. Each of us was to be happy, supportive, sweet, and encouraging when it came to our husband's courting and obtaining other wives.

Still, even the *idea* of Mark being with another woman, let alone the reality of such a thing, created a throbbing, breath-stealing ache I could barely endure. Even my religious doctrines didn't take that away. It was unfathomable God would require that kind of sacrifice of women. I thanked Him when that darling, scantily dressed gal who had walked up Dad's long driveway a few years back with her sister, decided to marry my brother Alan instead of Mark.

※

My father and his brother reluctantly conceded to the builders of the Fashion Place Mall. Dad gave in when he refused to live behind the giant concrete wall they intended to construct around his property if he wouldn't sell out. He signed a twenty-year negotiable lease and accepted a lump sum for the huge chunk of Plygville property on 300 east.

With the down payment, Dad purchased twenty-five acres of land in Bluffdale, and started building one of two large fourplexes for his elderly wives, his two most recent wives, and his young children.

※

In March 1971, after eleven hours of hard labor in my mother- and father-in-law's basement, I gave birth to Mark's and my perfectly magnificent eight-pound boy. No one—my mother, Francine, Amy, Doctor Fulton, Aunt Amelia, Mark, or my sisters-in-law (who kept peeking in to check on our progress)—was surprised to see Jake had a petite nose, long dark hair, and deep-set, alert, light blue eyes. All of those features, as well as his chubby, round face, were exactly as I had described.

Never in my whole life had I felt such joy, wholeness, and purpose as I felt that day. I wanted nothing more than to be a perfect mother to my perfect son—and to the other four boys and two girls (maybe three), Mark and I already knew we would have.

CHAPTER 17

A Meal Fit for a Queen
1971–1973

In May 1971, I proudly walked across the stage and received my high school diploma. Though I didn't graduate before I married, I was pleased to have finished school, not only for myself, but also because of the promise I had made to my father.

My "washing and anointing," or "mother's blessing," proved my incompetence as a servant of God. I was certain those blessings didn't take effect because I didn't have faith and the Spirit of God in me.

I wanted and planned to nurse Jake for at least nine months. No matter how hard I tried or how fastidiously I went through the LaLeche routines and followed everyone's advice, I had to quit. In his stymied efforts to nurse from my painfully torn and raw nipples, he'd end up with more blood than milk in his tiny mouth.

I was so naive. At the maturation class in junior high, the nurse told us you had to have a period before you could get pregnant. I didn't realize I could conceive before I had another period. Beyond what other people would think, I was elated to discover that another infant would soon be in my arms. I'd always wanted twins, and I figured one at a time was the best way to have them.

꒰

In the fall of 1971, Mark and I rented Dad's home in Granger (currently West Valley City). In March 1972, eight days before Jake's first birthday, our son Alan was born in our Granger home. Weighing just six pounds, he had a smidgen of blond hair at the nape of his neck and a round, adorable face like his brother's. The same good doctor who delivered Jake worked for a long time to get Alan breathing on his own, before he left for another home delivery across the valley.

Shortly after the doctor left, Mark said he was famished and was going out to get some food. While I slept for a couple of hours, Mom took care of the babies and wondered why Mark hadn't returned with some nutritious food and the fruit juices she'd asked him to pick up for his postpartum wife. Our cupboards were bare, as usual, so when Mark returned three hours later without any food for us, Mom was livid.

"There should be a few bags of beans or macaroni somewhere in the cupboards," I told her. "I've learned a few hundred ways to fix them without much effort."

Mom called my brother Shane, whose second wife lived close by. She gave him a list of groceries to pick up. When he returned, she got busy cooking. At last, when she brought a tray holding a steak, a salad, and a baked potato with the works, she said, "Here, my darling girl— a meal fit for a queen. And a queen you truly are!" My mother's cooking was always delectable.

꒰

Many times when Mark was at home to eat, he was upset with me for fixing the same kinds of food day after day. If I complained there was no money to buy anything but macaroni, potatoes, or rice, he'd get upset about how hard he worked and how there was never anything to

show for it. I reminded him it was because he was excessively generous and soft-hearted. He'd spend or give away most of our money
long before enough of it got home to pay the bills, let alone purchase
groceries which would cost way more than beans.

Mark was always too charitable, just as my mother and I were.
Everyone in the whole wide world was rightfully more important than
our own families. We were sure God would bless us for our unselfish
attributes, and in some miraculous way we'd get by because that's all
we deserved in His kingdom.

Nearly every day, a couple of my brothers and Mark's brothers,
who worked for Mark, would stop by with bread, milk, and "innards"
for their sandwiches. While I prepared their food, poured their milk,
and served them lunch, I'd suck in my fat belly and listen to our young
brothers with raging libidos discuss "big, beautiful breasts and sexy
asses," and say things like "Gee, how I'd love to have those in my . .
." and "Holy mackerel, how I'd love to take that brunette into the . .
." Mark laughed along with their jokes about the beauties they'd been
lusting after for days.

I'd be in tears. In fact, I cried all the time. I couldn't pull myself
together. All day long I nursed Alan and took care of my baby boys.
It was impossible to keep up with the laundry, the house, the meals,
and the never-ending diaper washing.

The messy cloth diapers had to be washed by hand at least two
times and then three or four times in my old single-wringer washer
before they'd be white. With each washing, the tub had to be drained
and refilled with hot, soapy water. Then the diapers had to be rinsed
a couple times with cool water. I had to hang them outside on the
clothesline to dry. Laundry days were the same arduous ordeal I'd experienced growing up.

When the diapers were dry, they had to be folded. Meals needed
to be fixed and the dishes washed, dried, and put away. Through all of
it I tried to stay sane. *No wonder Mom cried all the time!* I thought.

Mark, I was sure, was disappointed in me and wished he'd never
asked me to marry him. With all of my heart, I believed he didn't love

me and wished he were married to a few young, thin, beautiful sexy girls who would fulfill all of his domestic and male desires. Nearly everything he did and didn't say gave me the impression he would have been much happier without me and two babies to look after.

One cold day in October, I spiffed up the house, packed clothes for the boys and me, and left a "leaving you" letter on the bed. I was sure I'd go to hell, but I was already in hell and imagined Mark was also.

In Santaquin City, nearly two hours south of our home, I pulled into a long, winding driveway trimmed with fruit trees. Since Stuart left The Group and lived quite far away, I was sure no one would think to find us there. He was a friend of Francine's husband, but had no idea why I was showing up, unannounced at his place with my little boys. Still he welcomed us openly.

As he and I commiserated, Stuart gloomily told me the reason his wife had left him. He said Jon Thomas had convinced her she could never make it to heaven if she didn't leave her unworthy husband and marry him. I already had my strong opinion of Jon. He gave me the willies whenever I was around him. So of course I sincerely believed Stuart's sad story.

I told Stuart Mark was as miserably unhappy with me as I was with him, and he'd rather be anywhere but at home with his boys and me.

"Ah, men are just that way. Sometimes they're jerks and a-holes, but I'm sure he loves you, Sophia."

I'd already sworn Francine to secrecy regarding my whereabouts, but she called me three days later and begged me to call Mark.

"Everyone is worried about you," she said. "Mark is going crazy! I can't stand to see him like this. He's driven all over the valley the past two days, looking for you and asking everyone if they've seen you. He hasn't eaten or slept since the day you left, and he says he won't until he finds you. Please call him—you have to give him a chance to talk."

I called Mark. He asked Dad to drive him down to get us. Dad also brought his new wife and my newest baby sister, Dad's twenty-second child.

Mark and I talked all the way home, discussing our problems and feelings. He promised he'd try to show me how much he loved and appreciated me. I pledged my love to him and promised to keep up with things better than I had and to be more appreciative of his efforts. "You are my soul mate, Sophia," he said. "I've known we'd be together ever since I first saw you, remember? Don't ever forget how much I love you—way more than you'll ever know."

Why, I wondered, won't I ever know how much he loves me? It would sure make a difference in our marriage if I knew. I wanted more than anything to believe him and to have everything wonderful between us.

On the spur of the moment, I devised a scheme to guarantee better food on the table and how our bills would get paid on time.

A few days before payday, I let Mark know I'd opened a checking account and filled the cupboards and refrigerator with food. "And by the way, I filled the car with gas, paid the water bill, and bought some glasses. So you've got to cover those checks or they'll throw me in jail. If that happens, you won't have a wife or a mother around to take care of your little boys."

The best part of all, it worked. Mark said he appreciated some money management in his life. Every two weeks just before payday he asked me, "How much money do you need me to put in the bank to cover your checks?" For that piece of good fortune, I sincerely smiled.

❦

I rushed to Murray to watch the demolition of the home I grew up in. My father's basement home, and the later, upstairs edition, the one he built and paid for one step at time, was being bulldozed into a pile of rubbish. While I cried, Dad wiped his tears with his blue-plaid shirt-sleeve and reminded us, even though he knew this day would come, it still hurt. Dust, shingles, and drywall powder drifted into the sky in front of us.

Dad's quiet laughter gave way to some comic relief and another famous Allred pun: "It's all in the name of progress. I guess modern-day merchants need the Fashion Place Mall so they can *maul* customers who aren't in *fashion*."

We laughed, even if we didn't quite get his humor until later.

※

One of my many intuitive or telepathic experiences came long before cell phones were invented. Since Francine didn't have a phone on the west desert ranch her husband had moved her back to, we had already been sending simple, important messages to and from each other on a regular basis.

One gorgeous summer day in July 1973, Mark and I got a neighbor to babysit our little boys so we could walk to the bowling alley a few miles away. About halfway there, my sister Francine sent me a telepathic message. I heard her tell me she was in labor and needed me to be home.

Mark and I turned and ran all the way back home. We hadn't been in our house ten minutes before William pulled in our driveway with Francine and her youngest children I was going to tend while she went to the hospital; but she didn't have time to get to the hospital, so I got to help care for Francine and her adorable three- and four-pound twin boys who were born in our home.

While we lived in Granger, I got to watch her twins (the youngest of eight children) quite often, for over a year while Francine dealt with major health issues. As the four boys got older, I was delighted when people would ask how I happened to have two sets of twins.

※

During the past three years, I had wished Mark would buy me a diamond ring—all on his own accord. I mentioned it, hinted, and asked. A few times over the years, he took me to jewelry stores to daydream and hope some more. One of those times, I felt sure he would purchase one of the rings I fell in love with, and surprise me with it.

So I finally came right out and said, "Mark, I've wanted you to buy me a diamond ring set for years! How about rings for our third wedding anniversary?"

With the large jar of change he'd been saving, and some postponed bills, he decided to purchase the rings. The engagement ring we picked out had a diamond in the center; the wedding band wrapped the center diamond on one side, with three tiny rubies between three tiny diamonds. It was absolutely gorgeous. When it was finally sized and ready, I looked like the weirdest woman on earth, prancing around staring at my finger day in and day out.

✻

After their conversion, a couple of single women who'd been active participants in LDS Church programs initiated "girls' camp" in the Allred Group. They set it up similar to the LDS Church's program.

I'd known for a while my cousin Kenneth's daughter, Diane— Val's younger sister—had a crush on Mark. I thought that was why she and her good friend Norma wanted to be in my camp. At girls' camp we had a chance to get to know each other as more than just names. Everything we lost, forgot to pack, burned, or messed up only added excitement and new adventure. The pack of sixteen-, seventeen-, and eighteen-year-old fun-loving girls kept all of us rallied in fun. This kind of religious merriment had never been part of our younger years. Between the fun classes and great meals, we tubed down the river, jumped off a cliff into a cavern of deep, swirling water, and bathed behind shrubs and Indian grass in the river bend.

After camp and for several months, Diane came out to our house as often as she could. We enjoyed each other's company, just as my mother had enjoyed time with her good friend Alice so many years before. I felt Diane genuinely liked me, and not just Mark. She was smart and had a great sense of humor, which was an additional appeal to our friendship. Mark and Diane liked many of the same things as well.

I knew he'd have to marry another woman some day so we could be with each other, our children and our families in the hereafter—after our bodies die and our spirits live on. My sister-wives might as well be women I can love and get along with, I thought. Even though I was still jealous about the whole thing, I truly felt good about Diane being part of our family.

As time passed, we saw less and less of Diane. I was sad Mark didn't show more interest in her; I'm sure she sensed his distance and moved on.

🌿

Mark found out a member of our group had been asked by the priesthood council to be a mechanic for the people who lived on the Pinesdale Ranch. The man was eager to fulfill his calling, so he was in a hurry to sell his land in Bluffdale, close to the Utah State Penitentiary. The two acres of land included a large, dilapidated old house the family used for extra bedrooms, since the kitchen plumbing was totally useless. Two huge chicken coops were full of cars, windows, motors, and more junk than the universe had stars. Two more slant-roofed coops in front of the other two had been converted into semi-functional apartments.

There were only two good things about moving clear out to Bluffdale. We'd have a piece of farmland where we could raise our kids outside the gloomy, crowded, ghetto atmosphere of Granger City. We could have horses, a huge garden, and more privacy. Those things definitely appealed to me. However, the reasons not to purchase the land far outweighed the positives. It was the early 1970s, and we would be moving into the middle of nowhere, with a massive junkyard where absolutely nothing was finished. I couldn't see us ever having the time or money to make the necessary changes. Worse, was the land's proximity to the Utah State Penitentiary. I worried none of us would be safe from the convicts who seemed to escape on a regular basis.

After the fact, I was elated Mark stuck to his guns and held fast to his best judgment. He talked me into the move with wonderful promises of how we'd improve the land and the buildings. Dad let Mark and I sell his house, which we'd been renting from him. We borrowed $12,000 from Dad's equity, and purchased a quarter acre of grassland and one and three-quarter acres of junkyard.

In the fall of 1973, we moved into the better of the two slant-roofed, disheveled chicken-coop apartments—the same one the previous family had lived in.

The man of the house never had more than one wife, but many neighbors in the rural area presumed he had anywhere from three to ten. His wife wore her long hair wrapped around her head. Her dresses were ankle-length with long sleeves, and she openly advocated polygamy to anyone who would listen. By the time we moved out there, she'd already labeled us by association.

✼

Unlike my sister-in-law Val, my sister Amy, and the other "normal" young mothers I knew, I couldn't get my boys to obey very well. I was sure all the mothers but me knew what they were doing when it came to parenting, so I tried to follow their advice.

"You should make your boys take a nap, Sophia," my friends advised me. "It's the only time you have to yourself to get things done. No wonder you feel so overwhelmed."

In their tiny nine-by-ten-foot bedroom, Jake and Alan jumped up and down on their single bed. Listening to their precious laughter always tickled me inside and out. They got up a million times between my bouts of exasperation. As the time clicked by, the more swamped I felt. My work was demanding to be done, and soon nothing was funny anymore. I had to make them mind me—I had to get things right. My two- and three-year-old boys' noncooperation, even with my angry threats and warnings, added fuel to my vexation. I'd already smacked their little behinds a few times. They must've thought I was crazy. When had I ever made them take naps before?

Before I knew it, I'd gone insane. Their terrified and pain-filled cries finally brought me to my senses. I saw the redness on my hand, the redness appearing on their legs where I'd missed their little bottoms as they tried to squirm away. I literally wanted to die.

I squeezed down between my bed and the wall and called my mother.

"Come over and take my boys away from me right now!" I demanded. "I don't deserve them. Hurry! Please come get them now. I don't want to hurt them ever again! I know they'll be better off without me. I can't stand me! I can't live with what I have done! Come get them, Mom. As much as I love them, I don't deserve to have them anymore."

"No, Sophia, you're wrong," Mom shouted. "No one loves your boys like you do—no one ever will. You are a good mother! You do deserve them."

My boys' grandmother loved us as much as life. It took her quite some time to calm me. But Mom was right. I loved my boys more than myself, more than anything or anyone. I couldn't understand why I'd behaved so despicably and gotten so enraged. Where had it come from? What if it came back?

Months later, while Francine was driving me home across miles of winding, bumpy, dirt roads from the west desert, I unburdened a truckload of guilt. "Nearly every day to this very day," I told her, "I have mourned hitting my boys so hard. What will happen if I ever get out of control again? What in God's name came over me? How could I have ever done that to my precious boys?"

"You did it because you learned it from our mother," Francine matter-of-factly stated.

"Why would you say such mean, idiotic things about our mother?"

"Because it's true! Abuse can pass on from one generation to the next. If you don't stop it now, your kids will carry it on to theirs, and so on and so on. Mom did to us what her father had done to his children and what his mother had done to them, for who knows how many generations. It's not your fault, Sophia. In the depths of her self-loathing and turmoil, our mother beat on all of us kids, including you. That's what you grew up with, and what you learned."

Tears burned my eyes.

"Mom didn't beat on me, Francine. She didn't hit me like I hit Jake and Alan. She yelled and screamed at us, and I remember her pulling my hair and smacking me once in a while, but she didn't—"

"Yes, she did!" Francine yelled. Then she started crying and pulled off the road. "I was there, Sophia! I was outside the door. You weren't more than four years old. I could hear each snap of the belt on your little body in between Mom's scolding. I pounded on the door and screamed and begged her to stop. It seemed like forever! When I could no longer hear your screams and crying, I thought you might be dead. All I could hear was Mom wailing. When I finally got the door opened with a butter knife, Mom was holding you in her arms. She seemed catatonic, and her moaning nearly covered up your whimpers. She rocked you back and forth, back and forth in her arms."

I thought I'd suffocate from the pain of envisioning that story, let alone being the child victim. Francine slid over and held me. Together, we wept aloud as we rocked in each other's arms for a long time.

No wonder anger terrified me as much as suffocation and torture might. I had been there. And I never wanted to go there again.

❧

We'd lived in Bluffdale nearly six months. I was still frightened of the prisoners who might break out and come to our junkyard to hide. Even at my old age of twenty-one, I hadn't gotten over my fear of going outside alone if it was dark.

One ominously cloudy day while I was alone with Jake and Alan, I heard a loud pounding on the door. I was so startled I nearly wet my pants. The three of us peeked out of our window. All we could see was the legs of a very tall man—more like a giant man. He was standing one step above the platform where our door opened and shut.

Again, he banged on the door, harder and louder.

"Are those your damn dogs?" he bellowed as soon as I cracked the door open.

His six-foot-four stature, plus the eight-inch step above our door, made the barrel end of the shotgun he was holding even with my eyes. "Uh . . . uh . . . what?" I stammered.

"Listen, lady!" he yelled. "I've got sheep and cows over there in my field, and I'm damned—excuse my language—I'm tired of your dogs and all the other damn dogs in the neighborhood chasing and killing my damn sheep! So if you don't want some dead dogs, you'd better keep them locked up! You hear me? Okay?"

I bobbed my head up and down; feeling a little less scared knowing his wrath was about our dogs, not my little boys and me. Within seconds, the man's voice sounded like another man's.

"Hey, I'm sorry to be yelling at you, lady. I'm Leonard Swenson. You can call me Swede. You're the new neighbors we heard about, I guess. I'm glad to meet you. My wife hasn't been feeling very good so she's not very friendly, but you and your husband and the kids are welcome to come over any time you want. Get yourselves over for coffee and a good visit. Do you like playing cards? We'll play some poker sometime, and then we can chop the heads off those squalling turkeys and chickens of ours and cook them for supper, all right?"

"Thank you, Mr. Swenson," I said with a very relieved grin on my face.

"Well, shit, little lady." He stopped. "Guess it won't do to keep apologizing for my bad language. I'm sure it won't end after all these years. Anyway, I was telling you, don't call me Mr. Swenson—I'm Swede to you and to everyone else around here. Oh hell, I forgot to ask you what your name is."

I introduced my precious boys and myself. Then Swede invited them over for a piece of candy any time they wanted one.

CHAPTER 18

Birth Control and
Girls' Camp Anxiety
1973–1974

Birth control is the subject of many a religious debate. As with every doctrine, the rules change or vary depending on who is dispensing them or deciphering them. Opinions stretch to both ends of the spectrum. On one end, following God's laws to the T meant you live the "law of Chastity," where the only justification for intercourse is procreation. Many believe the most pure and special spirits come to those who abide by this law.

The extreme necessitated no birth control whatsoever. A married couple was to let nature take its course, and the frequent pregnancies were because one should have as many children as God wanted to send. Either way you looked at it, the main consensus, as I understood it among most Fundamentalist's, was (and is still), any manner of birth control other than abstinence is not acceptable to God.

In private, Dad told me, and probably his other daughters, not to have any more children than we could care for physically and emotionally. We should make sure each of them was planned and conceived in love. Yet, the amount of children a woman gives her husband to help build his kingdom, determines her value in the grand scheme of things. If we weren't strong-willed and righteous enough to use abstinence as our birth control method, we had to figure out other ways to make sure we didn't have unwanted pregnancies. Then all we had to deal with was the guilt about having sex other than for pro-creation, guilt about using another method of birth control, and God not sending us His most prized spirits.

My dad said he could not preach those things over the pulpit. He didn't want to get blackballed for teaching what many Fundamentalists would say was blasphemy.

"Too many of our people," Dad told me, "think God wants them to have a child every year, whether they can handle them or not. I wish they understood God expects quality before quantity."

I believed my father was truly a wise man about those things. He'd always taught us values that seemed wise, even though I sometimes had a hard time with them. Didn't God create humans to crave sex? Yet if He had His way, we wouldn't have sex unless it was to have a baby? Good grief, we'd already have to be gods or goddesses to make that happen! What if I couldn't "emotionally" handle more than my two boys—did that mean I should never have sex again? To me, it meant I wasn't as valuable as the women who could handle a dozen or more children—only having sex a dozen or so times. Yeah, right! Abstinence probably works for women who don't enjoy sex, or who feel guilty if they have a passionate relationship with their husbands.

There was always something to feel guilty about. It wasn't a righteous option to enjoy the powerful connection our lovemaking had come to provide. Mark and I knew we weren't, and probably never would be, strong enough to live the "law of chastity." The best we could do was to opt for the lesser of those evils. We would plan the conceptions of the rest of our children, use birth control, and have to live with the ongoing consequence—guilt galore.

One of my constant worries was Mark's aversion to attending meetings. As time went on, he spent less time at our meetinghouse. He had a list of reasons. Both of us despised Jon and Gregory, who were council members. Mark was critical of most of the men who were on the priesthood council.

Mark said he never felt welcome at church. "Your dad never did like me because I came from a family of Independent polygamists. I've never been good enough for his daughter."

"It's because you behave like an Independent polygamist," I'd argue. "You act like a law unto yourself, without priesthood leadership. If we're going to live the gospel, it should be lived the right way or not at all. We should live the lower laws first. We should attend meetings, pay our tithing, keep the Word of Wisdom, and have daily family prayer. If we can't even abide by the lower laws of God, how can we ever qualify or be worthy to live the higher law of plural marriage? If we'd do those things together, Dad would notice you are part of The Group and he wouldn't be so concerned about our eternal welfare."

"I have my own dad. He's my leader," Mark replied. "He still has the priesthood, even if your dad doesn't think so. I won't kiss your dad's ass, Sophia. If he can't see what kind of man I am without me following his rules, then he can shove it!"

I grieved about these issues consistently. They were exactly the things my father said he was worried about before I married Mark. A few months after he gave us permission to marry, my dad told me I would probably have to be the spiritual leader of our household.

As I already learned from dating Royce, most Independents were opposed to any kind of organized gathering. He said Lorin C. Woolley, one of our original prophets, believed and advocated Fundamentalist polygamists were not to organize or gather as a church. We were to carry out the covenant of plural marriage only. That's why most Independents claim no accountability to any religious leader or edict other than to live polygamy, and multiply and replenish the earth.

I remember asking Dad about those concerns, and he agreed. As usual, he asserted "valid" reasons why our latter-day prophets could change Woolley's rules and opinions. Needless to say, I went along with my family's opinions.

At church, I was embarrassed. I didn't want my family, relatives, or friends to know the real reasons Mark was inactive. Week after week I made more excuses for his absence. Once in a while he'd concede and attend meetings. Meanwhile, I hoped everyone would believe the good reasons I had for his not being an active member of The Group.

❧

In 1974, the economy and construction businesses were booming. Every time I saw one of Mark's finished masonry jobs, which were scattered across Salt Lake and Utah counties, I was proud. Anyone with an eye for quality could appreciate the artistry and perfection of the projects designed and completed by Mark and his crew of masons.

He and I borrowed $26,000 to build a home right in front of our chicken-coop apartment. It would be located where the old, run-down house was before Francine's husband bulldozed it and hauled most of it away. We chose a floor plan from Mark's boss, my cousin Kenneth, and planned to start building in a few months. It was so hard to imagine or believe such an incredible blessing could be ours.

❧

Diane's fifteen-year-old friend, Norma, lived close by. We asked her to watch Jake and Alan now and then. Over time, she and Mark developed an obvious crush on each other. She was darling, cute, and fun. *Maybe she would make a nice addition to our family*, I told myself. *I know we have to live polygamy some day and I'd better make myself give in.* Everyone else our age was expanding their families. We needed to move on as well. I certainly didn't want to be left out in the cold.

164

Many of the matriarchs in The Group claimed, "The sooner first wives live plural marriage, the easier it will be. The longer you wait, the more difficult it will be to share your husband with sister-wives."

It didn't matter how hard I tried to think pure, honorable thoughts and to be the supportive wife I should be. Even though Mark's (and other men's) flirting and attraction to other girls was justified by the precept of living polygamy, it always felt like a blow in the stomach to me. Still, I refused to let an evil spirit hold me back. For God's, Mark's, and our children's sake, I continued to put on my lovely smile in the presence of others. I held my head and shoulders high just like the other women around me did. I was pretty good at pretending and hoping everything would come up rosy.

※

Several young Independent girls signed up for girls' camp. The camp directors decided they couldn't all be in the same camp. That would be disastrous. The Independent girls had "apostate, alcoholic, smoking" parents and were considered wild if not completely way-ward. They could, and most likely would, lead "our girls" astray. So the directors decided they'd blend a couple of "goody-goody" Allred-ite girls and a few "middle-ground" girls with the three or four "wild" (Independent) girls. They hoped their arrangement would maintain a balance and help keep order. And since the leaders figured I'd had the most experience with the Independents, I got the privilege of being camp counselor for the mixture of goody-two-shoes and the wild-side.

At first there was an obvious gap and a major passive-aggressive struggle between the girls. Around the campfire, I asked them to list the things we all held in common. After we discussed those things, we listed things we thought were different about all of us and discussed why each of us felt the need to be right. In the end, the girls decided it was important for all of them to be kind and accepting of each other, even if they didn't agree. With renewed sensitivity and compassion, the girls were plowing through and making headway. I imagined these buddies would last until we all went back to our own narrow worlds.

Laura, one of Jon's many beautiful daughters had a bubbly personality and a gorgeous smile. In the middle of the night after all the girls were asleep, she began screaming. All of us woke up, petrified. By the time I crawled out of my sleeping bag, over all the other girls and got to her, she was wet with perspiration and shaking uncontrollably. Nothing I or anyone else said consoled her. Laura couldn't or wouldn't say one intelligible word.

We begged her to tell us what was wrong, to calm down and to talk to us. Everything we tried failed. Twenty minutes or more had passed and still we didn't know what to do to help her. The other girls were terrified and upset, and everyone was crying. So I grudgingly asked two of the brave girls to take a flashlight and find her father. I didn't want Jon Thomas near our tent, but since he was Laura's dad, I thought that was my only option.

When Jon, the girls' camp priesthood representative, came to our tent to get Laura, she became even more hysterical and combative. As he carried her away, she shrieked and cried, "No! Stop, I won't! No! Please, no!" Her desperate voice faded into the night.

We tried to guess what Laura's frenzy was all about—a horrifying nightmare, a desperate need for attention, an evil spirit? If only I'd have known.

With my whole being I wanted to console and love her. I hadn't wanted to ask her father, but I had felt helpless. "Forgive me," I begged God. "I am so sorry! I didn't know what else to do," I implored God at least a hundred times before I cried myself to asleep.

❧

Saturday, after the long week at camp, my ride dropped me off at home. I stood there in shock. All I could see were piles and piles of dirt around a massive, rectangular hole in the ground. As I got closer and realized the footings to our new home had been poured, I screamed in delight.

"We nearly didn't make it in time to surprise you," Mark called.

He hurried over, enfolded me in his muddy arms, and planted a bunch of sweaty kisses all over my face. "Whew! We just barely finished this part. We only have a little more to do and you can move in." We laughed and I held him tight.

*

"We've committed a cardinal sin!" I cried out. "I've got another period." I was sure God was punishing us for using birth control. Now that we wanted to get pregnant, I couldn't. It was God's way of telling us, "I told you so!"

My loving husband was pretty good at helping me understand some of my issues with God. Mark's intellect never ceased to amaze me!

"I'm telling you, Sophia, it isn't God punishing us. All we did was use the rhythm method to prevent a child from coming to us before we were ready. It's apparently not the right time for us to have another baby, and when it is, you'll get pregnant again. Meanwhile—" he beamed "—we'll have a lot of fun trying to make one."

Mark's body was so close not even air could pierce through our loving. "You see, Sophia," he said, "if God didn't want humans to enjoy each other as we do, He would never have created such pleasure for us. It's a damn good thing we didn't know how good this feeling was before we got married, or you'd have been pregnant for sure. I bet you are this time."

While in Mark's embrace, I felt tears slide down my cheeks. My heart heaved to release the weight. Not the heaviness of his body or the depths of soul connection we felt so intensely, but the excruciating pain always haunting me. How could Mark ever share this—our love, his heart, his body—with Norma, our babysitter, who was becoming ever more enamored with him? For that matter, how could he share this with *anyone* but me? Why would a *loving* god require me, other women, to suffer this pain?

CHAPTER 19

Evil Ervil

1975

Since the beginning of time, the world has been cursed with egotistical, grandiose men, each one claiming his authority over others was ordained by God Himself.

There's an obvious pattern with many of these psycho-fanatics: James Warren "Jim" Jones, of the People's Temple, who led the mass suicide of more than nine hundred cult members in Jonestown, Guyana, in November 1978; David Koresh, of the Branch Davidian religious sect, where fifty-four adults and twenty-one children died in a fire at Mt. Carmel, Texas, in April 1993; and Ron and Dan Lafferty, who slit the throats of their sister-in-law Brenda and her infant Erica in 1984, and claimed God commanded them to. The list of religious fanatics goes on, but another man at the top was Ervil LeBaron. As Irene Spencer wrote,

"Obsessed by his lust for power, Ervil LeBaron became intoxicated by his own self-worth" (*Cult Insanity: A Memoir of Polygamy, Prophets, and Blood Atonement* [New York City: Center Street Books, 2009], 207).

For many years, the Allred Group considered some of the LeBaron's to be "crazy idiots." Over a long period of time, several of them had displayed erratic and insane behaviors. Some of them had been institutionalized.

In 1956 Joel LeBaron asserted, just prior to his father Dayer LeBaron's death, his father blessed him with the mantle of leadership. Therefore, he began to establish his own church, which he called The Church of the Firstborn of the Fulness of Times. He maintained his father, Dayer, had received his authority from Benjamin F. Johnson, Joseph Smith's adopted son, who received his calling directly from Joseph Smith. It didn't take long for Joel to establish a group of converts and followers. He declared, within a twenty-year period, his clan would be holy and righteous enough Jesus Christ would return to the earth and reside with His flock of like-minded worshipers.

However as time went on, Joel's older brother, Ervil, used his authority as patriarch to justify his madness. He felt like a peon when his brother, Joel, gave him directions or told him what to do; and resented the love and attention parishioners gave his younger brother, which Ervil deemed should justly be his. In order to warrant his numerous outlandish and evil deeds, Ervil began to twist and use many of the early Mormon teachings that had since been rejected by the LDS Church.

Ervil stole and slept with other men's wives. In the name of God he molested, badgered, and coerced young girls to marry him. He borrowed money on the no-return plan; abused, abandoned, and discarded older wives; and demanded his followers support his luxurious lifestyle.

In 1971, after Joel excommunicated Ervil and his loyal patriot, Dan Jordan, from The Church of the Firstborn, Ervil began his own church—The Church of the Lamb of God.

The more Ervil read about the avenging angels, the Danites, in LDS Church history, the more grandiose he became. Before long, he aggressively took over the LeBaron ranch, homes, church building, and storehouse. Anything he wanted, he took. Ervil began to wield his sword of wrath by initiating a one-sided religious war with his brother's congregation. Anyone who wouldn't comply with Ervil's demands or got in his way would be exiled or put to death. In August 1972, Evil Ervil ordered the murder of his brother Joel. His henchmen shot Joel twice in the head, execution style.

At a sacrament meeting one Sunday afternoon in December 1975, Uncle Rulon warned his congregation, Ervil LeBaron had delivered more death threats to him and his first counselor, my father, calling them to repent and follow Ervil's demands or be killed. While we sat in shock and fear, Uncle Rulon read excerpts from the most recent letter he'd received from Ervil. In one of these excerpts, Ervil declared,

"It is a criminal offense punishable by death for an enlightened people to pay tithes and offerings to thieves and robbers."

"By this," Uncle Rulon told us, "Ervil means me, Owen, and possibly the brethren on my council. Ervil is commanding us to force you, my brothers and sisters, to pay all of your tithing to him."

Those of us who knew Uncle Rulon's humor were sure he was trying to display a little sarcasm in the midst of our grave concerns.

"He expects your total allegiance. It is your choice, my brothers and sisters." Uncle Rulon smiled. "If you would like to, please feel free to do so."

I assumed like me, everyone was thinking, "Who does Ervil think he is to really think anyone would do that? What an idiotic, senseless man!" The whole assembly snickered out loud, and Uncle Rulon read on:

"'The sword of vengeance will hang over the heads of those who should fail to hear the word of the Lord. Willful failure to comply with these requirements is in rebellion against God. Repent ye therefore or suffer destruction at the hand of God!'"

We listened intently as Uncle Rulon informed us that several members of his large family and The Group wanted him to go into hiding again. Then he boldly stated, "I told them I won't do that. If it is my time to die, then so be it!"

My father had the same attitude. Several of his sons began to hang close by, at least as much as they could. It was pretty hard to keep up with our dad. At first most of us didn't believe Evil Ervil was gutsy or

Dear Reader,

Thank you for purchasing and/or reading my book.

Before printing, my husband and I hired two editors, who were both very good; however, since we still found mistakes in the final product, I believe I accidentally sent one of the previous manuscripts to the printing company. After receiving our four thousand copies, it was cost prohibitive for re-runs. Therefore I ask you to pardon my blunder, and still appreciate the intended messages in my memoirs, as to the harms of polygamy to men, women and children.

Also, I'll be eternally grateful if you'd be willing to write and post a positive review for future readers.

With much gratitude,
Kristyn

crazy enough to send someone to Salt Lake to go through with something so horrendous. We hoped his threats were nothing but a bunch of hot air. But it wasn't so. The facts were proving otherwise as we received ongoing accounts of his daughter and other disenchanted friends' or family members' murders.

CHAPTER 20

Plural Wives and
Death in Childbirth
1975–1976

From the foundation to the final inspection, I thrilled at the house taking shape in our front yard right before my eyes. I felt like the most blessed woman in the world. In January 1975, we celebrated our move from our chicken coop into our new home. I couldn't help but pace from room to room and stare.

Every month I skimped on groceries and fixed more chili, rice, and macaroni so I'd have money for fabric. One month at a time, each window in our new home was adorned with my home-sewn curtains. I asked my sister-in-law to get me a few extra housekeeping jobs, and the two of us traded babysitting. With the extra money, I ordered professionally made curtains for our family room, which for Mark and me were expensive. With wood scraps Mark brought home from his jobs, I built and stained a frame for the boys' window, and matching picture frames for their photos. The dark oak stained frames accented the frogs on the boy's darling marshland bedspreads and curtains.

The next few months, after teaching school Monday through Wednesday and cleaning four to five houses on Thursdays and Fridays, I took an evening woodshop class at Jordan High School. With the help of the talented instructor, I designed and lathed eight- 4-by-4's and then stained them to match the boys' window and picture frames. With Mark's help I bolted them to two twin-size bed frames, and used second-hand springs and mattresses for the beds. Jake and Alan's rustic-looking bunk beds were durable enough to outlast their childhoods and possibly twenty more. I was pretty proud of myself, though I wasn't supposed to be.

Once in a while, the boys and I tagged along with Mark over to Kenneth's house. We'd hang out there while they looked at house plans for Mark's next masonry jobs. Since they had become pretty good friends, we were sometimes invited to dinner or other outings with them.

In the middle of Utah Lake, Mark and Kenneth fished off the side of the boat, while Diane and I visited and laughed. We mused over the fun times we had at girls' camp the previous year. Her occasional glances and smiles in Mark's direction made it obvious she was still interested in him.

"I know," Mark said, when I told him how she looked at him. "She's liked me ever since I started dating Valerie ten years ago. I'm sure that's why Kenneth has me come over there to work and why we've been invited to join them so often lately."

"She has a lot in common with you." I replied. "Both of you like country-western music, and she knows all of the songwriters and singers. Both of you have great singing voices. Besides being cute and talented, she is really nice and she's related to me." I grinned.

"I'm not interested in her, and that wouldn't be fair to her."

"Why?"

"I'm just not that attracted to her, I guess."

"The inside of someone is more valuable to a relationship than one's appearance is," I said.

"Yeah, you're probably right. We'll see what happens," Mark replied.

As she had before when we lived in West Valley, Diane began to come over quite a bit to hang out with us. Now and then Mark participated, but most of the conversations and activities involved only Diane and me.

It was still too hard for me to sit still for anything, even visiting; besides, there was always so much to be done. She'd visit with me while I cleaned, canned fruit, folded laundry, and performed a hundred other tasks. More often than not, Mark would go in our bedroom and shut the door, or leave the house. I could see the sadness in Diane's eyes as she again sensed his distance. It hurt me as well. She was a beautiful person, and I couldn't think of any girl I'd rather have as a sister-wife.

Diane gave up on Mark again. Later, Kenneth told him she'd married another young man as a second wife. I felt sad for Diane, left out, disappointed, and frustrated with Mark. We were still monogamists!

Because I knew Diane loved Mark, I supposed her unfortunate marriage happened on the rebound. Later, we found out she'd married into a "wayward and wacky" family. Dad told me he was worried for Diane because her husband upheld his father, who had gone off the beaten path. According to Dad and others, Diane's father-in-law was performing outlandish rituals—beating and hypnotizing a "disobedient" wife, and probably doing many more "wicked" and inappropriate things.

I thought of Diane often, hoping the reason Dad saw things that way, was just because he was so busy with his own life he didn't really understand or have the whole picture. I wanted his stories to be unfounded so Diane could be happy.

By then, three more women close to Aunt Amelia's age, and two women near Dad's age, had married him. Excluding Aunt Maryann, who'd left him, Dad had nine wives and several more children to claim and help rear. He was so busy building his new homes in Bluffdale, unless his family members were working with him, most of them only saw him at church.

❧

Alan was three and a half years old before I finally decided to ask a doctor about my infertility. In his medical office, Uncle Rulon told me couples often try too hard to get pregnant, and that alone could cause infertility. His simple and surprising advice was to abstain from sex for two months. Then we needed to wait until I ovulated between the third and fourth months to be together. "I'm sure you'll conceive then. If that doesn't work," Uncle Rulon said, smiling, "we'll go from there."

We were so anxious to be pregnant again we followed his guidelines explicitly. In November and December I missed my periods. Mark was right. God hadn't cursed us for using birth control after all. We took our soon-to-be big brothers to dinner and a movie to celebrate.

Our front acre of land was still full of junk. The three dump-truck loads that left the yard made as much difference against the remaining rubbish as wiping a flyspeck off a screen door. None of that mattered then. I was still in a glorious mood. I had space and privacy galore in our beautiful home, and another baby on the way.

☙

Gorgeous Carla worked at one of Kenneth's partner's offices in Murray, as well as with me as a part-time assistant while I taught second grade at our private school. Every chance Mark got, he talked and flirted with her. She'd flip her long black hair across her shoulders and flash her big brown eyes whenever she looked at him and other men. Before long, Mark began attending meetings with me on a regular basis. Even though he denied it, I was sure it was so he could visit with her before, during and after the meetings.

As always, rumors were spreading. Whenever a single girl was spotted sitting or hanging out with a married family, everyone had their assumptions. Before you knew it, true or not, the word was out. They'd assume another plural marriage had already taken place, or soon would.

This time when Mark accused me of being jealous, I said, "Yes, I am jealous, and I have a right to be! Your every thought lately is how, when, and where you can see Carla again. You come up with every excuse you can to see her without me around. You've pursued her more than any of your *hopeful* girlfriends, and I don't trust her one single bit. She doesn't want anything to do with us. All she wants is to win your affection and take you away from me!"

"It's not like that, Sophia," Mark insisted. "She likes you. She's just uncomfortable being around both of us at the same time."

"Big whoop-de-do!" I shouted back. "Now you want me out of your courting life because *she's* uncomfortable?"

"Dammit all!" Mark yelled. "I don't want you out of my life at all. You *are* my life! If we didn't have to live plural marriage, I wouldn't want anyone but you."

"I know. It's just feels like you are always looking at or for someone else; and no matter how hard I try not to care, it always hurts!"

❦

Previous to and during that time in our lives, I was grateful to God Norma finally quit watching our boys and hanging around Mark. Of course, I had no idea she would be back in Mark's life more than twenty years later. She started dating Jared, a married man who was many years her senior. While Norma was waiting to turn sixteen so she could marry Jared, she described their wild and heated escapades. She delighted in telling me how they had done nearly everything—how the two of them would get so turned on, they could hardly stop.

I knew about heated passion. But I was angry with her for fooling around with Jared before she became his plural wife. According to my dad's courting rules for married men, they were not to date or court a prospective wife without another wife present. They were not supposed to be alone together until they were married.

I told Norma their behavior was wrong and how sorry I felt for Callie, Jared's wife. "How do you think she'd feel if she knew what was going on behind her back?"

Norma appeared oblivious to anyone's feelings but her own, and just shrugged her shoulders.

"I'm sure glad you decided not to marry Mark," I told her. "It kills me to think what might be going on between you two if you were engaged to him."

Norma smiled and giggled sheepishly.

Jared and Callie, his beautiful and intellectual wife of fifteen years, were new converts to The Group. In public, Callie appeared to be elated, strong and completely accepting of their little teenage bride-to-be, who was only one year older than her oldest son. Yet, one day after church, Callie cried as she told me of the despair she suffered when her husband demanded she stay in her bedroom with the door shut. While she listened to the sounds of Jared "just" making out with teenage Norma in their dark living room on their opened couch bed, Callie piled pillows over her head and cried herself to sleep. But, as required of plural wives, Callie continued to publicly display her best-actress-on-earth smile and pushed forth in exemplary fashion.

❧

In addition to girls' camp, Primary had become a new resource for the Allred Group's children. My sister Amy organized classes for those in the Murray area, and I started classes for children in the South Valley area in our new home. The kids enjoyed the creative and fun ways our teachers presented otherwise dull stories from the Bible and Book of Mormon. On Primary days, I made sure my home was immaculate so the Spirit of the Lord could reside there, and it seemed well worth my efforts.

❧

Mom asked me to drive her down to Colorado City for her father's funeral.

"I don't want to be disrespectful of you, Mom," I said, "but I want you to know how I feel. Okay?"

She nodded.

"I don't want to go to the funeral, but if you need me to drive you down there I will. I can't pay my respects to Grandpa Cooke because I didn't *have* any respect for him. I didn't love him and he didn't love me. As you know, he was always mean to you and to your kids."

I hesitated. "He used to watch his girls dress and undress, and who knows what else he was doing. Mom, I don't have even one good memory of that old man."

Mom's breathing got heavy and strained. I hugged her and told her I was sorry I upset her for talking about her father like that, but it was true, and I thought by then she should know how I felt about him.

"My dad always hated me! He never once had a nice thing to say to me, either." My mother's words surprised me. She caught her breath and continued, "I never understood why he disliked me so much. Why me? What did I ever do to deserve his horrible treatment? When I was young, he would hit and slap me. He treated me like I was a dog!"

Mom started to say more, but she abruptly stopped herself. "This just isn't right. I shouldn't be talking about my father like this. It's very wrong to be so disrespectful. He was a good man. He did the best he knew how to do with his large family and . . ." Mom gulped, wiped her tears, and sniffled. "Do you know the reason he was like that, Sophia? A long time ago, his mother, who was a large woman, used to beat on him and everyone else in the family, including his dad. So my father had no respect for his mother. When he was just a young boy, he swore he would never allow a woman or anyone else to treat him the way his mother did."

"I'm sorry, Mom, but that's a sick excuse!" I snapped. "He justified his disgusting behaviors, and then treated you, his wives, children and grandchildren worse than shit!"

"You're right," Mom said calmly, ready to end the stressful conversation. "But it's like your dad always say's, Sophia—all of that is in the past and that's where it should stay. It's better left alone. I'm sorry I ever started complaining to you about my dad. We need to put our hurts and anger aside and keep sweet so we can keep the Spirit of the Lord with us at all times."

That was and is the Fundamentalist Mormon rule, especially for women. Nothing of discord was to be felt, acknowledged, or talked about—ever. We needed to keep a big smile on our faces and shovel our pain deep inside. If we were good, sweet, obedient, virtuous women and endured to the end, we'd be ever so blessed. We held onto the opinion that family idiosyncrasies and secrets were to be kept quiet and certainly never discussed. In the hereafter (if we ever qualified) we'd be able to trade any hell or anguish on earth for eternal happiness.

⁊

My labor pains came and went for nearly two full months. I was miserable. Uncle Rulon sent me to an obstetrician, "to be on the safe side." After some deep, palpating on my abdomen, the doctor told me I had only one big baby to deliver, and as far as he could tell, everything was all right.

I couldn't have an ultrasound, since they were rare and expensive back then, but the whole time I carried my baby, I was certain we'd have another son.

Doctor Fulton was also hiding out in Pinesdale, Montana. He'd been charged for practicing medicine in Utah without proper credentials. In two days, Uncle Rulon planned to make his regular monthly trip there, as well. He'd go to bolster his wives, congregation and disciples. And my baby was already twenty-two days overdue.

He told me I had three choices: I could wait longer and ask a midwife from the Kingston Group to deliver my baby, if she was available; I could take a castor oil and quinine mixture to start me in labor and get going before he had to leave; or I could go to the hospital, where they'd probably induce labor and/or do a caesarean section. He already knew I wouldn't choose the last option. Going to the hospital to deliver babies was out of the question for most women in The

Allred Group. No one in their right mind would go there to deliver a baby, unless they were desperate or in big trouble. We'd heard and spread numerous horror stories of unnecessary, rushed deliveries with forceps and episiotomies. But most atrocious, was our anxiety about the "mark of the beast" as is referred to in the Bible: "He also forced everyone, small and great, rich and poor, free and slave, to receive a mark on his right hand or on his forehead so no one could buy or sell unless he had the mark, which is the name of the beast . . .If anyone worships the beast and his image and receives his mark on the forehead or the hand, he, too, will drink of the wine of God's fury" (Rev. 13:16–18; 14:9–12).

All of us fundamentalists were worried the time was at hand for that to take place. We worried that if we fell asleep and left our infant in the care of a nurse, a barcode would be tattooed just under the skin of our infant's hand or forehead. There was already enough of God's fury in my life; I didn't want or need more.

I knew I couldn't persist any longer with my on-and-off labor, but I feared my huge baby would never be born if I waited. I'd already tried everything possible; so I administered the large dose of the castor oil and quinine mixture to myself early in the morning and counted on his birth before the day was over.

Around 7:00 PM. when my contractions became unbearable, Mom called Uncle Rulon to come to our home. While he checked me, he said he hadn't slept for three days and nights because he'd been so busy delivering four other babies in our Allred Group.

"Now, my dear, it's finally your turn." Uncle Rulon said tenderly. "The bad news is you still have several more hours before you will be dilated enough to push. If it's all right with you, I'm going to go get a few winks of sleep, as I still have to drive to Montana tomorrow."

For hours and hours Mom put cold, wet rags on my forehead and rubbed my back where I was sure my baby was trying to come out. This time around, there were no sleeping breaks between contractions as in normal labor. If I'd had any energy to scream, the whole neighborhood would have heard me. Instead my body was withering away in death. I begged God to stop the pains or at least ease them so I wouldn't die. I couldn't possibly go on one minute longer.

Finally I asked Mom to wake Mark so I could tell him goodbye. Within seconds after she left the room, I was no longer in pain. Close to the ceiling of my bedroom I could peripherally see every corner of all four walls at the same time. I was engrossed in euphoria for several minutes, it seemed when my spirit saw my dead body, swollen with child, lying on the bed below. Just as quickly I knew I didn't want to die. I wanted to have my baby and raise my children. In an instant my soul and body were connected once more; and I was again in tremendous pain.

Uncle Rulon, Mark, and Mom rushed into the room. Uncle Rulon checked me again. They had to move my exhausted and poisoned body to the end of the bed. When Uncle Rulon broke the sac my baby was still in, dark, slimy, brown liquid flowed from me. I heard him tell his wife and assistant, "This infant is in distress. He's had a bowel movement in the amniotic fluid, and some of it has entered his little body."

Melba hurriedly gathered syringes and the other necessary instruments and set them on the tray next to her husband. To ease my alarm he tried to lighten things up a little.

"No wonder this little guy is taking so long to get here. He planned to relax on his elbow and slide into this world with ease, but instead he got himself stuck. His right hand is covering his right ear and his little fingers are facing down toward his jawbone."

I heard a few sighs of merriment. In their concern everyone was trying to be optimistic.

After delivering literally thousands of babies over many years in his medical practice, Uncle Rulon knew exactly what to do so my son's arm wouldn't break during his trip through the birth canal. Each time I bore down, he turned Schuyler's head and shoulders to the right so his arm would slide down to his side. After twenty-two hours of agonizing labor, a dark blue, nine-pound, twenty-three-inch-long infant, silently entered this world.

Neither the baby nor I could move. After Jake's delivery I wanted to get up and run a mile. After Alan's I could have walked around the block a few times, but this time I felt paralyzed. Uncle Rulon finally got Schuyler breathing and handed him to my mother while he delivered the placenta.

Mark went downstairs to sleep, and Uncle Rulon left. After Mom had cleaned and dressed her grandson, she laid him next to me on the bed. Tears of joy slid down my cheeks as I stared at his perfect, pink colored face and thanked God he was finally here.

But within minutes, Schuyler quit breathing and started to turn blue. I picked him up, blew in his face, and screamed for help. The baby quit breathing every time his little body relaxed. For two more hours, Mom and I kept him awake and begged him to nurse and stay alive. She promised to take good care of him and pled with me to get some sleep. Though I felt run over by a train, I insisted on staying awake to make sure my precious infant wouldn't die.

I'd been awake over thirty-six hours. The twenty-two hours of excruciating pain had been caused by the impact of the castor oil and quinine mixture. It poisoned me and my baby's bodies, nearly killing both of us.

When I awoke nearly five hours later, Schuyler wasn't beside me on the bed where I had last seen him. I was sure God had taken him away from me because I'd been neglectful and fallen asleep. When Mom heard me cry out in anguish, she rushed in my room to assure me Schuyler was alive and getting better. She told me he had continued to stop breathing off and on for several more hours, so she'd finally called Uncle Rulon for help.

Mom kept Schuyler living through the night by giving him enemas of warm water and mild garlic to help remove the toxins. Though Schuyler's tiny arm still dangled for the next few days before his muscles gained strength again, he began to thrive.

CHAPTER 21

Guns and Murder
1976–1977

Six days after Schuyler's birth, Francine and William rented our unfinished basement while they waited for another home to rent. In lieu of rent payments, they decided to make the empty space as livable as possible without a big expense. They ordered natural, light wood cupboards and an ugly, bright orange Formica countertop. Just days before they moved in, William framed and put dry wall up for a bathroom, a long hallway, and three small bedrooms.

For another few rent payments, William bulldozed a couple of the old, dilapidated chicken coops behind the apartment we had lived in, which provided a huge space for a vegetable garden. With the huge scoop on the front of the bulldozer, he smashed the old, rotten wood and the concrete foundations into small pieces. Then he dumped the rubbish into a house-size hole he'd dug in the pasture in the back. Slowly, but surely, we believed our junkyard would be turned into a beautifully landscaped yard full of flowers, orchards, gardens, and play areas.

᯽

Nothing I owned fit me. Because Mark knew how hard it was for me to spend money on myself, he made me promise him I'd buy an outfit for me, not for our boys. When I saw the dimples behind my knees in the dressing room mirror, I sat on the bench and sobbed. I must have weighed a ton by then, since I never lost all the weight after having Jake and Alan. After having Schuyler, I felt like the cow Dad said I'd become if I didn't stop eating. It would have been nice to take after him. He seldom craved anything but sustenance for his tall, thin body.

A few years previous, when we learned the doctor had said Mom's heart was fibrillating, it scared all of us. We wondered if it was because of the extra forty or so pounds she carried around. Maybe I'd have to deal with all the trouble she was having if I couldn't get control of my weight.

My postpartum depression and all the fights with Mark continued to hinder my peace and spirituality. As usual, our fights were about his failure to participate in what I deemed necessary and appropriate religious behaviors and our differences in child rearing.

"My anger," he would yell, "comes from your inability to accept my choices and my beliefs! I shouldn't have to go to meetings, kneel to pray, and pay my tithing to your dad's group. I won't kiss people's asses in order to be considered a good person."

To add to Mark's long list of grievances, both of us knew a few council members, specifically Gregory Maynard, wouldn't work to support their massive harem that produced dozens of desperate, ragamuffin kids. He required his wives and devotees to provide clothing and sustenance for him and his family. To keep them humble, Maynard wanted his families to live in poverty and look like vagabonds.

Mark and I were told firsthand, he allowed his daughters to be molested and how he beat at least one of his wives for her differing opinions, and for trying to get away from him.

"Then there was sanctimonious Jon Thomas, who stole another

man's wife and . . . you already know the rest," Mark reminded me. "He's a major pervert of the worst kind."

When Mark was a teenager, he also witnessed Jon beat a horse with the blade of an ax. While its backside was split wide open, he still kept pounding on it because the horse wouldn't move the heavy load of logs he'd chained to it. Mark complained there were men in my uncle Rulon's "perfect group" who had committed adultery, cheated, and stolen. But all they had to do was kiss up and suddenly they were—and acted like they were—better than everyone else.

"Many of those men are held up as godly and honorable in your dad's and Rulon's eyes. And you know damn well I could go on and on So-ph-ia! So why in the hell would I want to be a part of that crap?"

I understood Mark's feelings. I too condemned all of that depravity. I couldn't understand why Uncle Rulon, Joseph Musser, or any of God's prophets could have been inspired to call immoral and corrupt men to be leaders, especially of His "chosen" people.

Still, in my ignorance I reminded Mark again what Mom always told me: "It's not the gospel that's wrong; it's the people and their sins that make it look bad. No matter what others do or don't do, we should still live the gospel of Jesus Christ to the best of our ability."

Mark snarled, "The gospel according to you! If I don't do things exactly the way you, your dad, or your mom think it should be done, you're mad at me and sulk for days!"

I was quiet for a few minutes while I fought the usual hot tears of defeat. Then Mark threw in another one of his grievances. "It's your fault Carla decided not to marry me!"

Already angry and hurt, I got defensive. "Oh yes? How is that?" I grouched back at him.

"She said you let her know in so many words she wasn't welcome in our family."

"Well, I guess she could be right. It was obvious from the get-go she didn't want *me* in *our* family. All she wanted was you. When she asked me questions about us, I was honest with her. So if she didn't like what she heard and took it as rejection; it's the way it's meant to be."

185

In the fall of 1976, I had our table beautifully set for Mark, Amy, her husband, and our children. Our house was spotless, and the aroma of pot roast and onions filled the air. I'd spent the day anxiously preparing for the evening, and was so grateful we were finally getting together again.

As our guests and our family were seated around the table, Mark, who was sitting straight across from me, griped about something. It hurt my feelings, so I ignored him. When I suggested we start passing the food to the left, he passed it to the right. A couple of minutes later, I asked him to please pass me the pitcher of ice water. He picked up his own glass of ice water, leaned across the table, and hurled it all over me. "Have some ice water!" he raged. "Do you have enough or can I get you some more?" The silence was deafening as everyone stared in shock. I kept my face down. No one knew what to do or say. By the time Amy got up to get a towel, I was on my way downstairs.

"He's either an angel or a devil," I cried to Francine, while we sat on her bed. "It seems he either deeply loves me or he intensely hates me!"

"What was he so mad about, Sophia?" she asked.

"I have no idea. Tonight it could be he thought I was being bossy. Maybe I sounded that way. He could have been mad because he had a bad day or I didn't do something he asked me to do. I'm so embarrassed I could die, but I've got to pull myself together and get back upstairs."

After I thought everyone would be done with supper, I tiptoed through the kitchen, hoping to sneak into my bedroom and change clothes without being seen. My uncontrollable tears came from emotional pain, but even more, they were tears of anger. I was so disappointed and furious at myself for caring what everyone else was thinking. How could I fix this mess? What kind of an excuse could I make this time for Mark's nasty conduct? My own need to make

186

things appear all right made me completely sick to my stomach, yet I didn't know what else to do. I'd always done things this way.

When I came out of my room with dry clothes on and swollen eyes, nearly everyone was in the front room. It was obvious they didn't know what to do either. Acting as if nothing had happened, I sat next to Amy and fed her some lame excuse for Mark's bad behavior, hoping she'd believe I was as happy in my marriage as I assumed she was in hers.

I slept with my back to Mark all night long. Most of the time, when we were mad and hurt; neither one of us talked about anything but the weather. He hoped I'd pass those kinds of things off and forget anything ever happened, but I felt sick to my stomach because of his evasiveness.

A few days later, he finally told me he was sorry for throwing the ice water all over me. "It's because you had been such a nag all evening," he said.

My guts were in knots. A request, an expectation—sometimes even a question for Mark felt like I was stepping into a minefield. You'd think I would have learned by that point in our marriage when to—and when not to—do any one of those things. The problem was there never was a "right" time. Like most women, I wanted my husband to see my needs and desires and to provide answers out of respect for me. Sometimes it was like that, but I couldn't for the life of me understand how he could call my desperate requests for help "nagging." No matter what his excuses were, my dejection lingered.

In those days and weeks, I wished Mark had a whole bunch of wives. He needed a real nag who constantly pouted and held deep grudges, so he'd know what a nagging and unforgiving wife was really like. He should have a wife who ragged on him when she was stressed or had a bad day, just like he did to me and his kids. Then it would be nice if he had a wife who would ignore *him* after *she* raged and cussed about everything. When or if he felt devastated because of her insensitive behavior, she would tell him he was pouting over nothing. Mark must also have a wife who wanted nothing more than to be my personal assistant and nanny so I, like Mark, could hibernate with a good book, get in the car and just drive around to de-stress without fretting over the care of the kids. Even better, Mark should stay home with our children day and night while I go about discussing life, liberty, and the pursuit of happiness with my prospective husbands. Maybe then he'd feel the bitter sting of this insane lifestyle.

On our way to sacrament meetings each Sunday for the past few months, members of The Group had noticed several police cars parked on the side of Redwood Road near the turnoff to our meetinghouse. We were told police were checking license plate numbers to verify the names of church attendees, as opposed to those who might be assailants. Some of us felt as nervous about having the police know exactly who was going to our church, as we were about Ervil LeBaron's threats.

His delusions of grandeur were in full force. He was still making death threats to anyone who wouldn't do his bidding. Because of the recent murders he had ordered, authorities were taking seriously Ervil's promises to "spill blood."

On the afternoon of June 10, 1977, Mom called in tears.

"Your Uncle Rulon has been shot! He is dead!"

For everyone in The Group, time seemed to stop. Everyone knew where he or she was standing when they heard the terrible news about President Kennedy's assassination. It would be the same for Uncle Rulon's contract killing, forever etched in our minds and hearts.

For days we watched the television broadcasts and heard the gruesome details of his murder. We watched the paramedics carry his dead body on a gurney from his office. More tears were shed when we saw his uncovered feet and knew they'd no longer carry him to and from his numerous labors of love. Why hadn't we taken Ervil's murderous intimidations more seriously?

Our usual Relief Society meeting on Wednesday evening turned into a general meeting where we assembled for strength and support. We wanted to hear the word of God from my father, to whom everyone looked up to as our new leader. Between his words of encouragement, Dad would stop to gather his composure. Few of us could control our tears as he told us of Aunt Melba's anguish. He described how she witnessed her husband being gunned down right in front of her eyes, and had no recourse.

Two armed women, dressed as men, had entered Uncle Rulon's office and quietly sat in the waiting room until they saw him appear. "Rulon Allred?" they asked. When he replied, "Yes," they filled his head and body with bullets from both guns.

Many church members sitting in general meeting were trembling in fear. Who will Ervil kill next—and when? Were any of our leaders safe? The hard, metal chairs I'd sat on hundreds of times before felt like crude, cold concrete grinding me further into conformity. My father's audience was riveted to every word he spoke. To us, Uncle Rulon was a martyr! Just like Joseph Smith, he died for his cause. Father admonished all of us to remain strong and become even more humble and vigilant in building God's kingdom.

"At least he got his wish. He got to die standing up doing the work of the Lord." Those words became our foundation of comfort and fortitude; we heard them and reiterated them for days, weeks, and years afterward.

Many people in The Group felt there would be no justice in his assassination. We were also angry about the media hype from reporters who continued to publicize, over and over again, Dr. Allred's death was the result of "rival polygamists" fighting over power. There was never a dispute between Rulon Allred and Ervil LeBaron over authority. He had nothing to fight about. Our leaders weren't trying to make Ervil's clan follow their regime. The Allredites were hardly protecting themselves, let alone planning to retaliate or fight for power. The murder was about Ervil's power-hungry insanity, using the old LDS "blood atonement" doctrine to perpetuate his own mafia like power.

On June 14, 1977, over twenty-five hundred people attended Uncle Rulon's funeral at Bingham High School. We were told a multitude of law enforcement officers we noticed everywhere had been strategically placed to deter Ervil's disciples who'd vowed to exterminate Verlan LeBaron, another of Ervil's brothers, and turn this scene into a blood bath.

About six weeks after Uncle Rulon's death, I was driving up our street with all the windows down and the radio on. Suddenly, I heard a loud pop and then felt an intense burning on my left cheek just below my eye. I slammed on the brakes and pulled over. Two young boys ran from a neighbor's back yard and charged into the house.

In the visor mirror, I could barely see the pellet embedded in my face, but I could feel it with my fingers and against my throbbing cheekbone.

I quickly drove around the corner and knocked on the door of the house the boys had entered. I rang the doorbell and pounded on the door some more. After quite some time I opened it and yelled at the teens to come out so we could talk. "So I won't have to call the police!" I hollered at them. Even after five minutes, they didn't show their faces.

I went back to my car and sat there waiting, wondering what to do next. I was angry, hurt, and embarrassed. Those two neighborhood boys had actually pointed their pumped-up pellet gun at me or my car and pulled the trigger! Fear came only after I pried the shell out of my cheek. Blood shot from the hole in my face and onto the steering wheel for three or four seconds, before it pulsated down my face onto my shirt and pants.

When I got back to my house, I pressed a cold, wet, cloth on my wound and dialed the Police Department. I explained I'd been shot with a pellet gun and asked if they would please come out and talk to the boys.

Within minutes, a loudspeaker warning bellowed throughout the neighborhood. Police cars seemed to have fallen from the sky. They barricaded the opposite ends of our street and the front of our home.

Lights flashed across the house and through the windows. I was so embarrassed I wanted to hide in my closet and ignore the pounding on our front door. I never wanted to be seen on the streets ever again.

"Are you all right, lady?" one of the three police officers asked when I reluctantly opened the door.

"Of course I am," I told them. "What's this big scene all about?"

"We had a call saying someone has been shot," he said. "We weren't sure what to expect."

The exasperated posse was called off after I explained again.

A couple of the policemen found the boys, after they decided to present themselves. An hour later the LDS bishop's wife, a neighbor who had never spoken a word to me in all the years we'd lived there (and not one word since), came down with her son and his buddy to apologize. As the policemen suggested, our neighbors offered to pay for an X-ray, if I would get one.

I told the two boys I was never allowed, and neither were my boys, to point even their play guns at people or animals, pretending to shoot or kill. It was my belief, that no one should touch a gun unless they've learned a great deal of appreciation for its proper use. "Most of all," I said, "I am hurt by your disrespect for me as a human being—even if, as you said, your intent was only to shoot at my car. If the pellet had hit my face one inch higher, your carelessness could have blinded me!"

A few days later the neighborhood gossip queen, who lived catty-corner from us, knocked on my front door. She had always been nice to us, at least to our faces, and she wanted to know what I had to say about "the entire ruckus." Then she told me everyone in her LDS Church ward knew I was Owen Allred's daughter; so she figured Ervil LeBaron's clan was out to get me also.

"Oh no, not li'l ol' me," I drawled. "I'm just a li'l ol' piss ant, not one tiny bit worth their efforts. I'll only die if I am among the crowd when their bomb explodes."

Then she admitted when she heard the gunshot on the street, right in front of her house, she called the police. "I thought they might be going after all of you polygamists," she said apologetically.

I knew she meant well. Even so, my embarrassment, shame, and notoriety chipped away at my ego. I despised the disparaging reputation that went along with our sect's belief system. I always took it personally.

✻

For the rest of the summer, Mark and I had to swallow our pride so we could take little Sky to watch Jake's and Alan's T-ball games at the park. We would try to go out to eat at least once a week. At night, while I was still cleaning, doing dishes, or ironing, Mark would make up more exciting chapters to the already-existing *Journey of Little Eagle* stories. He got the boys to help create the words, new characters, and animals. They laughed when they interjected their own juicy morsels into Mark's action-packed chronicles. I was elated when I heard their innocent giggles and voices, and I dreamed of a billion more of these pleasant father-and-son connections.

In the fall, Mark and I made another trip to Marysvale, Utah, where his dad had a mining claim in the beautiful mountains.

Down the hill, fifty feet or so from the huge cabin, I sat cross-legged on the cool earth and held two-year-old Schuyler in my arms. His soft blond hair pressed against my cheek while I watched Jake and Alan laugh and scream in excitement. Mark's younger brothers had strung a twenty-foot rope swing across a shallow ravine. It would carry the boys across and then back up the hill again. I embraced the wonderful panorama and mused over the romantic escapades, meaningful conversations, playful laughter, and precious times Mark and I had experienced there, off and on, for the past six summers. Those were some of the happiest days, feeling life was worth living!

CHAPTER 22

Courtship and a Sister-Wife
1977–1978

Kenneth told Mark, Diane and her almost two-year-old little girl had moved back to her mother's house. Dad's concerns had been accurate. Diane's soon-to-be ex-husband's first wife was openly favored as his soul mate, while Diane was relegated to concubine. In her short marriage, she had to ask her sister-wife for any privilege: for food items, personal needs, and apparel. She had to get permission to sleep with her husband and to visit her family. Often, the first wife refused Diane's requests.

When Mark told me about the situation, I was dejected. "If you would have noticed and cared for Diane a few years ago, when she was crazy about you, she wouldn't have gone through all that grief."

Mark warily agreed. Shortly after Diane's priesthood release, a divorce granted only under certain circumstances, Mark asked Diane's father if we could court her.

Up to that point, the heartache of courting another woman was caused by my imagination. Now it was haunting. For nearly four months, Mark spent every other night at Diane's mother's house with Diane. Often he wouldn't return until after one or two o'clock in the morning.

Though I dearly loved Diane and believed she belonged in our family, I fought off "the devil's" constant torments by keeping extremely busy. I was scared to death of what would happen if I let my imagination haunt me even more.

Now and then I had no control over my thoughts. I envisioned Mark and Diane kissing and fondling each other the way Norma had described what she and her married fiancé had done. *No!* I screamed at myself. *Stop it! Don't allow yourself to believe for one second either of them will let things get out of hand.* To retain my sanity, I accomplished a dozen more things, and crossed them off my never-ending to-do list.

When things got to be too much, and I was already feeling like an insane plural wife, I timidly complained to Mark I thought it was wrong for him to spend so much time—especially alone time with Diane before they were married, even if it was at her parents' home. He, of course, disagreed.

"She needs me there to reassure her. After the rejection she felt from me, and her ex-husband's crap, she needs to feel secure."

How could I dispute that?

One evening in the fall, I was finally invited to dinner by Diane's mother. After an absolutely delicious meal with Diane's parents; Mark, Diane, and I retreated to the basement family room to watch a movie. Mark claimed the huge reclining chair, while Diane and I sat on a nearby sofa.

It felt like a bolt of electricity pierced through my heart when I returned from a bathroom break and saw Diane, like a bear cub, snuggled up in Mark's lap, wrapped in his arms and kissing his neck.

I thought I might blackout from the horrendous pain imbuing me from head to toe. All my worries and concerns were warranted. Like a caged lioness, my grief wanted to be set free, as if aggression might be the only way I could stay alive. Instead I slumped down on the sofa behind them while my whole body quaked inside. Images of everything I believed they'd been doing for months on end filled my head. I wanted to shove the reclining chair they were sitting in over backwards. I wanted to have the strength to make Mark so angry he would pummel me senseless, to make me forget my heartache.

Silently, I commanded my heart to stop thrashing around in my chest and swore I wouldn't shed a single tear.

I wasn't supposed to feel like this. Not one plural wife ever warned me about this brutal pain. I had no idea such torment existed. The two lovebirds were totally oblivious to anything but the movie in front of them, and themselves, while I was dying.

I quickly wandered upstairs to the landing and out the front door. When I caught my breath in the cold night air, I took off on a dead run. I ran for blocks, until I fell down. Then I got up and ran some more. At the time, it didn't matter how far I went, if I ever stopped, or if I'd ever return.

After running away and then slowly walking back to Diane's house, I climbed into our freezing cold car to wait. I had no idea how long I'd been gone, or if I was even missed. All I knew was the shame I felt for acting out, for not being in control, and for letting my jealousy get out of hand. I didn't want to see Diane right then, and I certainly did not want her to see me.

On the way home, Mark said, "You know I love you, Sophia, more than anyone and anything in the whole world. I wouldn't be courting Diane if you hadn't encouraged me to. You know I never want to hurt you . . ."

After a long period of silence, I finally said in anguish,

"Just because I encouraged you to court Diane doesn't mean you two are justified in making out with each other! You don't have a right to break the rules! Nor does it mean I shouldn't or won't be in turmoil about your damn hurtful choices."

Mark apologized for days, while my imagination ran wild, stirring raw emotions and lack of trust. Like my mother's torment, I thought I would plunge into the depths of hell if I didn't get a handle on myself. Though it felt quite impossible, I drove myself into good behavior—more work, more crafts, more service.

A couple of weeks before Valentine's Day, Mark showed me the engagement ring he intended to present to Diane when he proposed. It was exquisite. And I was so happy for her. She deserved Mark's love, kindness, affection, and the gorgeous ring. But at the same time, I felt shattered. He hadn't bought me a ring when we became engaged. "Rings are no big deal," he had told me repeatedly. For three years after our marriage while I asked for, hinted at, and practically had to beg him for a diamond wedding ring, his comments were always the same: "Come on, Sophia, rings aren't important. It's love that makes a good marriage, not a ring. Why isn't your gold band good enough? Don't you like it? Besides, we can't afford one."

Even more hurtful, the wedding-engagement ensemble he bought for Diane without discussing it with me also had small diamonds and rubies. It looked way too much like the rings Mark had finally bought for me on our third anniversary. The reasons he'd used for why he couldn't, or wouldn't, get me a wedding ring when we were first engaged once again challenged my value and worth to him.

I slipped away to Swede's, my newfound safe house. He was my friend, my papa bear next door. With his help, I could usually talk myself into feeling rational again.

"We are no more financially stable now than we were then!" I cried to Swede. "It hurts so darn much that he is showing Diane more love and consideration than he did me. It seems he didn't care enough about me, when we got engaged, to forfeit something of value to get me an engagement ring.

At some point I had to calm down and get the spirit of the Lord back. "Mark tries every day to be a better person," I told Swede. "As he said, I'm sure his actions were not meant to be insulting or hurtful to me. I'm sure his intentions were to do the right thing this time around. I was the practice run. My poor husband; I've got to straighten up and get back to being a well-behaved wife!"

A week or so before the wedding, Diane took me into her bedroom to show off the teddies and negligee she'd purchased for her honeymoon with my husband. I dutifully smiled and approved of her eveningwear, all the while wondering how she could be so cruel and insensitive. If she loved and cared about me, why would she hurt me so much? I felt like she wanted to prove a point, as if to say, "I am here now. He loves me. And there's nothing you can do about it!"

⁂

Diane's sister, my friend Val, who'd already given my brother Charles another wife, told me, "You can't be alone on their wedding night, Sophia. We're going to have a sleepover, play games, and eat junk food until we're sick."

One week later Diane handed me an invitation to my husband's and her wedding celebration. Attached was this note:

Dear Sophia,
Thank you so much for your love and friendship. You're a very special person and I'm thankful to you for letting me be part of your family. I love you and I hope I never do anything to hurt you.
Love,
Diane

Two nights before the nuptials were to take place, I forced myself to hide my resentful and jealous feelings. I smiled graciously and treated myself sadistically. Mark and Diane flirted back and forth while the three of us set up and put sheets on their brand-new king-sized bed in the master bedroom, just below mine. Diane's room was the same one my sister Francine and William had shared just over a year ago.

At the wedding, guests sat in our living room facing us. Dad instructed me to stand on Mark's right side, and Diane to stand next to me.

Facing the three of us, Dad performed the plural wedding ceremony. At one point during this long, drawn-out ritual, he asked, "Are you, Sophia, willing to stand as Sarah [biblical Sarah, who gave her

197

servant, Hagar, to her husband Abraham to bear his children] and give Sister Diane to your husband as his wife for time and all eternity? If you are willing, please manifest your approval by placing Diane's right hand within the right hand of your husband."

I ignored the searing pain in my stomach. No matter how much it hurt I forced a thankful, gracious smile. Because I believed with all my heart that ceremonial sacrifice was necessary for our salvation, that it was my righteous, womanly duty, I placed Diane's small hand in Mark's hand. Then I stepped back next to his left side, while Diane took her my place on his right. To appear strong, I gave him a peck on the cheek and stepped back into my place to his left.

The rest of the day my thoughts were somewhere deep inside, while I portrayed the personification of a token first wife. I remembered watching my husband and his pretty young bride wave goodbye, heading off on their honeymoon. Of course, I'd never had a honeymoon. I quickly wiped the tears from my eyes so no one would see them.

Val and I watched a comedy and talked about the "blessings" of that life-altering day and everything else under the sun. Then we climbed into my bed and talked some more. After she fell asleep, I grieved in total silence, not wanting her to know of my agony. I couldn't let her know I wasn't as good of a first wife as she must have been when my brother, Charles, was justified in a new love affair with his beautiful new bride—his second wife.

My stomach was in knots as I kept hearing Mark's words of passion, the ones he had so freely shared in our lovemaking for the past eight years— expressions for only me. I trembled inside with nausea and anger while I imagined his and Diane's bodies entwined, pulsating in sensual rhythm, not just tonight on their romantic honeymoon, but in the morning, again and again, for the rest of our lives. I knew from that day forward the overpowering bond he and I had shared in our lovemaking would never again be the same. Why had I ever agreed to do this? It felt like my heart was being torn out of my chest.

The torture wouldn't stop. In the middle of the night, I woke to the sounds of Mark's and Diane's heavy breathing in a far off motel room. *How can he do this to me—to us?* Those torturous feelings ripped at my heart like he was cheating on me.

"He's not cheating, Sophia! You know this is the way God intended it to be," I heard my mother's words in my head. "Halt these evil whisperings from Satan's imps. They will stop at nothing to destroy you! Satan wants you to feel these repulsive, painful feelings so you'll give into them and fall from the graces of God. Stop now! Command them in the name of Jesus Christ to stop before they destroy you."

I reached for the medicine box in the hall closet. Through swollen eyes I searched for the valerian root capsules. I knew four of them would make me sick to my stomach, but it would help sedate my grief. Their atrocious smell and bitter taste gagged me. In between more outbursts of tears, I sang a few gospel hymns until I fell asleep.

Nearly every woman knows a husband's wife or wives are observed and scrutinized when a new one enters the family. It's like a brutal but necessary ritual polygamous women unwittingly thrive on. Either way, the older and previous wives get to be the theme of everyone's scrutiny and gossip after their husband's most recent nuptials.

"Oh, she's such a sweet wife."

"Look how kind and loving she is while her husband's attentions are on that pretty young girl."

"Well, how about that? She's doing great! We didn't think she'd be . . ."

"How can she put up with that?"

Or it might be:

"Good grief, does she ever need our prayers and help!"

"Oh dear! She's awful to her poor husband and his sweet, new wife!"

Val's mother had taught her well, how to deal with this psychoanalysis. The day after the wedding, my dear friend tried to help me save face with my newlywed partners and with the judgmental blather I would also have to undergo. Val couldn't help but notice my puffy, swollen eyes—she must've known I'd cried most of the night—but she didn't say a word. Before she left, she reminded me to practice everything I would say and do when Mark and Diane returned, as well as for the next few days, weeks, and months—especially in public.

"I'm telling you, this way is better than looking and acting the way you may really feel inside," Val said. She advised me to practice and visualize over and over again, until I had my gracious words and actions memorized. I should plan my actions, my hugs, and kisses—every step and every word. She promised it would help me feel better about myself and help me keep my dignity intact.

During the five days after Mark and Diane's wedding, I felt as if I accomplished a year's worth of work and play. To keep myself distracted, my little boys and I watched more VHS Disney movies, and went to the park and to friends' homes more than in any few months before.

When Mark and Diane returned, I flawlessly performed my routine. I said all the words and carried out all the actions I'd visualized and rehearsed a hundred times over—just like a perfectly programmed robot. I did so well I actually believed every single thing I said and did. I felt I'd passed my test with honors. "Act as if . . . and it shall come to pass." With my hugs, kisses, thoughts of missing them, telling them I was glad they were home—all the sweet, kind, gooey stuff—I was sure Mark, Val, my mother, and even God must have been very proud of me.

Mark stayed with me the night he and Diane returned from their honeymoon. Without a word, he and I held each other tight until morning. While he was asleep, I wondered if Diane was also. In the crevices of my mind, I saw them naked, holding each other.

Stop, Sophia! Don't ever let yourself go there, ever again, I demanded. *Think of other things, of happy thoughts, of the kids. You know Mark loves you. He's right here to prove it to you. You should be happy now—this is what you wanted. This is what God wanted, and He expects you to be happy and endure to the end. Be proud. You and your family are finally on your way to the highest glory of heaven—the Celestial Kingdom!*

A couple of weeks later around midnight, I woke up to thumping noises and whispering voices. "Please, God, don't let this be what it sounds like!" I heard myself cry out under my breath. Get up, I told myself. *Go in the front room and sleep on the couch!* The obvious noises got louder until I wished I could jump up and down on the floor, flush the toilet five hundred times, break a window, and die.

Then it got quiet. *Thank God I was wrong! They don't enjoy sex together. They never do. Just go back to sleep, Sophia,* I thought. Then, wondering if I'd been hearing things or was going crazy, I got on the floor and put my ear against the furnace vent. The few minutes of telltale noises gave me a vivid picture that knocked the breath out of me and made me dizzy. Somehow, I dragged my limp body to my bedroom door, down the hall, and to the kitchen.

"Get the knife! Get the knife, Sophia!" I heard a voice say. "You might as well die now. Just get the knife before you pass out!"

I reached for the butcher knife in the cupboard above the stove. It was there, thank God. "Now, all it will take is one swift blow," the voice told me again. "The stab can't possibly hurt more than you already do. Do it, Sophia! Go ahead and shove it into your heart, deep and fast. Then your pain will be forever obliterated. Do it! Do it! Do it!"

I pressed the end of the blade to my chest until it indented my dark blue nightshirt and burned against my skin. *One swift, heavy blow— that's all it will take.* I drew the knife a foot or so away from my chest, ready for the plunge.

Suddenly I heard Schuyler cry out.

"It's now or never," the voice warned. "If you don't kill yourself now, you never will, and you'll have to deal with this pain for the rest of your life." My baby's cries became louder and more demanding. I quietly set the knife back on top of the fridge, feeling guilty and grateful I hadn't been caught with it. When I reached Schuyler's crib, I thanked God for my precious little sons, for Sky's loud cries, for his precious smile and his infant arms that reached out to me when my soul came back for him.

I fixed his bottle and held him tight in the front-room rocking chair. My endless tears burned my eyes raw. I went through the scenario of my temporary madness as if watching a movie. *Was I really going to end my life and lose my children because of my jealousy over God's principle of plural marriage? How could I have been so wicked?* I knew then I'd never end my life. I would leave Mark, if I had to, before I would abandon my children over jealousy because of another woman.

In the morning I woke with Sky's little body curled up next to mine. Could he ever comprehend my love for him? Would he someday realize I decided to stay in this life to give birth to him and to raise him with my other children? When I heard his cries, I once again chose to stay for him, Jake, Alan, and the rest of the children I knew I would have with Mark.

CHAPTER 23

Nothing Sacred in This
1978–1979

Mark's adoration and affection wasn't only shown in all of the love-making we enjoyed, but also in his kindness toward me. We'd been spending so much "play" time together I tried to deceive myself into thinking he wasn't having any fun with Diane.

As long as I kept busy, ignoring anything and everything that looked or sounded suspicious, I was feeling I could survive our new lifestyle.

As is customary among most polygamous families, Mark's evenings were divided between his wives. Every other night he was with me, and every other night he was with Diane. A few months after she got settled downstairs, she asked me if we could split Mark's clothes between the two of us. Before I answered her, my mischievous mind got the best of me. Since I was already sharing him, my time, our food, his clothing, and everything else with Diane (including his genitals), I pictured myself with a pair of scissors, crazily hacking his underwear right down the middle from bellybutton to crotch and back up the crack. "There, now!" I'd snap at Diane, "you can have all the right sides and I'll take all the lefts, then Mark can 'hang out' with either one of us!" Those thoughts made me laugh so hard my face turned red and my eyes watered. Diane started to chuckle at my giggle, even though she had no idea what was so funny to me.

While Mark was at work we went through all of his clothes. Like two young girls picking out their favorite pieces of candy, we took turns choosing his shirts. We started with the best-looking ones and worked our way down to his grimy old work shirts. Then we did the same things with his pants, underwear, and socks. Once we each had a pile of Mark's clothes in front of us, we marked our initials on the - inside labels, as if his clothing were ours to disburse and claim.

"You should have asked me first!" Mark yelled when he realized his closet space in our room was half empty.

"You're right," I said. "But Diane needs to feel like your wife as well, and this will help her feel—"

"I don't give a crap about how she feels about this!" Mark cut me off. "Those are my clothes, not yours or Diane's. I want my things in one place where I know where they are and what I have!"

"I know that! But Diane wants to be able to wash and iron your shirts, and to have some of your things in her closet and in her drawers too. She wants to be—"

"That's just tough, Sophia! I can't believe you agreed to this! You need to get my stuff back up here."

"Listen, Mark. I really didn't want to do that either, and we should have asked you." I started to snicker a little, picturing his underwear cut in half, hanging lopsided on his skinny behind.

"But this is really the right thing to do. You know how much I hated it when Dad always had to leave Mom's house to get his change of clothes from Aunt Eleanor's house. I'd see the hurt look in my mother's eyes. Even worse, he'd often have Aunt Eleanor bring them to him, no matter what time of the day it was. She loved taking care of all of Dad's things. It gave her further control and information of his whereabouts. Besides—" I grinned from ear to ear as new, even more wild pictures entered my mind "—I decided it would be good to share washing all of your laundry, folding and ironing with Diane.

Just think, that will cut my wash load in half."

When I started laughing out loud, Mark probably wondered what on earth was happening to me. I stared at his crotch area. I blinked my right eye, then my left, then my right eye open and shut several times. "Let's see now, who did you sleep with last? Are you wearing the right or the left side of your shorts?"

Some of his father's wives had to deal with a sister-wife who was very much like Aunt Eleanor. "Every plural family has to have one or more antagonists," Mark often mocked. "That's how women get tested and refined, you know."

After all my laughter and explanations, Mark conceded, even though he really didn't want his clothing divided—or cut in half.

❧

For the first time in years I went to Doctor Fulton's office. He was back with a degree from Oregon, and we spent a few minutes catching up on our lives and what was going on in our huge plural families. I hadn't asked him for help since he'd delivered Alan, but for quite some time, I had vaginal pain and itching that was driving me crazy.

"It's a yeast infection, Sophia," the doctor matter-of-factly told me.

"What's a yeast infection?" I asked, feeling pretty stupid. He sounded like I should know the terminology.

"It's a Candida fungus. When the normal bacteria in the vagina gets out of control it causes the kind of discomfort you are describing. But don't worry, dear—it won't kill you. It's totally curable." Then he looked puzzled about my naivety. "You said you've never had this before?"

"Never! It's awful! How could I ever forget something like this?"

"How long have you been married now?"

"Just over eight years. Why?"

"Oh, my," Dr. Fulton said in a worried voice. "You just told me Mark took another wife recently?"

"Yes, but what does that have to do with all of this?"

"I'm sorry to have to tell you this, but Candida is often carried by men. A man may or may not have any symptoms of the yeast infection, but he can pass it from one wife to another."

As soon as I left the examination room, I rushed into the bathroom to hide my self-conscious, shameful tears. All the way home, I seethed with rage. Not only did I have to deal with blatant knowledge Mark and Diane had sex, now I had to deal with the reality that his penis had picked up a yeast infection from her vagina and deposited it into mine! Just thinking about it made me nauseous.

All the way home, I heard Dr. Fulton's words again: "There's not much can be done to prevent these sexually transmitted infections or diseases from happening in plural families. Cleanliness may help, but still may not stop the fungus from being passed back and forth. I guess the only way to stop spreading it is celibacy, or the use of a condom."

When I finally got the courage to tell Mark what the doctor had said, he felt bad, but he didn't know what to do about it either. "Just stop having sex with Diane! I was just fine until you married her," I wanted to scream, but I didn't.

"I'm sorry. I always make sure I'm clean, Sophia," Mark said. "Maybe you could talk to Diane about it and have her get some medication to clear it up."

"I don't care how clean you are! You and I have been married for eight years and I've never once had this infection before now. You brought this infection to me. It's sick and it's disgusting! You'd better use a condom with Diane from now on, or don't have sex with me ever again." By then I was sobbing. "My body was violated, and my soul feels desecrated! Not one single thing feels decent about you screwing another woman. Nothing about this feels holy, righteous, or sacred to me!"

No matter the rolling tension, I continued with every effort I could muster to live in a pleasing way before God. In many polygamist families I knew, sister-wives seemed to be happy and close. I too desired to be a perfect sister-wife. When it was my night with Mark, I invited Diane and her adorable daughter to eat meals, watch television, and hang out upstairs with us. When it was Diane's night with Mark, the basement door was shut and locked to let me and my children know we were to stay away.

Occasionally, when my boys or I wanted or needed to go downstairs to get something from our fruitroom, Mark would crack the door open an inch or so, as if we might see an orgy if it were fully open. Then he'd impatiently ask what we wanted. After too many months of rejection, I told Mark how hurtful it was to the boys and me. "It feels like a slap right in the face when you quickly shut and lock the door while I'm still standing there."

"I don't shut the door in your face," he responded. "I shut it to let you know not to come in or come downstairs. It might seem selfish, but that's the way Diane needs and wants it to be. I'm going to support her wishes for a while."

It looked and felt like I had encouraged Mark to marry a replica of Aunt Eleanor, and he was going along with Diane like my father always went along with Aunt Eleanor. I was worried and disheartened. Still, I was sure Diane would have some compassion and understanding about our displaced feelings and would compromise. After a few days of stomachaches and worry, I got brave enough to talk to her. I explained how unfair it seemed and how much their decisions hurt us.

"You've had him all to yourself for eight years," she replied. "Now it's my turn to have time alone with him!"

I didn't believe Diane's attitude and justification was the accepted norm in the plural marriages I'd heard of, at least in The Group; but I found it was common for men in the independent group to abandon their old wives for a given amount of time, claiming it was to give their new brides more time alone with him, "to get to know him better."

When neither Diane's nor Mark's way of thinking changed, my

gloom and disillusionment lingered; but my ego reminded me, "These selfish events can go both ways, you know!"

I got busy planning all sorts of games and paybacks. I could imagine a zillion ways to win. But it didn't matter how hard my ego tried to suck me into a war, my heart and soul knew better. All fighting would do is cause more rivalry and more conflict within me. I would have been very disappointed in myself if I had conducted myself the way I was tempted to.

Within a few months, Diane proudly informed me she had morning sickness. I gave her a hug and told her I was happy for her.

I really was. No matter how hard things were, I still loved and treasured Diane. It wasn't her fault my insides were on fire. At least her sickness was just in the morning.

With her happy news, I began to feel nauseous all day long. Why did that proof of her relationship with Mark make one bit of difference to me? Everyone on this planet knows conception usually requires intercourse; after all, that's what polygamy is all about. Mark was required to have intercourse with multiple women to help populate his own kingdom with "pure" blood. He was required to have an abundance of "special" children who were born under the covenant of plural marriage.

After several days of sequestered melancholy, accompanied with guilt for having bad feelings, I forced my way back to my busy life. No matter what or how I felt, I smiled. I grinned and smiled. I beamed so damn much sometimes my jaws ached and the skin on my cheeks felt like it would explode right off my face.

When Diane was about five months along, she started bleeding. After running some tests, her obstetrician said she had a complication called placenta previa. Diane was told to take it easy or she would lose the baby.

When the bleeding still didn't stop after several weeks of rest, Diane was ordered to stay completely down until her infant was born.

The little red devil jumped on my left shoulder and nudged me with his three-pronged pitchfork, saying, "Oh, this is good, Sophia—

this is really good! You can have some peace of mind for the next four or five months, because Mark and Diane can't be together."

Of course I didn't get my reprieve. I was worried from the get-go and couldn't bear the thought of Diane's sadness if she were to lose her baby. And unless one of her mothers or sisters came over to visit, I seldom got a break. Not one person asked me if I would be Diane's nurse and her daughter Carrie's caregiver for the duration of her convalescence. The responsibility was just plain expected of me, as her sister-wife. It was an automatic given with everyone, including myself.

I was good at serving. After all, my whole life's purpose was to have a bunch of children and graciously attend to everyone. It would surely get me closer to heaven! I was grateful to show my love for Diane by helping her with her needs, but at the same time I resented some of the demands and pressure.

Though I hated doing it, I quit teaching at our private school, enrolled Jake and Alan in the local public school in November, and commenced my duties. I served Diane meals, rinsed out warm washcloths over and over again for her sponge baths, and emptied her bedpan. Then I fed, bathed, and cared for our kids before I could finally get them in bed for the night. I'd get a few winks and start all over again the next day.

Some nights when I was so tired I could hardly move, I'd just cry myself to sleep. Sharing my husband with another woman was not what I had thought it would be. I wondered how many of my sisters and friends felt the same way I did, but like me wouldn't dare talk about it. From day one, I knew the law of polygamy was surely devised by a male God. If it were up to a woman, it would have been the other way around. Instead of being married to our sister-wives, we could be married to our brother-husbands or be monogamists. But like everything else I was committed to, I was passionate about serving our chauvinistic God. I wanted His love and His approval.

Aside from being dutifully required to love my sister-wife, I genuinely wanted to be kind, fair, and friendly. Since Diane and I were living polygamy together, I hoped we would always love each other, so

I did the best I could to care for her with love and compassion.

Most of the time, I was sad for her. She was a newlywed, a young energetic woman who had entered a very weird, dysfunctional, semi-established family. I tried to make time to visit with her and help her feel as comfortable as possible. As the days passed slowly by, she felt more depressed with the burden she had to bear. I suggested she read, knit, embroider, and write. I recommended several more things she could do to help keep her mind off of her situation, and felt frustrated when she chose to watch television all day and throughout the evening, which seemed to make her feel even worse.

❧

I was part of Mark's and my own huge polygamous families, yet much of the time I felt so alone—as if I had no family at all. Mom wasn't a social butterfly. She never had been. Whenever Aunt Eleanor or Aunt Amelia got their kids and grandchildren together, I was envious. By then, most of my dad's children had large plural families, just as busy as ours. We seldom saw each other, and I longed for the sibling closeness my mother's family never seemed to have.

Since Diane's dad, Kenneth, was a good friend to Mark, I secretly wished we would be welcomed as part of Diane's family. It looked like they participated in each other's lives on a regular basis.

After my fall canning season was over, I started making Christmas gifts for Diane, Carrie, and my kids. For Mark and our three boys, I sewed expensive-looking denim jackets lined with sheepskin. When they were complete, I monogrammed their names on the back of each one with bright orange thread.

For gifts from our whole family, I sewed matching nightgowns for Diane, Carrie, both of Diane's mothers, her sisters, and her sisters-in-law. For her dad, brothers, and all of our little boys, I made plaid country-western shirts with snaps.

On Christmas Eve, Kenneth and Mark carried Diane from the car into her mother Renee's house for the family Christmas party. The food was wonderful. I felt elated to be part of Diane's family, and grateful to present the pile of homemade gifts I'd created with love from the bottom of my heart.

After that complete rush of joy, my boys and I watched Kenneth, his wives, and their children dole out elaborate and expensive gifts to each other and to Mark. In less than five minutes I realized I was completely wrong. Mark had definitely become part of Diane's family, but his sons and I had not.

Back at home, I stayed up until 4:30 in the morning stuffing socks, finishing the last minute things for our family, and setting out a few more simple gifts I'd made for Mark.

By morning I was physically and emotionally exhausted from having pushed myself way too hard for far too many days and nights. I went downstairs for our family Christmas anyway. After Mark and the kids opened their few inexpensive gifts, there were two large, unmarked boxes yet to be opened. Mark pushed the largest one over to Diane. She opened it and was clearly elated about her new TV. She smiled at me excitedly.

"Now you can have your television back!" she said.

The family could hardly wait to see what Mark had purchased for me. We watched in dismay as he retrieved, and set that box on Diane's lap. She screamed with delight realizing she also had a new VCR to go along with her new television. My stomach heaved up to my throat and my heart surged with pain. Before Diane or Mark could see my crimson face and my tears, I got my boys busy disposing of the brown paper bags we'd used as wrapping paper. Sky and Carrie played with the few simple toys they'd received from Santa while Jake, Alan, and I despondently went back upstairs.

Of course my boys noticed the inequalities at Diane's family party, and here in our own home. Like their mother, they wondered why. Their resentment resounded in nine-year-old Jake's angry words: "If Dad hadn't married Aunt Diane, we would have had a good Christmas, and we would have the things we need and want!"

"And Dad would still take us places and do things with us like he used to," Alan mumbled with tears in his eyes. "It's not fair!"

Normally, I would have defended Mark's actions, decisions, anger, and second marriage. I would say, "Those things shouldn't be important in this life. Your dad is doing the best he can to provide for us. We're living God's laws, which are more important than anything else in the world." But my feelings were similar to Jake's and Alan's. Not one single rebuttal came to mind that time around.

I felt like I was going mad. All I wanted to do was to go to sleep and not wake up for months. But daytime sleep wasn't an option at our house. I put on my comfortable sweats and jogged down the path to Swede's house.

After two hours, I still couldn't make myself get up and go back home—my disgraceful emotions were too much to deal with. If I tried to talk to Mark, we'd just end up in another fight and I'd be wrong again. Even my mother would agree with Mark. "Your feelings are very selfish, Sophia. You need to nip them in the bud right now before the evil spirits cause you even more depraved thoughts and take advantage of you!"

There was no way I could make myself "nip it in the bud!" Besides, I hate that cliché with a passion. I don't know why, but I always have.

Diane didn't seem one bit grateful for anything I did for her. She didn't even thank me for the Christmas presents I had made for her and her family. My resentment lingered.

※

Since Diane couldn't go out with Mark every other Friday night like we had started doing, I told him it wasn't fair for us to go out on our Friday nights either. However, near the first part of January, I guess Mark decided he wanted to make up for Christmas inequities. Even more, he must have known he should get quiet, soft-spoken, "everybody's sucker," reticent, Sophia out of the house before her cover-ups got the best of her.

Mark asked Val's mom, Renee, to stay with Diane and Carrie. I got another sitter for our boys, and we finally went out to dinner and a movie together. When we got home, Mark stayed downstairs way too long, trying to console Diane. She felt devastated we went out while she still couldn't. So once again, we put our lives on hold.

In February, Diane delivered her chunky little miracle at the LDS Hospital. All the necessary emergency equipment was ready in case a Cesarean section was required, but thank God, the baby's head pushed the placenta aside as he entered the birth canal.

Three or four days after Diane came home with her adorable little son, her Aunt Renee, Val's mom, came to see her and the baby. After a while, she took me aside to talk.

"Thank you for being a supportive and loving sister-wife to Diane. She says you've been treating her a lot better lately. I'm so grateful you finally gave in to the idea you have to share your husband equally. These things take time, and you're finally learning how to be a good sister-wife."

Completely bewildered by her insult and falsehood, I couldn't say a word in my own defense. When Renee finished her "sweet" tongue lashing, my thank you was insincere. What on earth had Diane told her to cause her to have such a dreadful opinion of me? How could Diane have one thing to complain about? Maybe it was because our original long visits had to be "nipped in the bud" so I could get other things accomplished, or Mark and I had gone on a date once in five months!

Renee's belief in Diane's words and opinions broke my heart. Her comments haunted and angered me until I set off on a tangent of my own. My hurt turned to anger.

For nearly six months previous, and ever since Diane married Mark, my life had been a zoo. She should have been grateful I encouraged Mark to marry her, or she might not have been with him. I'd done everything I could to show my love to her and her beautiful little daughter. Most of my time had been devoted to *her* feelings, needs, and wishes. Often Mark and I avoided sex so she wouldn't hear us and feel even worse. I quit teaching at our private school and put my kids in a public school, which I hated to do. I seldom went anywhere with my mother, friends, or kids. Even worse, I seldom heard one thank you come out of Diane's mouth. Even after I "became the good wife" and continued to take care of Diane, Carrie, and her new baby, I didn't feel appreciated. What on earth could Diane have honestly complained about, other than her own malady?

Since I wasn't able to "nip the bud" from Diane's self-centeredness, I swore I would never again give in to her, or help her. When it was Mark's night with her, he had to take care of his wife and his new baby. I took my boys and Carrie sleigh riding. We built snowmen and visited with friends. I left our big, cold house as much as I possibly could.

Poor Diane; she probably didn't understand why I suddenly fell from my pedestal as "a supportive and loving sister-wife" and reverted back into the selfish sister-wife I'd apparently been for so long before.

CHAPTER 24

Poverty and
Dumpster Diving
1979

After living with Mark for nine years, I definitely knew all of his daily moods, habits, and rituals. One evening I told him our polygamous life was making me positively crazy.

"I always know when you and Diane have been fooling around, even if you're quiet about it now."

"You don't either," Mark said. "Why would you say that?"

"You've got to start changing things, Mark! You can't keep doing things the way you've always done them and then expect me to not know what's going on. How would you feel if you knew I'd spent time with my *other* husband, then I showered later the same night, after you knew I'd already showered, or again in the morning? You'd know it was because I'd had sex with him, wouldn't you?"

"I'll take care of it," he claimed. "It's not yours or Diane's business where I'm at or what I'm doing."

"Don't you mean to say 'who' you are doing?" I joked, with a pain in my gut.

Mark figured out how to miss showers or change his routines, for which I was grateful. I continued to get more involved in service, my children, friends, family, and life. If I could stay in my own head and my own space, I hoped none of his "doing" would ever matter.

※

By the summer of 1979, depression got its grip on me again. To add fuel to the fire, every time I wanted to make love, Mark wasn't interested or he couldn't. I was sure it was because he was having more sex with Diane while she was nursing and couldn't get pregnant—and I already was. He tried to assure me that my concerns were unfounded. He promised he'd never been repulsed by my body and would always love and adore me, no matter what size I was or would ever be. He maintained his reasons for our lack of intimacy were because of his own major stress level about finances, and swore his lack of ability was with both Diane and me—not any of the reasons I feared.

Francine and Swede told me I should discuss all of this with Diane to see if Mark was telling me the truth. They thought there was a good chance she was feeling the same way I was, and maybe there was no need for either one of us to feel hurt and rejected. But to have discussed anything with Diane could have made things even worse. I had a desperate need for privacy about such things. Whatever was or wasn't going on in my bed and in my personal life was for me alone to know.

If Mark was being truthful about things, I could feel some comfort and reassurance in his sexual deficiency. If Diane had the same worries I had, we could both feel some peace.

On the other hand, what if Mark had already advised her, "If Sophia happens to ask you if we are having sex, don't let her know. All it will do is hurt her."

He'd said similar things to me several times before. "Don't tell Diane this; don't tell her… If you do, she'll feel bad. She'll get mad and then I'll have to deal with all of her insecurities again." So why,

I wondered, would I not expect the door to swing both ways?

Regardless, it wouldn't work to talk about it with Diane. My sexual relationship with Mark, though not always perfect, had become the strongest element of our marriage, no matter my size. But since Diane was also at his beck and call, trying in every way possible to win his heart, I couldn't be sure of anything. So I chose to believe what Mark told me. I had to in order to stay sane.

If there were homes to build, Mark would be out doing the work. Then he'd come home and hide out behind closed doors again. But the construction boom had ended, and when there wasn't a masonry job he led a life of dismal leisure. He could sleep half the day and go out to breakfast, lunch, or dinner with a friend or by himself. A favorite pastime of his was crashing with a novel by Zane Grey or Louis L'amour. Mark would escape into his cave, only to reappear and then disappear again.

Every Wednesday and Saturday, just like many polygamous families, the children and I shopped at the local grocery stores—in their dumpsters. Jake, Alan, little Sky, and I climbed into the huge trash bins and hunted for anything we could salvage. Diane attempted the feat once and decided she'd never do it again. She never went without as a child, as far as I knew, and she still wouldn't have to.

My kids and I found all sorts of discarded food still packaged and sealed but outdated. Sometimes we discovered a gold mine of toys, coloring books, cereals, and crackers. Whatever we retrieved, we always offered to share with Diane and her children. If we didn't find enough, her parents would always chip in to help her.

When we got home, the kids and I would take a closer look at our "treasures." We went through every single thing. We cut spoiled parts off the fruits and vegetables, and ditched the slimy, moldy parts. Just like most of our Christmases in the past, our dumpster diving adventures were either feast or famine.

While I was grateful for Mark's efforts to provide for us, I resented him for not doing better. When it came to his ongoing struggles with Diane and me—our jealousies, insecurities, and character defects—I empathized with him. He was trying to be a polygamous husband, father, and provider while trying to muddle through his own list of personal issues—all of which contributed to his overall absence in our lives.

Now and then, if we discussed our dire situation, I'd ask Mark to take on even a menial job. Anything, it seemed, would be better than nothing.

"Every little penny helps," I'd say to him.

"If I commit to some damn peon job, I'll be tied down to it. If the weather is good and a higher-paying masonry job becomes available, I have to be able to accept it," he'd argue. His reasoning made sense to me.

I was seven months pregnant with my forth baby, and grateful I'd lost weight as fast as I'd gained it with the past two pregnancies. I needed and wanted a few things we couldn't afford, so I got a job taking care of an elderly woman who lived in uptown Salt Lake City. She paid me seventeen dollars a day. Three-year-old Schuyler could go with me while his older brothers were in school.

Since Diane had purchased a new car before joining our family, and I didn't have one, I asked her if she'd drop Schuyler and me off at the nearest bus stop at 8:00 every weekday morning. After her visits and errands, she agreed to pick us up at the same bus stop at 6:30 each evening.

On our seventy-minute bus ride up town, Schuyler and I read, drew, colored, talked, and played. Our exit was on State Street and North Temple. Sky's little hand would squeeze my hand until his legs would tire. Then I'd carry him as I trudged the rest of the six-block uphill trek to the retirement center.

I kept my employer's apartment clean, fixed her meals, and visited with her as much as she wanted. Sky would tug on the sheets and blankets when I changed her soiled bedding. He tried to help me with anything else she requested. When she napped, Schuyler and I would delight in a few moments of fresh air and sanity in the courtyard.

Six hours later on our long trek back to the bus stop, I'd carry worn-out Sky on the side of my bulging, pregnant belly. On the way I would pray God would save us a place on the crowded bus to sit down, so Schuyler could sleep on my lap while I rested. More often than not, we had to stand in the aisle nearly all the way back. Sky would cling tightly to my legs. To keep our balance, I'd firmly grip the top straps attached to the railing at the back of the bus. The bumps and stops jolted my belly back and forth. During those long rides, Sky would sit on my feet or on the floor of the bus and fall asleep.

While on the bus, I'd send Diane telepathic messages and hope she would hear me. "Please remember us and don't be late again. Forgive me if I've done something that hurt you."

Now and then a few tears escaped. What in God's name was I doing all this for? I hated having to depend on her—or anyone—for anything.

After one of those long, hard days, Schuyler and I had to wait for Diane during a fall rainstorm for nearly fifty minutes. I turned down three rides from good Samaritans because I hoped she would arrive any minute. I did not want her to worry, or look for us, or wonder where we were. In the meantime, I silently cussed and cried. While Schuyler and I shivered, he screamed. I didn't even have a quarter in my pocket for the pay phone to call someone else to come rescue us. I had no idea how much longer we'd have to wait.

Just like each time before when Diane was late, she had some kind of an excuse. I didn't say one word, though it was all I could do not to tell her off. I had decided to be loving and kind to her, no matter what. But on that day, I actually felt hateful toward her. Through burning, teary eyes I let myself glance at her as she nonchalantly sat behind the steering wheel and drove us home in total silence. She was in control, and I could only foresee more tribulations in my life if I didn't do something different.

In spite of all this, forgiving Diane and others never seemed too hard for me. It might have taken a while, but when I was ready, it was done. No matter what Diane did or didn't do, I held far less animosity toward her for her injustices than I ever did for myself. I always forgave and cherished her. I had no doubt I always would. It was far more difficult to forgive me—the sister-wife I wasn't—the one I wished I could be.

The day after Thanksgiving and seventeen days past my due date, I experienced the joy of a perfectly normal and fairly easy delivery, with only seven hours of labor. Our handsome Jack, was delivered by my sister Francine at her home. He weighed eight pounds, had round, rosy cheeks and patches of thin, blond hair. He was absolutely amazingly adorable! His soul smiled at me through his deep blue eyes, and I cried in gratitude.

CHAPTER 25

Temple Ordinances
and Blessings
1980

The Allred Group had finally finished a massive building in Bluffdale, Utah, where church services and private school would be held. When it was completed, it was dedicated as the RCA Building, named after Rulon Clark Allred, who was loved by thousands and was a martyr for our cause.

By June 1980, members were in a major quandary as word and evidence leaked out. My father and his councilmen had finished and dedicated rooms with a "temple-like" atmosphere. In the basement of an apartment looking building, original temple ordinances began to be performed for those who were considered "worthy" recipients. After the rituals were completed, most of those men and women began to wear the sacred, old-fashioned, long underwear known as garments, just like my parents had done. Mother said a few "qualified" ladies who had previously been through the temple had been "set apart" (given a special blessing) to sew the garments. It was important each of these seamstresses understood and respected the significance of the markings and the rituals associated with them.

This caused quite the controversy among some members. We'd been taught from the beginning the temple ordinances would and should never be performed outside of LDS temples. For years on end, we prayed fervently the "temple doors would soon be open to the worthy" (meaning we saints). But after LDS Church officials stated all worthy men of African descent could hold the priesthood and partake of the blessings, many Allredites felt LDS officials had allowed the desecration of the temples.

I never wanted to wear the "sacred gift," as I began to hear others call their garments. For so many years, I watched my mother's dis-ease with them. I already felt too restricted with having to wear dresses to school and struggle all day long on Sundays, and I was also concerned I'd have a heatstroke. The most confining part of the "gift" was couples were advised not to take them off, even during lovemaking.

I was in a physical and spiritual dilemma. Part of me was relieved Mark, Diane and I were never "called" or considered "worthy" recipients. While several families became pushy and demanding about getting their "temple work" done, the other part of me was perplexed and despondent for not doing the same. Over a period of time, we were surrounded by men and women who had their "ordinance work" done, while I continued to feel defective.

With several families in The Group, Mark and I both felt my father and other council members had begun to dole out those endowments as if they were prize money. They'd pretty much be granted to anyone who knew how to charm or beg their "work" be done also. Neither of us wanted to be placated. I wanted to want the garments and be worthy, but I didn't and wasn't. Mark refused to suck up to Dad so he'd be asked to serve the sacrament, speak in meetings, or be called for specific priesthood duties or functions. In fact, he said, "I certainly don't need to wear garments so others will think I'm a good man!"

I agreed with him wholeheartedly. We felt there were many who were granted blessings under the guise of being pious and devout members. My heart and head were in a dither. I didn't want that "gift," yet without having our ordinance work done; Mark, Diane and I couldn't receive the blessings of protection through wearing the garments. Neither would we be exalted into the celestial kingdom without them.

My father told me not to worry about it. He explained how pressured he felt by some of his council members, even though, he felt they should have waited until Christ returns to set His church in order. Dad said his brethren, the council members, felt there were too many righteous and faithful men and women who would benefit from those extra blessings right now.

"Our original intent," Dad explained, "was very few, under specific qualifications, would be 'called' for these blessings, but then things got out of hand. Men and women thought, 'If he is worthy, then I am,' and 'If she's laudable, then so is my wife,' and 'If they get to have their temple work done, why can't we?'"

Dad looked penitent as he continued. "Yes, now we're just as guilty of being out of order as is our mother church, who has ordained the blacks to the priesthood. We've done some grievous things. The Lord is very displeased with us for giving these holy ordinances to so many unworthy people. Those blessings may damn them—us—even further. And my brethren and I will be held accountable to God for our mistakes."

Though I felt like an alien around all my brothers, sisters, and friends who were wearing their "gifts," I thanked God that Mark and I were off the hook. I was elated that we didn't "qualify" as others had. Those garments would surely cramp our lifestyle, make me feel guilty for accepting ordinances I wasn't comfortable with, and damn us even further.

※

The fights and anger were not solely between Mark and me—not since week one of his and Diane's marriage. When I'd hear them argue, I was ashamed of my few seconds of glee. Moreover, I felt compassion for Diane's sorrows. I understood her battlefield well.

The rationale for our regular disputes was nearly the same. Like me, Diane felt she had to defend her children when Mark raged at them, called them names, or spanked them far too hard. Though we seldom dared talk about those awful moments, I felt sure she had the same needs, feelings, and fears I did. But neither Diane nor I had the courage or the know-how to change things. Not only that, if one of us balked about his behaviors, she'd be in the doghouse for who knew how long, and he always had the other wife waiting with open arms.

While Swede's brother, Chad, spent the summer of 1980 with him, I drank up his flirtatious attentiveness like I'd been dying of thirst. I'd lost a lot of weight during my pregnancy, and I felt wonderful. Chad's words of admiration made me feel beautiful. Every smile, laugh, and conversation we shared momentarily filled the gaps in my low self-esteem. His doting friendship became so addictive it was hard for me to stay away. It was even more difficult for me to leave after I'd already stayed there much too long. Through all of Chad's risqué propositions and promises of love, I knew his ultimate goal and assured him I would never give in.

"I'd live to regret it, lose my family and everything dear to me, and for sure go straight to hell," I told Chad. "More than any other reason on earth, though, I want to be loyal to Mark because I love him." The toughest guilt, was the craving I felt for Chad's attention, while Mark was so very absent in my life. On my way home, I'd swear to stay away longer and avoid him, (as my mother warned) like the plague."

※

I was so humiliated I wanted to climb under the table and disappear. If my dad and siblings knew I was asking the government for assistance, they would've been ashamed of me. Mark didn't want me to ask for assistance either, but I couldn't go on for one more minute wondering how or when our children would get their next meals.

"It won't pay for me to go to work right now," I explained to the service worker, whom I felt was asking too many snoopy questions. "I couldn't earn enough to pay for gas and a babysitter. And if I did, there wouldn't be any money left to feed or clothe my kids anyway."

After the painful interrogation, I promised not to exchange my food stamps for money, give them away, or share the food I'd purchased with anyone other than my own family. I knew I had no choice but to commit a lesser sin in order to live a higher law. There was no way I could have food in my cupboards and fridge, and meals on the table, and let Diane and her children go without—besides they were my family.

After she and I made a long list of groceries together, it took me hours to muster up the courage to go to the grocery store. Then it took me ten minutes to become brave enough to take my grocery cart to the checkout stand. I felt like a criminal who was stealing from everyone on earth. The crisp food stamp bills might as well have had noise sensors that shouted, "You slothful scum—you have food stamps!" My insides shook and I held my breath. The clerk counted them out and gave me "the look," or maybe I only imagined she was judging me.

I cried all the way home. Some of the tears drenching my shirt were from being so fearful and embarrassed, but most were from gratitude. At last, we had provisions from the grocery store rather than from the dumpsters. We would finally have balanced and nutritious meals on our tables and junk food ta boot.

❦

It seemed at times Jake and Alan argued every day over everything. They teased and tormented each other and Schuyler until I thought I could go ballistic and turn into a monster from hell. I'd plead, bribe, separate, ground, or restrict them from privileges they didn't really have. I was the most consistent mother on earth at being the most inconsistent.

I had a paddle and my hand, but whenever I smacked there bottoms to get their attention, they'd laugh. Spanking or hitting them when I was angry was not an acceptable option. It hadn't been for years.

If Mark happened to be reading in the bedroom when the commotion took place, he'd storm out and yell at them. "Do what your mother tells you to do! Get off of your lazy asses and stop acting like little shit heads!" Depending on his moods and patience level, he might add some smacks, punches or spankings to his demands, before he'd retreat again.

Since I could never be sure how volatile Mark might be at any given moment, I never wanted him to discipline our kids; but I hoped my idol threats of his wrath would suffice so they'd behave themselves. Sometimes it worked. Most of the time, not knowing what to do, I would withdraw further into my realm of inadequacy and cry.

❧

Diane walked up the stairs and leaned over the wrought-iron railing in my kitchen. I was sitting at the table writing in my journal. Mark was fixing some food near the stove while the three of us began to laugh about the adorable things our little kids were saying. I watched a beautiful ray of light pour through the south window. The rainbow reflection touched my right shoulder and bounced onto Diane's left. Mark smiled at me, and then at Diane. Then she and I smiled at each other.

"This is what polygamy is supposed to feel like," I said right out loud.

Diane loves Mark and me, and we both love her. There might be some hope in all of this mania after all.

CHAPTER 26

Cremation or Burial
1981

In the spring, two of the most beloved and respected women in our group told me they had prayed to know whom they should ask to be a girls' camp director along with them. They said they felt inspired to ask me.

I presumed they'd chosen me because another rule of the gospel was, if a person is going astray, the best way to get a person back on the straight and narrow path to God was to give him or her an assignment (calling)—or two or three. It's been said, "When you are busy serving the Lord, there is less chance the devil can persuade you into apostasy." I thought I was already as busy serving God as I possibly could be, but apparently I needed more direction. Also, the past few times I'd been a camp counselor, a few ladies said I wasn't a good example because of all of those "disgusting" pranks my girls and I were accused of doing. To a few of the women, I was too wild, light-minded, and definitely not spiritual enough. Therefore, I was quite baffled but flattered to have been "called." Though their reasons may have been for disciplinary purposes, I considered it an honor to serve in such an enjoyable manner.

At our first meeting, I asked Ellen and Myrna, "From the myriad of qualified women in our group, why did you choose me?"

"Your perception of yourself is inaccurate, Sophia," Ellen said. "You have always been a willing and active servant to the Lord. For years, you've been an excellent visiting teacher for the Relief Society. You are always in the service of the poor and needy. You faithfully attend your meetings." Then Myrna added with big grin, "You are young, creative, and full of great ideas. The girls love you. We prayed about it and feel you'll be a strong asset to our team."

I figured they were right to have drafted me. When I heard what others said earlier, it boosted my confidence and self-esteem. "If you want something done, ask Sophia. She'll not only make sure it's done, she'll do a great job!"

I was elated and grateful. I became so enthusiastically involved and dedicated to the camp's planning, it seemed I had three different lives, two of which I was becoming an absolute failure at. As a wife and mother, I couldn't seem to keep up. When I complained to my sisters in the gospel about my inability to fulfill my calling and still care for my home, husband and children, they assured me I was making the right choices. I was busy doing the work of the Lord, therefore, He would take care of things.

My mother always taught me, "Always place others before yourself. If others are in need, it's your duty to help." I watched Aunt Eleanor play that role to a T. Whether it was my time, energy, or God-given talents someone needed, I was there. I was everyone's babysitter and a good listener. I would cheer a desperate saint, or talk a woman out of leaving the gospel or committing suicide because of unending feelings of hopelessness and injustice. Whenever there were baby blessings, weddings, showers, girls' classes, school lessons, and funeral meals to prepare, I was there to serve, to assist, to give and to give.

My mother's tireless preaching had paid off. I believed with all of my heart, my singular value and only hope in qualifying for heaven was about serving God by serving others. The tiny bit of self-confidence I had was based on the service I performed.

Still, according to LDS Church President David O McKay, all of my service was null and void if I didn't put my family first. In Relief Society meetings, our instructor and group's matriarch liked to remind us of his quote: "No other success can compensate for failure in the home" (David O. McKay, [Salt Lake City, Utah: Deseret Book, 1971], 284). By that creed alone, I'd already blown to smithereens my "calling" as a mother in Zion. At home I felt like a complete failure.

No matter how many hours I spent cleaning, scrubbing, and picking up, my house always seemed to be a mess. I didn't think I had the time to teach my children housekeeping skills, either. I was a self-reliant perfectionist. It was so much easier to do things myself and get them right, rather than to fight with my kids to do them.

Even sadder were my never-ending expectations and promises I made to my children that didn't seem to change. "When I'm done with this or that, we'll play, or we'll go . . . or then we'll . . . When we can afford it, we'll sign you up for lessons or . . . When we can, I'll buy you a new . . ." My children, like me when I was a child, knew there was never enough time or money to go around. Of all my failures, the most disappointing; I was never the perfect mother I promised myself I would be.

One day, in the midst of my fear, guilt, and stress, I slumped back on my bed. *If the people in The Group really knew what a lonely, depressed, wicked mess I am. . . If they knew what a terrible, inconsistent mother I am . . . If the ladies I clean house for only knew what my home looked like . . .* Tears drenched my hair and the bed underneath my head. Then my precious seven-month-old Jack woke up and began to jabber up a storm. His pudgy little fists pinched and tugged on my shirt and arms as he crawled on top of my chest and planted slobbery kisses all over my cheeks and mouth.

I kissed Jack's chubby cheeks and his soft little neck.

There is nothing on this earth as precious as babies. They remind me of the miracle of life and the gratitude I should have. All I ever wanted, more than anything else in the world, was to be a good mother. I loved my children more than life itself, yet I continued to fail them and myself every day.

After wallowing in my guilt a while longer, I counted my many blessings as I'd done a million times before and went back to trying.

❧

I worked hard to keep my mouth shut and most of my opinions to myself. Things were much better between Mark and me when I didn't encourage him to join us in family prayer or attend meetings, and when I didn't mention God, Dad, priesthood, or "should" or "shouldn't" rules. When I didn't pressure Mark about my religious expectations he showed me more love and acceptance.

Our daily lives seemed black or white. On the white side, Mark's goodness and kindhearted ways deeply drew me in. We were strongly bonded by the fun sexual connection we enjoyed, and by his desire to be more spiritual and a better parent. On the dark side, I often felt shattered by his tirades against Diane, our kids, and me, and by his disdain for the religious requisites I believed in. When I thought about this side of things, my life seemed impossible, since I needed a man to get me to the celestial kingdom.

Mark's study of philosophy, and his beliefs and ideas about life, death, rebirth, religions, and gods and goddesses intrigued me. Everything he told me made more sense to me than Fundamentalist Mormonism ever did. I delighted in the possibility we had a loving, kind, honest God who gives us many chances to attain perfection. I could never understand why God would give us only one lifetime to determine if we'd end up in heaven or hell.

The new ideas Mark started to talk about were always considered blasphemous and damning according to the Mormon doctrines we'd grown up with. I was taught we shouldn't read unapproved books. To even consider something besides Mormonism meant we were "on the high road to apostasy." Unapproved books were tools of the devil and written to turn our hearts and minds from the truth. After all, that's what Satan was all about. "He'll tell you a million truths just to get you

230

to believe one lie!" Along with dozens of others, that statement sufficed to keep our minds focused on the doctrines we'd been taught all of our lives.

Even though my heart and soul felt drawn to certain philosophical ideas, most of them were considered evil. Embedded deep within my psyche were the dogmatic rules, vernacular, and systemic beliefs of twenty-eight years of life. They dominated my persona. The recorded creeds of seven generations of Fundamentalist Mormons would play in my mind, then rewind and play again and again.

"Just hold to the iron rod, the straight and narrow path to God. It's better to stick with your testimony and be wrong than to leave and find out you are wrong." Why? I wondered why a loving God wouldn't want and expect us to find the truth or know if our testimony was wrong, even if we made mistakes on the road to discovery.

My problem was I had a strong testimony of plural marriage. I certainly would not have committed myself to such insanity if I hadn't. But did I hold on to my testimony because a loving and gracious God had confirmed it, or did my testimony derive from the God of ever-present threats, eternal damnation and hell with no family ties? Was the God of my upbringing the culprit of my religious certainty? Was my confirmation of polygamy based on the list of menacing promises I'd heard a billion times since my birth?

All of that was a mystery to me. It was easier to close my eyes and just follow in the footsteps of my parents. If I didn't have the answers, I could simply fly by the seat of my pants on faith. I wouldn't have to study or have anything to think about. It was easier to stay in blinded bliss, where all of the doctrines I was raised to believe in could stay safe and snug in my head.

※

In June 1981, Mark's father died, leaving hundreds of descendants. His funeral, like most I had ever attended, turned into a church service. Those who spoke admonished his sons, daughters, and grandchildren to carry on the practice of plural marriage and bear as many polygamous children as possible; who would in turn continue to revere his name and carry out his legacy.

Someone spoke of his struggles trying to live polygamy, of his arrest, and the two terms he spent in jail for living plural marriage. Near the end of the service, Mark's eldest brother, who lived in Colorado City with his wives and oodles of children, made an unexpected announcement. He said many family members and friends had pooled together enough funds to buy a gravesite where their father would be buried. Anyone who wanted to join them for the dedication of the grave could do so.

While the brother was giving directions to the cemetery, Mark stood up and loudly declared to his brother and to the congregation, "I am sorry, but that will not happen! I promised our father I would carry out his wishes to be cremated. His body will not be buried in a grave."

"Yes it will!" Mark's brother protested. "The majority of our father's children believe his decision was wrong, and we're going to—"

"I am telling you, Dad's body will not leave this site! If it does, there will be hell to pay," Mark yelled before he marched toward the exit door near the front of the assembly hall. There, he stopped and looked back at his brother. "I will be right back with the funeral director. Let everyone know there is no need for them to go to the cemetery."

Their mother, Aldora, suddenly jumped up and called out, "Stop this bickering! Stop it right now!" She was sobbing and clearly mortified at her sons' irreverent display in front of her coworkers, friends, and family. I stood up and leaned forward to touch her shoulder. But before my hand could reach her frail, slumped-over body, she walked away and exited through the side door.

The crowd sat in deathly silence for a few minutes. Then Mark's brother started in again with what he claimed was "his priesthood duty." He told everyone God would be displeased with them if they didn't do their best to save their father. They should insist his body be buried so he could come forth in the morning of the first resurrection.

The funeral director announced his own decision. The body would not be removed from the premises until all of the brothers come to an agreement. Would there be a cremation or a burial?

Mark and sixteen of his brothers drew together in a large circle to debate the ramifications of their father's written, but not legalized, last will and testament. The rest of us women and children waited— and waited.

Eighty-five minutes later, the men dispersed, gathered their families, and quietly left the building. The votes had been cast. My father-in-law would be cremated. On our way to Aldora's home, Mark told Diane and me about their discussion.

"Everyone had a chance to speak," he said. "I told my brothers just what your father, Owen, told me. It doesn't matter what we want or don't want. It doesn't matter what we believe is right or wrong. Like all of us, our father had his God-given free agency to choose what happens to his body. Forcing our will would not guarantee his salvation even though all of you want it to. I told them Dad knew this dissension was going to happen, and that's why he wanted me to promise him I would make sure his wishes would be granted."

Immediately, Mark felt distance and judgments from some of his siblings and other family members. A few held on to their grudges for years. Most of the family, however, gained a newfound respect for Mark's courage to honor his father's choice, and stand up against the majority of his family.

Aldora was the first of Mark's father's six wives, and the only one still with him for many years before he died. She too, believed he should be buried; but most of her disappointment toward her sons ensued because of the ethical conflict that should have been resolved long before the services.

CHAPTER 27

Infidelity in Polygamy
1981

Our girls' camp planning, though long and tedious, turned out to be another validation of my abilities. I was grateful to God I had so much to offer.

Ellen and Myrna had a remarkable spiritual connection with God, which I envied. With all my "might, heart, and strength," I had fasted and prayed so I too would know what they claimed to know. I wanted to have the Spirit of God and His direction in everything, large and small. Every now and then, I thought I had it.

A few months before that planning meeting Mark, Diane, and I decided it would be nice to have dinner together on Sundays, as one big family. I would prepare the meal on my Sundays with Mark, and Diane would fix the meals on her Sundays with Mark.

We also agreed Mark's time with each of us would begin and end at certain times of the day. He said he would not be with either one of us if it wasn't our allotted time, and as sister-wives, we agreed to honor each other by not stealing his time when it wasn't ours.

During the drawn-out girls' camp meetings, I excused myself from the table to check the pot roast I'd been cooking for my family. I'd already cut up a pot full of potatoes and set out the ingredients to make a cake. I looked forward to our family dinner together. It was my day with Mark, and I hoped when the ladies left, he'd come in from his shop to help me with the rest of the meal and hang out for a while.

When the ladies left around 4:30, I sent five-year-old Schuyler out to the shop to invite his dad inside, and then downstairs to ask Diane if we could borrow a couple eggs so I could get the cake made. Sky returned with tears rolling down his cheeks. "Dad yelled at me and told me to go back upstairs!"

I held Sky in my arms for a few minutes and made up some excuse for Mark's anger. "I'm so sorry, honey. Maybe your dad is trying to sleep."

"No! Dad isn't asleep. He said I should get my ass back upstairs right now! Why is he so mad at me, Mom?"

Mark might as well have shoved his large arm and fist down my throat and pulled my stomach back up the same way. His frustration, I knew well, brought on another gut ache. He had used that tone of voice with our children when we wanted some privacy—some uninterrupted time in the bedroom.

I gave Sky some crayons and paper and asked him to draw me a picture, then went downstairs.

There wasn't one sound in the dark basement. I wondered where Diane's kids were. I knew what I was in for, but I was fuming. I tapped on Diane's bedroom door and waited, even though I knew no one would answer, at least for the first few times. While the two of them pretended no one was home, my heart was pounding. I knocked a little harder. Still, there was no answer. Then I banged on the door.

"Dammit, Sky, I told you to get your ass back upstairs!" Mark yelled. I heard Diane whisper something. There was no going back now. I pounded on the door, knowing there was a possibility I might get pounded on when it opened.

The door squeaked open about five or six inches. Mark's shocked face and naked shoulder were in my face. "What do you need, Sophia?" he asked, unable to disguise his frustration and guilt.

Even the anger in my voice couldn't conceal my horrific

heartache. "Just came down to verify what I already knew! That's what I needed!"

It was a struggle to climb the stairs. Every muscle and organ in my body hurt. I turned off the oven and the heat under the potatoes. Jack woke up when I changed his diaper and dressed him. After I splashed cold water over my swollen eyes, I marched across our back field with Sky, the baby in one arm, and the diaper bag across my shoulder.

I knocked on the door and waited to hear Swede's deep, warm voice. "Come on in!"

The delicious smell of Swede's corned beef hash and gravy permeated the air. When I walked in, there was Diane and Mark sitting at the table set for three. Miraculously, I composed myself long enough to ask Swede to loan me two eggs. In front of my cheating partners, it was difficult not to ask him right out loud, if I could borrow "two, bloody, stinking, fat-ass, cheating eggs?"

The two large suitcases on my bed were nearly full when Mark came in. Adrenalin-surged anger and pain had propelled me so rapidly I was still flying around the house gathering clothes.

"Where are you going, Sophia?" Mark finally asked.

I had no energy to speak even if I wanted to.

"I'm so sorry, honey. I didn't mean to hurt you," he said. "It's just that—"

I became faint from hyperventilating. I turned to go in the boys' room when Mark grabbed my shoulders. "Stop and talk to me, Sophia!" he demanded.

I pulled myself away to grab a few more diapers from the hamper. They unfolded all over the floor. Before Mark could bend down to pick them up, I grabbed them up in one heap and shoved them into the diaper bag.

Mark followed me into the kitchen. "Stop running around and listen to me!"

I snatched a few baby bottles, some baby food, and Jack's formula from the cupboards, stormed back to my room, and bustled around, looking for my old, comfortable shoes.

When I turned toward the bed, Mark forced me to sit down and again demanded I listen to him. But I couldn't sit. I sprang up again.

"I don't want to listen or talk about anything anymore! I am done!" I blurted. "I've had it! I am sick to death of Diane's shit and your shit! You can stinking have each other! I am out of here!" I yelled.

Mark pulled me back on the bed next to him and held me there. "Don't leave, Sophia. We can work things out."

Again I fought with him to get back up, but I had no more energy or strength left. I elbowed his arms off of me.

"Just leave me alone, Mark. I have to go. I won't deal with this shit anymore! I'm leaving with the boys before we die!"

Mark repeated every sincere and reasonable excuse he could possibly come up with to console and cheer me and get me to stay.

"Diane is really insecure. She doesn't feel like I love her as much as I love you. I made a big mistake by being with her today, and I am so sorry. She's always jealous because she sees what you and I have together and she wants to have that same relationship with me. You have Swede's place to escape to, and she wants to be a part of his life as well."

"She has her family and friends to escape to, Mark! I'm sick of her trying to take, copy, borrow, do, and have everything I have and do!"

"I know, and I agree with you. But when I was at Swede's place this morning, she walked over. He felt obligated to ask her to have dinner, like he does with you and me."

"I don't give a crap, Mark! We had an agreement. You two screwing around on my time was the most disrespectful thing you could do! And what were you two going to do, wait until I'd fixed all of us an elaborate meal, and then tell me you're not hungry? Or were you two going to fake it and pig out anyway?"

"You're right. I was very disrespectful and wrong in the way I was trying to console her insecurities. You have lots of friends, activities, and things to do. You're talented and beautiful. You see, Sophia, Diane sees and knows how much I love you, and it's killing her. Please forgive me, and her. I can't do this—I can't live this way without you."

I caved in to the sound of goodness coming from Mark. I knew he loved me, at least most of the time. For the sake of survival and right-eousness, I had to believe everything he said. I was sure he was try-ing to do the best he knew how to do, considering he had two insecure, berserk women to please. Besides, I had to be there for the long haul anyway. What could I do differently? Where would I go? Who would ever treat my four boys like their own? Who could ever love me as much as Mark did?

He'd tell me all the time. "No one will ever love you as much as I do, Sophia. No one will desire or touch you the way I do. I love you more than anything or anyone on earth! I am nothing without you and my kids—nothing!"

❦

It took me a while to forgive Diane and Mark again. In spite of all the hardships in our family and in those plural families all around us, Diane and I were still making strides. I knew we were feeling a deeper bond of sisterhood and camaraderie. In fact, it meant the world to me when she apologized for the hurtful things she did and said before she married Mark. In retrospect she realized how mean she had been by showing me her honeymoon lingerie and for sprawling herself all over Mark in front of me. She told me even the idea of Mark ever taking another wife was hard for her, let alone the reality of it. When she asked me to forgive her, I could honestly tell her I already had a long time before. But her awareness and caring meant a lot to me.

❦

It was a terrible sin to talk negatively about your husband. I knew better, yet I didn't stop. If husbands weren't doing what they should, wives were to pray for them until they did. "Behind every successful man is a good woman, or two or three." The male God I grew up with

238

had everything figured out. If Mark wasn't fulfilling his priesthood calling, it meant Diane and I were not faithful and qualified enough to change him; yet another way women are at fault.

In one of my particularly frustrated moods, I jumped down the stairs to complain to Diane about *our* husband, and to get some support from her. I had several things to say, but I began with the worst of my grievances.

"I shouldn't have to be cleaning other people's houses all day, and then come home to my filthy dirty house, and do everything else around here! I hate using food stamps while Mark sleeps or reads all day long and does very little to help and support us."

Diane threw in her two cents worth. She too said she hated the distance he kept between him and our children when he was home. He should take our kids places and do fun things with them.

"He should be our spiritual leader, Diane! How is he going to get us to the celestial kingdom if he won't even be the patriarch of our household?"

Suddenly I sensed Mark's presence and his hurt. "Quit now, Sophia," I heard my soul warn. But I didn't listen or stop. I looked around the room and continued to run amok.

"Mark could do anything, something to make some money. I've given him a hundred suggestions. He could go to work at night, so if he got a masonry job during the day he'd be available. With his talents, he could make things at home and sell them. Even a part-time job would be better than nothing!"

"Stop it now, Sophia!" My soul prompted me again. "If you don't, you will be sorry!"

Again, as I too often do, I ignored my soul and went on. "He should love us and care for us enough to—"

In an instant, Mark was at the bottom of the landing. "To what, Sophia? Care enough to what? I'll tell you what I care about. I care enough to get the hell out of here! I care enough to know when and where I am not wanted!"

I felt as though my body had been slammed against the wall. I was sure I deserved every bit of it.

Mark hurtled back upstairs. I chased after him. In our room he dumped three drawers of clothing onto the bed. His whole body shook from heartache and anger. While he urgently separated the socks, shirts, and underwear he wanted into piles, I begged him to forgive me and to please stay. "Please don't leave us, Mark!" I wailed. "I am so sorry! I knew better than to complain, and didn't stop. I am so sorry."

He didn't say one word to me. I sat on the edge of our bed sobbing. I muttered some more nonsense until he stormed out of our room and back down the stairs. Ten minutes later he reappeared with more clothing and an old metal suitcase. As quickly and tightly as he could, he crammed every inch with his things before he smashed it shut and snapped the metal bars over the latches.

The fire in his eyes scorched my soul. "I'm leaving Sophia!" he said somewhere between a growl and a whimper. "Maybe you'll hear from me in a few days—maybe not!"

Mark slammed the front door with such terrific force it sounded like a bomb exploded. From my glazed-over eyes, I watched the tires of his old white Chevy pickup fling mud and gravel against the garage door as he spun out of our driveway.

I could hardly function. Our kids were scared and wondering what happened to their dad. Neither Diane nor I heard from Mark for nearly five days. When he finally talked to me, his voice was cold, short, and snappy.

"I'm in California working for my brother. There's a lot of work here, so I'll send you as much money as I can, as often as I can. I'll keep only what I need to get by."

"Okay," I said, not knowing what else to say.

"All right, goodbye then," he said quickly.

"Wait, Mark! I really am sorry I hurt you so much. I was clearly out of line and I knew better than—"

He interrupted, "It's okay, Sophia. I deserved every bit of it. I am all those terrible things you said. I have been a real asshole. Now that I'm way out here, you and the kids won't have to put up with me anymore."

Grandpa—Byron Harvey Allred
with his second wife, my grandma,
Mary Evelyn Clark.

My parents, Owen and Vera when
they became engaged. They were
married in February, 1935.

At one, I am with my cousin Rebecca
in our unfinished front yard, in
Plygville.

Me and my niece, (right), who my
sister gave birth to at the age of 15

I'm two and a half, standing on Mom's
couch in our un-finished basement
home in Plygville.

My brother James is five and I'm three
on a glider in our back yard.

First Grade picture, after my mom cut off my long hair.

Me at nine years of age, the first birthday celebration I had or remember!

At thirteen, the year I met my boyfriend Royce and my husband Mark.

Me at "sweet" sixteen and a sophomore in high school. This picture was used as the cover of my first edition FYIP Book.

Left to right: My two full sisters, Lucinda and Francine, Aunt Eleanore's daughter Hannah, and me during the summer of my 'wild escapades' in Colorado City, Arizona.

Mom with her three daughters; L to R: Me, Francine, and Lucinda.

My wedding day. I was seventeen. Mark was twenty-four. My father performed our Priesthood Wedding in the front room of Mom's house.

My mother is holding my first baby, while I'm leaning down looking at him. Family and friends often gathered in her family room right after church.

Francine, Mom, Me and baby Karleen sitting on my lap, at Chuck-A-Rama at the Fashion Place Mall in Murray where our home in Plygville used to be.

Seven of my mother's eight children and seven of Dad's twenty-three: Jake, Shane, Darryl, Luke and Dean; Bottom: Lucinda, Dad, Mom and Sophia.

I had a tough time getting ready for this family picture where I weighed so much and felt so inadequate. Back L to R: Me and Jake; Middle row: Mark, Jack, Alan; Bottom row: Karleen, Schuyler, Keith and Anne.

This is a very recent picture of the AUB church. When it was first built, and when I attended there, it looked like a drab warehouse. Since I left, it's been remodeled, expanded, painted, and landscaped. The temple is next door. It too has been remodeled and looks like a huge apartment building. Attire is still the same: long sleeves and slacks for men and long sleeves and dresses for women.

Seven of my father's thirteen wives: L to R: Aunt Eleanor, my mother Vera, Diane, Ora, Ada, Amelia, and Brenda after "patriarchal blessings" at a couple of family friend's home. Dad is seated in the middle of new converts.

Two of my sisters and me on the right.
Something must have been really funny.
My top weight was 235 pounds.

I started at SLCC in 1991 with 5
children at home and while
teaching Head Start. Earning
my A.S Degree was rewarding.

An Over-Eater's Anonymous
Dress-Up Party. My friends and I
got to pretend anything. I wanted
cleavage, so I created a little to
(wickedly) show off.

L to R Back Row: My Children: Schuyler, Alan, Jack, and Jake. Front Row: Me, Keith, and Karleen. My daughter Anne wasn't able to be there.

My daughter Anne.

My wonderful mother and I, after Dad started calling me his "Troublemaker" — meaning anyone who asks questions or brings up issues and topics that aren't kosher. I no longer believed in polygamy; but for our families' sake, I still hadn't decided if I could or should leave our plural marriage.

I always had holiday angst; but after I "left," I gave in again, dressed up, and went to my sister's really fun Halloween Party.

Nothing can express the joy I felt at this moment of celebration: I was a 50-Year-Old Summa Cum Laude Graduate!

Below: Wedding pictures, in our back yard. We wished every one of OUR children and OUR grandchildren could have been there!

Above: LeRoy and I with three of his eight adult kids, their spouses, and four of his ten grandchildren.

Six of my seven adult kids with LeRoy and I; Ten of my 23 grandchildren were there. So far, we have 6 great-grandchildren.

"I guess you're right," I replied. "Now you won't have to put up with us, either. If I were a better wife and more grateful for all the things you have done and tried to do for us, this wouldn't have happened. You're not as awful as I made you out to be, Mark."

"I know," he said somberly. "I know exactly how you have felt for a long time. That's why I had to get out of there and come here to work. You need me away from you so you can heal and have your spiritual needs met without me holding you back."

"Will you be okay?" I asked. "How long will you be gone? What else can I say to let you know how sorry I am?"

"I'll be fine. I don't have any idea when I will be back. We'll see how things go and take it from there. Got to go now."

"Mark, Mark, are you there?" I asked into dead airspace somewhere between his hell and mine.

𝒴𝓁

On August 16, everyone in the Allred Group received the message; Ervil LeBaron had died in his cell at the Utah State Prison. While it was reported his death was from natural causes, many of us wanted to believe it was God's retribution for his evil deeds. Still some of us felt he got off much too easy and should have suffered. Either way, we were jubilant "Evil Ervil" was in hell where he surely belonged.

𝒴𝓁

We'd been living in our new home for six and a half years, but our whole yard was still a disaster. Over the years, most of the topsoil and fill dirt that used to be in three or four piles had been mixed up and spread across the front yard. It was scattered with Tonka trucks, Hot Wheels, and holes full of muddy water. The boys' bike trails and jumps also ran up, down, over, and between. What was left of the dirt piles was packed down as hard as rocks.

The only cheery thing about the yard was the bouquets of dande-lions the boys proudly picked from the weeds that blanketed the few spots of fertile earth around the perimeter.

At least a hundred times, Mark had described his big dreams for the front yard. Because of his plans, he didn't want me to do anything until we had the time and money to build a retaining wall. He wanted two layers of lawn, a sidewalk, a driveway, a flower garden, and more. But none of those dreams had come to fruition. As our lives had proved thus far, we would never have money to finish the yard. It was more important to put food on the table and clothe our kids.

Those years were way too long and one day too many. I was so embarrassed about our yard disasters I never wanted our neighbors to see me. I knew any more humiliation would surely turn me inside out.

Mark was gone and couldn't do anything to help. Nor could he talk me into waiting for the "someday" that may never come. With Ellen's encouragement and prodding me forward, I decided to make things happen, one baby step, one shovel, and one day at a time.

With Mark's old work gloves on both hands, I hauled a bunch of old cinder block from our junkyard in the back field, to the front. About five feet out from the front brick wall of our house, I dug a ditch eight inches wide and two inches deep. It ran the full length of the house. From the outside edge of our five-by-five-foot porch, going in both directions, I placed the blocks end to end in the trench. Then I lugged at least a hundred (it seemed) wheelbarrows full of rich, dark soil from the old pigpen and our chicken yard to fill the three-hun-dred-square-foot span.

A few weeks later, when the space was full and level, I purchased discounted, nearly dead plants from garden shops and solicited as many flower starts as I could from friends and family members. With tender loving care, I planted each contribution in my first, large flower garden.

By the middle of September, I had picked, shoveled, and spread only a tiny slice of the remaining topsoil. I still had at least nine-tenths yet to level.

One day, I rested on the porch to catch my breath. As I pressed my hand on my abdomen, I was overjoyed to feel my twenty-week-old baby squirming inside. On both sides of me were bundles of tiny sweet Williams ready to bloom. I sipped from a tall glass of ice water, letting it drizzle down my chin and onto my chest. My whole being felt soothed.

I recalled the first time I held Jake, my firstborn son, in my arms. I had stared in awe at the tiny human who had grown in my womb. That was absolutely the most exhilarating day of my life up to that point. Other than a few seconds now and then when people nagged me into mistrusting myself, I had no doubt my first baby was in fact a male.

With the exception of taking my baby daughter out of my womb and holding her like I did in my dreams with Jake, I was sure I was carrying our first daughter.

While Carrie, Sky, Jake, and Diane's toddler played in the dirt a few feet away, I thanked God for my tears of joy, and for the health and strength to be able to make a little progress in our front yard. I thanked God for the flowers that would soon be in full bloom, smiling at us. I also thanked God for our old dog, Brandy, and our six new ducks eating and pooping all the earwigs around our back porch. We would sell Brandy's litter of purebred pups to help us purchase school clothes. Our six or eight chickens gave us eggs each day, and we had a passel of adorable chicks. For all that was good, I thanked God. At last I asked Him for the strength and the money to get the rest of our front yard leveled and planted with grass seed before it got too cold to germinate.

"Come on, kids, let's get out those rakes and shovels and dig in again," I shouted. But the kids couldn't hear one single word over the sound of our neighbor's Bobcat. They ran up to the porch for fear Gary might run over them. He drove his Bobcat right up next to me and turned off the engine.

Gary had probably spoken a few words to me in the three or four years he'd lived next door. I was in shock when he asked, "So what is it you want done out here, Sophia?"

I wondered if this was some kind of joke. I felt sure his wife would rather we didn't live here at all. She often complained my children had or hadn't done this or that. Once she called the Division of Family Services on us "plygs." She told them we were giving our food stamps away and starving the children. The service worker just laughed after he saw our plump, tall, healthy children. He said our neighbor's "simple-minded" complaint came when she saw my older boys fight over a piece of candy.

From our front porch, the kids and I were encircled in clouds of dust for nearly an hour. All of us eagerly watched Gary level and grade the earth from my flower garden down to the road. When our live motion picture had come to an end, we meandered inside to clean up.

I looked in the hallway mirror just inside our door and laughed out loud. The dust powder had entered my smile lines and covered my teeth with grit.

The next day, when Swede and I were on our way to purchase lawn seed from our neighborhood Intermountain Farmers, I told him about Gary's good deed.

"Yeah, I know," he said. "I gave him a piece of my mind! I told him, 'You damned well ought to be ashamed of yourself sitting on your ass right next door to Sophia, watching her try to level the whole damned yard with a rake and a shovel. Dammit, Gary, if you're any kind of man, you'll get your ass over there and get it done for her. If its money for gas you're worried about I'll give it to you."

I was still so elated over the help, even if it was coerced, I fluttered around the store full of appreciation for Swede, for Gary, for the whole wide world. I splurged on a thin, five-foot maple tree and some quality lawn seed.

About five feet from the road and our bumpy dirt driveway, I planted my tree and nicknamed it "my Karleen tree," after our forthcoming baby girl.

I watered the grass seeds three times a day. I guarded our freshly planted area as if it were gold, and watched intently for the first pristine blades of grass to pop through the earth. As days passed, the mailman and most passersby commented on how nice the yard was looking. After seven years of that weed-patch-pile-of-rubble eyesore they'd been looking at, I could only imagine what they really wanted to say.

※

Mark started calling more often. We would have some great phone conversations, and the family sent letters back and forth quite often. We missed him, but things were looking up. We didn't have a dad or a husband around, but we were able to get off food stamps and not go back to dumpster diving. What a great source of pride for us.

Mark told me Diane was always anxious to get the mail so she could make sure each of our letters from him weighed the same and were the same thickness.

Every time we received a check from Mark, Diane and I would go through our long list of expenses and try to budget the money. There was still not enough. Often our conversations would get heated as we'd disagree on which bills must be paid, which ones would have to wait, and how we should divide a few personal dollars for our "sanity."

Diane felt any extra money should be divided fifty-fifty. Of course I couldn't see that as fair at all. She had three young children, and I had four older kids and another baby on the way.

"Dammit!" Mark said when I told him about the disagreement. "I don't know what in the hell either of you are thinking, but I've decided the way it will be. You two should pay all the bills first. If you can squeeze any money out for anything else, split it into tenths. You take six tenths and she can take four."

"Okay, sounds good. I can deal with that, and I think it will be all right with her as well," I told him.

"Well it damn well better be," Mark shouted. "If not, that's just tough. I'm sick of hearing you two gripe and whine about everything.

I can't ever do anything for you without feeling obligated to do the same for her. If I want to buy you something I have to get Diane something. If I write you a ten-page letter, I'd have to write her a ten-page letter—"

"But that's how Diane understands fairness and equality," I said.

Still, her perception of fair never worked for me. When Mark bought Diane her rings that looked too much like mine, it wasn't fair to me. Just one year after they were married, Mark, in trying to be fair, bought us identical heart lockets for Valentines' Day (their engagement anniversary). I didn't see that as fair. But Mark had done his best. He got gifts he liked and wanted to give to each of us. If they had been different, he worried one of us would feel the other piece of jewelry was more elegant or expensive. So he was sure if he got us the same or nearly the same things he couldn't be faulted.

A year later I had to tell Mark the truth when he asked. "Why don't you wear the heart pendant I bought you?"

I tried to explain it. "Apparently Diane likes to have and do the same things you do with or for me. When I got contact lenses, she wanted some. When I started fixing up my kitchen, she needed to fix hers. If you take me to see a show, she wants to see the same show. If we go to Lava Hot Springs, you have to take Diane to Lava Hot Springs. You just watch! When I buy a personalized license plate, she will have to get one also.

"On the contrary, Mark, if you take Diane to a Jazz game, I don't want you to take me to one. If you take her to the zoo, I don't want you to take me to the zoo! If she deep-cleans her house on Monday, I have to do mine another day. I am me. I need and want my autonomy. I don't want to be like anyone else. I don't want you to buy me the same things you buy her. I don't want you to take me to the same movies, restaurants, or hotels, either."

The Oak Ridge Boys' lyrics "Trying to love two women is like a ball and chain" seemed fitting for Mark. I felt sorry for him and for any polygamist men who really tried to be fair. It seemed they could not win, no matter what they did or didn't do.

CHAPTER 28

Guilt and Punishment
1982

My mother finally got to retire from nursing in 1981. She was sixty-six years old, and had more time to spend with her family and grandchildren. Dad and his sons finished another huge fourplex, on his property in Bluffdale, Utah. Mom got to move from her tiny home in Murray, that she'd been sharing with a sister-wife. What a treat it was to watch her choose all of the colors she wanted for her upstairs apartment. She was feeling like the Queen of Sheba in her new house.

Not long after she moved in, she told me she was going to move downstairs, because one of her new sister-wives wanted to live upstairs instead of in the basement.

"Why?" I snapped at Mom. "You love this house! It is yours. You chose all of the colors and carpet and paint you like. You're settled in and deserve this beautiful home, Mom. Don't allow them to do this to you. Ora can move downstairs!"

Her eyes were wet with tears as she said sorrowfully, "It doesn't really matter much to me, Sophia, I need to do whatever your dad wants me to do."

I knew it did matter to her. She'd only been in her home for six months and she was already being asked to move—booted out.

"It's always what Owen wants—what Owen needs, which really means what Aunt Eleanor or his other wives want or need! I exclaimed. "What about what you want for once in your life?"

I desperately wanted to shake some sense into my mother. I wanted to scream at Dad for his lack of sensitivity toward her dreams, needs, and wishes. Anyone could take advantage of Mom's goodness, since they knew she would give in to anyone at any time. I wanted to smack Dad and his new wife clear to the moon for their injustice. But nothing I did or said would matter one iota.

She moved out of her lovely home, the one she finally didn't have to share, after all these years, into the basement.

※

My sister Francine had become a certified midwife, and I was seeing her for my regular checkups. She assured me everything was going as well as could be expected, other than the constant discomfort and pain in my lower abdomen.

By the end of January I'd already gone into labor several times, just as I'd done with Schuyler. But this time my contractions were stronger and harder, so I called Mark and begged him to fly home. He dropped everything and got home in plenty of time. In fact, he had more than two weeks to spare.

One day, I went through six or seven hours of hard labor before it completely quit again. I was ready and willing to have this baby by C-section. If we could have afforded it, I'd have pled with a doctor to just cut her out of my miserable, huge body. My emotions were raw in every sense of the word.

Mark waited during the whole fourteen days his boss had given him off, before he had to leave again. During the nights he slept with Diane, my heart ached with jealousy. What would life be like if I could have a husband of my own, and not have to feel this kind of abandonment? Feeling ripped into pieces, was by far more unbearable than my pregnancy.

The night before Mark went back to California, we held each other, cried, talked, and laughed for hours. I tried to explain how difficult it was to have to share the two or three days he is home after he'd been gone for weeks on end. I was certain Diane felt the same way. But for this time, being so pregnant and feeling so vulnerable, this sharing was unbearable. Mark assured me it was hard for him to be home for only a few days and have to leave again, too.

We reminisced like we'd never done before. We laughed about the good, wild, crazy, happy times, and lamented over the many things that had not gone as we had planned or dreamed. Neither of us mentioned the innumerable fights and disagreements in the years gone by. Right then we wanted each other, and knew we'd do our best to make a go of things.

By the time we got to the airport, I wanted to lock the car doors and make Diane stay there and wait while I told my husband goodbye alone, in privacy, the way it should be.

I wished with all my heart I'd never encouraged Mark to marry her. What in God's name was I thinking? My huge, pregnant belly felt so tight I feared my horrendous grief would start me into labor. But there was nothing I could do; not one thing, except try to hide my agony and behave myself like a good, sweet, honorable sister-wife should do.

Diane, her kids, and my kids all stared at Mark's plane until it flew out of sight. I knew he wouldn't be able to come back for our daughter's birth. I knew he wasn't abandoning me—it just felt like he was. The throbbing pain pierced through my whole body. I was weak and sick all over. Even in my embarrassment, I couldn't hide my anguish this time around.

I couldn't move. From a bench next to the huge window, I watched Diane and our kids walk away. In a few minutes Alan returned to see what was going on. He looked so sad when he saw me.

"Go ahead and walk with Aunt Diane," I told him. "I need to be alone. I'll follow you to the car. I'll get there as soon as I can."

Early one morning during the second week of February, I woke up to a gush of warm, thick liquid pouring onto the bed between my legs. I'd never felt this sensation before, but remembered other women talking about the amniotic sac breaking and spilling the fluid even before labor began, so I stayed calm.

I wanted to call Mark, yet I didn't want to. No matter; he had already told me he couldn't come back so soon after his last long visit. I was angry, but not because I felt it was his fault. I was annoyed over the whole situation—especially as the labor began and progressed. I wanted him to know I was in labor so he could be part of it, at least in his heart. No, he should know so he could worry about me. It's the least the father of my baby could do. Then again, maybe he shouldn't even have the privilege of knowing his daughter would soon be born.

After my emotional battle, I decided not to ruin his day by telling him about a situation he had no control over. I'd wait and call him after the baby was born.

I finally got Jake up and had him go downstairs to tell Diane I'd soon be leaving to go to Aunt Amelia's, and would she please look after my boys as we had arranged. When she came up to see what was going on, I told her not to tell Mark anything, one way or the other. It was my right to keep him posted or not.

Aunt Amelia and Dad came to get me. All the way to her house, I still felt angry and abandoned. I couldn't quit sobbing.

Francine and Aunt Amelia made up the bed with sterile sheets and pads, and then put the blankets back on. As quickly as possible, I climbed under the blankets, lay in a fetal position, and cried some more. Francine and Aunt Amelia rubbed my back and talked me through each pain as well as they could. They tried to soothe my fears and anxieties by reassuring me everything would go well, even without Mark there.

My labor progressed rapidly. The contractions were excruciatingly brutal when compared to my previous deliveries. With every intensifying pain, I wondered if we'd make it this time around. At the transitional stage, I became so emotional I could hardly hold myself together.

I heard Mom and Auntie whispering, and then I saw their worried faces. Francine told them, "Go get Dad, now!"

In a short time, a brother-in-law and Dad came in and administered to me. Dad put a drop or two of consecrated olive oil on the crown of my head. With their hands placed on the top of my head, Dad pronounced a blessing for my unborn infant and me, saying we would make it through this ordeal perfectly whole and healthy.

For hours the labor pains continued without any progress. I'd never screamed during childbirth before, but I couldn't help but shriek with this intolerable suffering. I was scared!

Finally Francine told me my baby was presenting face first. Her cranial bones weren't able to compress, as would normally happen. She was caught between my pelvic bone and my tailbone. I had two choices. They could call an ambulance and admit me into the hospital for an emergency C-section, or we could continue to try at home, but risk one or both of us dying.

"I can't go to the hospital! We don't have time!" I told her. "We've got to get her out now, before we both die!"

Francine's hands, like forceps, gently tugged on the baby's chin with each contraction, still to no avail.

"I've got to push her out soon, or we won't make it!" I screamed.

For some reason, in nature's amazing and divine order, I knew what to do. "Help me get up! I've got to get up on my knees!" I told them. With Auntie on one side and my mother on the other, I grasped their arms tightly and bore down, long, hard, steady pushes, one after another.

"Push, keep pushing!" Francine and Mom said. "It's working," Francine shouted. "Keep going, Sophia, you can do it! Keep pushing! I can feel her forehead now! I just about have her chin out from under your pelvic bone! Come on honey, you can do it. Don't give up."

I screamed and cursed some more. I pushed until I thought my whole insides would come out with my baby. I knew it was a matter of life or death.

"Now, gentle, steady pushes," Francine coached me. "It won't be long and you'll have your baby in your arms!"

When Karleen was finally born, I fell backwards like a rag doll and sobbed. Francine got Karleen breathing and handed her to me, but my muscles wouldn't work enough to reach for her. I didn't have the strength to hold her eight-pound four-ounce body in my arms, or even to lift my own head up. My mother positioned Karleen on her side right next to me so I could stare at her.

I couldn't contain my gratitude for our lives, yet I couldn't let go of my guilt. In our religion, there was always something more to feel ashamed and guilty about. Again, I felt responsible for everything that had gone awry during the delivery. God, I was sure, not only punished me, but my infant child for my sins. Exodus 20:5 says, "For the sins of the parents are visited on the third and fourth generations."

If only I were a better person. If I hadn't encouraged Chad's flirting and attention a couple of years ago, God wouldn't have punished my infant. There wouldn't be bruises on her face and body. Her eyes wouldn't be so swollen she couldn't open them. She'd have a strong, healthy cry instead of her lethargic, barely audible whimper. I could hardly hear or see her breathing.

When she was at last able to open one little eye a tiny bit and look at me, I was sure she knew her suffering was my fault. Karleen should have been thriving and rooting about for my breasts, as any strong, healthy baby would have been by then.

Tears rolled down my cheeks onto the sheets. I asked God to forgive me for hurting an innocent child.

In an instant, I was full of resentment toward God. "It's not her fault." I said under my breath. "It's mine, not hers! How could you do this to my innocent baby girl?"

I slept for a few hours and then called Mark to tell him about his amazing daughter. He said he already heard about her and was grateful we were both doing okay now.

I pushed my anger toward Diane deeper inside. She should have let me tell Karleen's dad about her first. I also knew it wasn't Mark's fault he couldn't be there; but in spite of everything, I was resentful, and knew it would take me a long time to feel settled.

※

Not long after Karleen was born, Diane and I agreed I should watch her three children while she worked as a secretary. We needed and wanted the extra income. Since she had typing and shorthand skills, she could earn more income than I could, and I was happy I didn't have to leave my young children with a babysitter.

Things were going pretty well for a while. Diane and I were becoming "as thick as thieves," as the saying goes. We wanted to and we had to, since we were now sharing the same broken-down car and making all of the household decisions. With no husband at home to be concerned about or to share in the family evenings, we spent more time visiting with each other and our children.

As canning season approached, Jake and Alan helped me with seven-month-old Karleen, the usual household jobs, and the care of the other kids. During this time, we put twenty-five bushels of peaches, apricots, and pears in jars and processed them. Over the next few months, we picked twelve huge boxes of tomatoes from a neighbor's field and turned them into sauce, juice, and salsa. We picked ten 5-gallon buckets of Concord grapes from Swede's vines and processed them into grape juice and jelly.

On another of those inhumane, tiring days, Diane came home from work, gathered her kids, and disappeared into the basement as she had done nearly every day since canning season began. I sent Jake downstairs to tell her I needed to talk to her, and would she please come upstairs. Diane came up and leaned over the black wrought-iron stair railing.

"Jake said you wanted to talk to me?"

I continued to slip the skins off the boiled tomatoes before I cut and dropped them into jars. "I'm hoping you will help me get the rest of this canning done, so I can get some rest too."

"Well, maybe I can," Diane said, "but I am pretty tired from working all day."

My stomach started to ache. Even the slightest confrontation scared me. "I am tired too, Diane. My days never end. When you get home from work, you gather your kids and disappear into your house, sit in front of your television, and enjoy your kids."

"But you're home all day with your kids," she replied, "and you can take a break whenever you want to and—"

"There are no breaks, Diane!" I snapped back. "When can I take a break while taking care of eight kids all day and trying to keep up with the house, laundry, diapers, meals, dishes, and all the past months of canning and yard work that still needs to be done?"

Diane yelled back, "But I give you half the money I earn, and that's not fair! I have to leave my kids and work all day, and you reap the benefits!"

"I do more work in a day than you've ever thought of doing, Diane! You wouldn't have a job or any money at all if I weren't caring for your kids. Who would watch, feed, bathe, and love them like I do, for anything less? While you're at work in your quiet office all day long, my hectic, noisy days never end. When you're watching TV, I'm still working, doing everything I didn't get done while I tended your kids! If you can find someone else, maybe you should, and then I won't feel like a crazy maniac all day long, every day!"

"I don't see why I should have to help you with the canning you chose to do. I didn't buy all this fruit! I don't want to have to work all day and come home to more work," she exclaimed.

I calmed down a little. "Well, Diane, you and your children eat just as much or more of the fruit than we do, so if you want to relinquish that privilege, I won't expect you to help me get it canned."

Diane knew she and her children had been eating gobs of peaches as well as the other fruits and vegetables my kids and I had canned.

We sat on Jake's and Alan's twin beds, where we finally retreated away from lots of little ears, to finish our first and last real argument that finally wound down into a sane conversation. Diane agreed to help me wrap up our workdays together. She said she'd start making dinner for her own kids, or she would help out with the dishes whenever I made dinner for all of us. And I promised her I'd try to have more patience with her when she was having a tough day. We gave each other a big hug. With those promises, we renewed our love for each other and our desire to live the principle of plural marriage as sweet, loving sister-wives should.

CHAPTER 29

A Friendship from God
1982–1984

I wanted to believe. I convinced myself I was solid and making everything work out wonderfully without Mark. Apparently it wasn't true.

My ongoing battle with weight seemed to drag me down as much, or more, than anything else in my life. My compulsive overeating helped to numb my feelings of inadequacy as a parent, a wife, and a person. Over the years, with the exception of having my mouth wired shut, I tried nearly every diet I'd ever heard or read about, considering my lack of financial means.

I felt alone in crowds of people, among family members, and at church. When I was all by myself, visceral ghosts from every corner of my world would show up. On a wide movie theatre screen, in electrifying colors, they would recap my failures and harass me about my years and years of defeat.

I avoided full-length mirrors like they were demons. To me, they were. Those evil monsters punished and shamed me even more. If I happened to see the reflection of my 225-pound, grotesque, cumbersome body as I walked by a window, I imagined I should be vivisected and skinned alive. In my daydreams, I wished I could take the butcher knife to myself and carve and chop away until there would be nothing left of me but my medium-size bones covered with perfectly taut, light brown skin.

"God, if you are as powerful and omnipotent as we are supposed to believe you are, then why can't you make me stop eating? I have asked and begged, pled, and tried to make bargains with you! I have tried with every ounce of energy I can muster to have the will power to quit this obsessive overeating. Nothing works! You see, God, this is another reason I have such a hard time believing in you. In most of my requests and pleadings, you have abandoned and punished me. Why, God? Why don't you help me? Why can't you make me stop overeating?"

※

For girls' camp in 1982, my sweetheart of a mother agreed to stay in a camping trailer to help me out. Camping was not something she liked to do, so I was extremely grateful when she agreed to help me again. Three years earlier when I was a camp counselor, she watched Jack so I could keep nursing him. This time, it was my Karleen she'd help with. In between my duties as one of the three camp directors, teaching classes, and attending fireside meetings in the beautiful hills around Kamas, Utah, I could spend more time with my baby because of my mother's help.

On the second day at camp, I packed five-month-old Karleen in my arms and walked from camp to camp to see how everyone was faring with the mixture of personalities, needs and supplies. When I reached "Camp Gardenia," I visited with Michelle, an old friend who had dated my brother James when they were teenagers.

Karleen and I went back to Michelle's campsite at lunchtime. For nearly two hours, we sat on a blanket under the huge pines and quaking aspens, and got reacquainted.

A month after girls' camp, Michelle brought her five children over to my house for lunch as we had planned. During our visit, she told me she'd been praying for a long time to find a close friendship with someone who would care about her, and about whom she could also care.

Soon Michelle and I began to exercise, walk and diet together. We hung out with our younger kids and even began to plan our work, outings, meals, and holiday celebrations together. She became more of a friend to me than I ever knew was possible. She doted on me, my brain, my talents, and regularly reminded me of my potential. She raved about my abilities and attributes, and always defended my opinions and me. As the days passed, I discovered her constant and unflinching goodness and loyalty to my children and me. I began to think Michelle would make the perfect husband. We could enjoy everything in our relationship but the sexual aspect.

As time passed, Mark had a few longer breaks between his jobs in California. When he first met Michelle, he was kind and tolerant of our friendship. Before long, however, he began to despise and resent her presence in my life. With each passing month, his dislike for Michelle intensified.

"Don't you get it? She is a lesbian! She wants you all to herself," he said. "Michelle speaks and writes words of endearment to you the way a man would write. She wants to steal you from me, Sophia! She needs you all the time and makes you feel obligated to help her. There is always one reason or another why you have to rescue her."

"I'm telling you, she is so smart and manipulative she knows all the right words—the ones you want and need to hear—to convince you to trust everything about her. She'll continue to plot and connive to take you away from me, whether you know it or not! She compliments me to make you believe she cares about me. While you believe she has our best interest at heart, you buy into all her shit. She twists and turns those compliments around to make her criticisms of me sound and feel valid, then Michelle decides if what I'm doing, or not doing, is good or bad, and you believe her. She is as brilliant as she is sly!"

"You must really think I'm stupid!" I retorted. "Do you think I'm so dumb she could sway me and my thoughts enough to break us up?"

Of course, Mark adamantly believed everything he claimed, and in the quiet of the nights I'd mull it over and over in my heart and mind. He was right in many of the things he said. Michelle was brilliant. She had a knack with words and an incredible photographic memory. I couldn't blame him for his point of view. Even I was a little suspicious of the notes she'd written to me. The verses she wrote were a lot like a boyfriend's notes to his girlfriend. In many ways, I started to feel overpowered by her need for us to spend so much time together. Her demands definitely stole too much of my time away from my family and work. Still, I believed it was my duty to rescue her from her deep bouts of depression. She was there for me when Mark was gone. Who else would be there for her when she needed help?

I still couldn't or wouldn't believe she was a lesbian, or that she would deliberately do anything to steal me away from Mark. Even though her requests and actions were dragging me away from him, I pled with him to understand.

"Who will help her when she needs help? I can't just leave her and her children all alone when she feels like killing herself."

"She's not your problem, Sophia. You can't keep trying to fix her and everyone else. You are everyone's sucker—you always have been. They call, you jump!"

In my heart, I knew Mark was right about that part, too. I couldn't fix Michelle no matter how hard I tried. Leaving my kids and Mark to rescue her was only a temporary fix. I'd be exhausted, and within a few days or weeks, she was down again in another deep bout of depression—one right after another. For quite a while—because of Mark's insistence, I stopped hanging out with her and quit going over there every time she called. It didn't stop my constant worries, though. I wondered if I would also be held accountable to God for her death and the horrendous toll it would take on her children if she ended her life.

My sister Francine had finally had enough moving, sharing, and sister-wife grief. She left her husband of twenty-seven years, and our sister, Hannah. "There are at least a hundred reasons why I need to leave," she assured me.

I knew and understood her reasons quite well. It didn't matter that I had been her strength through her many trials the past ten or more years, or that I'd listened to her ongoing woes and rescued her from many debilitating physical and emotional traumas. I still felt abandoned and I was disappointed in her decision to leave the gospel, and me. Before the tables turned, it was her unwavering prayers and testimony; her talks of damnation and encouragement; her example of "enduring to the end," always nudging me back to my own dutiful existence.

"If we'll just hold to the straight and narrow path leading to God, there are abundant blessings in store for us, if we qualify," she would tell me.

Standing between my bed and closet, I stared at a picture of Francine on my chest of drawers. Right out loud, I proudly looked in the mirror and pronounced to God and Francine, "I will never leave polygamy! No matter how much this way of life hurts and how crazy it makes me feel, I will endure to the end! I will finish what you taught me to do, even if you can't or won't!"

Then I stared at the brave, bold young woman—or that crazy, altruistic mother—in my mirror and said, "Did you hear that, Sophia? Did you hear what you just said? Now you are stuck in this insanity forever, you idiot!"

※

Ever since Mark left for California, Swede had taken my kids and me under his wing, as if we were his very own. He never had any children. To have us involved in his life was as wonderful for him as it was for us. He was a godsend from the first day he brought his shotgun in hand to the front door of our old chicken-coop bungalow, to warn me to keep our dogs locked up. He and I were dear friends. We were like brother and sister, surrogate father and daughter, and he was a grandpa to my children, who adored him.

Early one early morning at Swede's house, he told me the same little red Opel we'd been tracking in the car ads had been marked down from $1,200 to $800 within a two-week period. He said, "Come on, Sophia, we're going to go buy that car right now!" He smiled teasingly. "Besides, I'm getting damn tired of you borrowing my damn truck. I'm not going to have you and your damn kids trailing me around town, having to go every damn place I go!" Then we laughed some more.

I'd been taught pride was not an honorable feeling. When I didn't buy into guilt, I discovered another wondrous sense of accomplishment. With the money I earned from extra housekeeping jobs, I paid off my loan for a brand-new Bernina sewing machine, a grain mill, and a Bosch bread mixer. Then I borrowed the $800 from the bank and bought my own little red Opel!

In February 1983, Mark made it home in time for the birth of his pretty and petite second daughter. Diane's lovely baby girl rounded out her family of two girls and two boys.

It seemed we were adapting to Mark's short visits. In fact, I'd become so independent, his short visits became somewhat problematic. I always felt like a single mother, whether Mark was around or not. In his two and a half year absence, I was adjusting to our curse or blessing. Since Mark wasn't there to help or to hinder, in the parenting department, things were more consistent. Whether good or bad, our days and nights had totally become our own.

Before long, Michelle was back in my life again. She reminded me of all the right things to do and to be. She encouraged me to hang in there with Mark since I was married to such a kind and loving man. I should show him how grateful I was for his efforts, more than I'd ever shown him before. She passed on lessons she'd been taught in Relief Society and meetings, since I had last attended.

"They're just things we've heard a hundred times over," she would tell me. "Pray for Mark, Sophia. Behind every good man is a good woman. If he's not doing what is right, it's because you aren't praying hard enough."

I wanted to slap her for repeating that compulsory statement, but at the same time I believed in its craziness; so I did what she said. I began to pray as I'd never done before.

Because I felt like my teenage boys had slipped off the straight and narrow path to God and were making such unwise decisions, I once again enrolled all of my children in The Group's private school. I hoped the influence there would help transform my boys, who were often angry and rebellious, into exemplary young bearers of the priesthood.

I also decided, as I had so many times before, if I wanted to be the good mother I ought to be, I would rededicate my life to the Lord. I'd get even more involved in church activities and in my religion. And for the hundredth time in my life, I decided if I was doing what I should, I would be happy. By my example, my teenage boys would have to comply and behave themselves.

One morning after I dropped the boys off at the RCA building, I kept nodding off while driving back down the narrow, winding frontage road toward home. *I only have a few more blocks before I'll be home,* I tried to convince myself. *Then I can take a nap with Karleen and Jack.*

Suddenly I heard shouting. "Wake up, Sophia! Wake up now!" My eyes opened just in time to see a huge semi-truck swerve to the side of the road. Almost too late, I realized my car had crossed into the oncoming traffic, heading straight in front of the truck and toward the freeway. "I'm awake now!" I called back at my inner voice. I pulled off the road. In tears of gratitude I thanked my soul, my God, for having rescued my children and me many times before. Like a swift kick in the butt, that experience seemed to grant me the fortitude to carry on.

⚜

One Sunday morning when Mark was home for a weekend visit, I begged him to Sunday school with me. How stupid of me. Of course he wouldn't go. I got to hear his list of reasons once again. He didn't need or want to. It wasn't for him and never would be.

All four of the boys argued, whined, and complained about getting out of bed and going with me. But then Jake started to vociferously re-gurgitate his father's lengthy list of excuses he felt should exempt him and his brothers from attending church as well. As usual, my stomach began to churn. What if Mark heard Jake's objections all the way into the bedroom? I tried to hush him, reminding him that his dad was home, but it was too late.

Mark stomped down the hallway into our front room and began to punch Jake. While Jake tried to defend himself, the rest of the kids and I yelled at their dad to stop. He stopped for only a few seconds, shot darts of disgust at me for interfering, and then started in again. He slapped Jake's head, back, or arms, saying, "Don't ever talk to your mother like that, you little shit head! When she tells you to do something, you do it! You hear me? Do you hear me, you fucking little shit head? I'm sick and tired of listening to your back talk and mouthing off at your mother!"

Mark's face was blood red. To protect himself from his father's blows, Jake curled himself into a ball. He wrapped his arms across his head and cried.

Mark carried on, "You hear me, you fucking little asshole? No more back talk, no more—"

I couldn't take it any longer. I grabbed Mark's shoulders to pull him off of Jake. He shoved me backward.

"You stay out of this, Sophia!"

He continued to hit Jake's chest, head, and back while the rest of us begged him to stop. By then, Mark was so enraged and incensed he didn't even feel my pathetically weak punches trying to knock him over.

When Mark finally stopped and left the room still raging, I tried to hug Jake, but he pushed me away and covered his face with his sleeves.

"I hate his guts! I hate him! I hate him," Jake bellowed as he ran out and slammed the front door.

With tears streaming down my face, I followed him out the door. "Come back, Jake! Please don't leave!" I called until he disappeared from my sight.

I was worried sick. I couldn't catch my breath, and I wondered if I'd ever hear from Jake again. I decided I would not speak to Mark until Jake returned.

Meanwhile, as Mark often accused me of doing, I sulked and grieved over his violence toward his son and his family. I searched for Jake for days. I couldn't sleep at night, wondering where he was and if he was okay. At last, three days later, he came home. He said he'd been in a safe place with a friend, waiting for his dad to go back to California.

I was still so devastated about Mark's abuse toward Jake I couldn't talk to him for days before and after he took his long journey back to work.

In trying my best to raise my children, I made a million excuses for Mark's temper, fits of rage, and his consistent verbal and oftentimes overly harsh discipline. Our children had more than their share of mental and physical anguish. They had written notes to their dad and me, saying, "Yes, Dad, you are right. I am a piece of shit, a dumb, lazy ass, a stupid . . . an idiot." I couldn't bear to save those devastating letters reiterating the words they'd heard blasted in their direction so many times over the years they could never be counted.

I'd hold my hysterical, sobbing children in my arms and push their hair out of their eyes and beg them not to be mad at their father who, "...didn't really mean to hurt you. He's just had a bad day. He really does love you. Your dad didn't really mean any of the terrible things he said. He just wants you to . . ."

I fed my children too damn many reasons and excuses for their father's bad conduct. In my ignorance and inability to know what to do differently as their mother, I thought my behavior was acceptable, normal, and justified. In that, the kids and I could continue to forgive and forget as we were always told to do.

A week later, I finally dared make an attempt to get through to Mark.

"Beating on someone isn't ever the answer," I said. All Jake was doing was repeating your words and actions about not wanting to go to church—behaviors he learned from you. His words of rebellion were exactly yours—the ones he's heard you say to me umpteen times in his young life."

"He deserved everything he got, Sophia! He doesn't have a right to talk to you like that," Mark exclaimed.

I knew better than to try, as nothing I ever proposed seemed to make much difference. Mark justified all of his negative behaviors by blaming Diane, our kids, and me for our inadequacies. "If you two weren't so passive, I wouldn't have to be so aggressive! If he or she wouldn't have made me mad, then I wouldn't have had to . . ."

Though many of life's ordeals are tragic, it's always rewarding when we can discover blessings among those disasters. I knew I could no longer make up excuses or reasons for Mark's, my own, or anyone else's mean, unkind, or abusive behaviors toward our children. There was no excuse! I wouldn't accept one, or make up one ever again. I had to do something different! The scary part was this was a concept and undertaking I knew nothing about.

CHAPTER 30

Birth, Deaths, and Suicide
1984

For three months I felt an urgency to get to Park City to spend some time with Mark's sister, my precious friend Ann. She had invited us to come up many times since her husband moved her into a beautiful new home next to his first wife's new home in the canyon. We met when we were eleven, at her mom's home where Mark teased us about using his game. The next time we met, she was skating with Royce, my first love, just before he asked me to skate. Four years later, I married her brother. Since Mark and I first started dating, my friendship with Ann had been solid and comfortable. No matter our visits were far apart and way too few, we were like best buddies whose love and respect took off right where it was before.

Near the end of February, I told Mark I was going to take the kids the following weekend and go see his sister. For the past two years he and I would plan to visit Ann, just an hour away, but for one reason or another, he would end up canceling.

"Ann and I both want you to come up, Mark, but if you decide not to, I'm going anyway," I said.

"Maybe next weekend," he replied. "My check should get here by then, and I'll be more relaxed. I just got home. I want to stick around a while before I go anywhere. I'll be here a few months, so we can go later."

"You've already put this visit off too many times," I said. "If you want to go up there later, you can, but I'm going to take the kids and go this coming weekend."

Minutes before we were ready to pull out of the driveway, Mark decided he would go with us. We met Ann and her two eldest sons at a gas station just off the highway. They piled our things in a small trailer. Our five kids, Mark, and I (with my nine-months-pregnant belly) climbed onto the back of three snowmobiles and hung on for dear life. Ann and her sons drove us up the snow-packed roads that wound around the hillsides. At the top, our boys begged them for more fun.

The three-day weekend with Ann and her family was the most pleasant event we'd enjoyed with our kids for a long, long time. I was more grateful than words could express for the wonderful time we spent together.

On our way home, Mark, the kids, and I talked about our deep love for Ann, and what a perfect person she was to us. "She's one of those perfect spirits who seems to be too good to be here among all us wicked ones." I said.

On Monday morning, the day after we returned from our visit with Ann and her family, I woke up to a warning voice in my head. "Get your things to your mother's house now—today."

As I had done a zillion times before, I debated with my soul. *I'm only one week overdue. I've got at least two more weeks to go.*

All of my babies but Jake had been born late by two or more weeks. To avoid further disappointment I added three weeks to this one, also. Still, I'd had plenty of occasions in my life to know, if I paid attention to and followed my sixth sense, I'd be grateful. If I didn't, I was usually in some kind of trouble.

The sterilizing process and list of things to gather for the delivery was almost memorized by now. I gathered the clean white bed sheets, the four large white bed pads I'd previously sewn together, a set of boy baby clothes and a set of girl baby clothes, cloth diapers, and sleepers, and tied them all in brown paper bags. Then I set the oven at two hundred degrees and baked them for one hour.

After lunch, I took Schuyler, Jack, Karleen, and my pre-natal packages to Mom's basement apartment and spent the rest of the day there.

For the first time ever, I fell asleep on Mom's couch instead of cleaning for her while we visited. She took my kids to play outside on the huge swing set Dad had built for his grandchildren. When she saw I was still sleeping, she took them to visit with their grandpa in his office upstairs.

When I found them after waking up, Mom said, "You must have really needed the rest, Sophia. You slept through every noise we made. As far as I know, you've never done that before."

In the late afternoon I rushed home. I wanted to spend a few minutes with Mark before he disappeared into the basement with Diane.

I had no sooner entered my kitchen from the garage, when I had a long, agonizing contraction. When the kids saw my white-knuckled grip on the countertop, I told them, "Your baby sister wants to get out of here right now!"

My infant's demands were more evident with each close, strong, and lingering contraction. I called Amy to let her know I was in labor. In the nice warm shower between the staggering pains, I smiled with gratitude. I was finally going to have an early baby, instead of three to four weeks late.

Amy arrived in time to coach me for forty-five minutes and then cut the baby's umbilical cord. While Mark, Mom, and Amy were busy fussing over Anne's beautiful skin color and face, I felt an uncanny separation between them and me. Barely above my newborn, I could sense and hear a young male voice. "I'll see you in a couple years! I love you! Goodbye, Sister."

"No," my soul told that little spirit. "You don't want to be here with us. I can't handle the children I already have! I can't be the kind of mother you deserve."

Again he tenderly declared his intentions. "I'll be with you in a few years, Sister. I love you . . . I love you . . . goodbye . . ." His soft words faded like the volume of a radio slowly turned down, down, and then off.

Because of my constant feelings of inadequacy, our family dysfunctions, and our lack of money, we had decided not to have another child we felt we could not do justice to. But I knew the unborn spirit talking to Anne would be the fifth son Mark and I always knew we would have. His little spirit's words were the motivation I needed to change my mind.

※

The horrible news that my Uncle Rulon's son, my cousin Louis, had shot himself in the head, spread like a tornado, leaving nearly everyone in The Group in a muddled frenzy.

I had thought of suicide on occasion, but the reality of it was vastly different than I could ever have imagined. Everyone's prayers and condolences went out to Louis's large plural families and his innumerable friends and relatives. Most of us were confused and horrified Louis would commit such a deed. After all, he was considered by many to be a perfect spiritual man, just like his father.

We always understood suicide to be a sin, equal to the murder of another human being. Still, in my own bewilderment I was infuriated by the know-it-alls who had already condemned Louis to hell for his "heinous crime." I was also frustrated with those who instantly forgave and justified him because he was Uncle Rulon's son, who had been such a "wonderful and righteous man." It made me consider all of the not-so-fortunate people who had taken their lives—the suicide victims who were never given the time of day, by those who exonerated Louis. "Oh, yes, they will be damned for sure, they'd insist."

Once again, when we needed to hear some consoling and uplifting words, many of us found solace from the pulpit. My father counseled us to show unconditional love for Louis, even in his self-inflicted death. "None of us know or will ever understand the turmoil or state of mind Louis was in when he took his own life," he said. "We should thank God we don't have to make any decisions concerning Louis's salvation. That is up to our almighty, all-knowing, ever-present God."

With all the pandemonium about Louis's suicide, more issues surfaced. Rumors of atrocities that had previously taken place on The Group's Pinesdale Ranch, started to recirculate. Six years before Louis's suicide, his stepson Adam had stabbed him. We heard only snippets of the repercussions of Adam's behavior, but apparently three men had "punished" (tortured) the young man for his "sins." We also heard a whole gamut of denials and justifications for their crimes.

The things I'd heard before troubled me back then, but now I felt the need to hear the other side of the story, "right from the horse's mouth," as the old folk used to say.

I knew who Adam was, and he knew me. He was under ten years old when his parents were first converted to The Group. His charismatic, intellectual, Hispanic father was on my list of short-lived crushes. A few years after I got married, Adam's father moved his rapidly growing plural family to the Pinesdale Ranch.

In 1973, Adam's father was killed in a freak tractor rollover some considered suspicious. Much too soon, according to Adam, his mother married Louis as a plural wife.

After Adam stabbed his stepfather, Louis, he was kicked off the ranch and warned to never return. He moved back to Salt Lake, where he worked for Mark for quite some time, making it fairly easy to look him up, which I did.

Clear back in 2003, when Adam and I met to talk, I told him I wanted to write his story in my book. I asked him if he would be willing to tell me the details about what had happened between him and his stepfather. Adam said he and Louis had battled for a long time over his long black hair and his assumed rebellion, which Louis described as "embarrassing to the family." To Louis, Adam's hair had to be cut because he said so. To Adam the fight was a matter of preserving his rights and his own self-will.

One freezing-cold day in January 1974, fourteen-year-old Adam returned from a campout in the mountains with his hunting knife on one side of his belt and his gun on the other. As he entered the house, Louis attempted to force him into a chair and tie his hands behind his back and to a chair, so he could chop off Adam's long, "wild" hair. In the heat of the skirmish Adam got his right hand free, grabbed the knife from his side, and swung it behind him. When it went into Louis's side, Adam bolted.

While Louis was still in the hospital in critical condition, as the knife had punctured his liver and kidney, Adam watched as three men stalked him for weeks. They watched his every move: what he did, where he went, and to whom he talked. Whenever Adam would look in their direction, they would duck down and pretend they were busy with another task. Adam said he was terrified they would kill him.

Just after Adam returned from a high school basketball game, the same three men kidnapped him, tied his hands behind his back, and chloroformed him. The men hauled him from the back of their truck, dropped him on the cold floor of a vacant home nearby, and left him there for hours. When the vigilantes returned, they stripped him. Two men held him down while one of them sliced three-inch long gashes into each of his forearms. After his head was shaved, they painted it and his face with Gentian Violet; a dark purple disinfectant that can permanently stain everything it touches. Adam said, "When those sadists attempted to circumcise me and found out it had already been done, they sliced me around the glans where the foreskin would have been attached!"

Then the men tossed Adam's nude body into the back of a truck and drove him into the hills. With a large safety pin, they secured a patch-work note to his bare chest. Like some ransom notes, the letters were cut from a newspaper and glued together. Adam said, "I believe the note said, 'Evil boy, bad blood.'" Lastly, the three self-proclaimed "Danites" rolled him off a fifteen-foot cliff and left him in the snow to die.

Adam said when he regained consciousness at the bottom of the cliff, it was his rage that forced him up. Ignoring the excruciating pain from his wounds and from the exposure to the cold, he made his way home, dressed himself, and retrieved his gun to go after his tormentors.

"Yes, I probably would have shot them," he told me, "but I was held down again by family members before I could get past my front yard."

"What did your mother do or say about all of this?" I asked. "Did you or she ever go to police authorities outside of Pinesdale?"

Adam blinked a few times to halt the rising tears. "She didn't do one thing to protect me, then or ever. Most of the time, I don't think she even knew what was going on all around her. All of her heart and love was given to Louis, not to the three of us kids, and I was too young to know what else to do."

I started to cry. "Did you get any medical attention?"

"A nurse on the ranch came over to stitch and bandage me up, but she said hardly one word to me. That was it. I stayed all alone in my room for days. I hardly saw anyone. And that wasn't the only time I was beat," Adam said sadly. "Many times I was smacked with a stick or thrashed with a willow and didn't have a clue what I'd done to make Louis or any of the other men on the ranch so angry. One time I got a beating for throwing rocks off the church's parking lot into the trees. At least, I thought that's what the beating was for."

Adam told me on another occasion Louis checked him out of class and told him to wait in the car all day until he finished work. Then, in front of his coworkers, Louis lashed Adam's bare behind with a willow. Again, Adam was not given a reason for the beating.

"The only consolation I feel in my heart for those kinds of evil deeds," Adam told me, "is about a month before Louis shot himself, he came to Salt Lake and apologized to me for all the beatings and trauma he'd caused in my life."

From the feelings Louis divulged to him on that visit, Adam reasoned Louis had decided his life had no more value—since it had been full of pretense and fraud. Adam said, "I think Louis felt he'd been deceived by dishonorable men and could no longer deal with his own mistakes and all of the wickedness around him."

Adam's stories solidified my own suspicions of corruption in The Group. At what point, I questioned, had "our" men started asserting such cruel and unlawful authority over others? They justified and hid their iniquities in the name of their earlier day prophets and God. How long will those men get away with such self-righteous, terrible deeds?

Was it really the "wrongdoings" of evil men that made the gospel look bad, as Mom had always said? I wanted to believe her. However, it started feeling more and more the other way around. Isn't it our gospel and religion, I wondered, that justifies and protects the nefarious under the guise of male supremacy, holiness, power, and priesthood?

To this day, no one has paid a penalty for the crimes against fourteen year old Adam. Then and after all these years, we can imagine the rest of the actions, lies and cover-ups that have been condoned and covered by some of those "holy men" in that little "kingdom of God."

҂

Six-month-old Anne was snuggled tightly against my breast when we were startled by an early morning telephone call.

Mark was calling from Diane's house.

"I have some really sad news to tell you," he said somberly. He swallowed, and I could tell he was holding back his emotions. "My sister Ann died last night."

"No!" I screamed. "That's not true! She's way too young to die. She's got eight kids. She's seven months pregnant. It's not true, Mark! You heard it wrong. It's not Ann, it's a mistake!"

"I am so sorry I had to tell you like this. I wish I were there so we could hold and console each other. I am so sorry," Mark said while we both cried on the opposite ends of the phone.

I couldn't quit crying. All day long, I envisioned the ghastly scene and the horror Ann's fifteen-year-old son must have felt while watching his mother die. Ann was lying on her bed when she choked on some antibiotics that had come back up and lodged in her esophagus. Her son tried in every way he could to help. By the time her husband got there from his first wife's house across the way, and paramedics arrived, it was too late!

The funeral was extremely difficult for all of us. Our only consolation was our belief that Ann was just too good to be in this world. "But what about her children?" I asked God. "Why was she meant to have so many just to die and leave them all?"

❧

Swede was ill again. I visited him the morning after Ann's death and didn't say a word about her. He seemed unfriendly and distant, which just wasn't like him, and I couldn't get him to tell me what was wrong. He was wearing thick navy blue overalls, and I poked him in the gut with the end of my spoon a few times. Then I fluffed his short gray hair with my fingers. Like I'd done before, I teased, we needed to find him a cute wife to keep him company. Still he wouldn't say a word. I gave in, sat quietly, and waited.

Just as I was thinking I should go home, he pushed a cup of hot water, the jar of instant Folgers coffee, and the powdered creamer in front of me. He finally sat down at his small, round kitchen table where he, his brother Merrill, Mark, me, and other guests always sat to visit and play cards. Swede lit up another Camel, took a few sips of his own mud-thick coffee, and inhaled a few more long drags of smoke. When he looked in my eyes, the first time that day, I saw the apprehension and sadness in his eyes. I decided I didn't want to know what he was concerned about. *He's probably terminal and going to die from some awful disease,* I thought.

"My brother Merrill died sometime in the middle of the night." Swede said. "His kid found him this morning, still in the chair with his television blasting."

My amazing Swede was never affectionate, but I walked over and wrapped my arms around his shoulders. Never before had I seen him cry, nor had he ever allowed me to comfort him.

In that ice-cold, treacherous winter, we had two more unbearable deaths to count before the year was over. My brother, James' third wife had just bathed her eighteen-month-old twins. She drained the tub and ran out to help her sister-wife get the car started, so she wouldn't be late for work. When she returned to the house, she found her babies floating in an overflowing tub of scalding hot water. One of the two-year-old siblings thought the babies needed some water in the tub. He had turned on the only faucet he could reach.

In all of my grief, torment, and pain, I prayed. This tragedy seemed more than I could possibly bear. Compared to the terrible ordeals others had suffered that year, my life was a soft summer breeze nudging fluffy white clouds across an aqua blue sky. I had no room to complain about anything.

CHAPTER 31

Forbidden Friendships
1985-1987

As usual, the lack of money plagued our large family and most others in The Group. Poverty lurked in every corner and contributed to nearly every disagreement, even behind closed doors. Now it was about my six children, Diane's four, and other various needs.

My little Opel was always breaking down, just like every old car we had owned. On lucky days, I could find a hill and park on top of it, with the front of the vehicle pointed toward the decline. I would load my kids into the car, and stand next to the open front door. With one hand on the door frame and the other on the steering wheel to guide the car, I'd push with all my might. Once my car got rolling fast enough, I'd jump in, turn over the engine, and pop the clutch out really fast. If the car started and kept running, we'd smile and sometimes laughed in relief. If not, we were in deep doo-doo again. If there wasn't enough room at the bottom of the hill to push any further, I'd hide my pride and embarrassment and ask a passerby for help. My jumper cables were the saving member between my car battery and someone else's.

While I raised my children, there were only a few years during which I had a dependable car. The vehicles I drove were seldom compassionate; they would die in the scorching heat of summer, the blizzards of winter, and anytime in between. A couple of times, when I found a payphone to call for help, I'd realize I didn't even have a quarter to my name. On those teary days, I'd pack the youngest of my kids in one arm, hold the hand of a toddler, and have the others follow close by as we walked home.

To add to my frustration, our telephone service, heat, or power would often be turned off for nonpayment. Michelle would notice and find the money from some undisclosed resource, to have the service restored. This was only one of the many things she had done for the kids and me, so I felt indebted to her for her ongoing kindness.

Throughout the spring and summer of 1985, Michelle and I, as the Primary presidency, created new Primary manuals that would teach basic values such as; honesty, cleanliness and work ethics. Not that the children weren't being taught some of those ideals in our families; we just felt the focus shouldn't start with the higher laws of the gospel. We believed it was important for children to live the lesser laws before they even thought of abiding by the tough, crazy-making law of polygamy, which would soon inundate every aspect of their lives.

I was still very entrenched in serving the Lord by helping mankind. While I continued to write lesson plans, I also led the Primary teacher's meetings, taught a Primary class, and taught a fourth-grade class at our private school. I attended Relief Society "area" meetings to help quilt and prepare various items for the needy. I made sixteen loaves of bread to sell at our regular Wednesday-night Relief Society meetings, cleaned house three days a week, and attended Sunday school and sacrament meetings. Through all those good deeds, I felt sure I should attain a glorious entrance into the kingdom of God.

However, even with all of those renewed convictions, single parenting was getting more difficult by the day. As the boys approached adolescence, it seemed one or the other of them had to be picked up from the police station every four or five months. Mark was never with me in those ordeals.

Being an insecure polygamous woman, I was still afraid of everything and nearly everyone. My awkwardness and humiliation, I assumed, were obvious to the authorities. The police always asked me where my son's dad was, after they'd already asked my son. Since the diamond had fallen out a few years earlier, I wasn't wearing my ring. During the times when I was obviously pregnant and had to retrieve one or both of my sons from the police station, I was sure they presumed I was an unmarried, wanton slut.

Even when the policeman would ask, "Do you want us to call his dad?" I felt it was a derogatory question and they were really thinking, "No wonder this poor kid is a juvenile delinquent! He has a hussy for a mother. He needs a dad around to teach him how to be a responsible young man."

Or they could have been thinking, "Oh, this poor, pregnant, polygamous woman. Here she is again, while her husband is off screwing one of his younger, more attractive wives."

I wanted to scream at them, "Yes, please call him now!" I wanted to flip out and madly tell them everything that crossed my mind during those incidents. "You're right. I wish he could be here, but he's not! He's either in California working to provide for his large polygamous family, or he's sleeping with his other wife when I have to pick up my sons; and I am sick to death of having to live like this!"

I didn't, of course. Even though in all of those situations I felt angry and ashamed, I forced myself to hide my tears until we were in the car. Then I let the flood gates open wide.

※

I stood under the street lamps around the corner from our home. It was 2:15 in the morning. I was sure it was already way too late to save my son Alan from the evil clutches of teenage Barbra. It was said, her goal was to deflower every young male in our neighborhood.

Barbra's two dogs would bark, growl, and bare their fangs every time I approached the locked gate to their driveway. A light flickered high and then dimmed in the huge red barn where my son Jake told me Alan was "getting educated."

I'd been taught a mother should be willing to sacrifice her life to save her children's virtue. Here was one of the greatest tests on earth. I should risk my own death to save my son from fornication, or I'd be held accountable to God for his sins. I would have to climb over the gate, run for my life, and hope the dogs didn't tear me to shreds. If I made it to the door, it would surely be locked. If not, I might be able to barge in and try to stop the evil deed that most likely had already happened.

For the millionth time in my life, I daydreamed someone would hurry up and invent a cordless phone I could carry everywhere I went. How stupid—as if I had anyone to call at that hour of the morning anyway! I paced, cried, walked back and forth, and stared at the barn, just like a chicken-ass momma, sobbing like a baby. I didn't have enough nerve, courage, or integrity to save my own son from a sin "as evil as murder."

We were taught we'd be accountable for our children's every action, good or bad. We'd pay the price if we "lost" them to the world. My mothers and those around us would often say, "I'd rather lose a child in death than to the world."

I pictured myself standing before God—if I ever made it even near Him.

"Where is your son Alan?" God would ask in His deep, accusing voice.

"Uhh . . . uh . . . I lost him, God," I would cry in anguish and disgust at myself. "Yes, Lord, I lost him to one of the most grievous sins of the world."

"That you did, Sophia, and all because you didn't have faith. You were not willing to sacrifice yourself to those dogs to save your son's soul. You failed him, too. What kind of mother would do that, Sophia? How pathetically selfish of you!" God would thunder.

"You are right, God, but you already knew that when you gave him to me," I'd have to reply before He condemned and sentenced me to eternal damnation where I would live for eternity without my children, without a husband, without my family.

For nearly an hour, I was in my self-inflicted hell. As I paced back up the street toward home, my soul spoke to me again: "None of it is true, Sophia! Not one single bit of it!"

"Really?" I asked out loud. My soul told me she was speaking the truth. I knew it from the top of my head to the soles of my feet. I started to laugh. Soon I was dizzy and lightheaded from the oxygen surging rapidly in and out of my lungs. I probably sounded like a laughing hyena, and for a moment I wondered if the neighbors might think I was drunk and call the police. But I didn't care. The God of love let my soul share a key of hope.

In my joy, I contemplated. *Why do I keep hanging on so tightly to all of those lies? Why do I keep on trusting the horrible God I was raised to believe in? A loving God would not destroy even one of His children over another soul's free agency, especially over situations we have no control over.*

When I returned home, I climbed into my nice warm bed, turned my son over to another deity of love, and slept like a baby.

❧

For a long time, Diane had wanted and needed her own place. She checked out a few possibilities she'd heard about and got help from a government agency to pay a good portion of her house payment, so she went house shopping.

When she took me to see the one she wanted to buy, we jumped up and down in excitement. We would both have our own homes and more space. Other than the distance between our children, and us, we loved the idea.

In June 1986, Diane signed a home loan. After eight long years of miserable basement living, she happily moved into a split-level home in West Valley. Mark was happy for us, but not at all happy about his travel time, or the extra cost for gasoline. He couldn't keep up with all the bills for one home, let alone another. He told me, "If Diane gets the house; she'll have to pay for her own expenses."

I was happy for each of us to be enjoying more space in our own homes. But I also envied Diane's ability to be independent and financially secure. With an extremely low house payment, her secretarial skills, a stable job with a good income, she was able to be her own families' breadwinner. At my house, we were barely getting some of our bills paid with the money Mark was sending me.

In my new gratitude for life and changes, I counted on things looking up.

❧

It was a beautiful, sunshiny day in August. My homemade, flowered curtains swayed in the breeze coming through the open windows. I changed the sheets on my bed and listened to Michelle's younger children (whom I was tending) and my three youngest laugh and play in the back yard.

Suddenly, my soul directed me to check on the kids. Since I was so disgustingly tenacious about finishing anything I'd begun, I decided it would suffice if I peeked out at them through my upstairs window. The yard was fenced in. I counted all six little children happily running around on the back lawn, so I carried on. In less than a minute I heard the voice again, this time shouting at me, "Go now, Sophia! Go outside and check on the children, now!"

By the time I flew downstairs and out the back door, the kids were all standing around a hole in the ground, screaming at me, "Anne fell in! She's in the hole"

Someone had removed the concrete cover from the septic tank clean-out, and all I could see was the top of two-and-a-half-year-old Anne's head.

Needless to say, while rescuing and cleaning her up, I beat myself up until I'd had enough agony to last a lifetime. She, I'm sure, was about to walk toward the hole when I first peeked out of the window.

If only I had gone outside the first time, she wouldn't have fallen in.

For months our family and friends made jokes to lighten our hearts. "Let's hope that's the deepest shit Anne ever gets herself into." Everyone laughed but me. I tried to, but the guilt was still tormenting me. How could I ever live with myself, after hearing my soul's voice, if I hadn't acted quickly enough?

***

By November, Mark's tolerance had maxed out. He'd had enough of my rebellion where Michelle was concerned. He was sure she was the cause of all of our problems. With her out of the picture, he believed things would work out between us. So he decided to recruit my father for assistance.

Dad tried to take the middle ground but leaned more in Mark's favor. He said he wanted me to limit my friendship with Michelle. "Mark is right," Dad said. "You are his wife, and your responsibility is to him and your children first."

"But—" I started to question.

"No 'buts,' Sophia. She'll be taken care of. I'll talk to her and her mom. We'll get her the help she needs, so your friendship can wind down."

At first, I was really angry with Mark for forcing me into compliance. My don't-tell-me-what-to-do mind wanted to rebel. I was also livid my husband had told my parents Michelle was a lesbian. After all, I was working so hard to stay in denial. *If I keep refusing to believe it, it won't be true, and the problem will just go away*, I must have told myself.

I'd tried many times to change Mark's mind. "She might feel attracted to me in that way, but as long as she doesn't act on her desires, she isn't a lesbian!"

"She is and has been acting on her gay tendencies for a long time now, Sophia! Are you blind?"

For a while, my pride held back my gratitude. But as several months went by, I recognized the value in Dad's and Mark's decisions. In Michelle's absence, I experienced a relief beyond measure. The pressure I'd felt to always be available for her happiness and to go along with her powerful, know-it-all intellect was finally alleviated. My life began to feel so much like my own, I lost nearly twenty pounds without even trying. Phone conversations and correspondence between Mark and me also improved.

※

In April 1987, while Mark was in California, three years and two months after Anne's birth, our precious Keith came into this world just as he had promised his sister right after she was born.

In the middle of his fairly normal delivery (other than the debilitating pains that seemed to be worse than ever before), the contractions completely stopped. By then Keith was in the birth canal. There was a grave possibility he could have severe birth defects if he wasn't born quickly.

"Are you going to have any more kids, Sophia?" Aunt Amelia asked in aggravation while my young midwife gave me a shot of Pitocin in my thigh.

I told her no. I was positive this was the last baby I'd ever have. My body's pain tolerance had gone far beyond the call of duty.

In an instant, I was in labor again, one contraction after another—faster, heavier, harder. My back hurt so much, I thought I'd scream.

There are no words on this earth to depict the relief my body and heart felt when my handsome Keith was at last born—with no injuries or birth defects. When I held my amazing son in my arms, I cried tears of gratitude. My childbearing years were finally over.

Mark and I had the seven children we always knew we would have. The basketball team I'd talked so often about was now complete. We had our five handsome sons and two beautiful daughters.

Everything about Keith's infancy was perfect. He had a knack for nursing; and unlike the rest of the kids, Keith weaned himself from nursing right to a drinking cup. I reveled in each stage of his development and celebrated when there were no more stinky diapers to change—at least until I became a grandmother, which I looked forward to a long time in my future.

※

Diane wanted to have Mark's first girl. I felt sad for her sake, I had that privilege. As per our religion, a woman's value is too often placed on how many children she "gives her husband," especially sons, so I was full of gratitude to have given Mark his first and last son, his first and last daughter, as well as four more incredible children in between.

Looking back, Diane and I produced ten children with Mark. One of us had a child every year for six years in a row. In all of those births, neither of us chose to invite the other to be a part of our babies' deliveries as some sister-wives do. Some of the things I felt I was "supposed" to do to be the altruistic sister-wife felt too intrusive. To hold onto my autonomy, meant privacy in any way possible. I especially felt that way with childbirth, which is such a vulnerable and intimate time. From my early childhood, I wanted my personal space away from everyone else. One way to keep my autonomy, and perhaps for Diane too, was to remain reticent at those times.

Underlying the respect and love Diane and I felt for each other after living plural marriage together for nearly ten years, was our unspoken resentments, frustrations, and jealousies. Always there, flanked by our good and happy times, was our acute awareness of each other—the other love in Mark's life. Each of us was, "the other woman" who wanted and needed his love—the one who would take his devotion, love, and affection and offer it back three-fold. With all of that rubbish in the forefront of our minds, when we dared let our thoughts venture, there were still the lingering, tormenting questions. Does he love her more? Does he enjoy sex with her more than with me? Does he wish he was with her or is he thinking of her when he's with me?

Therefore, communication was seldom sincere, and maybe not talked about at all, especially after Mark felt exiled to California. If either of us dared to try to communicate with him about our personal hurts and feelings, we risked creating a troublesome gap between him and ourselves. It was best for Diane and me to be as passive, agreeable, and as kind as we could make ourselves be. For weeks and months we'd hold on to our miseries so they couldn't turn into hostilities. We may have wanted to punch or scream at Mark for things he did or didn't say. It could be something he'd done, or not done, or possibly something created by our own imaginations. But if we dared bring up any hurtful issues, we risked our "good standing" with him. We might as well have voluntarily sent Mark off to his sweet, cheerful wife who was grateful to love and placate him, even if she knew better.

But after doing that for way too long, I couldn't deny and hold onto my grievances any longer, no matter the consequences. Things got so tough between Mark and me, I felt like I would suffocate if I didn't do something different. Even without Michelle in our lives, all we did was fight, whether he was home for a weekend or for several weeks. The issues were the same: money, plural marriage, religion, lack of religion, time, needs, his absence, his anger at me, verbal abuses to our kids, and my inconsistency when it came to disciplining them.

When I was a child and teen, I swore my children would never have to go through the distress of hearing or watching their parents fight. Yet our discord became so thunderous and unresolved, one of us would finally storm away, and I would cry until my eyes swelled nearly shut.

CHAPTER 32

Demoted to Nothingness
1988

Through my many years of service in The Group, I heard Mary, our Relief Society president, and those women who served with her, brag about my abilities to quickly and efficiently accomplish anything that needed to be done. The problem was my identity and value, were based on my service and the recognition I received because of it. I was thirty-seven years old, with an identity crisis wedged between my ego and my soul; neither of which were fully alive or real.

A few weeks before Thanksgiving, Mary asked me to prepare a meal for a needy family the next Friday. "Of course," I told her.

After our phone conversation I tried to figure out how I would get the food for this offering. It would've been a miracle if Mark could have sent enough money to pay all of our bills, let alone for us to be able to buy food for our Thanksgiving dinner. Soon it would be Christmas, and once again I'd have to swallow my pride and sign up for "Toys for Tots" or accept some other kind of charity. But I was too proud to shirk my responsibilities by letting Mary know how destitute we were.

Around 6:30 the next Friday evening, Mary's call woke me up. She wanted to know why the meal I was to take to the needy family wasn't there yet.

My horrible depression had gotten the best of me. I had forgotten all about the meal. I gave Mary an excuse. In my temporary insanity, I believed I was still a semi-capable person, and I told her I'd get some food to the family right away.

Dressed in the slippers and pajamas I'd worn all day, I wandered into the kitchen and opened our refrigerator and cupboards. I saw a few pieces of bread left in the bag, a quarter-gallon of milk, and some leftover macaroni. I knew there was no money in my wallet or in the bank. There wasn't even enough food for my own kids! I started to sob until I was wailing uncontrollably. Feeling only half conscious, I wandered back down the hall, climbed back into my bed, and covered my head with the blankets.

Mary called again around 8:30 or 9:00. When she heard my drowsy, melancholy voice, she said angrily, "Sophia, you sound like you don't care one bit about this! What about those hungry kids?"

When I couldn't say one word, she continued her rant. "How could you be so selfish and irresponsible? If you weren't going to make sure they got their meal, you should have called me or asked someone else to take care of them! I really can't believe you did this, Sophia. What on earth has gotten into you to be so undependable, so callous? How will we be able to trust or count on you ever again?"

Tears leaked from my already red eyes. I didn't even try to defend myself. Mary's words plagued me over and over. It was exactly as I thought. If they'd known I had no value and no worth, they wouldn't have trusted me in the first place. The tiny significance I dared think or hope I possessed, Mary had just assured me was a lie. In one day, I was demoted to nothingness.

I changed eighteen-month-old Keith, brought him to bed with me, and fell asleep. Other than for my children's sake, I never wanted to wake up again.

On one of those dismal and lonely evenings near the end of November 1988, everything in my life felt completely hopeless. All the kids were staying with friends or asleep. I crashed downstairs on the couch in front of the television with a huge bag of Peanut M&Ms to sedate my body and mind into oblivion. I popped one after another of those addictive morsels into my mouth, devouring them as if I'd never get another bite to eat.

Irritating voices blasted across the television, but I didn't want to get up to change the channel or adjust the sound. I studied the unpainted, filthy, dented drywall that had suffered nine years of wild living conditions with Francine's, Diane's, and now my kids. I gaped at the matted carpet square that barely covered the concrete floor, as I cried and kept eating the chocolate.

Soon, the bag was nearly empty. I had a terrible stomachache, and more tears rolled down my fat cheeks and drenched the front of my size 22 blouse. I hadn't left my house for nearly two months. I was afraid of what might happen if I left, and yet I honestly had no idea why leaving scared me so much. I hated my run-down house. I despised my huge body and myself; but I couldn't make myself stop eating. I was surely a failure as a mother, wife, sister-wife, and servant. I believed I was a piece of rubbish in every single way. I was going to puke, and yet I watched my hand reach into the bag of M&Ms and pump them into my mouth—one, two, three—as if they were drugs and I was an addict.

"God!" I screamed. "Look at me! Look what a horrible, revolting person I am! I am out of control in every way. I've begged you a million times to make me stop overeating. I've begged you to help ease my grief, my loneliness, depression, flaws, and unholy feelings!"

Even while praying, I grazed on a few more chunks of chocolate. "You've got to do something, God, before I kill myself, with food or without it!"

Finally, I lugged my pathetic body off the couch, turned off the irritating television, and slowly climbed up the long flight of stairs. Completely out of breath at the top, I cursed at my physical, mental, and spiritual noxious self. I got in bed, and as I lay there, my heart pounded so hard I could hear it in my ears. My bloated stomach castigated me. I knew I wanted out of my misery. Slowly but surely I was going to die.

Three or four weeks passed. I rejected phone calls from Mark, friends, and family. My older kids took care of my younger ones. Alan or Jake somehow found food, or money to buy it. They fed and dressed the little ones and played and fought with them. The only time nearly two-year-old Keith or any of the kids got hugs or kisses from me was when they'd climb on my bed, where I stayed day and night. I believed my kids and others would be better off without such a depraved, worthless drudge holding them back. If I stayed in bed long enough without eating, I could die without the shame of actually putting a gun to my head or taking an overdose of sleeping pills. In between tears, sorrow, and pain, I slept all day and all night, and then slept some more.

Then Michelle called. The kids told her I was sleeping again and still wasn't taking calls. She called again and again. When she told them to get me on the phone, they repeated to her exactly what I'd told them to say to everyone: "Mom can't come to the phone. She's resting and doesn't want to be bothered right now." They knew the routine. I'd gotten after them when they attempted to get me to talk to anyone. Michelle's demands and persistence became so annoying, I told Sky to take the phone clear off the wall.

Michelle showed up at the door and nudged her way past my children, whom I had ordered not to open the door for anyone.

"Sophia, wake up," I heard her soft, deep voice say. I hoped the voice I heard was an angel who was finally going to walk with me to hell and drop me off there. "Sophia, come on—wake up!"

When she saw my eyes she asked, "What is going on, my precious friend? I've been calling you for a week. Every time I call, no one answers or your kids tell me you're sleeping and they're not supposed to wake you up."

I was pretty foggy and didn't want to talk. Michelle refused to leave until I would tell her what was going on. After some coaxing, I felt obligated to give in. There wasn't anything she hadn't already heard before. The only difference this time was I had no more hope left that I could change anything. Every physical, personal, private, spiritual, religious, or emotional problem felt insurmountable.

"So why haven't you killed yourself by now, Sophia? You know how to do it. There are a million ways to take yourself off this planet, you know!" Michelle charged.

"Because it's against God's laws!" I snapped at her.

She laughed. "So you think starving and sleeping yourself to death is any different?"

Before long, the buckets of tears I still hadn't spilled fell like a downpour of rain. Between my headache from crying and deep breaths of air, I told Michelle, "I'm even a failure at this. I can't even die! I may be the shittiest mother on earth; but I do know that NO one on this earth will ever love my kids as much as I do! I'm sure that's why I couldn't will myself to die. I held on for them."

Michelle lay down next to me. She held me tight until I quit weeping and dozed off again. When I awoke hours later, there was a note on my nightstand.

Dearest Sophia,
I've taken your kids to my house to bathe and feed them. We'll all be back in the morning, so be ready to go with me to breakfast. I love you my sweetest, dearest, most precious friend!

Hugs and kisses,
Michelle

When Michelle got to my house in the morning, I told her I'd get up, but I wouldn't go with her anywhere.

"You've got to get out of your dark, gloomy house and get some sunshine, Sophia! If you won't go with me, I'll get Jake and Allen to help me haul you out of here. You can get dressed and walk out of here on your own, or we'll carry you out in your pajamas."

I knew Michelle well enough to believe that's exactly what she'd do, so I grudgingly complied.

When I was dressed and we walked outside, she opened her car door on the driver's side. I apprehensively squeezed my fat body under the steering wheel and slid next to the passenger door that had been smashed shut. The sun was going to instantly burn me up or the sky would cave in on top of us—one or the other. Anything and everything around me felt oppressive. While we drove up State Street, she said she was going to take her time so we could talk and then she'd take me to lunch.

"No, Michelle, just take me home now! I want to go back now," I shouted at her. "I didn't want to go anywhere in the first place!"

I wanted to escape and run back home; but she had me caged between her wrecked car door and her large, overweight body sitting behind the steering wheel.

Just then she pulled down a driveway next to a huge office building and parked in the back. "This doesn't look like a restaurant," I said.

"This is where Big Bear, my therapist's, office is. I've got to fill out some papers and ask him a few questions. If he's in another appointment, it might take me twenty minutes or so. Then we can go eat. Come in with me where you'll be warm.

Knowing the depths of my anxiety, Michelle walked close to me all the way inside the building. In the foyer, I sat next to her and watched people come and go. I stared at the walls while Michelle stood at the receptionist's desk filling out forms. As I waited and waited—I got more and more angry.

The receptionist took the brown clipboard from Michelle and told her, "Thank you. It will only be a few minutes."

"What's going on?" I asked. "What are we waiting for now? You said all you had to do was fill out some papers. Let's get out of here. I feel sick!" Again I was fighting tears and heart palpitations. "Give me your keys and I'll wait in the car."

"Just hang in here with me, Sophia. I need you to go in there with me. I'm sure it won't take very long. Breathe in some deep and slowly. It will help mellow you out a little."

291

I was up and ready to leave when a large, dark-haired woman with deep brown eyes stepped into the waiting room. "Michelle? Big Bear is with another client. He asked me to help you with your questions."

Turning toward the door, I told Michelle again I'd wait outside for her, but she grabbed my hand tightly. "Please come in with me, Sophia. I promise we won't be long."

I followed.

"Hello Sophia, I'm Linda," the woman said as Michelle and I sat down in a small room that made me feel claustrophobic. Michelle slid closer to me and smiled.

"So tell me what's going on, Sophia. Your dear friend here says you want to die and you've been feeling suicidal for a very long time."

I didn't answer her. My whole body was on fire, and I was ticked as hell at Michelle. I charged for the door, but Michelle jumped in front of me.

"Please, Sophia, please talk to her. If you won't talk to Linda for you, then at least talk to her for your kids' sake. Just tell Linda how you're feeling and what you're thinking. That's all you have to say." Obviously, Michelle knew exactly how to make me comply.

Linda asked what was going on in my life. She had way too many snoopy questions, and they felt way too personal. In my head, I knew this was not the place for me. Many people in The Group thought psychologists or therapists were the epitome of evil influences. We were sure they would talk you into leaving your religion, your God, and your family. Therapists would purposely "tell you one-hundred truths to get you to believe the one lie," that would ruin your life, as well as others.

Don't trust her! She'll talk you into leaving your husband and your family, I worried. But I couldn't help myself. Once I got started, I spilled my guts. I rambled on about how terribly unhappy I was and how I couldn't function any longer.

"Tell me, Sophia, what will make you happy?" Linda questioned.

"Well, that one is easy," I said. My heart had settled down. I was still nervous, but my soul felt surprisingly comfortable.

"Go ahead. Tell me."

I told her all of the things I could think of, that would make me happy: "If Mark was home more and always nice when he was. If Diane and I . . ." I stopped. I couldn't let her know we were polygamists. "Uh, and if my kids would only . . . If we had money for . . . If they didn't . . . If only I were . . . or wasn't such a . . ."

Linda interrupted. "Sophia, all of those things are about everyone else. What about you? What will make you, Sophia, happy?"

What did I just tell her? Is she dumb or something? I wondered. *I just blathered out a list a mile long. Doesn't she get it?*

"I just told you," I said, trying not to sound as grouchy and frustrated as I felt.

"Listen, let's just start with you and stay with you," Linda said calmly. Speak about only you—not if he, she, or they would or wouldn't, but what is it Sophia can or can't do to make Sophia happy?"

I couldn't think of one single thing to say. I had no idea what would make Sophia happy. That question was not religiously kosher.

When we finally left, I was so frustrated and angry I wanted to scream at everyone and everything. I was also afraid. It sounded as if a witch had entered my body; I certainly hadn't behaved like the normal, civilized Sophia everyone thought they knew. In all of my life, I couldn't ever recall feeling as angry or being as rude and mouthy to a friend as I had been to Michelle or to Linda.

Linda wrote my assignment on a piece of paper and asked me to bring it back to her in a few days.

CHAPTER 33

Courage to Heal or Die
1989

Since Michelle rescued me, I'd gone against Dad's and Mark's counsel. She helped me catch up on months of cleaning that my children had tried to handle, while I was depressed and at rock bottom. With her support and love, I started to feel alive and regain some sense of hope.

"Loving my children will keep me alive and going until I can learn to love myself," I told Michelle.

She kissed my forehead. "It's already working! Thank God for your children!"

I sat at the kitchen table and glared at the blank lines on my yellow, legal-size piece of paper—the homework I hadn't been able to complete. My therapist had written in print across the top, "Ten Things I Love about Sophia." I reread the directions Linda noted: "You may not use the words 'he,' 'she,' 'they,' 'them,' or 'others.'"

This is impossible! I fumed inside at the time and energy I'd already wasted, and I still hadn't written a single word on the paper. Anything good about me was because of him, her, they, them, or others. After fifteen minutes I finally came up with three things I loved about me that didn't use one of the non-allowed words.

1. I love Sophia because she helps everyone.
2. I love Sophia because she is kind to people.
3. I love Sophia because she tries to please God.

When I finished, I crammed the folded paper into my purse and started washing the dishes.

A few days later, Michelle picked me up to make sure I would keep another appointment.

"This is just the point I'm trying to make, Sophia," Linda said impatiently. "You don't even know who Sophia is outside of everyone else, do you? If you were all alone in this world, what would you like and love about yourself? Try it again. You can come up with at least five things for me now—before you leave."

"I already tried! This is just ridiculous!" I said.

"Okay, we'll do it together. I'll coach you."

Together we determined two solid outcomes that felt genuine to me. "I love Sophia because she is talented," Linda made me write, "and I love her because she is a good person."

It was important, Linda told me, to repeat those two reasons out loud over and over again with a conscious effort to believe them. After several times, my eyes filled with tears of comfort and relief. For the rest of the day I smiled. Not my previous public display—perpetual smiles exuding my "righteous" servitude and codependence—but smiles of true joy. There were at least two first-rate things about me I could at last believe in. For most people, I imagined, finding something to love about oneself would be effortless. For me it had always been a forbidden assessment. My inauguration into a whole new life derived from those two ostensibly simple statements.

※

In January, Alan—with Jake's brotherly support—asked me how I'd feel about being a grandma. I figured differently, I wanted his question to be *just* curiosity, so I passed his implication off as a joke.

"I'd absolutely love to be a grandmother, Alan, when IT IS THE

RIGHT TIME!"

He laughed nervously. "Well, it must be the right time."

I was silent while I stared out the big kitchen window into our still-unfinished back yard. Before I knew it, my emotions kicked in, and tears streamed down my cheeks.

"Mom." Alan put his arm around me. "Are you okay?"

I turned to him. "I'm way too young to be a grandma! Your baby brother isn't quite two, and I'm only thirty-seven. Good grief, Alan, you and Allie are only sixteen! You're way too young to be parents. Don't you know I already feel like a crazy woman? What if your baby turns out to be a lunatic like its grandmother?"

Nervous, angry, and worried, I paced around the kitchen. I was barely holding myself together after all these years. How could these teens possibly stay sane and be responsible for a new baby?

"What in the world were you thinking, Alan?" I finally yelled at him. "I told you a million times to keep that thing in your pants!"

"Yeah, I know you did, Mom. You taught me right from wrong. I promise it's not your fault."

The reality was there was nothing I could do about it. I began to laugh. I jumped up and down and screamed. "I'm going to be a grandma! Me—wild, crazy me—a grandma!" I gently backhanded Jake in the stomach. "Can you believe it? I'm going to be a grandma."

"Yeah, I can believe it!" Jake said snidely. "Alan hasn't kept that thing in his pants ever since he discovered it!"

❧

At the beginning of my six-week crash recovery course, paid for by Medicaid, Linda and I set some goals to help me build a personal foundation. She promised me I would discover who Sophia was outside of the belief system I subsisted in.

Linda also suggested I start attending Overeaters Anonymous (OA) classes at least once a week. In a large room, fifteen women and one man took turns speaking. They were forthright about their years and years of binging, stealing food, shame, self-loathing, hiding, purging, fad diets, starvation diets, bulimia, and anorexia. All of the participants spoke with a level of candor I'd never heard before.

I'd always understood this kind of blatant, shocking, truth would only be revealed if we ever met the Lord. At that point, we'd be asked to review our whole entire life with the utmost frankness. Only then would we dare divulge any deep, dark secrets and flaws. Then after God's judgment, we'd be guided to hell or to heaven. But here on this earth, in that OA meeting, I heard confessions about matters I thought were reserved for God, on that Judgment Day.

Not only had members admitted to their mistakes in this life, but also to the foul treatment they had inflicted on their bodies. I learned about wooden spoon handles—how well they worked to cause gagging—and how laxatives helped keep the weight down. *Well, that would obviously force you to stay near the "throne" and keep you from grocery shopping.* I smiled.

At my first OA meeting I heard of more desperate things to do and to try than I ever imagined; and I thought I'd done it all. When it was my turn to speak, I was nervous and somewhat shy. The leader said I had to say something, even if it was, "I pass."

To end the deafening silence, someone prompted, "Just a few honest words."

I finally found courage enough to say a couple of sincere words. "Hi, my name is Sophia. I am a compulsive overeater. Hmm . . . Honest words . . . well, frankly all I can say is, even though you are strangers to me, I feel like you know me better than anyone else on earth. It sounds to me like you understand my pain, my heartache, my plight, and my desires, more than anyone in my family [and in our religion, I was thinking]. I believe all of you know me more than God does. Now let's get out of here so we can go home and eat!"

Everyone laughed while they clapped for another newcomer.

Michelle and I decided to experience some marijuana she'd somehow obtained. "We just want to see what it is like, and we need to see why our kids enjoy it so much. Then we'll know what we're up against," we justified.

The springtime rapids swirled and pounded against the massive boulder the two of us sat on, before the river split on either side and crashed on down the mountain. The pot ignited every sensual aspect of our beings. We thought the poetry and songs we created in our state of mind were amazing. Our laughter galloped in all directions before it bounced against the mountainsides and echoed back at us.

On the drive down Little Cottonwood Canyon, Michelle abruptly pulled off the side of the road. "Sophia," she said slowly and seriously. Whenever she sounded, it scared me. "You know already Big Bear, my therapist, and I have been working together for months."

"Right," I said.

"He said I can't hold back any information from you any longer. I am going to come out of the closet. You know what I mean, don't you, Sophia? You're the first person I am telling this to, even before my husband. I've tried with every fiber of my being to deny myself these feelings, but I've felt attracted to girls and women all of my life, for as long as I can remember."

Of course I understood what she was saying! Still, I was sick and disheartened. "Why didn't you admit to this a long time ago?" I grumbled. "I feel betrayed and embarrassed! For nearly four years you and I told Mark you are not a lesbian. I told him you are not attracted to women of the same sex because you are married and have a good sex life with your husband. You have five kids together! Now what, Michelle? What about the kids? What about our religion and our friendship?"

She didn't say another word. Her silence always felt like a punishment. After a long time, Michelle slid next to me and took my hand in hers. "You know the worse part of it, Sophia? I'm in love with you. I've been in total denial about it all along." Then Michelle leaned in and kissed me on the lips.

I wanted to tell her I didn't like it at all, that it made my skin crawl, but I didn't want to break her heart. I'll just keep my distance, I told myself, to make sure it doesn't happen again.

"Sophia, talk to me. You are really mad, aren't you?" Michelle asked when I pulled away from her.

"I don't know what to say, Michelle. Guess I'm in shock and afraid. You know I don't feel the same way, and it's going to be a kick in the, you-know-what having to tell Mark about this."

⚘

For the next few months, therapy came in mega doses at my OA meetings, but without my therapist, Linda. I'd completely taken chocolate out of my diet as an alcoholic does with drinking. The forty-five pounds of fat that was melting away was nothing in comparison to the emotional sludge being ripped from my guts and slowly but surely dissipating. On the outside, away from the oppressive "be good or else" community I'd grown up and lived in, I felt more love and true friendship than I knew existed. Best of all, contrary to my mother's belief that it was not okay to love yourself, I was learning it was absolutely mandatory to genuine happiness.

However, the more I was learning, and the better I felt about myself, the worse things got between Mark and me. He'd never known a Sophia who stood up for herself much, especially one who was learning to like the person she saw in the mirror. Even worse for Mark, Michelle and I were on the road of progress together. She helped save my life. She cared when no one else even noticed my years of decline into hellish darkness.

While attending regular OA meetings, I also started going to Codependent Anonymous meetings and an extremely intense course based on the book, *The Courage to Heal.* Our discussion group was for me and four other women who had been molested when we were children. But none of us knew the importance of having a professional facilitator to guide our progress. We wanted healing, and we felt we'd courageously walk through the traumas created by our perpetrators.

All of us realized how much the abuse continued to adversely impact our lives and prevent us from reaching our potential.

With other loving and understanding victims, we could purge. During recall and re-experiencing the trauma, we wrapped our arms around each other, feeling each other's sorrow and remorse. We allowed ourselves to let go of the racking agony and shame we'd carried for too many years.

Some women fell into a fetal position or convulsed or thrashed as they wept uncontrollably. Some of us screamed, rocked back and forth, and trembled. Some pounded on things with their fists while they sobbed and wailed. Some recollections played out in vivid, bloody detail, while some couldn't and never would be spoken out loud.

We wanted to recover from those abuses, no matter what it took. We wanted to become confident, emotionally secure women. And we knew until we got past the actions of our perpetrators, as well as any unwarranted feeling of responsibility we carried, our healing would be restricted.

The classes permitted me insight into my newlywed traumas. I began to understand all the negative feelings about bodily fluids, which was everything about sex. My subconscious anger of being exploited when I was a child, along with guilt from the belief sex was wicked unless used for procreation, often interfered with Mark's and my pleasures and new discoveries. I was sad about the fights that occurred because of our naivety and misunderstandings. Neither Mark nor I had any idea we were dealing with the repercussions of sexual trauma.

My convictions that I was ignorant, stupid, and inferior were also exacerbated because of the many episodes of abuse in my life. The fact that I wasn't mentally there to participate in thousands of elementary school lessons was beginning to make sense as well. I remembered I could hear my teachers' voices but couldn't understand what they were saying. My mind was outside of me, flying in the sky, running down the road, or hiding in cornfields so no one could find me. I was busy; it just didn't look like it. I was actively preoccupied with survival. To avoid my constant fears—of the world coming to an end, of our family being ripped apart, of the devil coming to get me, of the emotional and physical cruelty from peers at school and in our neighborhood, and from the sexual abuse—I became skilled at disappearing while my body stayed to meet the blows of life.

When I returned from those "safety flights," I felt a loss of being, memory, and orientation. I also experienced time lapses. No wonder all of that intensified my feeling of stupidity, which my peers readily accused me of. No wonder I missed so much of everything going on all around me. A simple, natural teenage kiss or touch would be grotesque rather than pleasurable and would often cause me to rage inside.

During my search for awareness, it hit me how risky such behaviors were. I had subconsciously tried to claim power and control over situations I'd been too small to deal with as a child.

We had been warned by professionals not to attempt to evoke the pain and raw emotion without someone trained to walk us through it. But we were broke, self-reliant troopers who felt we had all the love and support we would need from each other.

Before I knew it, I was falling into a deep depression again. My sad realizations about my past sucked me backwards at an alarming rate. Abandoned, unkempt, chunky, snot-nosed little Sophia was at the bottom of the abyss, sinking in muck and darkness. She could no longer fly off to her subconscious state of well-being. The terror was in plain sight.

With Mark still gone all the time, I was overwhelmed again. I had another new, self-imposed responsibility: a damaged little Sophia to deal with. She was screaming and begging for help and healing, and I felt completely incapable of caring for her. I barely had enough skills to care for my kids and myself, let alone an insecure, abused, neglected child inside me. She was angry and relentless. "If you won't take care of me, who will?" she would challenge.

It had never been about having an affair or about promiscuity or adultery. I was clear about that. When a man, old or young, wanted to take me to his car or take me home after dancing and one too many drinks, I was mortified and disgusted he'd even ask. On the other hand, maybe, just maybe, he'd "adult-nap" me and knock me clear out of my wretched melancholy—out of polygamy and out of Sophia's painful memories. I fluttered dangerously, like a moth too close to a flame. Poof! We'd be gone—taking the easy way out.

My descent into hell ripped at Mark's guts while he was too far away to comfort or stop me. My misbehaving little girl, full of self-destruction, was raring to create some chaos before all the sadness sucked the life out of her. When I would check myself and try to stop us from annihilation, we remained even more defeated.

The first night of Mark's weekend home after another seven weeks of absence, he stood by the bathroom door, looking heartbroken. He watched me pile some of my long blond hair on my head, put a little too much makeup on, and put on some gaudy-looking earrings.

When I tried to leave the bathroom, he stepped in front of me. "I know you're going bar-hopping again tonight, all dressed up in those tight jeans and sexy blouse, and you keep telling me you're not going out to get picked up! You might as well wear a sign that says, 'Come and fuck me!'"

I tried hard not to pay any attention to Mark's chest as it rose and fell with his breaking heart. Nor did I want to hear his gasping breaths or see the tears forming in his eyes. I didn't want to hurt him, and I didn't have a clue what to tell him anyway.

Trying to force myself back to numb just wasn't working anymore. Loving him, and sharing him hurt way too much. His short visits from California felt like torture. I didn't want to leave him, and I didn't want to stay living with him in polygamy. The only way I knew how to get out was destructive to all of us.

For a few seconds Mark wouldn't budge from the doorway. Then he stepped aside. "Just go ahead then, Sophia! You might as well reach in and rip my heart out of my chest and stomp on it. I can't stand the thought of you in another man's arms!"

From years of hearing and knowing of his sexual encounters with

Diane, I already knew far more pain than he could ever comprehend. But his light blue eyes glistened with tears and began to draw me in. None of my behaviors were aimed at hurting him. I wanted to stop what I was doing, undress for him from head to toe, melt in his arms, and stay there with him forever. But I couldn't. He would be sleeping with Diane that night. It was her turn again.

"At least I won't be fucking any of them!" I yelled. Tears poured down my face and as I finished the blow. "While you're out there screwing Diane, I'll be dancing with whomever I damn well please!"

❧

My mother should have been there for me! Where was she when I was molested over and over again, when I was alone and hurting? I could hear her angry screams at Dad, and then her lonely sobbing into her pillow. Her absence tangled and twisted in my guts. As a child and teen I watched her act like a martyr. I heard her calling out to Dad, Aunt Eleanor, and anyone else who would be happy to take advantage of her. "Here I am, all of you precious, more-deserving-than-I-am folks! I'm ready for you to come on over and crap on me and my kids while I keep on kissing your __." But no! My mother wouldn't dare say that word!

My mother's demeanor followed the "perfect" code of ethics for women in our religion. The most "qualified" women were those like her—those who were full of humility and who practiced constant servitude and sweetness to their husbands and to others.

Mom didn't seem to give a wing-ding about her kids going without a room, clothing, meals, their father's time, her time, money, Christmas, and birthdays. Mom was too busy worrying about pleasing Owen, Eleanor, and God! She was busy doing the work of the Lord—as if the Lord was needy. She sacrificed everything so others could have, and was so busy people-pleasing we children too often went without and were abandoned.

I visited Mom only a few times, compared to nearly every week. On those occasions I took her grocery shopping, watched *The Price*

Is Right with her, and cleaned her house. If I had to talk or listen to her, I felt more frustration and resentment toward her.

For just over three months, those black clouds lingered. It seemed they'd never leave. Like my mother's fight with the devil's imps so long ago, they obviously hadn't passed me by either. As a young girl and woman, all my desires were to be the mother I never had. I was going to be a perfect mom and a perfect person. Yet all of Mom's infirmities were epitomized in me. Like her, I had even become a perfect saint in public, but a self-loathing nothing in private.

Early late evening, after another dangerous episode of my "self-will run riot," I woke up with my old suffocating chest pain. It felt like someone had grabbed my heart and squeezed it so hard it couldn't beat. I was sure I would die physically, spiritually, and emotionally if I stayed in so much grief.

Mark could hear my anguish. On the other end of the phone, I could hear him cry with me. He wanted to be there holding me again. He begged me to stay, even though he too knew the umpteen reasons for living polygamy were making less and less sense to both of us.

But he told me, "I can't ever leave Diane. We made commitments to her we shouldn't break."

"I know, Mark. I'd never ask you to leave her. I never will! I know you can't let go of your duties, but I'm not sure how to survive if I stay."

Like a maniac, I fixed dinner, did the dishes, got the kids ready for bed, put a VHS movie on for noise, and dropped into my big bed next to Keith. For days I couldn't stop crying, even though I felt emotionless.

Back at the Salt Lake County Medical Clinic, I attempted to explain to my newly assigned therapist, Scott, the "who," "why," "when," and "what" of my life. "Little Sophia and I, need to find the courage to live or the courage to die," I told him.

Between floods of rage and tears, I told Scott, along with Little Sophia's horrendous pain and my adult tribulations, we were busy inciting dangerous situations that I wasn't sure how to handle. If I couldn't pull myself together, and keep Little Sophia safe from her pain, we'd both die.

Scott reassured me. "Sophia, you are going to become clear again. As long as you stay in touch with life and with me, you'll be running smoothly in no time."

I gave all of my kids who were home super-long, meaningful hugs, and cuddled two-year-old Keith on my lap. Every day, all day, I repeated my new affirmations. "I am a valuable asset to the adult me, little Sophia, my children, and the universe."

Scott was right! One gorgeous morning, after a few weeks of intense therapy, I awoke to gems dancing through the multifaceted prism dangling in my window. They sang of joyous days, weeks, and months ahead. The sunbeams of hope flickered across my pillow, danced around my room and across my face. I knew I would be able to pull my priorities together. I vowed to put Little Sophia first in every thought and action. Until she was well and happy, none of us would be. I told her I would honor her. Even though I was still a little afraid of the bullies on the outside and the inside of our lives, I would do everything in my power to protect her, me, and my children—and other children—from ever being disregarded, rejected, ignored, neglected, or abused.

Deep inside, I knew the anger I'd directed at my mother for all her imperfections was really aimed at me. She was my scapegoat. Mom had already been way too harsh toward herself for her defects of character. I knew her absence in her children's lives was the only way she knew how to deal with her own constant heartaches. Even though we didn't ask her to, every day for years she had been doing her best to make up for those days gone by. She would continue to make amends for the rest of her life. In time, I understood she'd done her best with what she knew. As I forgave her for not being perfect, I was learning to forgive myself for not being perfect. And I too would continue to do the best I could do, even amid my own inadequacies.

$\mathcal{U}$

In June, our oldest son, Jake, ditched his miserable life with our family and moved in with his beautiful girlfriend. While I was happy for him to be away and in love, his moving felt like a confirmation of every inadequacy I ever felt. I was grateful I had already begun to establish a support group, and had Scott's support in my life, while I beat myself up for my numerous flaws and mistakes.

CHAPTER 34

Reconciliation
1989–1990

When Michelle at last braved her convictions out loud—"If you will leave Mark and go with me, we will be happy ever after"—I knew our friendship, what she called "a friendship from God," was in big trouble.

"She is worse than the devil to me!" Mark shouted. "I hate her! I don't want her in this house, around you or my kids, ever again. Michelle knows every twisted, conniving, deceitful thing there is to say to take you away from me, and she's succeeding in doing it. This is worse than having a man after you, Sophia. If she were a man I could beat her up, or at least kick her clear across the parking lot!"

Though I told Michelle she couldn't come over to my house any-more, I was afraid of losing her friendship. I was like a child who wanted to dip her fingers into the pot of melting chocolate and keep tasting it, even knowing how hot it was getting. Although I regularly reminded Michelle I was not a lesbian, I sometimes ignored her illu-sions about "us." If I pretended long and hard enough I could keep her friendship anyway, and everything would be okay.

Mark and I continued to fight, to no avail. Each hoped the other would see what the real problems were in our marriage. And I wasn't sure how to end my friendship with Michelle, which had lasted nearly eight years. She was yanking on one of my arms, while Mark pulled on the other. They were ripping me apart.

I had terrible stomachaches. I fought with my loyalty to Michelle as her friend and tried to resist the sexual experiences she wanted us to try. She was determined to win my heart as her partner and lover. She'd beg and bribe. She tried with all she could muster to convince me she would love and care for me more than anyone ever could.

Michelle's whole world was rapidly falling apart. As directed by her therapist, she had tried to work things out with her mother. But her mother refused to help her or to take any responsibility for the sexual, physical, and verbal abuse she allowed Michelle and her siblings to suffer from their so-called perfect father.

Six or seven year old Michelle remembered her mother was leaving for another man, again. She chased her mother down the street screaming, "Please Mommy, take me with you! Don't leave me. I'll be a good girl. Please don't leave me, Mommy, please! I promise I'll be good."

The rejection and agony of "coming out," and the coldhearted responses she received from her family and relatives, was destroying Michelle. She'd been told there never was nor ever would be a place in God's kingdom for gays and lesbians—especially not for those who had been taught the fulness of the gospel, accepted it, and then refused to live a life of celibacy, preferring to give in to their so-called evil desires.

Michelle cried in frustration. "According to our priesthood doctrine, I can't even have my children in this life or in the hereafter!"

Just like my eldest brother's first wife who divorced him, Michelle would also be considered an apostate. She too would be required by priesthood law to leave her children with her husband. Michelle would have to be forced into another realization. She couldn't have me either—now or ever.

At South Valley Mental Health, Michelle's psychiatrist invited us to have a seat across from each other. I was sure Michelle's stomach was as tangled in knots as mine.

"Michelle," Big Bear started, "Sophia has some things she has to tell you, and you need to hear her out."

Michelle already had a good idea what our meeting was about. To hide her pain she kept her head buried on top of her knees.

"Go ahead, Sophia," Big Bear said. "Remember you will need to be unequivocally honest with Michelle so she will hear you."

I started with, "Well, Michelle, Scott, my therapist, required—well more like demanded—I had to start being honest with myself first, and then I could be honest with you and others."

When Michelle's eyes met mine I saw her anger. My voice began to quiver, and my heart pounded so hard I couldn't speak. Big Bear moved his footstool next to me, put his bulky arm around my shoulders, and pulled me next to his chest. "I'm here, Sophia, go ahead."

I started again. "Michelle, I've been trying in my lousy, inadequate, stupid, codependent way to let you know my feelings and thoughts. I've tried in every way possible to—"

She cut me off. "I know what you're going to tell me, Sophia! Just spit it out!"

"That's just it! Your anger and pain scare me! It's always been hard for me to express things you don't want to hear. You always seethe in silence, flip out and barge off, or talk me into doing something different from what I really need or want to do. One way or another, you always win!"

"Just say it! Spit it out, Sophia! I am a big girl! I can handle it!" Michelle shouted.

I stammered on. "Well, I already knew—and so do you, if you will admit it—I am not a lesbian. I can't be and never will be, no matter how much you want that. I won't leave my kids ever, for anything or anyone. I won't go with you, Michelle. My feelings will never change. No matter how much I love you and you love me, I will always be me—a heterosexual woman!"

"I don't believe you, Sophia! You enjoyed my affection and the messing around we did!"

I waited to compose and express myself the right way. After a few minutes of silence, I tried again. "Most of that was a lie, Michelle. I didn't like you to kiss me. I never did feel comfortable with your hugging or holding me close like I do with Mark."

Michelle leaned in toward me and exploded. "Then why the fuck didn't you tell me all this before?"

"I did! Every time I tried, you would yell or try to convince me my feelings and thoughts weren't real! You'd say, 'Love and affection doesn't have to come from a man, Sophia!' You'd cry or freak out when I had an opinion different from yours. You wouldn't hear anything I had to say unless it was what you wanted to hear. That's why I had to ask Big Bear for help."

"Then why did you let me kiss and hug you, Sophia? If you hated it, why did you fucking go along with it?"

"I just told you! You already know the answers! In every way possible I tried to avoid situations or places that might entice you. Everything about my life thus far has been about everyone else. What you, Mark, my kids, everyone else needs and wants—what I should and shouldn't do to protect all of you. I thought I had to save you from your pain, from falling apart, from feeling rejected, devastated, and suicidal."

"You're full of shit, Sophia! Even here in front of Big Bear you still haven't got the balls to tell me the truth!"

Big Bear asked. "What are you talking about, Michelle?"

"She enjoyed the affection part—I know she did."

Big Bear looked at me and waited for me to respond.

"There was only one time I was really turned on, Michelle. The time you touched my breasts and between my legs after we had a few too many drinks. The rest of the times when you tried to kiss or hold me, I pretended it was okay, or I pulled away. I was just too afraid of hurting you! I am so sorry, Michelle. I hated being dishonest with me and with you. It made me feel sick, inside and out. I didn't know how to get you to hear me. Remember about eight months ago when you and I first talked to Dad about touching each other? He told us to 'repent and sin no more.' I felt a relief beyond measure because I thought you would stick with it. I counted on you to respect his advice as well. But you started in again, pressuring me to test myself, to see if I was really gay or not when I already knew I wasn't! I have no choice but to end "us." That's why we are here today."

"You know what, Sophia?" Michelle jumped up in front of me and glared daggers. "I fucking hate you! I'll never trust you ever again! And I never want to see you again!" She stormed out of Big Bear's office.

I sobbed. "No matter how much relief I feel in telling her all of that, I still feel responsible for her pain and feelings of rejection," I told Big Bear.

He put his large hand over mine. "Scott will be proud of you! I sure am! And Michelle will be all right, Sophia. She'll get through this. It took a lot of courage for you to be honest with her. Let her go. Stop feeling responsible for her feelings, her dysfunction and hostility toward you. Don't let yourself buy it back! Keep honoring yourself, Sophia. I am proud of you."

※

After another of Mark's raging, name-calling fits at seven-year-old Karleen and five-year-old Anne for childhood laughter and games he didn't approve of, we ended up in yet another horrible fight. I called him the next morning at Diane's and told him I needed him to move out of our house for a while.

"Your kids have had more than enough abuse," I told him. "I should have stopped your verbal attacks a long time ago! I don't want to fight with you, Mark. I've had more than enough fighting, and it never does any good."

We were at a stalemate. During our separation our phone conversations were always the same old, same old. We'd banter back and forth before one of us would get frustrated and hang up.

≈

The phone rang at least ten times before I finally picked it up.

"Mom, what are you doing?" Jake asked urgently on the other end of the line. "I need your help!"

"What's going on, Jake?"

"Jenna and I are on our way back from Montana. We got stranded here in Idaho Falls. Can you and Dad come get us, or help us get going again? Listen, Mom, I wouldn't impose on you, but we don't know who else to call."

"There's nothing I'd love more than to get away! I want to help you and see you two again. I'm so happy you're coming down. But I don't have a car that will—"

"Mom," Jake interrupted, "we have to hurry! The guy here said we can leave our car for a couple of hours, and then we have to move it."

"I'll figure it out, Jake. Give me ten minutes then call me back."

The last thing I wanted to happen was for Mark and Diane to go get my son. I could call a friend or one of my brothers to ask for a ride up there to rescue Jake. Then I realized this might be the chance I'd been hoping for—a way to open the doors of reconciliation with Mark, especially now that Michelle hadn't been in the picture for months.

Her absence from my life was another exchange process in my recovery. Her consistent loyalty had wrapped me in blind security, giving me false self-esteem as I saw myself through her opinions. Her friendship kept me from opening my heart and soul to a higher power outside of the absent and wrathful God I grew up with. I allowed Michelle's well-meant, intellectual, and biased opinions to be my higher power. Her disappearance tossed me back into the lonely vulnerability of the unknown. I had no choice other than to figure out how to get back up on my own.

As my OA program recommended, I'd began giving my will over to a higher power I could trust. I still wasn't sure who or what form that was. But I begged my deity to pour out some unequivocal wisdom about my past "self-will run riot." I began to give up believing everything was Mark's fault and not mine. I asked my invented Creator what I should have done differently. What was the best thing I could do from here on out, every day in my future?

That nearly three-month-long separation from Mark and Michelle offered the opportunity for soul searching. In what part of our lives had I been wrong? I'd been so busy blaming him for countless wrong-doings. I'd blamed his failures for the shambles of our marriage, when both of us were responsible. I hoped Jake's rescue would be ours, too. This might be the opportunity for some one-on-one time with Mark to make amends. If we were supposed to be together again, it would work out. If not, I would have at least made an effort amid a critical transition period in my life.

Mark agreed to borrow Diane's new car. He and I headed toward Pocatello, Idaho, with hopes of a grand reconciliation. We knew it would take both of us to break down years of barriers, as well as our own stubbornness. The silence in the miles already gone by was excruciating. My heart wouldn't stop its nervous, disconcerting rhythm. Even after twenty years of marriage, my stomach convulsed at the thought of talking with Mark about our problems.

"I might as well go for it," I finally said in a lighthearted tone. "It can't be any worse than it's ever been."

"Yeah, go for it." Mark smiled at me.

"Before you came to get me, I wrote all this down so I wouldn't chicken out or say things I hadn't thought through." I opened the envelope. "I'd like you to listen to me read all of this, without interrupting me. Then when I'm all done, I'll listen to you without jumping in. Okay?"

As I started to read my letter, the pale blue stationery shook in my hands along with my voice, but I kept going anyway.

> *Dear Mark,*
> *When we first separated, I felt a lot of pain and sorrow for both of us. Neither of us understood or accepted each other's stand. This short but quality time without you or Michelle in my life has been a gift to me.*

You blamed our troubles on Michelle's presence, and I blamed it on too many years of non-communication, with our major contention being religion and child-rearing differences.

I'm sure you know as well as I do we are both right and both wrong. Michelle came into my life during another crisis in our marriage. She tried and did in many ways fill many of the empty and missing pieces in my life. And even though I felt an "unhealthy sense of being" in that friendship, it was better, I believed, than no relationship at all. She loved and validated me as a mother, woman, and friend. She believed in my intellect and potential enough to pull me out of the depths of my hell. She rescued me from my desired death, and nurtured my ego and soul with love and adoration. Many times, when we were without food, and our phone, heat, and power, was about to be or had been shut off for non-payment, she came through there as well. She was there for me in many ways when you weren't.

But, as you've said so many times before, and as I have realized—hopefully not too late—Michelle is so smart, she knowingly or unconsciously persuaded, manipulated, and controlled me in contrary directions, away from you, and away from finding me.

I know you despised her. I can't blame you; but I will always love her for the good she's brought into my life during, before, and after all the hours, days, and months and years you weren't there for us.

But most of all, Mark, I dearly love you! You've given a huge chunk of your life to our children and me. You have made many sacrifices for us. And even in the midst of your frustration and anger you cared and loved us every day of our lives. I love you because you love me. In between our conflicts, you are tender, caring, and giving. You are the man I made covenants with. You are the man I want a deep friendship with—the one I need and want for the rest of my life.

By the time I'd read most of the letter, tears filled Mark's eyes. He pulled off the freeway, wrapped his arms around his head, and rested them against the steering wheel.

I slid closer and caressed his back with my fingernails. "How can I tell you and show you how much I love you? I wish I could reach into your heart and fuse the broken and missing pieces of your life back together, so you'll feel whole and strong again."

After a few more minutes, I read the rest of my letter to him.

For all the years of my life, I thought my duties were to others before you, our kids, and me. I've been away from home way too much, caring for everyone but you and my kids like I should have been doing. I've tried in many ways to control you religiously because I believed my dad's way was the only way to salvation. I am so sorry.

I want you and our marriage and our family to be united. I want to be open and honest with you. And I want you to be honest with me. We have to communicate! Since our relationship has proven neither of us understands the "Latin" the other is speaking, please get some help with me. Let's see a marriage counselor. Please do this for me and for you. I do not want to be an old married couple who are still as pathetically inept at communication as your parents were, as my parents are, and as we have been. Let's make these changes and take steps together, hand in hand, heart in heart. Please, my love, please.

Yours forever,
Sophia

Mark and I talked and listened like we'd never done before. Just before we reached our destination, he profusely apologized for his anger, raging, absence and complacency for so many years of our lives. He said he wanted to make it up to me and our kids—to be a better father and husband

On our return from helping Jake and Jenna get back on the road again, Mark and I indulged ourselves in a private pool at Lava Hot Springs Resort. We basked in each other's arms while the hot, bubbling mineral water enveloped us. In our room we cried, laughed, and languished in each other's embrace. Our lovemaking shifted deeper than the realm of our bodies. The soul-deep consummation shifted us far beyond our first nights of desperate passion—further than the innumerable tender and lustful rendezvous in all the past years of marriage.

❦

As always, word traveled like a wind-driven fire. In the fall, Gregory Maynard was at last excommunicated from the priesthood council. My father and other council members could no longer "see no evil and hear no evil" when it came to "brother Gregory," on their council. We knew from firsthand witnesses of Maynard's cruelty to at least one of his wives, of purposely keeping his wives and children in dire poverty, and of his own depraved behaviors. Now, they finally listened to a few of Maynard's daughters tell of the years of sexual abuses they had suffered. For years they'd told their father, their brothers were molesting them. And for years Gregory sanctioned his sons' illicit behaviors with one excuse after another. Others reported he'd welcomed vile men into his home, to "use" young girls in "supposed" holy rituals. In silent arrogance, Gregory sat across from his judges—his priesthood peers. On the hot seat of accusations he still claimed Godhood and righteous domain over his family.

The abuse and Gregory's complicity wreaked havoc with the lifelong stability of many of his girls.

Some of us were relieved when a few of his utterly despicable actions had finally been acknowledged by the council, but we worried about the other terrible things, known, told and ignored. My soul was correct. From the very first time she met Gregory, she knew there was something vile about him.

※

Clothes never smelled as nice and fresh as when they were airdried in the summer sunshine. The fresh breeze and aqua blue sky held me in awe. One piece at a time, I hung laundry on four 20-foot lengths of clothesline, just as I'd always done. I thought of the past year of change in my life, of newfound friends who loved me unconditionally, and let me speak and feel without judgment or condemnation. My heart was full of gratitude.

In February, my precious OA friends celebrated one year of physical and personal healing with me. My amazing new therapist, Scott also helped me finish the list of ten things I loved about myself as I was slowly unmasking them. Until I could comprehend my personal value outside of service, and unless they were in my immediate family, he forbade me to say yes to anyone who would most certainly continue to ask me for help. A little at a time, he would allow me to say yes to something I really wanted to do for someone; but only if the request was not accompanied by any of my past feelings of obligation or guilt.

Quite often, especially in the beginning, I questioned this antipodal theory of my upbringing. "Me first" had not only been unthinkable but was considered "downright dishonorable and wicked."

The cool breeze blew my hair and chilled the tips of my wet fingers. As I began to hang sheets and towels from a basket of laundry, a sense of peace and joy engulfed me. I wanted to savor my newly found gift! Every day, all day, I wanted to discover more of Sophia. I wanted to reach deep into her heart and soul and find out what made her such a tenderhearted, gentle, trusting, and loving person. I could hardly wait to figure out where she was going from there. Why had it taken me thirty-seven years to begin to cherish her?

The love and acceptance I was beginning to feel for Mark was also delightful and heartwarming. Our renewed love was still blazing and thriving even after he went back to work in parts of California. Our many significant phone conversations and lengthy, evocative letters paved the way to even more devotion between us.

In the long process of showing love and respect for myself, I realized others' derogatory actions or words could never diminish my authentic value.

CHAPTER 35

Our Honeymoon and Questions for God
1990

The year 1990 helped make up for the many years of loss and heartache. Mark and I had fallen in love with each other between his long stays in California. The growing economy and our reconciliation set in concrete his decision to come home to stay.

In the spring, our seventeen-year-old son Alan and his girlfriend Stacie graduated from high school. They decided to get married so they could raise their beautiful daughter together. They planned their wedding for August. And just before their wedding, twenty years and four months after our marriage, Mark and I finally went on a honeymoon. We decided to spend money we'd probably never have enough of anyway and take a road trip to northern California to the Mount Shasta Pageant. Two of Mark's brothers and a sister were acting in the phenomenal depiction of Christ's life.

On the way to California, our old Chevy Cavalier broke down four times. But we forbade ourselves to think about our lack of money, or to acknowledge the car was so damn old we were crazy to be driving it down the street, let alone on a long trip. We refused to let "the old beast" get us down. As Mark and I waited for the car to be repaired, we had some wild escapades, making love in the root bed of a massive redwood tree next to a railroad track as a train sped by, and on top of a massive, moss-covered boulder.

Near our destination, when the car died again and we wanted to light the damn thing on fire, we chose to start another fire instead. We nearly suffocated during our "afternoon delight" in the back seat while waiting for Mark's brother to come tow the piece of junk—and us— into the town of Mount Shasta. Including all the repair times, most of our nine-day vacation turned into the most adventurous, romantic, enjoyable trip I'd ever been on. Of course there weren't many to speak about, but that one seemed to make up for the lack of travel over all those years.

Mark's and my open-minded conversations were enthralling and supportive. We couldn't remember when we enjoyed each other's company and laughter more. Our eyes melted each other's hearts. We felt and behaved like newlyweds. After all, it was our very first honeymoon.

Our developing love was so much stronger and superior to the young, inexperienced love we'd shared before. I imagined I was Mark's only girlfriend and his only wife. In the giant redwood forest, we renewed our marriage commitments with a mock priest and behaved like those days would never have to end.

I hadn't been so deeply in love for so long I couldn't remember if I'd ever felt that way before. Without the soul connection and passion Mark and I had begun to share, I'd been able to block out most of my jealousy and despondency, at least to some degree. Every time I thought about how Mark and I were together during our "honeymoon phase," I imagined our partnership was like that all the time. So when he told me, "You know I'll have to take Diane on another honeymoon to make things fair," I felt a chunk of my heart break away and die. Why did he have to ruin my illusion by bringing that up? I wished she had someone of her own, so I could have Mark all to myself. Diane and I each deserved our own man. Mark deserved to be a monogamist as well. Then he wouldn't have the anxieties caused by trying to please the two of us.

In the eight years before Diane married Mark, there were times when he and I felt a strong, deep love—an exhilarating passion—in our marriage. None of him, I was beginning to believe, should have ever been given to anyone else. I wasn't sure I could make it much longer. Falling in love again was making polygamy intolerable. Caring about my husband hurt way too much.

Near the end of our long trip, I still wanted to pretend Diane didn't exist in our lives as Mark's wife, but I couldn't help being concerned for her feelings. I suspected he had slipped away to call her, and I hated for him to, since it never turned out good. But I pictured the fear, loneliness, and the turmoil she must be feeling. I'd start to cry when I put myself in her shoes. How would I feel if the tables were turned? I'd be in so much grief I probably couldn't function.

On our fifth night away, and just before Mark was ready to shower, I finally asked him if he'd called Diane. "No, I haven't called her," Mark said angrily. "And I don't want to!" He was quiet for a moment before adding, "I've been putting off the inevitable—the crying, yelling, cussing-me-out session I'm in for."

"You should have called her days ago, and then it might not be as bad," I suggested.

Still, after all those years, even on our honeymoon, I, just like my mother had taught me, was trying to help keep the peace between Mark and Diane. I had always done that to some degree, and was sure I always would. But deep inside of me, on our honeymoon, I wished polygamy had never been our way of life.

I plopped down on the hotel bed and found myself worried about Diane again. I knew exactly how she must have been feeling. She was surely feeling as suspicious and resentful as I had felt many times before. Her guts must have been tearing her apart. I, too, was sure she'd get angry and upset at him. She always did. But he still had to call her. The stupid part was I hoped she would control her emotions for everyone's sake like I did when she went on her honeymoon. At least, I wished, she would wait to explode until it was her turn with him.

Tears filled my eyes and overflowed onto the pillow. "I'm so sorry! I am sorry to be the cause of your pain!" I wanted to call out to Diane and have her really hear me. "I'm sorry I am the woman who is away with your husband. I am sorry for both of us to have to go through all this stinking, irreconcilable-differences crap. For what, whom, and why? Do we really need to have all this pain in our lives so we can continue to be servants to our husband, if or when he or we ever make it to the celestial kingdom? I doubt it!"

I screamed inside my head, as if Diane could hear all of it. "This is insanity to the max! I still can't believe a loving God would require this of His children!"

The shower stopped. After a while Mark went outside to call Diane; I heard his quiet mumbling and then his angry, defensive voice preface a yelling tirade.

Even though I felt bad for Diane, I wanted to haul myself out the door, grab the pay phone from his ear, rip it off the wall, and fling it across the gravel parking lot. It never failed—she expresses her jealousy and insecurities, throws a fit, and ruins things for us.

When he finally came back inside, his body was tense with anger. "You see now why I didn't call her, Sophia. Well there's the damn proof I shouldn't have!"

His response didn't surprise me at all. I'd heard his complaints about Diane's insecurities, and his justifications because of her demands and jealousies, so many times over the years, they were practically engraved in my mind.

"Diane keeps count and track of everything I do, and every second I spend with you. Any time I take you somewhere, she expects me to take her there too. If I go to the store with you, I have to take her to the store. If I buy you something, I have to buy her something. She thinks she's got to have everything you have! And now I'll have to take her on a long, drawn-out trip I can't afford! I get so sick of hearing her crap and ruining things for us, I could—"

I dried my tears, reached across the bed, where Mark was still ranting and tickled his sides.

"Mark, please stop bitching about Diane's complaints. You're doing the same thing. Don't let your issues with her ruin our time together. We've had a wonderful time up to now. Let's keep it this way."

Our planned five-day trip turned into nearly nine days. We'd already spent a fortune on car repairs and rooms on the way to and in the city of Mt. Shasta. Just before we reached Susanville, heading south on Highway 89, the car broke down again. Mark had to come up with $800 to repair the catalytic converter. Then the damned old Chevy's engine blew up fifteen miles west of Elko, Nevada. Mark and I hitched a ride into the city with the tow-truck driver and got a cheap motel room where we could wait out the long, hot day and part of the night to be rescued.

I begged Mark to call anyone but Diane. I didn't want her involved in the end of our honeymoon—even the car's demise. We'd had such a wonderful time. I felt chopped up inside when Mark had no regard for my feelings. I was sure there were several other people who would've come to our rescue. Diane's emotions had already come way too close to spoiling the last several days of our honeymoon together. During the second phone call the night before, she had accused Mark of unfair treatment, of lying and making excuses for taking longer than we planned. In her jealous rage she screamed, cried, and carried on until Mark was so upset he could hardly be decent to me.

No matter how hard I encouraged, coaxed, and tried to seduce Mark into giving in to me, so nothing could ruin our last day and night together, he was no longer able to spin our mishaps into happiness. His positive, amiable attitude was exhausted. While he complained and slept through the day, I walked and cried. Our honeymoon had no promising ending; instead it came to a close in an abrupt and brutal crash landing.

"Why did you insist Diane come and get us?" I finally dared ask Mark. "Even you agree every time you call her when we're away, she ruins our time together! No matter how jealous or hurt I've felt, I haven't ranted at you when you two have been on trips together."

Mark defended his decision as if his masculinity and survival depended on it.

Damn! How I wished I had a Tom, Dick, or Harry I had to call while I was away with Mark. How would it be to hear T, D, or H, bitch and moan about me spending too much time away from him, and how unfair I was treating him?

In fuming retrospect, I not only wanted to slap the phone right off Mark's ear, I wanted to pound him with it while Diane listened! In all of those fights, I resented both of them for being so disrespectful of me.   .

While Mark slept, I caught the casino shuttle and went into town. I thought it was a female prostitute's world, so I was shocked when three male prostitutes tried to proposition me before I got to JCPenney's. There I purchased a cascading, bright pink dress for Alan and Stacie's wedding, which was only two days away.

With my nerves flying high and raw, I decided to burn off some adrenaline and walk the ten blocks back to our motel room. It would also save me from having to deal with male harassment again. When I arrived at our room, I opened the curtains a little and smooched and caressed Mark's body again. He knew I wanted one last go-round before Diane showed up and it would all be over. Too soon, we'd be back to the time-sharing grind tearing away at my guts while we tried to qualify to live with a God that I didn't even like or trust.

Mark might as well have flung me out the door and into the arms of those twat-coveting gigolos when he angrily rejected me out of concern for his insecure, lonely, dejected second wife's expected arrival.

I didn't speak another word to him for the rest of the evening. At first I relapsed back into my old patterns of codependency. I began to wallow in Mark's misery and his depression. I was supposed to be sweet—to kiss up to him, hug him, and let him know he was the boss and doing the right things. It was my duty to make everything and everyone feel better. But I didn't want to! I decided Mark could have his "insecure, lonely, dejected" wife. I would start looking for another life—with a man of my own.

When Diane finally arrived, I waited under the covers in the dark, dreary room while she and Mark hooked the piece-of-junk Cavalier to her dad's van with a rented tow bar. They hauled out our suitcases, and when they were ready to go, Mark told me to "get off the bed and into the car." I wished to God and the whole nation I had the money and time to take a bus home. If it were safe, I'd have hitchhiked. How on earth, I wondered, could either of them behave like such insensitive asses? During their honeymoon days I'd stayed as far away as hell is.

On the way home, Diane snuggled so tightly to Mark she might as well have been on his lap. I sat in the back seat, feeling desperate for a deep, dark sleep that would put me out of my wretchedness. And I wished I was the kind of first wife who could have reached up and banged my inconsiderate sister-wife's and husband's heads together with one swift knockout.

As Diane draped herself all over Mark, it seemed she was making a statement about the position she held in our lives. And though I would have kept my distance and never rescued them during their honeymoon, I knew how she must have felt while Mark and I were gone; with her imagination going full speed ahead. I didn't blame her for any of those feelings. All of us sister-wives who were not numb, celibate, or lesbians already knew those depths of hell. We just didn't dare admit it to anyone.

※

While cameras snapped photos of our large polygamous family all dressed up for Alan and Stacie's wedding, my head was full of mixed emotions. My stomach swirled. How on earth could I live with my resentment of the lifestyle that was smothering all of us?

I loved Diane—I would always love her. I just didn't love her in my husband's heart, face, arms, and life. This lifestyle was so much more tolerable when he and I were fighting all the time, when I had a strong religious reason to numb myself and oblivious to anything going on around me. None of that meant diddly-squat to me, because being an unconscious zombie was so much easier.

No wonder the God of polygamy requires women have a zillion church duties and children to wear them down. It keeps them too busy, tired, and depressed to care when, where, or whom His righteous sons are busy serv(ic)ing to help build God's kingdom.

For years, excruciating menstrual periods with excessive bleeding held me prisoner in my house every month. Those six long days were not at all conducive to my sanity. My tired, worn-out uterus that had served its wondrous purpose seven times had to go.

My doctor warned, "If you try to have another child, there's a good chance your uterus will come out with the baby, and both you and your baby might not make it."

Even though I believed I shouldn't and wouldn't have any more children, the drastic and "evil" decision to destroy my body's ability to procreate was so final, and considered damning by some. Many Fundamentalist men and women believed a righteous woman would choose to risk death in childbirth rather than stop having children for any reason.

Again Dad gave me his uncensored advice. "I can't and won't teach this to our people, and I may have hell to pay for these comments, but it is my personal belief God is very displeased with so many men and women who have more children than they can physically, financially, and spiritually care for. I don't believe, as many do, that when John Taylor told the brethren to make sure not one year passed by without a child born under the covenant, that he meant every woman should have to give birth to a child every year.

My father went on,

"The same goes for plural wives. A man should never marry more women than he can provide for. It's a dreadful injustice to women and children, and more so to God! Well, I'd better get off my tangent and get back where I was before. When Eleanor had her last baby, her uterus came clear out with the baby. It's a miracle they both lived! Listen, my darling. You and your husband have to make this decision, but it is in my heart to tell you to take good care of the beautiful children you've already got. If you were to die, you wouldn't be here to raise them. I feel assured you've completed your calling when it comes to having children."

No more periods! Finally I'd be free of pain, discomfort, accidents, and embarrassment. I wanted to sing and dance all over town. Along with the physical gift of a hysterectomy, Mark and I could enjoy sex without worrying about an unwanted pregnancy. And there was no better time than while Mark and I were falling in love.

Though I felt sorry for Diane because she'd still have to worry about getting pregnant, since she too didn't want to, I took tranquil relief in her plight.

"You are terrible, Sophia," my guilty conscious yelled at me. But I couldn't even wallow in that pleasure without being concerned about Diane's feelings!

"Leave me alone, at least this time!" I bribed my soul. "I'll be a better sister-wife with another issue."

With the smidgen of remaining testimony crumbling apart from the soles of my feet to the tip of my head, I still prayed that Dad, Mark, and I were making the right decision.

In the middle of November 1990, I had the hysterectomy and some repair surgery. I had one problem after another. Mom was sure that during my reconstructive surgery, the doctor damaged my ureter. When I walked, the pain was horrendous. Each new attempt to urinate on my own ended with me having to be re-catheterized.

"To be 'cathed' usually makes someone a little uncomfortable," Mom told me.

But for me the pain was so excruciating I'd go into cold sweats and nearly black out. To stay sane while I forced myself to hold still all the time, I read, sewed, watched television, wrote, and wished I had more visitors.

More horrifying than anything, I was sure the God of my upbringing was punishing me for permanently getting rid of my ability to reproduce, and for relishing the idea I had "one up" on Diane.

I was infuriated with family, friends, and relatives to whom I'd been a "sucker" (helped), as Mark had said so many times before. Miss Do-it-all, Helpful, Rescuer, and Giver had been at everyone's beck and call whenever they wanted or needed me, yet not one of those people was there for me during my recovery from surgery. My total care was left to my kids, my mother, and Mark, when he was home.

I was also frustrated with Diane. Rather than help my children and me like I'd helped her when she was down for so many months, she took off to Oregon for Thanksgiving.

Nonetheless, I was full of gratitude for holiday time with just Mark and our kids. He was amazing. With the kids' help, he cleaned the whole house, cooked a perfectly delectable, full holiday meal, set the table with flowers in the center, and then cleaned up the food and dishes afterward.

❧

In my nightmare, one of those hideously distorted, evil imps I'd heard about all my life came to get me. He closed in on me. With his outstretched, deformed, purple fingers he zapped my chest and electrocuted me. I began to suffocate and drop to the floor. "You have sealed your doom in everlasting misery!" I heard his guttural groan. "Forevermore you shall dwell in the pits of hellfire and brimstone, never to be united with . . ."

Mark's face was right next to mine. "Sophia, wake up!" He tugged on my arm. I screamed for a few more seconds while the revolting monster yanked me backward and threw me off a cliff into purgatory. HELP!" I screamed and cried all the way down.

"Sophia, you're all right! You're here with me!" Mark held onto my flailing arms and legs. "I've got you. I'm here, Sophia. You'll be okay."

"No, I won't! I am going to go to hell, Mark. Now I know I am!" I cried out. "I was supposed to have that severely disabled little girl we thought we might have. I should have sacrificed my freedom and my life to give birth to her, and to raise her. I forced her into a family where she won't thrive!"

"It's just not true," Mark insisted. He wiped the tears from my eyes with the sheet and snuggled with me. "You know it's not true. You and I, and even God, knows bringing her into our life would not have been fair or good for her."

"But, maybe—"

"There are no maybes about it, Sophia! God knows we made the right choices. Your dad was right when he told us we've already done our part—we've already got more children than we can do justice to. It's all those insidious tapes playing a billion times in your mind, telling you to feel guilty and bad. They are all lies! It's all a bunch of lies! The God you and I are learning about wouldn't damn you to hell for choosing to take care of the blessings you already have."

In Mark's arms I felt secure. I wanted to believe everything he claimed was the absolute truth. In peace, we drifted off to sleep.

Then, I was flying across the vast cornflower blue sky—this time with Mark and our children. We were touring the Salt Lake Valley, Superman style; clear from the Rocky Mountains to the Oquirrh Mountains. The Corner Canyons of Draper, to Butterfield Canyon, in Herriman, clear to the capitol building were visible from our height. The wind blew in our eyes, forcing out droplets of water and splashing them back across our temples. As we picked up speed, the swift currents of air stretched and contorted our cheeks and mouths. We laughed at each other's geeky-looking faces and nearly tumbled down from the sky.

But six weeks after the surgery, I still couldn't pee on my own.

Forever, it seemed, I wanted to ask God a mile-long list of questions my dad could never satisfy. Most of them would be about His inequitable rules for women and men. Number one would be: why can men have more than one wife but women can't have more than one husband? Two: why can't women hold the priesthood and men have the babies? Three: if it's true, in general, women are more spiritual than men, why can't we be the leaders and have the final say in priesthood and family matters? And then there was question number four. It surely wasn't the last one, but ever since I was a young tomboy trying to compete with all my brothers and the neighborhood boys, this one was another of my trials. "Okay, God." I'd ask, "Why did you make it so guys can stand up to pee anytime and anywhere there's no toilet, while women have to ditch the scene, hunt frantically for bushes or trees or some kind of a hideaway to cover their naked behinds?" If we are lucky enough to find a place where we are able to get our pants down in time, we are still apt to drizzle all over ourselves and our clothes!

But after all of my recovery problems, I was more than ready to take back question number four! I decided my bladder problem was surely that "prankster" God's continued, unfair, and cruel way of demanding my undivided attention.

By Christmastime, I thought I'd gone totally bonkers staying home and down all the time. So I would endure a few hours of pain to walk around and purchase some small, inexpensive items for the kids' socks.

Long before they came up with the little motorized carts in shopping centers, I had Mark push me around ShopKo in a wheelchair. In the ladies restroom, of course, I dropped my pants to the floor, stood in front of the toilet, and twisted the little valve at the bottom of the full bag that was strapped to my right leg. I pointed the spout to the middle of the bowl and listened to the recognizable male-sounding stream of liquid pour into the bowl. Surely the lady sitting on the throne in the next stall was able to see my tennis shoes facing the toilet. "God, of every punishment you've ever given me—and for who knows what—this is one of the worst," I bitterly complained.

The woman took ten minutes to wash her hands. I knew she was waiting to give this pervert man a piece of her mind. I held out longer, and waited until she finally left.

Sure enough, when I exited the bathroom, there she was. She stared at my shoes and did a double take of my face, and then my shoes again. Her jaw dropped to her chest, and her face turned yellow.

I guess the woman had never seen, nor would she ever again see such a completely real-looking transvestite as I appeared to be.

Every day, all day, I repeated, "Oh, Lord, I promise, promise, promise if you will let me pee normally again I will never again complain about your favoritism toward men—at least in that area of my anatomy! I promise, dear Lord. Amen."

After forty-six days of torture, and wondering if I'd be attached to that pee bag forever, God finally took pity on me. He must have felt He'd inflicted enough agony on me to make His point and gave in to my plea. My urologist finally prescribed a wonderful drug to make the swelling go down and made me stay flat on my back for three or four days so as not to irritate the tissues. And sure enough, my ureter was finally functioning again!

I slugged the doctor on the shoulder after he said, "Congratulations, Sophia, you've set the record! You beat one of my previous patient's inability to urinate by four days."

CHAPTER 36

Work, College, and Mom's Confessions
1991

When I enrolled Keith in the Head Start preschool program in September, it opened up a half day for me to pursue my college education. I had quit trying to fulfill my dreams. All of my life I believed that if I tried and failed the results would prove my stupidity. But my newfound friends were helping me realize that my dreams were worth pursuing and that I was smart enough to make them come true. If I didn't try, I was failing myself. Two of my dear OA friends literally supported my jittery, nervous body and walked me into the Student Center at Salt Lake Community College (SLCC) to take entrance exams.

I'd been out of school for twenty years. And since I was mentally absent so much of the time, I felt I hadn't learned very much. Just like everyone else with lousy grades, the system pushed me through. Even though I knew a lot of the reasons, I still felt unintelligent. I was sure I would fail the math tests. Maybe, just maybe, I'd barely pass the language arts exams since, I loved to hang out and listen to intellectual, articulate people. As a kid, while I'd rub Mom's feet after her hard days at the hospital, we'd take the vocabulary quizzes in the Reader's Digest. I loved them.

After hours of text anxiety, I was amazed with the test results. I had aced the language series and would get to register into an English 101 course. Not surprisingly, my math scores placed me in remedial classes. I had to learn all kinds of basic math before I could take any of the five required college math courses. No matter what, I swore I wouldn't let my fear of failure stop me from trying to move forward.

At the flourishing age of thirty-nine, with five children still living at home, and with funding from a Displaced Homemaker's grant, I started my first few college courses. My life-long dream was still the same. I planned to become a certified elementary schoolteacher.

In between my classes, I volunteered in Keith's Head Start Class and my other children's classroom whenever possible. One afternoon, Keith's teacher told me, "I think you should apply to be a substitute Head Start teacher. You are really great with children."

There wasn't nearly enough time in a day to accomplish all that needed to be done. How could I possibly fit in a job? But we could sure use the money, and it would give me a lot more experience. Wondering if I'd truly lost my mind, I applied for the job in November and turned it over to God—the nice one I was learning more about.

I was called to sub across the Salt Lake Valley a few times. By January 1991 I was offered a full-time assistant teacher position at Millcreek Elementary School in Salt Lake. I moved my three, day classes to night, and took the job.

Every day amid my progressive joy, I was still petrified about the ongoing lies I thought I'd have to tell to feel and keep safe among "the outsiders."

No matter to whom I talked—my college peers, instructors, the teachers I worked with in Head Start, and the parents—I was frantic about how to cover up my lifestyle. I'd come to hate lying and dishonesty with a passion. For years, I'd been hashing out, separating, and dissolving all the supposed necessary and completely unnecessary lies from my life. A lie was a lie no matter which way it was or wasn't told, and neither was acceptable to me. However, by choosing to live and thrive in the midst of "outsiders," I thought I had to protect my family and myself with deceit. As an embryonic "normal" adult, I felt I had to lie more than I did as a student for thirteen years in public schools.

Working and associating with normal, every-day, monogamous people was incredibly fulfilling, and at the same time, completely terrifying and nerve-racking. The risk wasn't only about losing out on friendships, as it had mostly been when others found out I was a polygamist kid. Now it was about having no value, or being judged as stupid, ineffective, a bad influence, or a derelict of a human being. It may have been my fear of not being hired, or possibly losing a job.

I feared I'd forget what I told coworkers about my past eighteen years of on-and-off teaching experiences in our group schools. What would I tell them if they wondered why my husband didn't come to staff Christmas dinners? How would I explain how and why I felt so inadequate and naive about appropriate, normal systems others were accustomed to living with on "the outside"? What would others think about how inept and scared I was when it came to normal social skills?

All of my concerns jabbered incessantly in my head. It haunted me in my college classes, with my instructors, in study groups, with my Head Start students' parents, and with other Head Start and public school staff where I worked. Yet each day seemed to convey more reward, gratitude, and peace. I was slowly feeling more comfortable and credible.

I'd come to respect and appreciate Phoebe, the head teacher I worked with. She was an incredible example. She helped fill my developing esteem with acceptance, adoration, approval, and love. And every day, on pins and needles, I wondered if she would treat me as well if she knew about my background and what I was really like. I decided I needed to protect my friendship and job no matter the stories I had to fabricate. I was finding, thank my higher power, there were hardly any to come up with.

In the fall of 1991, I was offered an assistant job close to home. I had the privilege of teaching with Keith's Head Start teacher, with whom I'd already worked in the Jordan School District.

One day, the principal came all the way from her office to our Head Start classroom to insist I go to the auditorium to get my picture taken. "The photographer said there was someone in Head Start who didn't want to pose for a picture," she said.

"It's okay," I replied. "Shawna took her picture with the kids. I'm just an assistant teacher, and I hate having my picture taken."

"No, it's not okay!" the principal barked, pushing at my shoulders in the direction of the door. "Now get yourself down there! Can I trust you to go down on your own, or will I have to walk with you?"

When the picture packets came back, I stashed mine inside my book bag with the intention to chuck it in the dumpster on my way to the parking lot. But I didn't. Behind the steering wheel in my car, I decided to brave a peek. Chagrined about what I might see, it took me a few minutes to pull my photos from the package. These pictures of me, I was sure, like the few others I had seen, and the ones I hadn't dared look at for most of my life, would prove again how unattractive I was, and remind me how much I used to look down on that person.

The first glance led me to believe the woman in the duplicate pictures wasn't me. I had never before seen Sophia in the reflection of my mirror as I saw her in those photos. I was stunned by her deep blue, sensitive eyes. They held compassion for the Sophia of years gone by. I saw the pretty woman Mark and others had asserted—one I never recognized before.

I was a forty-year-old woman the first time I allowed myself the gift of physical acceptance. The woman in the pictures was the beautiful woman I was learning to love, honor, and appreciate. In her, I could see and feel her love for life, others, and me, clear to the depths of her soul. Tears of overwhelming gratitude and wonder traveled down my cheeks, into my mouth, and onto my lap. My soul reminded me she'd believed and trusted in me when I felt no one else did.

Looking back, I'm reminded of the constant opportunities my soul was giving me to learn. The principal's demand felt rude and demeaning, yet having my picture taken turned out to be a blessing in disguise.

Dad entered Mom's kitchen, where she and I had been visiting. "Oh, dear, my troublemaker is over here again!" he said, sounding frustrated and cynical. He filled his glass with water, plucked an apple from the fridge, and went back to his headquarters which consumed all of my mother's living-room space. A few years previous to this, Dad had allowed Mom to move back upstairs—this time on the south end of the fourplex, after one of his wives passed away.

We ignored Dad and kept gabbing while we ate Mom's delicious tuna salad, thickly spread on whole-wheat toast.

"Mom," I said, "in Leviticus 19:18 it says, 'Love thy neighbor as thyself.' Well, you've probably quoted that one to me at least a million Allred-exaggerating times in my life. What do you think those words really mean?"

"Well . . ." Mom hemmed and hawed for several moments. "I guess it means, uh . . . well, it means to treat other people at least as good as or better than you would treat yourself."

"That's exactly what I thought you might say, Mom. So how is it you can truly love your neighbor as yourself, if you don't love yourself?"

I waited a few seconds before I pointed at her and then myself. "You and me. We have to come first! You learned it backwards, and then I believe you taught it to me backwards. It's supposed to be the other way around."

"I guess I've never thought of it that way," Mom said.

"Before you die, Mom, I'd love it if you learned to love yourself as I am finally learning to love myself. It's really the right thing to do, you know. Believe me, God wants us to love ourselves first. In fact it's necessary! Every day I am finding the more I genuinely love myself, the more capacity I have to love and to offer others."

Mom looked at me sadly.

Changing those concepts was as difficult as learning a new language. All of our lives we'd been taught one way. We were to think, believe, and act the same: one thought, one mind, one straight and narrow path to the kingdom of God. That was pretty much it. If we obeyed, we might make it there someday. Asking my seventy-five-year-old mother to learn something outside of her fundamentalist box was like asking her to forget the English language and start speaking Latin. Still, her heart was open to my ideas because she saw tremendous changes in my life.

"Sophia, you have a glimmering, bright light shining through your eyes every time I've seen you lately," Mom told me excitedly. "It's like something wonderful has happened to you and you're coming alive. I don't see any signs of the depression you were feeling. What is going on?"

My new, positive attitude was starting to show as I took what felt like baby steps to happiness. This emerging insight and outlook were sometimes too freaky for those who knew me—my friends, family, and children. Either I was ostracized and called a weirdo, or I was described as full of the Spirit of the Lord—or the devil, depending on who was speaking.

I was so grateful Mom wanted the kind of happiness and energy I was discovering. It was something she'd seldom felt or claimed as her own.

"It's okay," I continued. "Don't be sad now. It's not your fault you believed it wasn't good to love yourself. It's what you were taught by your parents, so you wanted us to believe."

Immediately Mom's cheeks turned bright red, and she looked like she might cry. Her chest heaved up and down until I worried she might explode with emotion.

"How can I ever love myself, Sophia? I have such a profound hatred for myself, sometimes I can hardly bear it. I've always felt it there—it won't go away!"

Mom pressed her palms to her forehead.

"My father always hated me!" she cried out. "He always treated me worse than garbage. He never had one kind word to say to me, not one. As hard as I try, I can't remember one kind word that ever came out of his mouth about me. I always wondered why." My precious mother began to gasp for air, as I cried with her. "Why? Why did he hate me so much?"

For a few more minutes, mother spoke about some of the false-hoods and garbage she had embraced her whole life. "My dad always put me down! Even as an adult I could never please him. He hated me. He . . ."

Her grief and tears turned her words to mumbling before she started to choke. She drank some more of her water and then grabbed a handful of tissues from the box on the table. She balled up the soft paper, blotted her eyes, and blew her nose.

Before I realized what was happening, Mom got quiet. I was sure she could hear her dead father's voice yelling in her head, "Keep sweet, Vera! Keep the Spirit of the Lord. It's a matter of life and death!"

Mom swallowed hard, took in several long deep breaths, and then muttered, "I'm so sorry, Sophia, I have no right to talk about my fa-ther that way. He was a good man. I know I shouldn't ever bring up the past. All it does is cause trouble and hurts me and others even more."

"I know it hurts to talk about it, but the more you do, the sooner the pain starts to dissipate and go away. Talk about it as many times as it takes to eradicate the heartache you've held inside all these years. Then you learn you are worthy of love from yourself, your dad, and everyone."

Mom wiped her eyes and face. She looked around the corner to see if Dad was nearby, and then she whispered insistently. "Your dad says we shouldn't live in the past. The past is done and gone."

"That's just my point, Mom. As long as that sickening garbage is inside of you—and it is—you are living in the past! It's not healthy to keep shoving it back down by claiming you'll lose the Spirit of the Lord. What you hold inside becomes poisonous. You have to purge it, so you can heal."

I put my arm around Mom's shoulder. When Dad came around the corner he looked at her swollen, red eyes. Then he looked at me in anger.

"You see, Sophia?" he snapped. "Every time you come over here lately you get your mom all riled up over something or other! Then she gets all upset or mad at me and I have to deal with it."

"You don't understand," I tried to explain before he was off, side-stepping us again.

My father didn't have the courage or know-how to deal with Mother's heartache and guilt. All he knew how to do was persuade her to keep the lid on tight and pretend there was nothing brewing. It was much easier for him, and the rest of us polygamists, to move into a realm of make-believe. There couldn't possibly be any real problems or troubles in the prophet's plural kingdom! Outbursts by any one of his nine beautiful, perfect, sweet wives were trivial. And they knew they should deal with their sins of the flesh by more fasting and praying—more pleading with God to take away any feelings that weren't conducive to godhood. With my father's wives trying to handle their own issues, he could be encouraging his church members to bury their never-ending issues, and get on with life. With most of them he would have a say, and with the majority he would surely be heard.

Just before I left, I said to Mom,

"Ever since Dad became Uncle Rulon's right-hand-man and then The Group's leader, most of us kids have no longer had a dad. When I was a little girl he'd hold me on his lap and rub my cheeks with his whiskers and tell me how much he adored my dainty little neck. I miss the times when our family was smaller. Dad only had fifteen kids' names to try to remember back then. Now he doesn't know who I am, and he doesn't seem to care."

Mom tried to cover him with her usual cloak of charity, like we were all supposed to do. "You know his calling as our prophet takes precedence. He has to—"

I knew where she was going. I'd heard it a thousand times and had explained it too many times to my own children. As I walked away I told Mom, "Just because Dad's calling is God's will, it doesn't give

338

our dad back to us, nor does it stop the longing."

On the back road toward home, I started to giggle. I realized my dad did know something about me. Since I started wearing a little makeup and was the first girl in The Group to get my ears pierced, Dad knew me as his daughter who wore "Indian war paint" and "fishing lures for earrings." At least I had a distinction from his other fifty-plus adopted and biological kids! And it was truly an honor to have a title, even if it was Troublemaker.

CHAPTER 37

Religious Perpetrators
1992–1993

Nothing turns my stomach or tears me apart more than the mistreatment of children. Everyone, it seemed, either knew or believed that Gregory Maynard had committed and allowed horrendous acts against women and children. We were haunted and sickened by such despicable and criminal behaviors, and wondered why Maynard had been able to be an abuser for so long.

Now, the other man on the priesthood council whom I had despised my entire life, Jon Thomas, was also accused of vicious and terrible acts. The story going around was that he had raped and molested some of his own children, as well as many others outside his family over the last twenty-plus years.

Shortly after this horrific news, and while I was caring for my aging mother, I was jolted awake by my father's loud, haunting cries. I crept out of bed, trying not to wake Mom, shut the bedroom door behind me, and tiptoed down the hallway toward the kitchen. I heard Dad's tormented, drawled-out words.

"She tried to scream, but . . . and then he threatened again . . . to kill . . ." Dad stammered between his sobs. I peeked around the corner. He was crouched over his old black tape recorder in front of him on the kitchen table. "My dear God . . . Oh dear God!" he cried out. "What have we done? What have we done?"

My father's body trembled in horror.

When he mentioned the name Laura, I felt faint and nauseous. I realized Dad was recording a journal entry and I wasn't supposed to hear it. But I was riveted.

My father tried again to compose himself and speak clearly. "She told me when he withdrew his bloody penis he pointed to the huge knife by the side of the bed and once again warned her she would be killed if she ever told anyone."

This was only a portion of Laura's account of her father's monstrous deeds. Her father was Jon Thomas.

My remorse was unbearable. I felt extremely dizzy and fought to keep my breathing under control. Then my legs collapsed underneath me, and my head hit the wall and then the floor.

Suddenly Dad was sitting next to me. He pulled my limp body to his chest and leaned against the wall. We both sobbed for a while. My body was boiling over with anger at Jon, and compassion for Laura. I was sure the pain would devour my heart.

Through blurry eyes, I saw my mother leaning on the wall next to her door with tears welling in her eyes. Then without warning, my forsaken, dejected little girl and young woman who had never been respected enough to be listened to finally let go of her rage.

"I told you I've known ever since I first saw Jon Thomas when I was just a young girl he was a creep! Even then I felt he was looking through my clothes. His presence always made me feel sick. I told you it was nearly impossible for me to sit through his monotone, tedious, sanctimonious sermons while feeling something was evil about him. Mark and I both knew something wasn't right. We felt the same with Gregory Maynard. But who are we? Just stupid, idiot peons! Our complaints and opinions held absolutely no value to you or to Mom! No, something was defective about us. You once told me Jon had a few problems, and the brethren had to call him to repentance for going over their heads. 'Oh, but don't worry Sophia, it's nothing serious you should fret about. Pray to have an understanding spirit, to help soften your heart toward Jon. We don't always know or understand what it is we feel. But we know he is a man of God.' You taught me to 'listen

to the still small voice' of the Holy Ghost. Then you told me not to!"
While Dad listened to me, tears continued to stream down his pale
cheeks. For a long moment, he stared back at me through red eyes.
Then he dropped his head and shook it from side to side.

"I just don't know, Sophia. I just don't know anymore."

"Dad, if Mark and I—just dumb little peons in The Group—had
this witness, then why didn't you, and Uncle Rulon, as prophets? Why
did Joseph Musser call Jon Thomas in the first place? Why would God
ever 'call' vile abusers to be His 'chosen' people's leaders? You believe those men were called in the name of God, right? And all of
you—including the council members—upheld, defended, sustained,
and harbored those two evil men, and believe me, there are still more
evil perverts in The Group, yet to be discovered."

In my childhood, I endured only a minimal amount of terror, sexual, physical, and verbal abuse as compared to so many children in
polygamous families. Though my own memories haunted me, my
greatest anguish was for Laura, after hearing Dad talk about some of
the barbarities she'd suffered from her own father.

I remembered with agonizing clarity, years before at girls' camp,
when she had awakened us with her bloodcurdling screams and fits of
terror. She couldn't tell a soul what was wrong, fearing she or someone else would be killed. She had no way, no words, no clue how to
plead for help and safety. In my ignorance, I believed the opinions of
my parents and others over my soul's warnings. I was told I was the
one with the "evil" attitudes toward Jon and Gregory. It was I who
was told to pray for help and understanding. But the reality was I had-
n't learned to honor my soul above everyone else, and I let Laura's
despicable father take her away into the night.

"As if you could have stopped him, Sophia," my therapist told me
a few weeks after I heard Dad's recording. "You need to forgive yourself for not knowing what to do differently. None of you were taught

how to defend yourselves or anyone else! No one, even in your own family, noticed your subconscious disappearances as something to be wary of. And even when many of the victims themselves continued to tell their own parents about the abuses, they weren't believed by those who should have made a difference."

For many days and nights I continued to feel a sense of responsibility and remorse beyond description. If only I could have known what to do, maybe I might have made a difference for Laura and others. I had to make amends. I sent a long letter, asking her to please forgive me, as I was working on forgiving myself.

Beautiful, courageous Laura said she had nothing to forgive me for. With love, she encouraged me to get my own forgiving done very soon.

I was breaking the Fundamentalist, womanly, sister-wife rules of servitude and obedience. I was no longer adhering to the creed of, "therein holds my womanly virtue and value." Jon Thomas's countless sermons about our womanly duties—of blind obedience to our husbands and priesthood leaders—made me sick enough to vomit. I was thankful I'd already begun to honor my soul.

For years, we'd heard of all sorts of promises and blessings, including more plural wives and endowments for "worthy" recipients. While in reality, those "approbations" were quite often given to those who were good at "kissing up" and winning spiritual "brownie points." They were for abusers, adulterers, men who were laundering money, embezzling tithing funds, trading daughters, and marrying relatives. Those "gifts" went to men who already had more children and wives than they could or would financially or emotionally sustain. The blessings had been and were still for all of the Jons and Gregorys who had been sheltered and protected under the auspices of religious piety and kinship.

My list of reasons to leave Fundamentalist Mormonism had become longer and more valid than my motives for staying. I'd begun to see the numerous flaws in a religion said to be perfect; I was beginning to discover and honor my soul's integrity; and lastly, I was discovering the meaning of real happiness.

For too many years, I'd observed the mostly unhappy, but righteous loved ones all around me. I noted too many broken and changed rules, deceptions, and lies. In the end, it was the false God of my fundamentalist religion who had called Gregory and Jon to be leaders, and it was their sadistic behaviors that finally spurred me to completely abandon the God of Fundamental Mormon beliefs.

How could I trust the God of my childhood who "called" those evil men as council members?

My childhood soul had spoken the truth to me since I was tiny. My adult soul saved the lives of my children and me. She honored, loved, and valued me. Even as a child my soul whispered in my ears to tell me I was valuable and good when no one else did. My soul was always truthful. When I listened to her rather than to my people-pleasing ego or the good intentions of the Samaritans in my life, my soul prodded me in the right direction. She awarded me with love, truth, and happiness. She knew where I'd been and where I needed and wanted to go. My goddess soul would be the God I would trust—at least for the present time.

I'd spent too many years of anguish, watching myself and others constantly fail a life fraught with impossible rules, and laden with bribes and threats. I decided to choose heaven. I quit attending church meetings on a regular basis. Without the constant coercion for blessings we could never earn, and the fear of damnation expounded from the pulpit, Sundays with my family became mellow, joyous, and rewarding.

CHAPTER 38

Life and
Runaway Karleen
1994–1997

Whenever possible, between my classes, teaching Head Start, Mark's work, and our multitude of duties, Mark and I met for lunch, dinner, a movie, lovemaking, and more gab sessions to discuss and debate anything and everything. I began to appreciate and respect some of his philosophical beliefs and thoughts I'd considered so hideous while cemented to my Fundamentalist ideals. With our newfound physical and emotional intimacy, we became renewed friends, lovers, and comrades—far more than we'd ever been before. Mark was forever delivering flowers to me in fun and crazy ways. We craved and appreciated each other in the many ways each of us gave and received.

In the past we were never able to live in peace, because my strong religious views always came between us. However great it may have been to no longer be divided in that way, I now lacked a religious reason to share the man I loved. The only reason to continue being a plural wife, other than for our children's sakes, was my newfound love for Mark. That became the ultimate irony.

Still, nothing stopped me from being concerned about Diane—her feelings, her life, or Mark's taking or stealing her time for our escapades. The first few months when I'd bring it up to him, he'd reprimand me.

"It's my life! My money, energy, and thoughts are mine. They are mine alone unless I decide to share them. Where, when, why, how, and who I spend my time with is no one's business but my own. So quit worrying about it, Sophia."

It took me a few more times to realize he was absolutely right. It was the same with all of us. I was not accountable for Mark's relationship with Diane, his kids, or anyone else. I was discovering my only responsibilities were to my underage children and myself. That was part of my new understanding about life, but changing my beliefs was quite different from suddenly being able to alter my actions, feelings, and habits.

I was working really hard to "let go and let live." More and more, I openly joined Mark in his disenchantment with and defection from the religious dogmas we'd been raised to adhere to. Unless I felt our children were being abused, I stepped aside from their conflicts with Mark as well. It was tough, but I was refusing to be our family's "relationship-fairness monitor" any longer.

In the past, I was too worried about being fair to Diane to consciously take part in a torrid love affair with Mark. Lingering in the back of my mind was always "the turnaround." I would wonder, "If Mark spends this much time with me when it is Diane's supposed time; he has probably done things the other way around when I was too busy in survival mode to care or notice." I figured if the tables were ever to turn, I wouldn't stick around.

I envisioned, not only for myself, but because I loved Diane, she would have courage to find the happiness she deserved with a man who would love and be with only her. But I felt sure she'd never go in that direction, no matter how many inequalities she felt there were between us.

Friends wondered why Diane seemed to be in denial about Mark's and my love affair. But as I had often done before, she too may have moved herself into survival mode, choosing to keep her eyes closed tightly to anything painful or threatening. No matter what she knew or didn't want to know about what Mark was doing behind her back, she loved him too. She always would.

It certainly wasn't her fault I resented her mental presence in the middle of our love affair. The more in love I became, the more difficult it was to stay. When I'd express that unease to Mark, he'd remind me of the allegiance I owed him, Diane, and our family.

"After all, you're the one who persuaded me to marry her, and both of us made commitments to her," he'd say emphatically. "We have to honor them." Or he'd say, "You know I can't leave Diane," as if he thought I was asking or demanding he leave her. "But I can't and won't do this without you Sophia! I've always believed in plural marriage. I've known all my life I'd live it. I will always be a polygamist."

"Your remarks sound like all three of us have to stay in polygamy just because we started there," I told him. "And you know darn well I am not asking you to leave her! I'm ticked off you would even insinuate for a split second I'd ever expect you to. I might like you to be able to, but we both know neither of us could live with ourselves if you left her for me. If the day ever comes I can't live this way any longer, I will have to be the one who leaves."

"I know, Sophia. I wish I could help you more, to make things more bearable for you, to love and kiss all of your heartaches away. It's hard for me too. Sometimes even I cry when I have to leave, but you know I have to."

꿏

During my first two years attending SLCC, Mark's perseverance was sometimes stronger than my own. His encouragement and assistance with our kids, the housework, and the meals were not only appreciated and admired by me, but by everyone else as well.

Teaching and going to school part-time was holding me back from graduating as quickly as I needed and wanted to, so I decided to quit teaching and become a full-time student. For the next two years I took twelve to eighteen credit hours per quarter.

Those days and hours were grueling. Along with mine, Mark's patience started growing thinner by the day. We hardly had any quality time together. When I could be home with the kids, he would steal me away alone. Of course, I felt guilty for leaving the kids, for buying a muffin on campus, or for going out to dinner without them when there was too little food at home. I missed my kids so much! I wasn't playing with them and helping them enough. I felt so guilty for feeling guilty I was cracking again. When I tried to study at home, I'd often hear Mark lose his temper with the kids. I'd rest my forehead on my textbooks and notes, and sob. I dreamed of a good-natured, patient, doting child-sitter for their sakes so I could relax, learn, and get my schooling done without feeling such torment for being away from them so much.

To top it all off, I became suspicious when Mark was gone from me and our home at times that were once considered "my time." Maybe Mark's "turnaround" was already happening. Yet, it didn't' feel right to try to change him or his decisions, so I moved into distraction and my own life again. I did what I always did to stay sane. I kept my mind, body, and heart busy in other directions. But this time was different. If Mark could have a love affair with Diane, I could have one too.

When a staunch-LDS philosophy professor and I passionately debated religion and philosophy, we began to justify our flirting around my marriage situation. Before long, we found ourselves creating intellectual and emotional highs before and after class.

The great part of those brain-teasing rendezvous was, no matter how much we cared for each other, we were both very safe. I knew he would never ask me to commit adultery with him. His were religious reasons, and mine were based on my personal values. While I foolishly tested the possible grounds of freedom from Mark, while he held to his convictions to forever be a polygamist, I participated in crazy, advance-and-retreat experiments, until the professor had finally had enough.

Another instructor at SLCC told his students about his Boy Scout outings and Church callings, but his prejudice and blatant disdain toward polygamists was manifest in his words and his cruel treatment of me.

My name and our address must have been the dead giveaway from the first day of class. He delighted in setting up situations and then snatching every possible opportunity to ridicule and embarrass me in front of other students. When I attempted to refute his accusation that I had cheated on a test—which every student in class knew wasn't true—and of being immoral, he rudely interrupted and meted out more unjust and vile comments.

His malicious behaviors tore open and salted a myriad of not-so-ancient and recurring wounds. In his classroom I never felt safe. Sometimes I'd go in the ladies room and cry in the stall. I wasn't brave enough to explain to my peers the reasons behind his contempt when they'd ask me, "Why on earth does he treat you so harshly? How does he get away with that? Why don't you report him to the Dean?" I could no more go to an authority then, than I could as a child and teen. After kindergarten, I'd had no protection from principals or teachers.

My childhood fears and distrust of outsiders—especially Mormons, who had been my archenemies throughout my lifetime—were still holding me at bay. I wanted to get out of his class, college, homework, and stress. I wished I could have run until I felt like a cougar again, until I'd run so fast I could take flight and never return.

Already overwhelmed, it took me nearly three months to pull through that thrashing. But with my Twelve-Step friends on my side encouraging me to keep going, to not listen to "the nasty old man's crap," my inner drive egged me on.

"You'll have to deal with someone's shit no matter when, where, or how far you go, Sophia." One precious Twelve-Stepper, an outspoken LDS soul sister I trusted, told me in a private conversation, "Just remember, Sophia, they are the ones behaving like a horse's ass." Then she giggled.

In June 1995, at the age of forty-three and a half, I proudly and finally graduated with an associate's degree in early childhood and elementary education. Other than giving birth to my children, that was the second time I'd felt such a grand sense of accomplishment and satisfaction. Mark, most of my children, my sisters Amy and Jolie, and a few other friends were there to watch me graduate with a 3.8 GPA, and on the Dean's list.

❧

I had the privilege of working full-time at Children First as the Education Coordinator's assistant. Many privately owned, as well as state and federally funded day cares, were beginning to require their child-care providers to complete 120 hours of training to obtain a childhood development associate certificate. All Head Start teachers and assistants were required to have a Child Development Associate certificate. With my Associate degree in Early Childhood Development, I'd already completed those valuable CDA courses through Head Start staff trainings and with Children First.

It was the most rewarding and enjoyable job I could have ever imagined. In the evenings we taught classes with an emphasis on competency-based curriculum that would be individualized to the needs and experiences of families and children. During our busy prep days, we wrote grant proposals for ongoing government assistance, and set up CDA classes across the state of Utah.

In addition to those jobs, I observed and took anecdotal records of each prospective candidate's teaching techniques, actions, and qualities, or the lack thereof, in the day care or Head Start facility they worked at. After several of those appointments we'd meet with the providers to discuss the outcomes. Working with those amazing women and a few men was fun and rewarding.

However, I found I was discouraged and annoyed nearly everywhere I went. In the past few years at SLCC, I'd taken a zillion wonderful, early-childhood classes on developmentally appropriate practices, places, and activities—and learned pretty much everything research professed was best for young children. I was especially concerned about the school-age children who were at day care while their regular school was not in session. What they needed and deserved wasn't happening. When I complained to my boss, she agreed.

Thanks to those classroom observations, the seeds were planted for me to start dreaming of a children's college. I envisioned a place that would accommodate elementary-age students in the Jordan School District. Fees would be charged on a sliding-scale based on a family's income. The children would have the opportunity to learn and enjoy countless subjects within their realm of learning style and ability. In 1995 and 1996 there was nothing for Utah children that even compared to my archetype—at least that I was aware of.

For the next year and a half, while my kids were at school, I enthusiastically worked on my ideas. I spent time at the library learning how to write a business plan. I researched already existing day-care charges, locations, community-based statistics, and every need imaginable. I volunteered to work with the Utah State School Age Child Care Association. For the state of Utah to receive federal funding, we set up focus groups for parents across the county to determine their needs and what they desired from child care centers. Part of this research paved the way for my opportunity to fly to Washington DC to attend a three-day National School Age Child Care Seminar and Conference.

The first week of November 1996, with much trepidation, Mark and I put our house up as collateral on a massive loan. After twenty-two years of payments on our home, the balance was only $16,000. I remember wondering if we'd ever get that paid off. Back then, $16,000 seemed like a billion dollars! Now we were hocking it for more money than I could fathom. Not only our home, but also two others were required as collateral for our half-million-dollar SBA loan. After bringing in two financial partners who also risked their homes, we purchased 1½ acres of land with a 2,400 square-foot building where a semi-functioning day care center was taking place.

Over the Thanksgiving and Christmas holiday, we remodeled the entrance; we planted flowers, a couple more trees and shrubs, and detailed the yard. Some of our friends and relatives helped paint, and scrub carpets, furniture, and walls.

We did everything else required by the state of Utah to update the codes for childcare licensing. Mark was incredible. For the next five grueling weeks he worked all day long at his regular jobs, and then worked late into the night and every weekend with me. Our ultimate plan was to slowly and progressively revamp the place into the outstanding children's college we would desire for our own grandchildren.

About the second week of December, shortly before we would reopen, Mark's resolve and energy came to an abrupt halt. I saw him every other night for the few hours I could go home to sleep, and for a few minutes every other weekend. He said he'd already done all he could do to support my dreams and goals, and now all he could do was deal with the financial worries. I continued to prepare for the opening of the center.

I purchased all the necessary food, school supplies, and toiletries, and hired eight Day Care Providers who'd completed their Child Development Associate certificates, and were ready for eighty-five children to show up.

When we opened our doors on January 7th, only twelve of those eighty-five children listed on the rolls the previous director had given me, showed up for care. In the next few months I found several more significant problems. We had to spend over $2,000 to repair the basement cracks after it filled with two feet of water; and the faulty heating and cooling systems. I also discovered I'd been given false information about the previous day-care center's functionality and numbers.

According to my figures, as well as my bookkeeper's and banker's figures, we should have been at break-even point when we opened and in the profit area with new enrollments within a few months. I had no other choice but to use our small amount of "working" capital to fix things and try to stay afloat. We were quickly sliding into the red by thousands of dollars.

Through all of our dread, our enrollment rapidly increased the first month. Children were so happy there, they didn't want to leave at the end of the day, and parents were delighted to leave their children with our superior day-care providers.

☙

Karleen, like her dad and me, had always taken the side of the underdog. She loved them all and desperately wanted to fix and save them. She brought home victims of abuse (real or imagined) who had been kicked out of their homes by their "horribly mean" parents. But before we were aware, a few of her supposed friends talked fourteen-year-old Karleen into getting "fixed" with a few drugs. While all of my time was consumed with my business, struggles with Karleen became worse by the minute. She quit helping at the center, and when she got permission to go somewhere with her friends, she often didn't return for hours or days. She would sometimes call to tell me she'd be home, and still she wouldn't show up.

From the middle of December to the end of January, my life was totally consumed with my day care center. Both partners held full-time jobs, Mark had quit, and I was trying to do everything myself. My jobs were teacher, driver, director, janitor, bookkeeper, cook, and manager. I had to show up at the center at 5:00 am and stay until nearly midnight every night but Sundays. With Karleen taking advantage of my insane workload, my other children's needs and concerns, my fragile marriage, the long hours, and financial stresses, I lost twenty-three pounds in six weeks. My body trembled, and I cried nearly all the time. I knew I couldn't keep going alone. With credit card money, I hired an assistant bookkeeper/director/bus driver, and a part-time student janitor to help us survive.

My assistant director was great. With her help, I had a few minutes to breathe. But no matter what I tried, by the end of January I knew I couldn't keep my dream alive without massive amounts of working capital. We had absolutely bottomed out all personal resources as well. My banker said they had already loaned me the maximum amount possible, and every other seemingly plausible option was negated by another problematic issue. There were several wonderful families who pled with me to make our place stay afloat. Those grateful, caring, and generous parents' loan offers still wouldn't have been enough to pay our bills and pay someone to take over for me while I left to go find my missing daughter. With every review of our budget and situation, the bottom line was, Karleen, my other children, my marriage, and my health were my first priorities. I'd have to let the center go.

In April 1997 my dream of a children's utopia ended about as quickly as it had started. Most of the teachers and the families of the forty-seven day-care children we'd enrolled were distraught. Some were even cantankerous they'd been let down after such a dynamic build-up. As soon as my Utah School-age Child Care Association conference in Florida was complete, I ended every obligation with them, closed the center's doors, and set out to get Karleen back home.

While I spent my days and nights searching for her, more pangs of anger and resentment toward me and God filled my heart. The whole time I had planned and visualized the children's college, I begged the God I still held a tiny residue of hope and belief in, to let my dreams fade away. "Please do anything it takes to halt this thing. Don't let it survive in my heart if it isn't meant to be," I'd pray. But as in the past, to add to all of His previous, villainous, traitorous deeds, God had also allowed Karleen's wayward insurrections. My dreams were gone, and my precious Karleen was on the streets.

I carried a few pictures of Karleen. At some of the homes where I believe she'd been hiding out, people told me they didn't know who she was. Those who did admit she'd been there would tell me, she must have just ditched me again. With the help of other drug-using kids or adults, she was long gone and in another hideout by the time I arrived. After a week of searching without any luck, I reported her missing as a runaway.

I kept in daily contact with the Salt Lake and Sandy City Police departments to give pertinent information or to receive any news. Three or four times, the police picked up Karleen and her friends for truancy and dropped them off at Youth Services. Then I'd pick her up from there. She would stay home in her room for a day or two while she slept off another crystal-methamphetamine-induced stupor, and then she'd be gone again.

With each disappearance she was gone for longer durations and called me less and less. I searched her drawers for numbers and addresses. A few lucky times when I got a mother or another person to put Karleen on the phone, she'd rage at me.

"You're a crazy, insane, mother! Just leave me the hell alone and let me have my own life!"

"I won't let you stop me from finding her and getting her back!" I screamed at the God who'd prodded His way back into my life. My determination to save Karleen, and God's resolve to punish us yet another time became the ultimate dispute between me and the deity of my childhood. "I will win!" I told myself before I made several more calls. I'd buckle Anne and Keith into the car, drive all over, and hit the streets again.

During all of this, my business partners, Mark, and I sold literally everything in the day care to make our monthly $1,500 payments until the building sold. All of us tried to not freak out too much about the possibility of losing our homes.

For a few more months I walked more neighborhoods from one side of the valley to the other. I asked everyone for leads, and left pictures of Karleen with our phone number. At the homes where she'd been hiding out, I was either shunned or revered as I continued to warn her alleged friends, their siblings, and parents not to harbor my underage daughter or I would press charges.

Mark's and my relationship was full of disaffection. His fury toward Karleen and her ongoing absence was more than I could stand.

As unsuccessful days turned into weeks, then another month, I continued to castigate myself for the derelict mother I believed I'd been. In the videotapes playing in my mind, I regretted the fights between Karleen and me, regretted not spending more time in laughter and play, regretted not standing in between her and her dad's fights and the malicious words he often directed at her. A million of my shortcomings haunted me.

On many of those long, miserable hours and days of worry, my eyes would again be so swollen from tears I could hardly see where I was driving. My only solace was my precious children who were home with me, and available to love and enjoy. I would never give up on Karleen! No earthly acquisition would ever be worth more to me than my children. I'd give up everything for them if I had to.

CHAPTER 39

Court-Appointed Recovery
1997–2001

One evening in the fall, after months of not hearing from Karleen, she called to tell me she was alive and okay. Actually, she'd called again to insist I stop looking for her. "I don't need you or Dad in my life right now!" she insisted. "Just leave me alone and stop bothering my friends and their parents!" She told me she loved me before she hung up. Even though she was probably under the influence of drugs and only said it to get me to back off, it still sounded great.

I picked up the wall phone and dialed *69—the best service the phone company ever came up with. I'd tried it several times before when Karleen had called, but she always blocked the numbers. This time, I swooned with joy when the operator gave me the number Karleen called from and told me pay-phone numbers couldn't be blocked.

With my heart nearly jumping out of my chest, I waited twenty minutes before I called, hoping Karleen wouldn't answer. The phone rang about fifteen times before I finally heard a young man say hello.

"Hi. Is Anthony there?" I said in the sexiest voice I could muster.

"No, ma'am," he said. "This is a pay phone. Ain't no An-tony here."

"Well, where are *you* at?" I asked. "You sound like a nice guy. Maybe you and I can meet up and gab for a while."

We chatted a few more minutes, and then with excited anticipation of meeting up with me, the young man gave me the address to the 7-

Eleven store where he said he'd wait for me.

The next morning as I drove nearly twenty-five minutes from our home, I was more hopeful than I had been in a long time. I smiled when I thought of the young man whom I'd intentionally stood up, and wondered what he must have been thinking. I hoped, if he knew Karleen, he'd waited for a long, long time after I told him to "give me ten minutes to get there," and I'd ticked him off royally.

At the 7-Eleven, I handed a kind-looking clerk a picture of Karleen, explained who I was, and asked if she'd seen my daughter. She told me she saw her at least every other day, and she came into the store quite often. I started to cry.

"The next time I see her, I'll ask her a few questions and watch to see where she goes when she leaves. Then I'll let you know," the clerk promised.

I waited on pins and needles. It was hard to leave the house even for a few minutes, fearing I'd miss the clerk's call. She sounded so sincere. I hoped with all my heart she wouldn't let me down. A few days later, the clerk called to tell me Karleen walked to and from a nearby trailer park, "sometimes with the kids she's tending."

The manager I talked to at the trailer park was just as affable as the clerk at the 7-Eleven. When I got home, I called the police to let them know how close I was to finding Karleen, and I'd soon need their help. I was full of hope and gratitude while I waited endlessly for another call from the park manager to let me know Karleen was for sure there, and which trailer she'd gone to.

Again, as I had a million times over the years, I contemplated how perfect it would if I had a phone I could take with me in my car. When would someone ever get them invented? I wondered. But of course, how could I ever afford one anyway?

Three days later the manager called to report she'd seen Karleen return to the trailer park. She knew exactly which trailer she went to. The police dispatcher took down the address I gave her, and I waited a tortuous three more hours while my imagination went berserk. Finally a policeman let me know they'd picked up Karleen, and I could get her from Youth Services again. "God," I shouted, "what will you do this time? Will she be home and be gone again in a flash, just as before? No! Something different will happen this time! I know it will!"

When I arrived at Youth Services, they sent me to the Juvenile Detention Center close by. There, I saw Karleen for the first time in nearly four months. She was pathetically thin and gaunt—she must have only weighed ninety pounds. She didn't want to hug me, but for the policemen's and guards' sake, she did.

A police officer told me the couple who lived in the trailer where Karleen was picked up had several outstanding warrants for their arrest. They were giving drugs to my daughter in exchange for her tending their children.

When the police dropped Karleen off at Youth Services, she was stripped and searched. They went through her clothes and everything she had in her backpack. Between the foil wrappers of a cigarette carton, they found some crack. She was booked in jail for possession. Karleen insisted the drugs weren't hers, that she grabbed the pack of smokes off of the entertainment center as she was leaving the trailer house. It didn't matter to me or the law.

"Yes!" I screamed inside. "Thank you, thank you, thank you, goddess of our souls!"

Nothing we'd ever done or tried to do to discipline Karleen had made one bit of difference to her. In the past six months, I'd waded through piles of shit. My heart was scalded from the terror a mother experiences while searching for her missing, possibly tortured and murdered daughter.

She had always known how to flash her beautiful, blue eyes, parade her bright smile, and sweet-talk her way out of the consequences of her wrongful actions. Though it hurt me as if I were being whipped with a willow when I recommended the judge come down as hard as possible on Karleen, it was also as cathartic as a debriefing from a bloody war zone. My last hope was there'd be consequences tough enough to get my daughter's attention.

After spending eleven days in juvenile detention, Karleen was released early on good behavior. The judge also sentenced her to six months of house arrest, and random drug testing. The best gift was he also ordered twelve weeks of therapy—for both of us.

While I attended Karleen's first court-ordered counseling session with Dr. Kris Branson, she was mean, tough, cold, and bitter. Some of the things Karleen revealed to us in those sessions seized my breath and doubled me over in agony. But as the drugs wore off and Karleen listened and talked to Kris and me. Our gorgeous, kindhearted, sixteen-year-old Karleen began to show up for life again. We got to experience and appreciate her divine soul more than ever before. When her court-assigned therapy sessions came to a close, she eagerly took leave as a stronger, more secure person.

Dr. Branson kept Karleen's file open so she could return if she wanted to; and so she and I could delve into my lifestyle, guilt, and shame that were still halting my progress. As time passed I knew the judge's soul had been directed to include me in those services. We had no health insurance of any kind, and no money for therapy. Dr. Branson's guidance was a bequest that would have otherwise been impossible.

The fact that my therapist, Dr. Branson, never encouraged me to divorce Mark was appreciated. She felt my desperation for someone genuine and consistent to help me process the constant turbulence in my head and my heart. Nothing there was new. The big questions were: Can I ever live a fully productive life without Mark and the love he so ardently claims to have for me, and can I fully commit to and be satisfied with half or less of his love, time and energy while we live polygamy?

Every hour I spent with Kris gradually offered me more life, and a fighting chance at living the rest of it to the fullest. She astutely took my side and Mark's side, listened to me, and sometimes cried with me. Until I heard or saw evidence of another client, I always forgot I wasn't her only one.

By fall, the day-care center still hadn't sold. Mark had already put his business on the line and borrowed more money. By November, that loan had maxed out. Our homes and everything we had were going into foreclosure. Just in the nick-of-time the God of love found us a good realtor who found us a buyer, and we were saved by the seat of our pants—at least to a minimal degree. After being ripped off via the buyer's bankruptcy the following summer, and false promises, we ended up starting all over again. Instead of the payoff on our home being $16,000, it ended up being $98,000.

In abundant gratitude, I thanked my interim God, Buddha, our partners' homes were free of liens, back where they were before my turbulent adventure.

Even though Mark was gone more than usual, things also seemed better at home. He reminded me I shouldn't count on him—not his presence, his time, his undivided love, attention, or his life. His life was his, not ours! Therefore, my time and life had to become my own, as well. Most of the time, as newly developing individuals, we were able to bring our uniqueness together and stay good at loving and caring, but my struggles with the same-old familiar resentment, suspicions, and envy made me desperately want to ask Mark, "Where have you been? What took you two or three extra hours to come home? Who have you been hanging out with?"

Sometimes those squelched words made their way clear to the tip of my tongue. I'd gulp them back down and soldier on. I reminded myself not to delve into anyone's business but my own.

To really love Mark while we lived polygamy felt more impossible by the day, so I continued to keep really busy. I made new friends, hung out with my kids (kidults) and grandchildren, and enjoyed my new job as a Head Start Teacher and Home Educator in the Granite School District. But the best thing about staying busy was it kept my mind distracted from Mark's other lives. While those were rebuilding, as well as staying techniques for me, Mark saw them as me avoiding and withdrawing from him.

Several times a day, I mentally reviewed the reasons to stay and the reasons to go. *Should I stay with Mark and Diane and our kids and try to graciously accept the things I can't change? Or should I try to find a man and a life of my own and leave Diane in bliss with her own husband?* On secure days I thought I would be okay with the latter, but on insecure days that thought made me envious.

"I won't live plural marriage without you, Sophia," Mark tenderly reminded me once again as we sat across a cafe table. "You and my kids are the reasons I lived plural marriage in the first place! I love you more than anyone ever can. Don't you know that? Please don't leave. I can't and I won't do it without you."

"That doesn't make any sense, Mark. You and I both know it was only our ingrained testimony of plural marriage that started all this pain in the first place. You know you don't have to have me in order to stay with Diane."

Mark and I, and even Diane—though she wasn't aware of the extent of it—were facing the crossroads of our lives. None of us had any clue which way we'd go. Maybe he was right when he said, "Yes, our family is dysfunctional, but why trade this craziness for another one? At least we are crazy about each other in all of this."

I'll make us work I decided. "For better or for worse," I reassured myself.

CHAPTER 40

Test Angst and College
2000

"**I**t's better to have tried and failed than to have failed to try, Sophia," my dear friends encouraged. "You'll be forty-nine even if you don't get a bachelor's degree, so you might as well be forty-nine with one."

In the summer of 2000, I studied for the Praxis Test until I was sure my brains would fall out. At Southern Utah University (SUU) in Cedar City, after hours and hours of the most grueling, terrifying test I'd ever taken, I sat in my car and sobbed. I was sure I failed. All those young brains testing with me looked brilliant, lighthearted, and full of self-confidence.

Before the test I had already told the SUU Education Department's student adviser, "Please don't bother calling to tell me I failed the test—it will be embarrassing. When I don't hear from you, I'll know for sure."

"We'll call you either way, Sophia," she said. "You'll know in a few weeks."

Since I didn't trust in my abilities, I was sure I didn't pass. Aside from the sections I felt confident about, I guessed the answers on too many of them, and didn't have time to finish the history and math sections.

❧

On the other end of my phone, the student advisor's voice was monotone. "Sophia, this is Tammy. As I promised, I'm calling to tell you—"

"I already know, Tammy," I interrupted. "At least I tried. I've been telling myself it's all okay."

"Well, I'm sorry too," she said sadly. "If you hadn't missed so many questions, maybe you'd have gotten one hundred percent, rather than eighty-eight percent!"

I wasn't sure exactly what she meant. I guessed, just like the last Praxis test I took a few years previous, I'd missed the grade by a few points. "I'm okay Tammy. I wasn't sure I would make it. Now I'll have more time at home with my kids."

"But you did, Sophia," she said excitedly. "You got eighty-eight percent! You passed. You're in!"

Our phone receiver flew clear across the kitchen before the cord stopped it. It sounded like our floor would cave in from my jumping up and down. I screamed and pounded on the countertop. "I did it! I did it! I'm in! I'm actually in!" I chanted.

When I remembered Tammy might still be waiting, I found the phone and thanked her profusely.

For the rest of the summer, I had to do double time to get ready to go to SUU for a year. I was determined to finish the basement I'd started pounding down, gutting, and hauling out clear last spring. I wanted to finish things so I could come back to something complete, comfortable, and beautiful. To remodel our basement was a dream Mark and I'd held onto ever since Diane moved out.

Aside from the remodeling, I kept busy with friends and family. I hiked in our foothills nearly every day with my dear friend and neighbor, Racine. She, unlike most of our neighbors, always treated me with kindness and respect.

The past several years, though difficult in many ways, had also been beautiful and full of joy. Amid my pandemonium and sorrows, my decision to stay with the man I loved and wanted to spend my life with had been worth it all. In the summer of 1999, Mark and I flew to

Oregon and drove to Mt. Shasta for a second round. We rented a car and drove up the coast to Astoria and back down Interstate 5 where we spent a few amazingly romantic nights at a beach house. We were still doing great, so I felt really secure about leaving 255 miles south of home, for more education.

Before I was off, I desperately wanted to spend a couple weeks with Mother Nature, reading, writing, listening to the waterfalls, and meditating in our grand Rocky Mountains. It had been way too long. I bought groceries and packed the tent, camping gear, and everything else Anne, Keith, and I would need. I hoped Mark and the rest of our adult kids, (kidaults) and grandchildren would make time to come up as well.

On Friday, the second day at camp, Mark showed up with a huge surprise. He said he'd bought Diane and me a pop-up camping trailer. Our whole family had wanted some "easier" camping, so I was elated when Mark replaced the old tent I'd set up at Tanner's Flat Campground with our new-used small but comfortable camping trailer before we settled down for the night.

On Saturday afternoon, when Mark came up again, he bitterly complained, "I am sick to death of Diane's disgusting, selfish attitude about you using *her* trailer!" I tried to dissuade his anger, so we could have peace for the rest of the day, and Sunday before he went down to the city again.

When he came up on Tuesday afternoon, he was still fuming. "I told Diane I bought the trailer for both of you, but since she's the one who found it in the ads in the paper, she insists it is hers. She says you always get everything you want, so she should have the trailer for herself. I've had nothing but hell to pay ever since I brought the damn thing up here for you to use! All she's done is scream and cry about the stinking thing. I'm sick of her attitude! I bought it for all of us—but no, she has to be a selfish bitch and keep it for herself."

During his tirade, I did my best to stay calm. My anger and resentment toward Diane came from the comments Mark said she'd said about me, more than her desire to be the sole owner of the trailer. I told

365

Mark I didn't blame her. I knew how she felt. She also loved camping. She would have more opportunities to use it than I ever would. Besides, I knew all along there was no way I would sleep with Mark in that camper after he and Diane slept in it. If only I'd have known that's how Diane felt before Mark brought it up, I would have refused to use it in the first place.

By Thursday evening, Mark's constant agitation was making me livid and sick as well. He wouldn't let up.

"I'm sick of hearing about this!" I finally snapped. "Your ranting about all of this has ruined my plans for a calm, quiet vacation. I've had enough of it, Mark. I don't want to hear another word about any of this, ever. What do you expect me to do about it? Why are you telling me all this crap? If the camper is hers or even if she just thinks it's hers, I don't want to use it now or ever again. I'm going to unpack tomorrow morning so you can take it to her. I'll either go home or set the tents back up and stay. I'm sick of hearing about it, and sick of you putting me in the middle of all this crap! Just give her the damn thing and let it be!"

Mark tried to talk me out of unpacking the camp trailer. I did anyway and stayed a few more days with the kids in our tents. The rest of the family, who came up to visit and to stay, had a wonderful time before we called it quits.

✠

Our Thanksgiving celebration was huge. Mark, Diane, and I, all our kids and some of their partners, our grandkids, my brother James, my sister Amy and her husband, other friends and their kids all met in our completely empty, unfinished, basement family room.

As usual, during our years of family-and-friends gatherings, I enjoyed the company, food, and visiting, just not the responsibility of the long, drawn-out preparations. We'd get it all setup, just to have it over with in a few minutes, and still have to clean up after the huge mess.

That Christmas, we again decided it would be less expensive to draw names for a family gift exchange. We divided our large and growing family of twenty-one into three age groups: adults, teens, and kids under twelve. Gifts were opened, starting with the youngest child on up to the oldest adults. When Diane opened her movie passes and gift certificate for a motel room, she looked at me, then at Mark. "Ooh, honey!" she cooed, "now you and I can have a romantic night on the town!"

After Mark opened the road atlas I purchased for him, Diane snuggled into his shoulder. "Oh, baby, now we'll have directions when we take road trips together." I thought Diane must still feel so insecure that she wanted to spite me with those little pokes and jabs.

According to Norma, she thought I intentionally flaunted my affection for Mark in front of her. I was really surprised. I'd always done my best to be the opposite around her. I remember only once carrying out a premeditated plan to intentionally cause Diane some major discomfort. When she had her own car and I was totally dependent on her for transportation, she often left my kids and me stranded and helpless; often without a good reason or any apologies. It was the same when we had to share a car. So, when I had a chance for a payback, I took it.

She had someplace she wanted to be at a certain time, so I took my time with our car. "As long as you please . . . come on, Sophia . . . hold out a little bit longer," the imp on my shoulder coaxed. "If you give in now, you won't have made your point," the devil had to insist, since my stomach was in huge knots. "Just stay long enough for her to know exactly how it feels."

By the time I got home, I was mortified and filled with guilt. When I saw Diane's angry tears, I knew exactly how she was feeling. I also knew my little shenanigan was a foolish blunder. It served to make me feel like a heap of dung!

In the weeks before I left for Cedar City, I reminded my precious mother she couldn't get sick anymore, "at least for a whole year, until I return in December to help take care of you again."

Mom had been deathly ill off and on with congestive heart failure and profuse bleeding. Three times in the past five or six years, our family had gathered to say our final farewells to her. With each recovery, she'd giggle, smirk, and say, "Well, I guess it must not be my time to go yet."

She also had severe dementia. While most of her long-term memory was still intact, her short-term memory worsened by the day. No matter how many times I explained my impending absence, she'd ask me repeatedly, "Now where did you say you are going? When are you coming to see me again? Why are you going way down there?" Each time I'd repeat the answers and tell her to stay healthy while I was gone, she'd reply, "Okay, Sophia, I'll do my best to stay healthy and wait for you."

CHAPTER 41

Following My Dreams
2001

My sister Jolie and I originally planned to trade homes for a while. She'd stay in ours while she attended SLCC in pursuit of her nursing degree, and I'd stay in hers while I went to SUU. But by the time I was about to head south, she moved into a room in her daughter's basement in West Valley City, Utah.

Jolie didn't ask me to give her any money for the use of her home, because she wanted a house sitter, and would need the heat running through the winter. But I talked Jolie into at least letting me give her one hundred dollars a month to help with the utilities I'd be using, though she might have to wait until I got a job.

❦

I'd often talked with friends about changing my name. I'd always wanted to. My choices, feelings, and beliefs had changed so much I no longer felt the name Sophia fit the new me. I also detested the name Sophia because it was a constant reminder of the mishaps, the name-calling, the abuses, the abandonments, the imperfections, and the ruthless God in Sophia's life.

Mark's and my newly remodeled basement was nearly complete. Alone in my serenely of my beautiful bedroom, I began to meditate. Snow completely concealed the bare tree limbs around the house. The moonlight's reflection spun off the snowflakes and danced on my lavender walls like stardust. I looked back at where I'd been since birth and where I was going from now on. The only constant about Sophia was her soul and her sincere desire to make better choices in her life. That was it! I would change my name and be thrilled about it. People would condemn me, but I didn't care. In a new city and school, I could test out a name I'd always loved. I chose to be called Kristyn.

✢

The first week of January 2001, I kissed and double-kissed and hugged my family goodbye. I didn't know anyone at SUU or in Cedar City, other than one of Jolie's full brothers, who I hadn't been in contact for a long time, her ex-husband's family, and a few more Allred Group people who still lived in the area.

Driving to Cedar City, I tested and listened to my new name. I said it out loud, softly and quietly. I even yelled it as a happy "KRIS-TYN! KRIS! KRI-STEN!" And I tested it with an angry tone. No matter how I said the name, it couldn't sound nearly as horrible as I'd heard "Sophia" used before. My name had been used in mean and disgusting ways to spite, hurt or threaten me. The most hurtful sound of my name was when Mark used it in anger or rage. During those times my name was more offensive to me than any four-letter swear word he could ever use.

Two hundred thirty-five miles south of Bluffdale, I exited I-15 at the golden arches of McDonald's. My stomach was queasy as I turned west on Highway 56, heading all alone to the middle of nowhere. But my apprehension was accompanied by hope. My longtime goals of becoming an independent woman and a teacher were finally within my reach!

Two and a half miles west of town, I rolled down the window to read a street sign. The ice-cold January breeze carried the comforting scent of sagebrush. When I pulled into Jolie's driveway alone in the dark, I took several deep breaths of the fresh air and told myself,

"Have no fear, Sophia my dear! Oops—I mean Kristyn dear, have no fear. From this moment on, you are a woman with endless possibilities!"

I used the code to open the garage. Then I pulled my car in, found the light switches, turned up the thermostat, and began to unload my car.

Later, in the bedroom, Jolie's venetian blinds let in shafts of moonlight. I was happy—I knew I was. But when I climbed under the cold sheets and cuddled with my own pillow, I cried myself to sleep. During the night I woke over and over again. *Will Keith and Anne be all right without me? Will their dad make sure they are taken care of and their needs met like he promised? Will they be happy—will they miss me? Will they come to believe I'm a shithead mom for leaving them?* I wished I'd made them come to Cedar City with me. Already I missed my family so much it hurt. *Where are our married kids and grandchildren? What am I doing way down here in this dark, deathly quiet, all by myself?*

On my sixth day in Cedar City and my fourth day of classes at SUU, Karleen called to tell me she was in labor. I attended my literature class without really being there. My first daughter was giving birth to her first baby!

After my last class, I hurried north. All I could think about was Karleen. She'd married a wonderful Hispanic man and was safe, happy, in love, and having a baby. Wanting to be with her during the delivery, I broke the speed limit all the way back to the Salt Lake Valley. I arrived at the hospital in South Jordan to find she had hours to go before she'd be pushing.

I tried to be strong, or at least to look like I was. My daughter's every pain and discomfort were mine as well, so I was grateful I'd somewhat come to terms with her having an epidural.

Though things were going smoothly for Karleen and her unborn baby, I couldn't help but worry for them. All the familiar smells and sounds, along with the anticipation, made me reminisce about Karleen's delivery. The prolonged and excruciating labor that took place previous to her birth at Aunt Amelia's house almost nineteen years earlier was fresh in my mind.

Karleen's handsome husband nudged my shoulder. "Why are you crying, Suegrita? Are you okay?"

"Just memories." I hugged him. "I'm so happy my gorgeous girl is with you and going to have a handsome, brown-eyed prince!"

❧

Back on the campus at SUU, I was in total awe. There were so many beautiful young women and handsome young men who had recently graduated from high school. Most of them appeared to have the world on a string, expecting nothing but perfection in their lives. Without a friend to hang with or talk to, I felt like an alien among hundreds of personality-plus, techno kids. They must have wondered what on earth this grandma person thought she was doing back in school, particularly when I'd try to fit into one of their youthful discussions. At least, my wizened, hard old sponge of a brain started sending more beta signals every day. I began to squeeze into my brain every shred of information it could possibly retain.

Never had I expected to feel so lonely I'd actually miss the hustle, bustle, and commotion of our city stomping grounds. Nor did I think I'd long for the messes and the noises. It also surprised me how much I missed the crowds of teens and adults who lived in and frequented our home day and night. My loneliness was the only reason I could come up with as to why I lost nearly fifteen pounds in just over five weeks.

When I talked to the kids and Mark on the phone nearly every evening, they told me they were doing fine. A couple of times I reminded Mark to finish filling out the Children's Health Insurance Program papers and get them turned in to Workforce Services so Anne and Keith would have medical coverage while I was in school.

The few times I talked to Jolie on the phone or when she came down, I asked her for names or phone numbers of her friends, or of people I might meet and hang out with. She ignored my inquiries and went on her merry way as if I didn't exist. After I moved back home a year later, Jolie apologized. She said she had always been envious of me, and while I stayed in her house those feelings had tormented her again.

Near the first of February, I found a social club ad in a local newspaper, inviting new members. When I called the number, a guy named Greg told me the group of middle-aged men and woman met on a regular basis to bowl, hike, dance, and meet up for meals, or "…whatever else we decide will be fun."

At Denny's restaurant, I waited for a group of people to come in. At least I should have seen a few people gathering or looking for others. When a husky, black-bearded guy asked me if my name was Kristyn and then sat down across from me, I wondered if I'd been set up.

"Sorry, gal, but no one else can make it tonight, so I guess it's just the two of us," he said, then introduced himself as Greg.

What the heck, I thought. I'm alone with nothing better to do right now, and I drove all the way into town to get out for a while. I told Greg I was married, had seven kids and thirteen grandchildren; I hike, study and attend college every day and most evenings, but want a social outlet and some activities to attend now and then.

In less than two weeks, after a few phone chats and a walk in the public park, I let Greg know his expectations were not going to be met. "I won't be calling you, and don't you call me," I said.

※

Nearly every night for three and a half weeks, Mark told me how much he missed me, but his words were getting more and more difficult to believe. After I left for Cedar, he had an opportunity to spend six nights in a row with Diane, yet he wouldn't spend three nights in a row with me while I was home helping Karleen and the new baby. Whenever I asked, he had one idiotic reason after another to postpone a weekend trip to see me.

"I've been back down here for three weeks now, and you're telling me you won't be able to come down until next weekend? Why? What do you have to do that's so important?" I asked.

His evasive answers bothered me more than if he'd just flipped me off. Even an honest reason that hurt me would've been better than another of his excuses. He tried to make it sound like his concerns were about Diane's feelings. I'd heard his genuine concern about Diane's feelings enough times over the past twenty-two years to know he wasn't being truthful about that, either. Also, since he had ninety percent more time to be with Diane after I left, none of his bull made any sense. I didn't really believe she could justifiably complain about him spending a few days with me.

For over a year, it seemed Mark's life had been changing more and more, especially with all of his weird and unexplained absences. He'd begun adamantly proclaiming, stronger than ever before, his time and his life were his own, and what he did with them was no one else's business but his own. He'd become noncommittal and evasive, and his decisions totally bewildered and frustrated me. What was going on with him? If I didn't know better, I would've thought he was having an affair with a third woman. What I really thought I was hearing from him, was coming down to see me was nothing more than a pain in the butt and a drain of his pocketbook. Debating about it only got him riled up, which brought him to more vehement claims of independence.

Mark finally made it down to Cedar City five and a half weeks after I started school there. He arrived on Friday evening and left Sunday afternoon. I took advantage of his company and didn't question his evasiveness that had become more obvious since my departure. We made up for the lack of time together, had some long visits, and took a short road trip. I loved the time we had together, and hated him to leave.

A few weeks later when I answered the phone, I heard a deep voice on the other end of the line say, "Hi, is this Kristyn?"

"Yes."

"My name is Graham," the man said timidly. "I know this might sound weird, but we have or should I say had a mutual acquaintance in common—Greg.

"Yes?"

"Well, Greg said you may want to have a friendship with someone to uh . . . just have coffee and gab with." Graham hesitated. "Greg says he got too pushy, so you told him to take a hike. He said I might be the kind of friend you are looking for. I am a *good friend* kind of a guy, and that's all."

When I laughed at his shy but convincing tone and words, he laughed too. "Wow, I'm not really sure what to say. Did Greg tell you I'm married and have . . .?"

"Yes. He said that's why you dumped him, but like you, I'm not looking for anything more than a friendship either. Do you think you'd like to meet me for some pie or something and we can gab for a while?"

I smiled. At last I might have someone in Cedar City to hang out and talk with.

※

The first week of March, a week after I'd been up to Bluffdale for a weekend, Mark came down with his two best friends. Before they came down, he'd explained for quite a while, he and Diane had been double dating with Norma and Jared. The foursome had been spending a lot of time getting reacquainted. Mark told me Diane had done her best to keep him away from her lifelong friend, Norma. After all these years, according to Mark, Diane still felt jealous because she knew of Mark and Norma's long-ago crush on each other.

"Until lately," Mark said, "all Jared and Norma heard was Diane's opinion of you. Now that they've heard what I have to say about you, they want to come down with me so they can get to know you better."

"No!" I immediately said. "In the first place, Norma and Diane are best friends, so I don't trust this idea at all. Norma probably wants to hear what I have to say, so she can tell Diane everything I do or don't say. And secondly, I agree with Diane. It doesn't matter how long it's been since Norma babysat for us and you two wanted to get married; for some reason, I just don't have a good feeling about it either."

"There's nothing for you to worry about," Mark persisted. "Just give them a chance. They're great people. I know you'll like them."

I always liked Norma—I just didn't trust her in *my* life! It could have been because of her fling with her husband before they were married, when neither of them seemed to give a rat's ass about Jared's first wife, Callie's feelings. Also, years previous, my sister Francine's sister-in-laws warned her not to trust Norma, since they felt that while she acted like a friend—she was busy chopping you into pieces behind your back. But more than anything, my reservations were because I didn't want to hurt Diane.

"Give them a chance, Sophia," Mark said. "I'm sure you'll find out you're wrong."

To please him, I gave it a go.

In the early afternoon after Mark, Norma, and Jared arrived; the four of us sat in Jolie's family room and visited for hours. We laughed and discussed life. We shared our philosophies, thoughts, and feelings. We talked about all of our kids. And we discussed Diane—about whom all of them claimed to have become an expert. Mark, Norma, and Jared flooded me with information about Diane's kids, her insecurities, her life, and what they felt were her defects of character. I cried, when according to their claims, Diane felt everything gone wrong in her life was because of me. I knew she and I had normal jealous feelings, but that news cut me to the core.

Most of what they said about Diane was more than I ever wanted to hear. I hurt for her and her kids.

"Just in case you were worried," Norma said." The information they confided in me was intended to smooth over my concerns. They said I could trust them to keep quiet about anything I might say and anything that would go on between the four of us. However, it created the opposite effect. They—especially Norma—had been bad-mouthing her dear friend Diane, to me. So why would I think it wouldn't or hadn't already gone the other way around?

The next morning, Norma and I hiked to the foothills and partway up the mountain paths I'd frequented and grown to love. There, she told me her spirit guide had revealed to her that Mark was to be her best friend and support. The reason for Mark's special calling was because she'd also been told by her spirit guide she would die sometime within three years. Not only could Mark help her cope with her imminent death, but he would also be able to care for and comfort her three little boys more than anyone else. "Since he lost his own mother at a very young age, he knows and understands what my little boys will be going through," she said.

Suddenly I knew why Mark had been absent and evasive for so long. No wonder he'd been too busy to come see me for five weeks! I bit my tongue not to scream out loud. I was angry he hadn't told me about their "divinely bestowed friendship?"

Her death, Norma said, was so Callie, Jared's first wife, would go back to him. Norma explained, her guide said the only way that would ever happen was if Norma was no longer in Jared's life. Norma said she was willing to sacrifice her life for Jared and Callie's sake, since she believed they were soul mates or "twin rays" and should be together forever.

"If Callie ever wanted to go back to Jared and it was about you being in the way, then why don't you divorce him? To die and leave your family and kids just doesn't make any sense."

"I don't understand it all," Norma replied. She thought perhaps Callie wouldn't feel comfortable going back to Jared if she, Norma, was still alive. She was just going with what she was told by her spirit guide, and would need a lot of love and support during her coming ordeal.

Norma wanted to know how I felt. It sounded crazy and ridiculous to me, but I knew I had no right to spurn her beliefs. They were hers and she had a right to them, no matter whether I thought she was right or wrong. I was sure everyone would feel the same way about me changing my name. All I could do was be truthful with her.

"I think your spirit guide is off her rocker." I laughed teasingly. "But just because it doesn't make one bit of sense to me doesn't mean your plight isn't real. And in spite of your concerns and deep fears about dying and leaving your boys, I believe the death you're feeling isn't a physical death at all, but a huge change in your life—possibly a divorce or the death of your marriage. And as far as your friendship with Mark goes, you are both grownups and old enough to make your own decisions. In fact, it looks like both of you already have, even without Diane's or my approval. But believe me, Norma, what really bothers me the most about all of this is you two have kept this secret from me, Jared, and Diane. If this 'friendship' is really appropriate, there should be no reason to keep any secrets about it. Jared especially has a right to know about all of this! He is your husband and the father to your boys!" I paused, then told her from the bottom of my heart, "Norma, in all the years Diane has been married to Mark, I've known of too many times he has lied to her, or kept things from her to avoid conflict or jealousy. He would justify it when I'd get mad. I told him I wanted and needed him to always tell me the truth no matter what! I'd tell Mark, 'It doesn't matter to me what you do, did, or didn't say that would ever break my heart or cause jealousy and pain. I'd still want you to tell me the truth, because I know I'd be wounded a million times worse if I found out you lied to me, or were deceitful like you have been to Diane. Any day, I would rather hear the truth from you even if it causes me excruciating pain, rather than ever have you lie or be deceptive to me!' That's how serious I feel about it, Norma! I think Diane, and especially Jared, have a right to know what's going on."

"They just can't know about this, Sophia. They won't be able to deal with it or understand the information," Norma claimed. "It's just not the same with Diane and Jared. I just can't tell them, at least not right now. Besides, Diane isn't like you. She doesn't want to know about anything hurtful. She keeps her head buried in denial. Maybe someday things will be different."

No matter how many reasons I gave for Norma to tell Jared and Diane, she came up with just as many to cancel them out. Not one of those reasons for her secrecy felt reasonable or acceptable to me, but that was Norma's way of thinking.

All weekend long, and for the rest of Sunday before they returned to Salt Lake; Mark, Norma, and I listened to Jared's sometimes entertaining stories, which he embellished and elaborated with each retelling.

A few weeks later I met another friend on the phone. Lyle called to talk to Jolie. They talked once after an online dating service connected them, and then Jolie started dating someone else. I explained Jolie was living in Salt Lake to get a nursing degree and I was staying at her house to get my teaching degree from SUU. That phone call set in motion significant changes in both Lyle's life and mine.

CHAPTER 42

Cedar City and
My Mother's Death
2001

My plans were to take several classes during the summer so I could finish school in the fall rather than in the winter. Things weren't meant to pan out that way. My soul knew there were other things in store and I had to be home, and it miraculously worked out so I ended up with a six-week summer break.

On my way home I met Mark in Salina at the gas station. He was on another camping trip with his new large family of friends: Jared, Norma, Diane, their kids, and some of mine. He and I headed up a canyon for some afternoon delight, but for the first time in ten years Mark was impotent again. Some of our most thrilling times were out in the wild, which was an aphrodisiac for us. I was hurt and angry while he tried to guess why he just couldn't make things happen. He had a dozen reasons. Among them was his angst about what everyone else thought might be taking him so long. On the drive back to my car I asked him if he and Norma had ever been tempted and wanted to have sex together. He hesitated then answered. "I'm married to you and she's married to Jared!"

"So, you didn't answer my question, Mark," I said.

"Yes, I did. Anything that goes on or doesn't go on between me and Norma—or anyone else, for that matter—is none of your business! If we keep it like that things will be okay."

"No it won't be okay!" I yelled. "Just because you think you can keep your life a big secret doesn't mean everything will be okay!"

I climbed in my car and left without hugging or kissing him. I started to cry. The rest of the way to Salt Lake, I listened to the radio and sang to my heart's content.

Since leaving in January, Mom had been minimally healthy. On my previous weekend visits home I'd spent as much time as possible with her. This time as soon as I got home for the summer, Mom started a rapid downhill slide. It was as if her body and soul were telling me, "We waited as long as we could. Now it's time for us!" Mother couldn't breathe or sleep well at night. She complained of pain nearly all the time, yet couldn't identify it or where it was coming from.

On July 26th, my sister-in-law Ruth, (my mom's nurse/caretaker), my father, and I sat with a hospice facilitator while she explained the processes and care we could expect from them. Dad signed all the necessary papers, while I walked outside with Ruth before she went home. Then Mom and I waited together while a hospital bed was delivered. Aunt Eleanor dictated where she thought it should be set up, and then we made up the bed and tucked her in. Other than Mom's episodes of not feeling well, she was her usual happy, precious, tired, thankful, restless, forgetful, beautiful self.

Later in the day, a nurse came to discuss the medications Mom would be given to help her relax and to be pain-free and comfortable. I held my mother's hand while I sat next to her on the edge of her hospital bed. The nurse asked her if she was allergic to morphine. She said no.

She asked me if my mom was allergic to morphine, and I said I didn't think so. But within minutes of the morphine injection, Mom's arms started jerking and flailing up and down. Her eyes start rolling in her head, and when I screamed at the nurse to do something she didn't seem at all alarmed. She said Mother's reaction was common—that it had something to do with her muscles relaxing so much.

"She'll be okay. Her jitters will soon subside and she'll be resting like a baby."

Her words didn't help at all and I panicked. Mom was fine ten minutes earlier and she was getting worse by the minute.

Ruth returned within minutes and started yelling, "Did the nurse give Mom morphine? Did she? Mom's allergic to morphine!" Then Ruth asked the nurse, "How much morphine did you give her?"

"Twenty mg's," the nurse replied.

"That's way too much morphine to give anyone!" Ruth shrieked. Her nervous, aggravated words directed at the nurse became a jumbled-up mess in my shocked and confounded mind.

"Dear God!" I cried out. "Oh, dear God, what is going to happen to Mom?" Amid Ruth's ranting, I remembered Mom had told me many years ago she was allergic to morphine.

When Dad came back and was told Mom had been given morphine, he too was appalled. "I didn't remember to tell the nurse," he wailed over and over again.

He lay next to Mom, holding her, and explained how close she'd come to death when she was given morphine during my sister Lucinda's delivery. Ruth called the nurse to come back, but the nurse assured her Mom would be okay. With good news, and Mom finally calming down, I rushed a few miles into town to get some lunch for everyone.

How could I have forgotten Mom was allergic to morphine? I scolded myself over and over again. I couldn't shop. By the time I'd rushed back, her room was full of people, all gathered around her bed. My knees nearly buckled under me when it dawned on me what was happening. I screamed, sobbed, and moaned. "No! No, this can't happen! Mom was just fine! No, she can't die yet. She's got more time left!"

Ruth held me tightly and whispered, "Our mother has been waiting for you to come back, so you can tell her goodbye."

I backed up. "No! Don't just stand there Ruth—do something!

Give her back her oxygen! Stop her from gasping! She isn't supposed to die yet. Help her, Ruth! You know what to do."

Calmly, and as true to love and life as she is, Ruth told me again, "Sophia, your mother isn't in any pain—she's unconscious."

"I don't want my mom to die now. I ran to her and fell over her chest. "I'm sorry we didn't remember your allergies Mom. I'm so sorry I left you! The nurse told us you'd be okay. Dad thought you would be okay. I want you to stay alive!"

"Please, Sophia," I heard my brother Shane whisper as he placed his large hand on my back. "Our precious mother needs you to let her go now. Tell her goodbye."

Sobbing, I hugged Mom and kissed her shoulder, her face, her eyes, and her arms. I was sure she didn't care. "If I have to . . . if I have to let you go . . . but only if it's really your time, Mom. Is it your time to go?" I gasped and sobbed. "If you know it's really your time to go this time, then I have to tell you goodbye."

I sat in my mother's sitting room on her favorite pink reclining chair while her body was getting cold and rigid on the hospital bed in her room. Every inhale and exhale sliced away at my lungs and throat. I felt so remorseful and crazy, I needed to slither out of my skin and disappear—to become null and nonexistent. My head throbbed and my eyes ached from crying so much.

Everyone was sure things had happened just as it was meant to. "Because all three of us forgot about your mother's allergy to morphine, I believe it was nothing less than a gift from God. The nurse believed Mother would be okay in a while, and even Ruth, who did remember, was gone at the very time her presence would have stopped the injections and prolonged your mother's life," Dad told me.

"Just know this," Auntie Amelia said. "She no longer has to stay and suffer in bed and in this life any longer. Now your wonderful mother can be with her family and loved ones on the other side. Everything that happened today—the whole day of events—were part of God's divine plan. Everything went exactly the way He intended it to go."

After many long weeks, months, and years I finally accepted those explanations. Maybe it had something to do with her soul's decisions, more than the God she still revered. Either way, one day I saw Mom's eyes twinkle, and heard her giggle. "Hey, Sophia, wasn't that great? My soul arranged a top-quality escape artist for me! Can you believe that amazing feat—to mess with your minds, and make all of us forget about my allergy to morphine? One minute I was there and the next minute I was gone. Wow, all in the blink of an eye. I hope it goes fast for you when you're ready to exit this life."

I giggled out loud, knowing she could hear and see me smiling too. She'd done her time. My mother definitely deserved a death that was as quick and painless as possible.

※

In the middle of August, during my return to Cedar City, the "powers that be" adorned me with an incredible gift. I received a call that rocked my world. (Oh, yeah, I finally had one of those traveling telephones I always dreamed of.) If I could move in right away, I could live in an apartment, since no one above me on the waiting list could relocate for over a month.

Sometime back in May, Jolie had moved back into her home with her kids, and I needed to find another place to stay. For four or five weeks before I went home for the summer, I got to stay with my precious sister-in-law and her husband in St. George. The long drive and gas was a hardship, so I did some more legwork. I applied for a student-housing apartment as an unemployed, self-reliant mother and student. When I was at the bottom of the list of twenty-five or so, I visited the homeless shelter and made arrangements to stay there and in my car. Nothing but my children would stop me. I'd come this far and I was determined to get my bachelor's degree. The apartment offer was a grand gift from the universe. I was so grateful, I cried happy tears for weeks as I moved in and set up my own quiet study space.

Up to that point in the year, my suspicions were confirmed. It had been and was obvious to nearly everyone in our lives how inseparable Jared, Mark, and Norma had become. With information from the three of them and other family members and friends, I knew the majority of Mark's off-work time—his days, nights, and weekends— had been and were still being spent with his bosom buddies and confidants.

Throughout my spring, summer, and fall visits home and phone conversations with Norma, she told me about the feelings and behaviors of just about everyone we knew. She assured me her knowledge was because she knew these people better than they knew themselves.

It didn't take me long to find out, of course, this included me, my kids, my friends, their friends and their spouses, Diane's whole family, Jared's first wife who'd left him and remarried quite some time ago, her children, their children, their friends—everyone! Norma said she knew everything there was to know about all of us. Before long, Mark also began to claim the same expertise about people and of course he included me also.

To Mark and to me, Norma proclaimed her love, devotion, and dedication. "She supports us and wants to help keep us together," Mark repeated. "She knows we are 'twin rays'—soul mates. She says we have been forever and always will be."

With his strong, persuasive assurances, I swept my apprehensions and perceptions under the carpet and tromped all over them.

Near the end of September or first part of October, the threesome came down to my apartment. I hadn't seen Mark for twenty-two days. He said he came down to spend "some quality time" with me.

No matter where we went or what we were doing, Norma was always pissed at Jared. She was angry with him for everything he did or didn't do. That time it wasn't just because of the turned-on sounds Jared made when he showered or enjoyed his food, or because he talked way too much. I felt sorry and embarrassed for him. Norma's fits of anger toward Jared were carried out right in front of my visiting friends and me.

A friend of mine, who hadn't known Norma for more than an hour, whispered, "Gee, Kristyn, it looks like she hates the guy! Bet a divorce is in her plans."

On Saturday, the four of us decided to drive the loop through Cedar Breaks and travel through Zion National Park on our return. On our way through Cedar Breaks I wanted to show off the beautiful bristlecone pine trees I'd been telling Mark about ever since my friend Graham had introduced them to me earlier in the summer. Mark and Norma acted like an engaged young couple who couldn't keep their eyes or bodies away from each other. It was obvious neither Jared nor I existed, other than as intrusive passengers. Mark snapped several pictures of Norma in a variety of poses under the bristlecone pines before they frolicked off on another trail, leaving Jared and me behind.

At our last pull-off, just before dusk, Jared and I stood by his truck in a quandary, watching Mark chase Norma as she jogged around a red-rock hillside, traipsed close to a dangerous-looking ledge, and ran down a pathway on the other side of a ravine before they disappeared into the canyon. While they were gone, we waited like puppies waiting to be drowned. We walked around a little, sat in the truck, and leaned on the truck, wondering. How I wished Jared had a girl "friend" with him and I had my friend Lyle to take off with.

I thought about Lyle and our nonstop laughter, the deep conversations about our families and our likes and dislikes. I wondered how his kids and grandkids were, and if and when he'd meet the right lady of his dreams, who loved horses and would live with him on his ranch someday. *If only he lived closer, I daydreamed. If he were here today, I'd definitely go the other direction with him. I would even—*

"—their proclaimed friendship?" Jared said.

"Sorry, Jared, what did you say?"

"Oh, I was just asking you how you feel about Norma and Mark's proclaimed friendship?"

"It's okay with me," I lied. Then I said, "The truth is, it has to be okay even though it hurts like hell! I always wanted Mark to have close friends who would appreciate his value, intellect, wisdom, and goodness. I'm honestly grateful you two love him and treat him as good as you do. I just have to trust them, Jared, because a long time ago I chose to let go and let live. I've told Mark several times how his decisions often cut me to the core. But I can't and won't try to change or manage him anymore. I am not in charge of his life—only my own."

Contrary to his normal diarrhea of the mouth, Jared was silent for a long time after I spoke. I'd never known him to contemplate anything I said, let alone really hear it. Then he said, "Guess that makes sense, Sophia. What else can we do?"

When Mark and Norma returned a little over an hour later, I was more angry and hurt than I knew what to do with.

The rest of the miserable way back to my apartment, I sat clear across the back seat, mulling things over. In the first place, Norma's actions contradict her regular assertions that she knew Mark and I should stay together.

"You and Mark are twin rays, Kristyn!" she'd often said. "He's in love with you! He loves Diane, but he is *in* love with *you*! You two are meant to be together forever."

Norma won again where Mark was concerned, which had been typical all year long. Whatever Norma said, did, thought, felt, or believed was the way it was, with no *ifs, ands,* or *buts*! Not one thing I brought up, felt, or cared about mattered anymore to Mark. To complain about anything only lengthened a fight that wasn't worth having. His ongoing denial and defensiveness of Norma's intentions and his day-and-night need to serve her every need and wish were obviously far more important than his professed loyalty or love for Diane and me.

By fall, even before Mark's claim that he came to Cedar City for some "quality time" with me, I'd already heard about Norma and him spending a lot of time together—holding hands while shopping and dining out, playing footsies and flashing their eyes at each other, and of having been caught in suggestive situations. Folks all over the Salt

Lake Valley came out of the woodwork to tell me or my friends of things they'd witnessed and of their concerns for what was obviously a fling going on behind my back while I was away. They'd say, "What we don't understand is how they get away with all that right in front of Jared and Diane! Are they blind? How can they be so dumb, or act like they don't know things are going on when it's practically right in front of their faces? Guess it's their choice if they want to believe Norma's and Mark's stories, and live in denial. What about you? What are you going to do about it, Sophia?"

In my heart I knew things between Mark and Norma were not always on the up and up, but I wanted to believe in their integrity. I also wanted to believe they hadn't "done it." Still, it was blatantly clear Norma's "friendship from God" was rapidly moving beyond the point of friendship. Not one thing I would say would make one bit of difference to either of them.

Earlier that spring, Norma told me, Mark was pretty much the most perfect man she'd ever met. Nothing he'd ever done, did, or would do was wrong. What I considered abuse, she said was nothing more than discipline our children deserved. She gave more reasons and excuses for his behaviors than even he'd thought of until they got their heads together. Who else had ever satiated Mark's male ego like that? No one else connected so intensely to Mark or esteemed every word that dribbled from his intellectual brain by way of his mouth. Mark said Norma also had the capacity to help him recognize and honor the wonderful man he really was. And who else needed his sacrifice and kindness in times of crisis more than she did?

Those lengthy thoughts reminded me of the way Michelle idolized and needed me, and how much she sucked me into her life.

All in all, none of that really mattered. Maybe that's why I didn't try to beat the boogers out of them when I felt like it. In everything going on between them, I knew I couldn't possibly continue in Mark's polygamous lifestyle he was obviously not going to leave, and would be expanding.

By the time we arrived back at the apartment, all of us were exhausted. I was filled with emotion I couldn't speak or express. I went right to bed.

In the middle of the night, after my feeble attempt to tell Mark how he and Norma's vacation made me—and probably Jared—feel, Mark surprised me. He asked me to forgive him, saying he didn't even realize how he'd behaved.

"Of course you didn't—that's my whole point, Mark," I said. "It's been like that ever since you two have become friends." Again he convinced me there was nothing going on between the two of them other than Norma's desperate need for solace and friendship in fear of her pending death.

I couldn't be there other than physically. As I'd done so many times before, I fell into the "make love and everything will be better" mode. After Mark fell asleep, silent tears poured from the corners of my eyes and drenched the pillow all around my head. I wrapped myself in a blanket and sat on the lawn under the floodlight. How on earth had I let myself fall into the same old daydreams and longings? All that wishful thinking and our newfound love had kept me with Mark for the past ten years.

At first, when we fell in love again, I'd shifted into workaholic mode in order to deal with living polygamy and to be able to stay. Even with that and a myriad of ongoing hardships, we were still in love. I thought I'd go to school and then go back home, and life would continue that way. Apparently it was another vicious joke. Then I tried to be happy enough living my own life to accept Mark's choices and his ongoing absenteeism. In our desire to maintain peace and joy in our lives while accepting each other's choices, we still weren't dealing with the real issues. In my case, I needed and wanted more, and Mark obviously needed Norma to need and want him more than he needed or wanted me. He told me many times how satisfying her love, appreciation, validation, and acceptance of him were. It was tough enough to deal with Diane in his life. Now he had a girlfriend as well. By then I was certain Norma's spirit guide would also direct her in how to divorce Jared and come out looking like a goddess to him and to her family. And because I believed she'd not die, I was sure she'd come by an honorable explanation as to why she wouldn't be required to die, but would be expected to let Jared go. I need to get the hell out of this picture fast, I thought. *If I leave, Norma can share Mark with Diane. Callie will never return to Jared, since she is deeply in love with her husband, but I can be on my way out to find a life and happiness elsewhere. My soul might even direct me to a really amazing man. But I am quite sure that man doesn't exist.*

CHAPTER 43

Calling It Quits
2001

Our fighting separated us for five days during the end of the summer. It seemed I'd never forgive Mark for spanking our three-year-old grandson so hard it left bruises on his behind. In my opinion, there was no excuse for spanking a child in the first place, let alone hitting his little bottom that hard. Again, Mark used every reason in the book to justify his behavior. I'd already separated twice during our ten-year honeymoon phase because of his displays of anger toward Anne and Keith. I hoped Mark would never spank a child again, especially one of our grandbabies. And even after we got back together way back then, I wondered why. How did I accept his justifications and forgive him? Or did I just push away the heartache as usual? It haunted me forever and a day.

To add to everything else, my resentment and anger revisited me like a punch in the stomach when Diane appeared uninvited at my home on my birthday. I'd felt similarly about her presence several times before, as I was sure she had felt about mine, but that time I was sure she had intentionally disregarded my wishes. I had already written her a letter several months previously, telling her I loved her dearly as a person, but I needed her to give me some time and space. For my own sanity I wanted and needed my home to be independent from the reality and appearance of polygamy, which she, as Mark's other wife, represented.

Diane didn't bring a card or a gift or say one word to me all evening long. She hung out and observed. Her presence was as invasive to me as a burglar casing out my personal belongings. She pored over my actions, the dynamics between Mark and me, and the gifts I received from others. And even though I felt assaulted by her disrespect of me, I surrendered my pride just to be kind and behave graciously.

Norma was the one I was really infuriated with. She'd already told me and others how she loved to cause trouble—how fun it was to toss some huge piece of trouble in the middle of people, then sit back and watch the mayhem she'd caused. Then Norma would do her wicked little chuckle that made her chuckle at herself some more.

That night must have been another of the jolly bombs she tossed into the wind and sat back and gloated about. Norma knew my feelings, and still she brought her friend Diane to my birthday celebration! Norma even said she could change and arrange things. According to her own words, she needed to be in control of everything and everyone around her. She'd bragged several times about how she could advise or persuade Diane to do or not do whatever she wanted. Norma took pride in that; and whether Diane knew it or not, she appeared to be one of Norma's puppets. Along with her very questionable relationship with Mark, it was also times like those that led me to completely distrust Norma's public declaration that she loved me.

While I cleaned up the dishes, I felt physically ill. I knew I'd dishonored myself by passing that injustice off as I'd done multiple times before, just to keep the peace, avoid a scene, and to help everyone else feel happy, safe, and guilt-free. Until the last several years, I had often gone out of my way to support peace between Mark, Diane, and our children. In my lifetime I sagaciously lived by the fictitious-but-real-in-my-head manual called *How to Completely Dishonor Oneself.*

I could hear my therapist's voice again. Kris told me to create and hold onto my own serenity. Nourishing my mind, body, and spirit was not in keeping with my old, negating, pointless patterns of dysfunction.

The next morning, on my birthday, Mark and I made love and cuddled for a long time; yet my stomach was still queasy. As always, I felt extremely anxious about expressing any deep feelings, needs, or thoughts with him. Like a million times before—like a dog waiting to be kicked—I tried again. Things moved along fairly peacefully as I revealed my discomfort with Diane's presence at my party. What was new there? Mark said he felt the same about her neediness and insecurities as he always had. But the tides changed sharply when I explained how Norma's decision to ignore my requests, were also offensive to me.

"I wonder," I said out loud, "if last night was one of Norma's sinister, antagonistic pranks she proudly claims to engineer so she can sit back and delight in her manipulative powers. You've heard her brag a couple of times about how she loves to do that!"

"Diane has always been insecure when it comes to my feelings for you, but Norma didn't do anything to create the problem! She loves you!"

"Then why did she bring Diane?" I asked. "What other purpose would she have, when she knows exactly how I feel about Diane coming to our house? If Norma were my friend as she claims she is, she wouldn't have brought Diane. If she were really my friend, why does she behave otherwise and continue to sabotage us, so often?"

In Norma-defense-mode, Mark yelled about how perfect she was before he began listing my horrible offenses of the last thirty years. Some of his perceptions and feelings rang true—a lot in the past, not so much in the present. With every effort I made to defend or explain his explosive accusations, they got more intense and vile.

"Don't you get it?" I finally cried. "Norma wants you! It shows in everything she says behind your back to me or behind my back to you. She needs you all of the time. Her God has made you her hero-friend—the one who is obligated to walk the path of death with her. There are always a million reasons she needs you! Can't you see what a genius she is at manipulating you? She knows exactly what to say and how to say it to get you to trust her. She compliments me and criticizes herself. She tells you, me, and others, she loves me, to make you think she has our best interests in her heart. You believe that so much that when she wants to twist and turn those compliments around to make her criticism of me sound and feel valid, she always wins. Norma decides if what I'm doing, you're doing, or Diane is doing is good or bad. Then she lets us all know her decisions, and you support her!

"I am not stupid!" Mark retorted. "Hell, So-ph-ia, you are the controlling, selfish bitch here! Nothing I ever do is good enough for you. You're always mad at me. You never appreciate me. You don't want me to have any friends or happiness unless it benefits you. You're always jealous of the time I spend with Jared and Norma, and all you care about is you and what makes you happy!"

By then I was sobbing. I already knew it was a hopeless cause. The more I asked Mark for details I knew he didn't really have, so I could understand his accusations, the worse it got until he was gone.

After he left, I threw my shoes on, slammed the front door, dashed across our street, and jogged up the road until I reached the narrow trail of the muddy foothills. I pushed the play button in my head, then rewound and played those shocking words again, in deep contemplation. Where did those shocking, repulsive words spewing out of Mark's mouth come from—Norma, or straight from hell? Mark had never before attacked me like that, even in his most tyrannical rages.

In the afternoon before I had to leave back to Cedar City, to school, Mark returned to apologize. In this long-overdue conversation we were able to discuss some of our differences in a fairly calm manner. He tried to explain away his wrath toward and complaints about me, blaming them on stress. Then he listened to some of my explanations. I told him that aside from him allowing his "new friends" to consume his whole life, his decision to back out of his family's life the past year had unraveled my trust in him.

"You not only vanished from me. When you encouraged me to go clear down to southern Utah, you promised me you'd make sure Anne and Keith had their needs met. You said you'd take care of their health insurance, our yard, the bills, the house payments, and even send me $300 a month until I could return to help financially. You did it all for a few weeks and then you just quit! It's a blessing others were able to stay at our house in your absence. At least Keith and Anne could count on them a little to help with food and transportation! How could you let everything slide until shit was flying in all directions? What on earth did you do with all of your income, Mark? We're three house payments behind—it's in foreclosure again! I had to charge our house payments on credit cards and get a student loan to get me by after you quit sending me money, and—"

"I just couldn't function with you gone!" He cut in. "I didn't feel at home at our house. I didn't have any energy or desire to take care of anything without you here. You've always been leaving me, Sophia! From the time we got married you've been looking for greener grass on the other side of the fence."

In many ways he was right. Living polygamy was all that was religiously necessary to Mark. From everything I'd ever been taught to believe, his attitudes and actions didn't qualify him as my priesthood head. According to my dad's Mormon Fundamentalist God's rules, Mark would never be able to take me into the celestial kingdom, where I could dwell with my parents, siblings, and our children for eternity. That was certainly my number-one fear and reason for praying that God would either make him a righteous man, or let me out, so I could marry a man who could get us there. But I loved Mark! I *wanted* to be with him, so I begged and cried. I tried to kindly and "sweetly" sway him into "honoring" his priesthood like other "good" men in The Group.

A man has to have at least three wives to get even his big toe into heaven. And the way things were going; Mark wasn't going to make the grade as far as my dad, our prophet, was concerned. I had a reputation to get and keep. Everyone else our age was on their way to attaining their plural wives and their celestial kingdom. I pushed and encouraged Mark to get another wife, and when he tried, I would freak out again. So he'd stop and I'd get miffed. Then, like the "good wife"

I was required to be, I'd nudge him even more, and where did we end up?

After about twenty years of this off-and-on, of finding ourselves and doing some inner healing, I'd finally fallen in love with Mark. Then I started leaving him—a good man—because he had to honor his commitment to Diane and plural marriage, and I couldn't. There certainly was some truth in his charges against me. My compassionate, trusting heart also wanted to believe his reasons for abandoning us. What else could he do without assurance of my never-ending love and devotion?

Accepting Mark's justification for bombing out on all of his responsibilities and us wasn't easy. In every thought, I tried to; but the more I thought about his excuses, the more unreasonable they were.

The whole year I was gone, the threesome was busy dining out, working on projects together, camping, vacationing, and going on various other outings. Mark and Norma often came and went by themselves. Whenever I asked him why he didn't have time, money, or energy for us, his reasons were never clear. His refusal to answer my questions, in it-self was deceitful. Now, his claim that he couldn't function without me felt like a cop-out, contrived so he could continue to do whatever he wanted to do with his time, with no responsibility or accountability to his family. If his reasons were valid, why hadn't he been honest about everything in the first place, circumventing all this confusion and anger? We had such a long list of problems; it was no wonder we were on a dead-end street going nowhere.

I was grateful Mark didn't ask me what he could or should do to make things better, like he'd done so many times before. We both knew it hadn't done any good in the past. I was quite certain it wouldn't make any difference now.

Mark's next words took the breath out of my lungs.

"Sophia, as of today, I am divorcing you. I am releasing you from any and all marriage contracts or commitments we have ever made together—religious, legal, and celebratory. The only thing that will put our marriage back together is love. Our love will have to be strong enough to take us through anything and everything, or we will never make it."

I'm not sure why I wept so copiously. As my body was doubled over in sorrow, my soul was set free. The dent in the side of our bed when Mark sat down drew me into his hip and back. He tenderly rested his left hand on my shoulder. Then, not surprisingly, he used another of Norma's favorite sayings to sanctify his necessity to end our marriage.

"Sophia, you have come out of your chrysalis and turned into a beautiful butterfly. If I hold onto you, as I'd like to, you may smother and die. But if I let you go—let you fly away—and then you come back to me, you will truly be mine."

Then, to top it off, Mark told me he'd already divorced Diane. "But I will never go back to that marriage," he said. "I am done with any and all of my past commitments there. I married and stayed with Diane because I believed in the religion our parents convinced us to live." He said he'd done the best he knew how to do in caring for and loving Diane and their kids. Now that they were all over eighteen, he was through living polygamy.

My three-and-a-half-hour drive back to Cedar seemed endless. Mark's furious, earsplitting charges; his presentation of our past few years, both fact and fiction; and especially his abrupt end of our three-way marriage were all trifling with my sanity. One moment I was apathetic and grateful, and the next I felt sure my anguish would crush me to death. The things he had told me cut deep into my heart.

"That is insanity from the get-go!" I complained during our long, drawn-out discussion a couple weeks later. "How can you ask me to be married to you without Diane being married to you? It would break her heart and mine! It should be the other way around, you know. She will be completely happy to have you to herself. She'd have her children, my children, and her best friend Norma, and even Jared—if he's still in the picture—and all of our kids for family gatherings. Mark, Diane is the one who will continue to be the *good wife*; the one who will stay loyal to you forever. According to Norma, that would make Diane's dreams come true! You and Diane are supposed to stay together! I am the one who's been leaving you all those years! God only knows how many times you've told me you won't ever leave her!"

I wished Diane really knew my heart—not the stories I knew she heard. Gossip was coming back to me from several angles as well. I wanted her to understand me and the remorse I was feeling for what she was going through. If she'd talk to me, or write, or call I could tell her I always wanted her happiness and never tried to hurt her—well, other than the time with the car. I regretted not being a better friend and sister to her. I was sorry I hadn't gone ahead and mailed the notes, letters, and cards I wrote and wanted to write to her, and didn't because Norma told me not to send, telling me Diane didn't want them and or to hear from me. Right then I wished I could have forced Mark to take Diane back so she, our kids, and I could stop hurting. As if I could.

In the next few weeks of dealing with my emptiness, longing, and memories of so many wonderful days in Mark's and my marriage, I wished we could be in each other's arms. I wished nothing had ever gone so crazy and never again would. In those moments I wanted to plead with him to take Diane back so he could take me back, or the other way around. I'd promise him, "I'll be good—I won't be jealous or cry anymore! I'll make myself be happy in our misery and not trade it for another misery, like you said."

However much pain I felt, nothing compared to my life's consoling blood, flowing in abundance. The personal freedom I had embraced away from too many years of conflict helped solidify my decision to finally let go.

My lingering pain was not so much for myself, but for everyone else: my kids, Diane and her kids, Mark, and our friends. Because of too many wounding assumptions and spiteful words, all of our hearts were aching. With time, I hoped our grief would dissipate and all of us would someday be able to heal.

CHAPTER 44

Leaving My Sanctuary
2001

Finals were tedious and simple, other than math, of course. As always, I was the last student to finish the test. Fighting tears, I told my professor I hoped his long, drawn-out test from hell wouldn't ruin my grade point average and haunt me for the rest of my life. I'd done the best I could and hoped it would all pan out. I arranged to finish my last early childhood class through correspondence. If all went well, I'd finish that class in the next four months while I was doing my student teaching from home and I'd officially be a certified teacher.

My apartment seemed to cling to me for dear life, as I clung to it. Leaving my sanctuary seared my heart as would the death of a beloved pet, yet I was taking with me knowledge and self-esteem I'd never known before. I didn't want to move back home, or be done with school, or leave my apartment. Neither did I want to cope with the wrath of my now-distant family and friends who knew little or nothing of my life and feelings. In an effort to make sense of my "soul flip," which they called a midlife crisis, many believed the mostly mistaken rumors they'd been hearing about me.

If I had my druthers, everyone I loved and honored, who loved and honored me, would move down to Cedar City away from crazy-making people and the big-city life.

I decided to stay in Southern Utah for four more days just to celebrate—to honor myself with an appropriate closure to one of the most difficult yet incredible years of my life. Also, I hoped some quiet alone time would cement my decision to return to Mark, and make my transition back a bit easier. I spent time gabbing with a few friends and took some bereavement time at my favorite cliffs, caves, and trails. I left offerings of gratitude everywhere I went for Mother Nature's generous gifts of love and healing.

Still feeling somewhat down, I decided to head farther southwest on a day trip to Pa Tempe Hot Springs, and go to Colorado City to see my sister Lucinda, my nieces, aunt Maggie—my friend—and her kids, my cousins.

"Lucinda is not down here anymore, Sophia," Maggie said matter-of-factly when I first saw her. The way she sounded, I knew it must be bad news.

"Why?" I asked. "What's going on with my sister?"

Maggie explained how Warren Jeffs had ousted several of the Barlow brothers, including my sister's husband Wayne. One day in church, Warren, without warning, told them to stand up, called them sinners and told them to leave, send him their money, and repent from afar. He took all of their wives and children away from them and gave them to other men. "I'm pretty sure Warren moved Lucinda to Texas where she's been assigned to be a caretaker to all of the children Warren has taken from their mothers."

I was furious. Fire from my core ran through my body until my skin tingled. I'd already been sickened by too many of Warren's heinous crimes; now his evil really hit home.

"How totally brainless can those men get?" I yelled. "Wayne is a stupid idiot!"

The Barlow men were always looked up to as leaders, serving in many high-ranking capacities ever since John Y. Barlow had been the group's prophet, in the early 50's. They'd been mayor, bishop, and counselors, among other positions. That family line had run and shoved the whole show at the Crick for nearly a hundred years. "How can any one of those chauvinistic, outspoken men just stand by and allow sick, little, man-creep Warren to take over the whole community, kick people out of their homes, tie their family jewels in knots, prostitute their wives, steal their children and give them to a more "worthy" dad or mom? I've completely lost the tiny ounce of respect I had left for Wayne!" I ferociously complained.

My uncouth response probably burned Maggie's ears. I don't feel at all bad about how I'd described Warren. To me, he deserved far worse, maybe even to be called "the devil in disguise." It certainly wasn't my intention to personally offend Maggie or her beliefs. I wasn't sure exactly where she stood after her prophet, Rulon Jeffs, died and didn't come back to life. The clan's irrational claim he'd never die, created a glitch in many testimonies, including Maggie's. Like all of us, she too had been, and still was, caught in the clutches of her religious beliefs while being torn by the myriad of injustices she'd seen and endured. For as long as I'd known her, she always wondered which of her many trials might set her free or ban her straight to hell.

I'd started down a path that was obviously becoming more natural to me. Ever since I was old enough, I'd questioned the FLDS priesthood leaders, and now I had the audacity to place Warren in the same class as the devil.

"Sophia!" Maggie's voice brought me back from my thoughts. "Those men are just following his directions because they believe they're being tested by God!" Then she threw in another obligatory rule programmed in our heads from the time of conception. "You know we've always been taught God will never allow the prophet to lead his people astray. God would destroy him first!"

"Warren is nothing more than a narcissistic, egocentric, perverted man, just like Evil Ervil LeBaron!" I snapped.

My skin crawled as I thought about how many men and women still held on to edicts that empower evil men in high positions to abuse and nullify their followers' rights and freedoms.

"Testing?" I asked angrily. "Testing them by morbid game playing? If their God is really testing them, it's to see if they have balls enough to fight for their children and wives instead of letting Warren sell them into more slavery than they've already been in!"

I needed to quit. It wasn't my business to change her mind about a mad-man "prophet" who had already and would continue to pass edicts of insanity. He'd continue to gloat as thousands of generationally programmed puppets, would smile as they jumped off a cliff, just because he told them to.

We knew of many terrible crimes that had been covered up in the FLDS and other polygamous sects. In every visit with Maggie over our forty-nine years of friendship, she had divulged many more. Now things were getting worse by the day. I couldn't stop myself. "What else is that crazy man up to?"

At first Maggie didn't answer my question. I wondered if she was again striving to conform to the famous FLDS-Colorado City mantra: "Keep sweet, keep sweet, and keep sweet"…which really means; shut-up and smile about any and all maltreatment; or you'll be severely penalized!

Maggie verified and despised many of Warren's father's decisions. Now under Warren's direction, parents were told to remove their children from the public state-funded schools, but regulated by "priesthood" authority. All of the FLDS teachers and staff members, who were the majority, were also told to quit; causing the schools to close down. The clan kept taking money sent by Arizona to fund the education of children who were no longer receiving any. Warren shut down the city zoo and parks. After one child was bitten by a dog, he ordered all of the dogs in town to be killed. Many families watched their beloved pets shot right in front of them.

Jeffs also demanded that a monument Wayne had built and dedicated to Leroy Johnson be demolished. Leroy Johnson had been the FLDS prophet during the attempted rescue of women and children, in 1953, by the State of Arizona. John Howard Pyle, Arizona's governor at the time, had support for his action from his state as well as from the state of Utah. The attempted rescue was also sanctioned by the LDS Church, to try to stop the human rights violations taking place among fundamentalist polygamists. Even back then, authorities knew men were breaking the laws by living polygamy; of abuses and poverty; and of young girls (some between the ages of twelve and fifteen) being trafficked and assigned to old men. In the same timeframe Warren Jeffs demanded the statue of the former prophet was idolatrous, he announced, "I am God's anointed." Every one of his clan had to place pictures of him in every room in their homes to remind them of Warren's scrutiny and whom they'd really better be worshipping.

I believe Warren knew from day one he was a charlatan. His nemeses were anyone who presented the slightest threat to "his kingdom." Parents were not to talk to their wayward children, or any family members who'd left for any reason. They were directed to no longer converse with anyone outside their sect. Folks were discarded for not spying and ratting on anyone who disobeyed Warren's tyrannical rules. He promised more wives or other rewards ("blessings") for those who did his bidding—particularly if one snitched on a close family member for insubordination. The surest way to one's demise, was to question anything Warren did or said.

After Maggie's oratory, I understood where her loyalties were. She still believed in plural marriage and the Book of Mormon, but would no longer follow any man who claimed authority over others. She'd already been through hellfire and brimstone. She'd suffered through too many hellacious times trying to stick up for her own rights as a "low-life" woman among "god-like" men, who'd wielded all the power from day one. When she'd asked for a release from her adulterous husband, she was counseled to give in to his demands, so he wouldn't have to get it from other women. He got a verbal slap on the hand, continued his infidelity, and became physically and verbally abusive to her because she'd told about his nasty little secret.

I completely understood the blinded and brainwashed women and men who continued to follow every proclamation coming from their prophet's mouth. Like my mother, and me for a while, they too believe in the need to die miserably happy. While women live like perfect robotic Stepford Wives, their husbands and fathers can do as they please; thus a straight shot guarantee they can become Gods of their own worlds someday.

On my drive back to Cedar City my head was inundated with chatter that wouldn't stop. I worried about my sixty-year-old sister Lucinda and the hundreds of relatives who would continue to follow and condone all of the behaviors of their depraved, insane god, Warren Jeffs. I feared I'd never see my sister, her children, or her grandchildren ever again.

I sang as loudly as I could and bounced and twisted to rock-n-roll tunes blasting in my ears. I listened intently to the world news, but nothing could block the stinking thinking swirling around in my head. How on earth could I go back to Mark now that I had been with Lyle? I had to talk to someone I could trust!

At the park, I spread my car blanket across a wooden picnic table, lay down, and let the wonderful sunshine warm and comfort me while I waited for Graham. Since we first met, our friendship stayed platonic and strong, and both of us cherished that incredible camaraderie.

I listened to the ice crackle as it slid from the riverbank into the water. Twenty minutes later, Graham's approach was given away by the snow crunching under his shoes. He pulled my sweater off my face and moved quickly to block the early afternoon sun from my eyes. His handsome face smiled.

"What's up, Kristyn?"

I got up and gave him a big hug before we sat down on top of the table side by side. "Thanks for coming, Graham. You're the sane man I trust and need to talk to."

"Ah, you knew I'd come over! You've been around plenty of times for me! What's up? Are you okay?"

"No! You already know Mark divorced Diane and me . . . anyway I was through with all of it! I've been really happy and settled between the swells and waves of pain."

"Your family and Diane are having a hell of a time, and you're still getting the blame?" he guessed.

"Yes, but that's not my biggest dilemma right now," I sighed. "Do you remember me talking about my friend Lyle—the guy I met on the phone and then at Hart's Gas Station right before my summer break?"

"He's the guy who owns a ranch in Colorado Springs?"

"Yes. We met each other again, at Denny's sometime in October when he traveled through town with a buddy." I smiled. "All in all we've probably talked on the phone over a hundred hours."

"You slept with him, didn't you?"

I felt a little embarrassed. "Good grief, Graham. You sure made that easy!" For a minute I forgot where my thoughts were going. "Are you upset and disappointed in me?"

"Of course not! Why should I be? You're a beautiful woman! Why wouldn't he want to be with you and love you?"

"Thanks, Graham. I know Lyle loves me, and that's why . . . well, when things . . . my relationship with Lyle was tender and benevolent, a rewarding experience I will never regret."

I started crying, and my thoughts dissolved into mush. The old song by Terry Jacks played in my head. Tears streamed down my face, and I began to sing the lyrics in my head. *We had joy, we had fun, we had seasons in the sun. But the hills that we climbed were just seasons out of time . . .* Then it was quiet.

"I'm here, Sophia. I'm still listening." Graham's words and the feel of his arm placed around my shoulder drew me back.

"It was wonderful! I cared about Lyle for five months. We fought with and resisted every stupid, wild, crazy emotion one could imagine so I could make my marriage work and stay with Mark. Lyle and I were sure after we met in the summer, things would never work between us even if I was single. I knew darn well I didn't need any excuses, but I used them, just in case. Mark divorced Diane and me. He knew what it was like being with more than one woman. I always thought what was good for the gander was good for the goose. Two and a half weeks after I got home after my birthday, I gave in! I wanted to know if I could love someone else and if he could really love me. Mark would say, 'No one can touch, caress, or love you like I do, Sophia,' Mark would often remind me.'" I found that wasn't at all true.

"Now you're feeling guilty?" Graham said.

"It's not so much guilt. It's plausible deception I'm more concerned about. Maybe I should tell Mark, even though I know he doesn't want to know. Then he can decide if he still wants me back or not."

"Kristyn, what are you talking about? You told me you were done with that marriage. He divorced you! You don't owe him an explanation!"

"I was done, Graham! That's why I needed to talk to you. Mark begged me to come back to him, to try to work things out. He's called me nearly every day for just over a week. The first four or five days I told him no. Besides Diane's feelings, there were a hundred more reasons. But we talked and listened to what each of us needed, wanted, and didn't want—our dreams and expectations and the things we could and couldn't count on. We discussed just about everything we hadn't ever made work, and how we'd be able to make things work now that we could have a monogamous marriage."

Graham looked confused and angry, but I kept talking. "Mark assured me all that matters to him is being able to make us work. So we decided we'd both be willing to do whatever it takes. We made promises we want and intend to keep."

"It sounds like he sucked you in again, Kristyn." Graham's deep voice was tense and choppy. "Do you really trust him? Won't he just keep seeing Diane?

"No, Norma," I said.

"Norma?" Graham's blazing eyes pierced mine. "Is Norma still in the picture?"

I nodded.

"I think he still wants to be a polygamist like he told you so many times! Aren't you worried he'll be with them behind your back and pretend he's only with you? What about the hell he put you through this last year? Have you forgotten?"

Graham paused. "Listen Kristyn, it's just . . . Well, I'm not sure I'm trying to change your mind, even though it sounds like I am. I know how you feel about Mark. I'm just worried about you. And what about Lyle? You just told me he loves you. It sounds like you love him too. Does he get a say in any of this? Are you two . . .?"

I gently pressed my finger over Graham's lips to shush him. "Yes, we're over. However I told him about Mark's proposition two or three days after Mark's first call, when I was sure I wouldn't return to him. Lyle will be devastated when I tell him I've changed my mind."

"So what will you do?"

"That's a good question. All I know is, even after all the pandemonium we've been through, I still love Mark. We might have a fighting chance."

"Are you going to tell Mark about Lyle?"

"The only reason I should, I think, is because I would want him to tell me if it was the other way around. But Mark hasn't wanted me to know anything about his "personal" life. And he made it clear he didn't want to know if I were to ever have an affair. Maybe that's his way of letting himself off the hook."

"But you didn't have an affair. He divorced you."

"Yup, I guess that lets me off the hook," I smiled.

"Won't your feelings about Lyle get in the way of working things out with Mark?"

"I don't know. But I won't know if I don't try. Lyle is a very good friend! We both felt safe with each other. We adored each other. I loved his sense of humor and his love of life and nature. But both of us know it could never go beyond there."

"Kristyn, several times you told me to listen to my heart," Graham said. "So now I'm telling you to do the same. Listen to what your heart is telling you."

"I've gone deep so many times this past week I might become stoic if I'm not careful," I explained. "My heart tells me if I don't do everything I can do to make our marriage work I'll be sorry."

"You've already done everything you know how to make it work," Graham insisted.

"I know, and I still waver back and forth. Part of me feels it's just plain selfish of me to try again. I worry every day about Diane and our kids. They'll hate me! But Mark promises he'll work things out. In the torrent of pain I've been in for so many months, I've withered away from Mark. After the past few days, somewhere deep inside, a tiny spark ignited my hopes again. Maybe that's crazy, but under the right circumstances that flicker might be so powerful it will burst into a magnificent flame—enough to keep our kids and grandchildren intact. That alone would be worth every effort in the world, wouldn't it?"

Graham waited for quite some time before he responded. "Sounds like you're sure of what you want to do. You both want a happy life together. Now you may finally have a chance."

🌿

My bedroom closet was nearly empty. I'd packed everything I wouldn't be using for a few days. The last thing I saw, way back on the top shelf, was a small white box dotted with tiny red and blue flowers. My heart pounded as I took it down and held it in both hands. *Where is Lyle now?* I wondered. Is he feeding his horses, gathering the hay, or playing his guitar? I have to tell him I'm going back to Mark.

My thoughts meandered back and forth from Lyle, to Mark, to Lyle. What would be different with Mark this time around? We promised each other we'd do all we could to work on our relationship, but both of us had already done that more times than we could count. *Will it really be different now that our kids are all nearing adulthood and heading in their own directions? Can we create a new life together without living polygamy—without Diane?*

One minute those dreams felt so good, and the next things felt terrible. How could I be in panic and in hope all within the same few minutes? "Get busy and do something! Don't think!" I commanded myself.

I stuffed my last batch of laundry into the washer. When my phone rang and I saw the 829 prefix on the caller ID, my stomach tightened.

"Hi, sunshine!" Lyle said. I nearly cried at the sound of his voice. "We stopped by Mom's so I could call and tell ya ga-bye again. Me 'n' Corry are headin' to Lake Powell to play, and . . . uh, I . . . mmm . . .I'm sure missin' ya, baby. I'm not sure I can live without ya."

His voice faded. I could tell he didn't know how to say what he was thinking, but he went on. "It's just, well, this is just bullshit, us bein' apart like this. I can't let ya leave 'n' go home now! I need ya, and want us ta figure out how we can be together. Listen, Kristyn, just come down here and we'll work it out! I've been figuring things out and . . . just get a paper—I'm gonna tell ya how to get down here, okay?"

Even five hundred miles apart, Lyle and I loved and supported each other through one of the toughest years of each of our lives. We prized the times we laughed and buoyed each other through difficult times. The possibility of me moving to Colorado, or him to Salt Lake or to Cedar City, was only a dream. Neither of us could leave our careers, our children, or the new lives we'd been creating. From the time we met, we planned on being "telephone friends" forever. The real difficulty for us came after the intense closeness we shared through our long weekend together. Saying goodbye was hell.

"Lyle," I said as quickly as I could, "we both know—"

"I know, hon," he interrupted, "but thingser different now. I know we can do this!"

"I'm going home, Lyle!" I said as strongly as I could.

"I know ya are, honey, but we—"

"I'm going back to Mark so we can—"

"Just stop that bullshit, Kristyn!" Lyle cut in. "I won't hear it! No way! What the hell's gotten into ya, baby? Are ya crazy? It's taken ya years ta leave and now yer finally free from that cockamamie cult crap and from Mark, and yer talkin' like yer goin' back? Good hell, Kris, ya can't go back to him!"

Lyle's rage in my behalf opened the deep wounds in my heart. As hard as I tried not to, I broke down. My body slumped to the floor. When I could breathe again, I tried to persuade him, my decision was for the best.

"Please listen to me, Lyle. Mark asked me to give us another try again now that we can be a normal monogamist couple, and I think we can—"

"Bullshit! Ya know damn well it won't work. What the hell are ya thinkin', girl? He's gonna rope ya in and pretend he's left his other wife, but ya know he'll be doin' her on the side while yer up there trustin' away!"

By then I was nauseous with my influx of raw emotion.

"Listen to me—listen good," Lyle went on. "This is really pissin' me off! You've been doin' so good. You've been so happy down there away from all that shit. What can I do ta stop ya, baby? Is it money? If you need some, I've got some. I'll send ya as much as ya need. Better yet, I'll come up an' get ya. Just don't go back! Please, Kristyn, I'm beggin' ya, don't go back to Mark!"

Through my tears, I mustered enough courage to end his pleading before I jumped in my car and drove the five hundred miles to his waiting arms and to a perfectly wonderful dream world.

"Please stop, Lyle! I've got to go now. No money! No more calls! No more letters! Promise me, Lyle. Nothing!"

He still didn't hang up. I should have. I listened to his heavy breathing and envisioned his chest in its exhausted rise and fall in cadence with mine. Together we struggled for air—something we might have power over.

"Ya know I love ya, don't ya? I do love ya, baby. Please wait for me!" He was pleading again, through sniffles this time. "Ya know we can figure it out. We can—"

His words were ripping my heart out. "I love you too, Lyle, and I am so sorry."

"I'll always love ya, Kristyn. Promise you'll call if it don't work out. And call me if ya need me or some money or anything. Promise me, baby. I need ta hear ya say it before I can hang up."

We had a beginning. We had to have an end. We had joy and we had fun. We had a weekend in the sun. "But the hills that we climbed

411

were just seasons out of time"—and a gift we'd forever treasure.

I dragged my weary body into my bedroom and crashed on the bed.

In the morning, my eyes were almost swollen shut from crying so much. Lyle's own torment and words filled my head. Would my move back home be like moving into an abyss of darkness? My endeavor to find myself and feel complete was still an ongoing process. I'd gained a great deal of self-esteem and self-reliance. Lyle was right. I'd never felt more alive and empowered in my whole life. I'd never felt such safety and serenity. Were Mark's pleas just another ploy to draw me back to insanity? I didn't think so. It certainly hadn't felt that way.

But what about this past year?

There were too many contradictions in his behaviors and his words. I saw how he looked at Norma and how she looked at him. They'd both made it so workable and convenient to go everywhere together—to come and go alone and in their three-way friendship with her husband. It wasn't Diane I thought he might be "doin'," as Lyle suggested. I also knew from my own experience and Mark's own theories, male-female friendships more often than not lead to sexual relationships. *Why in the hell am I going back?* I thought. When it came to Mark, Norma's thoughts, needs, feelings, opinions, and ideas superseded mine. Over the past week, he had promised me several times it wouldn't be that way anymore. Along with his big words and promises was his assurance of Norma's deep love and devotion to helping us work things out so we could be together without hurting Diane.

My love and affection for Lyle would remain a joyous memory. But wouldn't the reality of Norma and Mark's physical and emotional connection stay with them forever?

❧

Graham returned my call on his lunch break.

"Hi, Graham, bet you're surprised to hear from me again," I said as cheerfully as I could.

"Yeah, I thought I wouldn't hear from you for a few weeks."

412

"I panicked and was sick all over after Lyle called yesterday. He was shattered and angrier than I thought he would be. All morning long I couldn't get your warnings and his out of my head. I'm afraid I'm making a big mistake. What if I'm not doing the right thing?"

I must have succeeded in converting Graham to the pros of my reconciliation with Mark, when we'd talked before. He convincingly spoon-fed them back to me. He reminded me of how elated I sounded when I recounted my recent fantasies of Mark and me doing the Texas two-step without missing a beat, and of hiking the back side of Mount Timpanogos again.

Graham reminded me of the wondrous images I conjured, which after four days of Mark's pleading caused me to say yes to his determined proposal. In those daydreams, Mark and I danced and made love on a beach in the Cayman Islands. We traveled, worked, and played together in all the ways we'd ever talked and dreamed of. Our children, grandchildren, and their children hung out with us. They laughed at our old-age dementia, and helped us back up when we fell down.

"Sophia, remember the other day when I took your hand and set it against my heart?" Graham asked tenderly.

"Yes."

"Do you remember what I said?"

"Yes. Tell me again, Graham. I want to hear it again."

"Well, I told you, I know you love Mark, and he loves you. You both want a wonderful life together, so give it a try! Go for it!"

"Thanks, Graham. It means more than you will ever know to have your support and understanding."

"I care about you, Kristyn. I want you to be happy. You of all people deserve happiness!"

I quietly placed the receiver back on the wall jack as if I might wake a sleeping baby. I replayed Graham's words over and over, hoping to inscribe them in my mind so they could encourage me until everything was as perfect as I contemplated.

CHAPTER 45

Burning Bridges
Winter 2001

On the edge of my desk was my white letter box full of memorabilia. Its content was extraordinary—possibly lurid to others—and drummed up a metaphorical dance of turmoil. In the middle of my front-room floor I examined the handful of notes, letters, and pictures one last time. How I wished that segment of my life with Lyle was just a figment of my imagination. If only I could take it all back and change the timing! Why did Mark wait so damn long to make such a mind-boggling decision after all these years? He told me at least twenty times in the past ten years he would never leave Diane. Now that he wanted us, I'd be the bad wife and mother!

For my grown kids, it was already terrible enough I was leaving their dad. They didn't know he'd divorced us. Norma said Diane believed I had given Mark an ultimatum, saying if he didn't leave her, I would leave him. What on God's green earth was I thinking? What Mark and I wanted would create a war inside and outside of all of us. Nevertheless, he swore somehow, by some miracle, we would be able to work things out.

I wanted to create a special ritual with the few but tender notes from Lyle and the pictures. I couldn't just tear them up and throw them in the garbage can. Tears filled my eyes as I looked at my favorite photo of us. The towel was wrapped around Lyle's hips, and his right arm held me close. My right arm was crossed over my breasts and across Lyle's hairy chest, hugging him tightly. Neither of us wanted our weekend to end, which was obvious by the tears in our eyes as we stared longingly at each other in the mirror when he snapped the picture. I laughed and cried as I read every word of the few letters and cards I had printed from Lyle's e-mails. "Let me be able to say good-bye to Lyle forever!" I said to my higher power. "Help me to let go of him as if nothing had ever happened. Please, Creator, don't let this come between Mark and me."

I dumped the dirt and what was left of my crumpled pansies out of a twelve-inch clay flowerpot and stuffed the contents of my box into the pot. I would haul it to my back porch, light it with a match, and watch the ashes and smoke rise up into the universe—my higher power would, I was sure, take care of everything from there on out.

The cold December breeze doused the first match, then another and another. Finally I drew a sheet of paper out of the flowerpot, lit the corner, and stuffed it below the others. I gently blew on the paper until sparks ruffled black and red edges around my risqué collection of pictures. Within seconds, fifteen-inch flames and huge ashes sailed toward the roof. I panicked. "You stupid imbecile," I yelled at myself. "The neighbors will call the fire department for sure!"

For considering myself such a safe pyromaniac, I was totally inept that time. Within seconds the flames were nearly two feet in the air! Crumpled, flaming chunks of computer and Kodak paper tried to forsake my ceremonial ritual as I frantically tried to snatch them back into my caldron.

That's all I need—to be forced to chase bits and pieces of photos of nude bodies down the stairs and grab them from the hands of good Samaritans who might offer to help.

"Criminy sakes Sophia!" I heard my mom holler from somewhere in the sky, "Good-Heavens, are you trying to light us on fire?"

I thanked the universe when the flames finally leveled back to the top of the pot. The ashes flashed brilliant red and blue colors before they smoldered at the bottom. I had no sooner taken in a few deep breaths of gratitude, than the suffocating smell of rubber burned my nose and the whole porch filled with black smoke. The pot was melting itself to the outdoor carpet! I charged into the kitchen in search of something to douse the whole thing with. *For sure someone will call the fire department now! I'll be arrested and be fined! I'll owe money I don't have! Bad choice, Kristyn, you stupid, dumb, totally inept pyro!*

The fire was out by the time I got back. I hit the side of the scalding hot vessel with a wooden ladle. It didn't budge. Using a hot pad, I grabbed the rim of the pot and pulled upward with all my might, but it still didn't shift. Standing back next to the wall, I gave the pot a swift kick with the sole of my shoe. Still no luck. Finally, I sat down, planted both feet firmly against the container and my back against the porch wall and pushed as hard as I could. The pot came unstuck, but clinging to the bottom like tentacles were stringy globs of melted carpet fibers and tar that had once surfaced the floor. All that was left was a circle of scorched particleboard where the dark blue carpet used to be.

When the pot and fibers cooled off, I trimmed the remaining carpet with my scissors and laughed right out loud. How would I honestly explain this crazy episode to my landlady? In spite of everything, my deepest concern was whether or not the proof of my wild fling made it up into the Universe for safe keeping. Or would someone find a few remains and try to use them to sentence me to hell someday?

❧

Only three of my five Cedar City friends were able to make it for the "thank you" dinner I planned for my last Friday evening in Cedar City. I'd invited the few, but good friends I'd made, to thank them for being such an integral part of my life the past year.

My first try at mixing margaritas turned out great. I found the vodka, triple sec, and tequila in three different stores. A friend gave me the recipe on the phone and told me how to mix and freeze it ahead of time so it would be nice and slushy.

During and after our meal, I served the best margaritas on earth—at least all of us thought they were. We were flying so high on just one glass of those delicious spirits, there was no need for any more. My jaws ached from laughter. And while my heart felt truly satiated with the love and kindness those friends had shown me, I already missed them terribly.

By Saturday afternoon, I had everything packed and ready to be hauled out, other than my kitchen and bathroom things. When Mark arrived with Norma in his truck, and her husband Jared pulled into the parking lot right behind them in his truck, I talked myself out of acting on the anger I felt. But they picked up on it anyway. Mark said he and Norma "had to talk," and that's why she rode down with him. She continued to tell me she and my husband had nothing more than a God given friendship, and added another excuse for spending so much alone time with him. "You and Mark are twin rays, and you two should be together forever."

The four of us sipped leftover margaritas and munched on goodies. Then Mark massaged Norma's feet and back for over an hour while I packed the bathroom and then scrubbed it. Jared recounted another of his many tall tales that got more and more elaborate with each recap. When I'd finally had enough of Jared's, Mark's, and Norma's insensitivity, I shifted into high-gear workaholic mode, ignored my jealous feelings, and again wondered what in the hell I was going back to. I must have been totally crazy.

Before long, powered by a sugar-induced, margarita super buzz, I danced to and from boxes; swirled around with my cleaning rags, whisking away dirt and debris; and had the whole kitchen packed in less than forty-five minutes. I was so high on the possibility of a wonderful future, I successfully convinced myself Norma and Mark were being honest, and our love was divinely planned and ordered to remain as such.

Without my request, a couple of friends returned Sunday morning to help Jared and Mark load my boxes and furniture into their trucks. Then I wandered back in a few more times to say farewell to my sanctuary of five months. As we pulled away I stared at the apartment building until it was out of sight and I prayed for a glorious new beginning.

CHAPTER 46

For Better or For Worse
2001–2002

Mark drove while I snuggled tightly against his legs and torso. Nearly all the way home we planned our new, happy life together as we dreamed it would be thirty-two years ago just before we got married. Again, we reviewed our list of ideals and made new pacts and promises to each other. We'd always be considerate, discuss and stick together on issues. We'd be completely honest, choose each other over others, and fall in love again. That day, all of the horrendous, regrettable, and mundane trials that shattered our marriage seemed totally illusory in our minds. "All we have to do is love each other enough," Mark repeated a few more times while we travelled northward. With all my heart I chose to believe him.

Piles of snow concealed most of the yellow grass and overgrown weeds in my flowerbeds. The first glance reminded me of more things left undone and gone to ruin. Pangs of resentment flooded in.

Mark, Norma, Jared, and I haphazardly parked most of my things in the middle of the front room until I could decide where everything should be put. Then I took a tour of my home as if I hadn't been there in years.

Other than a vase of yellow and orange daisies Keith and Anne placed on the table with a "welcome home" note my upstairs kitchen felt icy and impersonal, Their bedroom arrangements reflected their personalities and comfort zones. I just smiled.

I was saving the best part of my tour for last. I could hardly wait to move back into my beautiful new basement again. Like a child in anticipation of Christmas morning, I descended to the bottom of the stairs. I could barely push the door open all the way. The whole room was still full of my sister Amy's household furnishings! My gorgeous bedroom was filled with her belongings as well. I sat on the only bare space of my beautiful purple carpet and cried. She'd known for months I was moving back home in December. Apparently she didn't care one single bit. She'd taken her body back to her marriage and left everything else in my way!

Mark sat next to me on the floor. "Don't worry, Sophia [he said he just couldn't call me Kristyn] we'll have all of this out of here in no time.

When I called Amy, she said she and her husband had Christmas shopping to do and a zillion other things that had to be done. They wouldn't be able to move their things out of my way for at least two weeks.

Mark and I cuddled under a pile of soft blankets in our wonderful king-size bed. While I cried in anger at my sister for being so obtuse about my situation, I tried to smother my overwhelmed feelings with sleep. *My to-do list is a mile long: move all my stuff back in, move Amy's things out, clean, scrub, do laundry, buy groceries and a few Christmas gifts, plan a family party . . . with whom—angry kids? With what money? Just shut up, Kristyn! Just shut up and go to sleep.*

The next day I packed Amy's things as fast as I could while Mark, Jared, and Keith loaded and hauled two heaping truckloads of boxes and furniture back to Amy's house. When we were a half truckload away from being finished, Mark said he had to leave. The threesome had a dinner date, he said. I needn't be worried—he'd help me get the rest of Amy's things moved out of my way within a few days. I must have stood there in shock, with my jaw dropping to my chest. I was so used to Mark's ill treatment by then, I must have begged for it. Just like my mother, I too must have exuded "victim." "Here I am Mark. I came back to you so you can tromp on my heart and wipe your feet all over my face!"

If his and Norma's big plan to help us work things out while protecting Diane's friendship and happiness meant keeping us apart, along with lies, secrets, and deceit like the whole previous year was full of, Mark should have been honest and decent enough to have told me right up front. At least I could have consciously agreed or disagreed with their plan, before I went back to his bedlam! And if I'd have been listening to my soul as much as I wanted to believe I had been, I would have told Mark right then, "Enjoy your life without me!"

For the next three weeks before Christmas, Mark's waking hours with me were infrequent. He spent most of his time working with and hanging out with his best friends. He said he was sleeping on Norma's couch. Now and then he'd climb in bed with me in the middle of the night to cuddle, make love, or just sleep. He convinced me to believe the reason he couldn't stay with me more was because he needed to make his divorce from Diane as easy as possible on her, so she wouldn't fall apart.

"She's a good person, and I just can't hurt her more than I already have," Mark said. "Please hang in there with me. All I want is for us to work this out. It will take some time, but it will happen. The sooner I can finish things with Diane the right way, the faster we can be together forever."

I reminded myself he liked and deserved his space and freedom, and that's what I wanted for him. And in the too many minutes my heart was breaking from his ignorant choices, I determined not to have any expectations. I would have to agree to deal with things the way they were, or I would have to move on.

On Christmas Eve, Mark took Keith and me to Norma's house to see her ornate and elaborate Christmas village. Mark showed off every detail of Norma's collection of many years, while Jared bragged about the nonstop, days-on-end collaboration it took Mark and Norma to lay out her beautiful arrangement. The cramps in my guts from anger and jealousy were masked by my *oohs* and *ahhs*.

Then, on the wall behind me I noticed a picture of Norma posing under a bristlecone pine tree—one of the many, Mark had snapped many months ago. She fussed about how Mark had it enlarged and framed . . . something this and something that. Most of her words came and went. The proof of "their" lovely vacation, Jared and I were so privileged to chaperone, cut and sliced at my stomach. I was busy holding on so I wouldn't throw up.

I was so good at keeping sweet and pretending, that I resented the hell out of me.

At 3:00 in the morning, tiny green Christmas lights reflected on my wet cheeks. I set a few more gifts next to our grandchildren's under the tree. I knew Anne and Keith would understand. So would the other kids. They were used to our meager holidays, interspersed with excessive or sufficient ones through years gone by.

All morning long I smiled, silently reviewing my long list of things to be grateful for. I even conjured up some more to help dissuade my blues. No matter how hard I tried every single year to change my frame of mind and experiences, especially for the kids' sakes, Christmases were always full of anxiety. Around 9:30 on Christmas morning, I held in my tears and asked Mark to, at least, get up long enough to watch the gift exchange.

Anne opened her snowboard and helmet from her boyfriend, and the costume jewelry Mark and I bought her. Keith got to unwrap a few pairs of pants, a couple of shirts, and some desperately needed underwear. Then Mark went back to bed.

Throughout the morning all of our kids arrived, except Jake. He hadn't spoken to me since I became the "witch who ruined our family." Around noon we had our traditional Christmas brunch of ham and egg sandwiches. Mark got up, ate a few bites, and socialized for a little while before he announced his planned departure to Diane's for her Christmas dinner with Jared and Norma's family.

By 2:30 all of my children and grandchildren had gone in different directions to celebrate with other loved ones. I encouraged Mark to take Keith with him so he'd have something to do and family to hang out with. When Mark left, he said he'd "be back in a few hours."

In the quiet solitude, it felt as if a hundred-pound bag of sand had dropped on my chest, preventing me from breathing. For the first time in my whole life I was completely alone on Christmas Day.

Other than having Mark to herself, Diane's secret dreams appeared to be coming true. My kids, grandchildren, Diane's kids, Jared and Norma's kids, and Mark were all together at her house without my presence.

In the frozen silence my head throbbed from the past three weeks of restrained emotions. I plopped down on my bed and gave myself time and permission to lament every morsel of rejection, hopelessness, and self-pity I'd been feeling for so long. Then I'd kick in the reality department and pulled myself through again. I had so much to be happy about!

From the past many experiences, Marks words about returning in "a couple of hours" really meant five or six hours, or not at all. So I wouldn't expect him until much later—maybe eight or nine. To expect or hope for anything had been my mistake from day one in our marriage! Either one of those verbs got me in big trouble on too many occasions. So I strove not to care about or to count on anything. I didn't dare expect, wish, or even hope Mark cared enough to keep his word that time either.

Around 6:30 Mark called to tell me he was almost ready to leave, so he'd be home soon. By 9:30 I was exhausted and satisfied. I proudly noted my sum of grand accomplishments in the six hours since I'd dragged myself up and decided to keep busy. Trying to remain sane had helped me rearrange my room; clean out drawers, shelves, and cupboards around the house; wash and fold piles of laundry; and scrub and wax the old linoleum floor in the kitchen on my hands and knees.

I showered, put on my pajamas, and desperately tried to ignore the pounding, throbbing, pain making me want to scream out loud. I watched TV, read, and wrote to rid my mind of the angst I was feeling all over again.

From our picture window, through the pasture in our back yard, I saw the lights were still on at my dear friend Racine's home. Though it was 10:30, I called her, threw on some sweats and a coat and ran over. While she poured raspberry wine into beautiful Christmas goblets, I knew I wouldn't be able to say one word or my emotions would explode.

"You're dying inside, Kristyn. I can see it all over you! What on earth is going on?" She asked. I lost it. After five minutes or so of uncontrollable sobbing, I confessed more heartaches than she'd ever heard during our therapeutic hikes and walks over the past few years.

By 11:30 I'd gathered strength in the warmth and safety of Racine's friendship to meander home. I was glad Mark looked and sounded like he was asleep. The old, familiar nausea was back again. I didn't know how I was supposed to feel or not feel—what I should or shouldn't say. No matter how I might attempt to express my feelings I'd be in trouble. So I wouldn't. I gently climbed in bed, hoping not to touch or wake him. I didn't want him to touch or hug me, either. He didn't, thank God. The energy was cold and tingly. All I could think of was getting to sleep as fast as I could so the day would be over and gone.

"What did you do today?" Mark asked suddenly.

I couldn't answer. My mouth wouldn't even open. Does he really want to know, I wondered? Can't he see? Does he really care?

Finally, in an effort to "keep sweet," I told him, "Just kept really busy."

"What did you do?" he asked again.

Are you an idiot? Are you blind? I wanted to scream at him. Instead, I said in a trembling voice, "A whole lot of things that needed to be done. I'm really tired and want to get some sleep."

"You're mad at me!" he snapped.

"I'm not so much mad as I am—"

"I know you're mad! You're mad because I didn't stay home and kiss your ass like you wanted me to. Norma said you'd be really pissed because I stayed longer at Diane's than you thought I should and you weren't invited!"

After a few minutes of silence he started again. "You wouldn't have gone even if you were invited, So-phi-a!"

"I don't think I am as mad as much as I am—" I tried to explain again.

"I know you are. Don't even try to deny it."

"I was really hurt and alone—"

Mark intruded. "You are too, mad at me! I can tell you are. You're always mad if you don't get your way. If I'm not where you think I should be when you think I should, then you're mad. I'm sick to death of kissing your ass. If you don't get exactly what you want when you want it, you go into one of your pouting fits! Well, I'm fucking tired of it! I'm not putting up with your bullshit any longer!"

I was appalled by his hostility toward me and the accusations that spewed from his mouth. He shot out of bed and stuffed some things into his carryall bag, then walked out the bedroom door and slammed it. Soon, I heard his truck door open and slam shut. The engine revved up and gravel flung across the driveway.

I cried all through the night and into the wee hours of the morning. Mark had slammed the door on my heart again. What, I wondered, were his anger and deception really about? Why did he say he wanted us if he couldn't and wouldn't honor even one of his renewed commitments?

Maybe Lyle was right about what he told me last fall. "Mark can't see yer feelin's past his nose cuz his ego and his dick's doin' the thinkin' when it comes to Norma!"

Mark had loved Norma when she was a teenager, and it was blatantly clear he loved her now. Men who were having affairs were known to flip out. Also, some men who were once nice to first, and previous wives had also become crazy and abusive to them after taking another wife. Two of my close friends had gone through that very thing. Their husbands had sudden outbursts, made terrible accusations and behaved outrageously—particularly when a woman tried to confront or question her husband about his conduct. It had become clear;

425

even if Mark wasn't having intercourse with Norma's body, he certainly was with her mind. So what in the hell was I still doing there in their way?

The day after Christmas, my puffy, red eyelids drooped so much I could hardly see. Mark was right about one thing he said the night before. I wouldn't have gone to Diane's house even if she had invited me. I had no doubt I wasn't welcome there. She hadn't been welcomed in my home either. At least I didn't show up uninvited. I chose to respect Diane's wishes, and that was the only truth in Mark's five-minute-long tirade.

Christmas Day and night, Mark set the precedents for the next year. I began to realize with every aspect of my being it didn't matter what I felt, said, or did. A force much more powerful than Mark or me, had already invaded our aspirations of reconciliation. It was obvious neither one of us was wise enough or courageous enough to wrangle with "Gods" persuasive control, and fight for our marriage.

CHAPTER 47

Places in Hell
January–June 2002

Throwing a huge New Year's party for my grandchildren was the best way to avoid the feelings and conflicts hounding me. It didn't surprise me, Mark stopped by to see what was going on. He said he had a few more of his things to pack, and he'd be back in the morning to at last haul the rest of Amy's boxes over to her house.

I was sure this was just the introduction to another apology. The next day, in anticipation, I canceled my morning hike with Racine and waited for Mark's arrival. By 3:00 when he still didn't show up, I ran a few errands and returned in haste, hoping we could spend some time together. When I got home he said he wasn't feeling good. He slept until nearly seven, and then hurried off to another appointment he said was none of my business.

Mark returned after midnight. He asked if he could climb in bed with me and talk. He apologized again for his bouts of anger and his ongoing absence. My insides felt twisted and tangled while he explained or dismissed his behaviors and choices with almost the exact same words Norma had used the previous day. Obviously they'd already discussed his fight with me in detail.

Norma begged me to meet her for lunch so she could "explain a few things and make them clear." I was still pathetically gullible and people-pleasing, and I wanted her to understand where I was coming from. So I showed up. She declared she knew and understood all of the difficulties and issues between Mark, Diane and me. She also claimed to be extremely keen about the particulars and the personalities of everyone involved, including our children. Norma said she and her siblings had gone through her mom and dad's divorce when she was a child, and had to suffer through Callie's (her ex-sister-wife's) divorce from Jared, nearly twenty years ago. Therefore, Norma said, "Its best to keep Diane and all of your kids in the dark concerning his decision to keep you in his life, while choosing to divorce her. It will kill her if she finds out he wants you to stay with him, when he has tried so hard to make it clear to her he is through with their marriage."

I sighed. "Norma, I told you when you first talked to me about keeping your death a secret from Diane and Jared, and I've told Mark a zillion times: truth to me is always better than lying under the guise of protecting someone. I would rather have the opportunity to make a decision based on truth rather than to deal with lies I might find out about later on. If Mark wanted to stay with Diane and not me, I would want him to tell me. That way I could move on, go through the pain, get over it and live in truth."

"It's not that I don't try to get her to wake up," Norma said. "I tell Diane or at least hint to her a little at a time, Mark won't be coming back to her and she needs to take care of herself and move on. But Diane refuses to hear it because she wants to believe Mark will come back to her once he gets over you. She doesn't want to know the truth. Believe me, she couldn't handle it. We need to go slow and protect her and the kids from finding out about Mark's feelings, or it will break all of their hearts."

"I can understand both of you—all of us—wanting to protect Diane from her pain, and I certainly don't want to hurt our kids either. However, all of the cover-ups remind me of nothing more than the same old 'plural marriage lies' polygamist men regurgitate and their wives agonize over. Husbands, I'm sure, have to lie to one or more of his wives to keep out of trouble with the others. They make up stories to save face, appease each one, and avoid unwanted pain. Such are the normal idiosyncrasies of plural marriage. Each wife hears the same old stories from him. She believes she's the most loved and adored while the other wives are the troublemakers and selfish ones. And she, in most cases, wants to believe his defensive fabrications. She goes on trying to keep sweet for the sake of survival and to be in harmony with her husband."

It didn't matter I disagreed with Mark and Norma's choice to mislead Diane, or about any of their decisions. Just how long, I wondered, would they continue that duplicity? Would it ever end? It would probably never make a difference in Diane's heart. All three of us were sure Diane would never be able to accept Mark and me together without her.

So, at lunch on the first day of 2002, Norma adamantly claimed her authority as a marriage counselor. She knew the ins and outs— everything plausible and even impossible—when it came to living and ending polygamous relationships. She had already been, and was still very busy endorsing her own advice for the supposed good of everyone involved.

Mark fumbled around his words while he tried to express all of Norma's strong opinions in his own words. I tried to stay tuned in as he continued to explain in a variety of ways his misconduct was all due to his level of stress; his worries about the kids; Diane's feelings and mine, which were more than he could handle; his inability to make ends meet; and the sad fact he just couldn't be with me as much as he'd like to be.

My thoughts had returned to Norma's sermon the day before when I wanted to reach across the table and slap her face. The ridiculous explanations she used to justify Mark's mistreatment of and cruelty to me, made me sick. "He's just weary of trying to protect Diane's feelings while trying to work things out with you," she said. And now, on my bed, Mark was repeating the same justifications as to why it was okay to treat *me* like garbage while he was so concerned about protecting Diane.

"But more than anything," he said after a while, "I want you and me to be together forever! I want us to work out. Please wait for me, Sophia. Don't hop on that runaway train again. Wait for me to finish things up with Diane, in the right way, so I won't have to hurt her more than I already have. She can't know I'm with you, or that I want to stay married to you. It would tear her apart."

"I know it will hurt her," I told him. "But how can you expect our marriage to work if you're hardly ever with me, and you're cussing angry about made-up crap when you are here?"

"I don't know how to do all of this," Mark replied. "I just know I want to grow old with you. Norma always says we're 'twin rays' and you and I should be together forever."

Like most totally insecure, addicted to abuse, crazed women in unstable relationships, I melted. Mark's words of love and passion, of grief and longing, found their way into my dream world. Again, we conversed for hours about our long-term goals: a smaller home out in the country, retirement, visits from our kids and grandchildren. We made new vows and commitments to each other, and I fell back into his arms to stay, hope, and wait.

When Mark granted me fragments of his leftover time, I made every effort to be with him. While *his* time became less and less *our* time, I filled my life to the brim with my on-line class, student teaching, dancing, family and friends. I determined I'd do anything to be happy, healthy, and strong while I waited for him to "finish things up with Diane in the right way." Near the end of February, I was amazed when Norma decided Mark could stay with me for four nights in a row before I left for Oregon. *How will they hide this one from Diane?* I wondered.

My brother, James, bought me a "getaway" ticket to visit him and his wife. They took me everywhere. We compared our perceptions of being raised in the same household with the same two parents, under the duress of Dad's other wives. For the first time in my life, I heard an in-depth version of the pieces of hell, only a polygamist husband knows. My heart ached as James recalled his past marriage to his three wives.

"From the outside, everyone thought things in my family were great. All of us put on a good front so no one, not even you, would know how bad things really were. But my wives fought like cats and dogs," James said. "They didn't want to live together and were seldom happy. The very people I loved the most had little or no love for each other. The more tension there was at home, the more I wanted to run away and leave."

Tears filled his eyes. "And you know what, Kristyn? No matter what I did, no matter how hard I prayed or how many meetings I attended, or how hard I tried to be a good priesthood leader and to do everything right, nothing ever worked. Not one of us was really happy. If I wasn't doing what they thought I should do, they'd fume for days. No matter how many hours I worked, no matter how much money I made, or how much time I did or didn't spend with someone, there was never enough of me or my money to go around! Someone was always pissed, jealous, and wanting to leave. And most of the time," James almost shouted, "I was so damn depressed I could hardly function! I felt like such a failure, I wanted to be out of that lifestyle or die. Sometimes I truly envied the dead."

James's remorse shifted through my guts like an auger with razor blades. In his feelings and words, I saw a lot of resemblance to Mark's life with Diane and me. I always knew Mark needed and deserved his freedom from that kind of craziness. Diane and I were both insecure and needy women. We wanted his devotion to God, his love, and his attention. In many ways, Mark, as a good man, brought up to believe he had to live polygamy, was just as unsatisfied, tormented, and full of grief as we were. My sister-wife and I felt and watched him flee the scene over and over again. He too had been depressed, angry, and dying. James's words keenly extended my perspective of a male polygamist's torment. It brought to my awareness much more than my own sorrows and woes.

Mark and I were still "together" when I got home—at least in heart and spirit. Nothing had changed in the six days I'd been gone. Every day, all day and most nights—aside from his job—he was gone. He continued to work for, travel with, and mingle with Norma, Jared, and their children. He made himself readily available to comfort and soothe Norma's broken heart any time she fretted over her advancing death. If her spirit guide were right, she had less than a year to live. If her spirit guide were wrong, Norma would surely come up with another explanation to explain Mark's spiritually required friendship and devotion to her.

In between all of the drama, I was sure I'd made a mistake trying to be in Mark's life without Diane as his wife, and with Norma running the show. But he guaranteed me it wouldn't be long before things would be resolved.

"If I take things slow, Diane will be secure enough that we can soon be open about our relationship," he said.

Though somewhere in my soul I believed our efforts were in vain, I clung tightly to his promises and forgave his continual distance and neglect.

Through March, while he stayed in our daughter's basement, Mark and I acted like lovers on the make. We got together whenever, wherever, and however we could. In private, we enjoyed our delicious conjugal visits immensely. In public, around those we knew, we were back to acting as if we were divorced. We immensely enjoyed those times of lovemaking, with no fighting and no disapproval.

Whenever I saw Jared, he'd tell me how much he appreciated Mark's validation of his stories and his wisdom. Mark assured me of his appreciation for Jared as well.

"They love me, Sophia. They are the friends I've never had before."

He was absolutely right. I certainly didn't want to complain about him having friends. For as long as I'd known Mark, I had longed for him to have the gift of true friendship. He deserved loyal friends who would honor and love him. Norma and Jared filled his empty cup and his ego to the brim. In their eyes, he was near perfection. No matter what he ever did or didn't do, he was and would always be justified.

Still, I couldn't understand why he continued to spend so much time with them and away from me, and why he was so deceitful about it. I'd plead with Mark to explain things to me.

"If you want our marriage to work out, why do you lie and keep secrets from me? Why am I excluded from ninety-eight percent of your life and time? It would be easier to wait with even twenty percent of your time. Instead, the only time we get alone is if you want sex. Why do you let Norma run your life and make our decisions?"

Asking for any clarification didn't work. It made Mark angry and defensive. I forced myself to ignore my concerns and disapproval and kept on keeping on with my own life.

The few times Norma decided I could be invited to join her, Jared, and Mark, she reminded me of the importance of not letting Diane know we were all together, especially that I was with them.

"She's too jealous, and all it will do is cause trouble," Norma would say. But within minutes she would boast again of her skill at eluding Diane in any way she wished to.

"She never knows what I'm up to unless I want her to know," Norma bragged. "I've told my kids exactly what they should and shouldn't say whenever Diane calls the house. They've gotten really good at it. You just watch." Norma laughed. "She'll call while we're sitting here eating. She calls me several times during the weekend to check up on me."

This was just exactly as I surmised. Norma admitted Diane never knew about their outings, yet she and Mark continued to exclude me. With that factual information (verified by Mark) I knew I could no longer trust any of their contrived reasons to constantly exclude me.

Finally I asked Mark, "What does your secret life with Norma have to do with making things easier or better for Diane? And how does your whole life being consumed by Norma, help you, Diane, or me? None of this is right, and you know it, Mark!"

As usual, he accused me of being nothing but a selfish, jealous bitch again. He raged at me as if I were a crazy lunatic while he defended Norma. "Nothing she is doing or saying is wrong. She loves you Sophia. She would never do anything to hurt you."

But each time Mark launched his pile of toxic refuse at me, slammed the door, and left me covered in his vile debris, it was more evident why he said such mean things. And whose words were really coming out of his mouth? That was not Mark's vernacular. It hadn't been in years. He began to eat, think, breathe, and speak "Norma." He doled out her exact words and phrases every time I saw him.

Between his new gobbledygook, new perceptions, abusive accusations, and my pain and tears, we couldn't tolerate each other anymore. We'd fight; he would disappear. Then he'd come back anywhere from a few hours to a few weeks later to repeat his worn out, old apologies. When we were alone, he'd tell me he never really meant the terrible things he said. He knew I wouldn't do and be all the horrible things he accused me of when he was raging mad. As always, he promised to be loyal and more attentive. And as always, I forgave him. We'd make up, have sex, and fall in love with the idea of being in love, and with the idea of living the rest of our lives in bliss. Then we were fighting again.

My student teaching, planning, and assignments and job hunting kept me away from social activities and friends. I was and felt so alone! The serenity prayer became my constant mantra during those four long months. I nurtured myself as best as I could with nutritious food, exercise, meditation, and breathing. But beyond and above all, I told myself as often as possible, "Don't *ever* expect anything from anyone anymore, ever again! Take life one day at a time, and take care of yourself, Kristyn! No one else will or should."

It seemed each one of our kids, as well as Diane's had a different take on the bombshell that had been dropped in their pathways. They were used to years and years of the old familiar polygamous lifestyle—of their parents hanging in there through thick and thin. But according to some, Aunt Kris—oops, I mean Sophia—had blown it to smithereens.

My son Jake hadn't talked to me since the last part of November unless he had to. I never heard from Diane's kids. On the other hand, the rest of my children seemed to keep on loving all of us while they made an effort to stay in the middle ground and not take sides. I told them I hoped they would never feel they had to choose between us.

In April, Mark and I didn't celebrate our thirty-second anniversary. He said he couldn't. He was too busy remodeling Norma's kitchen along with all her other projects and requests. "It's no big deal—we can celebrate it later when we have more time and money," he told me nonchalantly.

I didn't even try to debate it with him. If he didn't care enough to make some time for us, I didn't want to make it happen. I buried myself in a tubful of hot water, and allowed myself to lament.

When Mark and I were communicating, we decided it would be best to sell our dream house and buy a smaller home—one we could keep up with and pay for. Since our bills were still unpaid and our debts were beyond belief, we agreed selling would be the best way to go. I'd already maxed out my credit cards to keep us afloat, and something had to be done before we lost the house completely. We knew there was no way anyone would want to buy our junkyard for anywhere near what we needed. Something had to be done about the back half-acre that was still an eyesore and an embarrassment. Over the years, I'd laboriously cleared portions of it off for the planned little playhouse, swing-set areas, sandboxes, gardens... Those areas were nowhere to be seen. They'd done nothing more than serve as more open spaces for "Mark and sons, family, and friends" to pile more rubbish, scraps, batteries, and broken-down "good for someday" refuse and masonry equipment.

Mark's brother in-law, our knight in shining armor, came to our rescue. He drove down our long driveway and hauled his bulldozer off of his glistening gold trailer. He'd driven all the way up from St. George (in southern Utah) just to help conquer our junkyard battlefield.

It took him three long days to rip out the elm forest that had taken over like weeds. With his front-loader, he got rid of four or five dump-truck loads of garbage and completely leveled the back half of our land. Watching twenty years of rubbish disappear brought me to tears. I was overwhelmed with hope, gratitude and relief.

Mark and I owed our hero more than a king's ransom. But he knew we didn't have it, nor did he expect it. After his hard work and expensive labor there was a good chance someone would want to purchase our place, which now had endless possibilities.

When Mark came home and saw his battlefield had been overthrown, he was livid. He wanted the blocks, the cans, the old wheelbarrows, and the junk trees. He felt beaten and wounded. I had taken his brother-in-law up on his offer to help without consulting him first.

I made the decision. It was planned and set in motion before Mark could balk and refuse the offer. I knew from 29 years of past experiences, and Mark's "someday" dreams and promises, the property would never be cleaned up and turned into the wonderland we always talked about. It was the complete opposite. It got worse by the day! We would never have money to hire it to be done. Mark was also too proud to accept any offers of help. He was at least a hundred times angrier with me that time, than when I accidentally mutilated the large lilac bush in our back yard.

As time passed, it was more obvious the months and years Mark had been spending with his new family was creating a total stranger out of him. His thoughts, words, and actions were *their* thoughts, words, and actions. His unpredictable rages toward me began to scare me, and created ever more mistrust for Norma's claimed good intentions. Things Mark had loved and appreciated and things he complimented me for, were now twisted and contorted into me being a selfish, conniving, manipulative bitch—all expelled from Mark's mouth like projectile vomit.

Right from the start, Norma started telling me those things. "Oh, you're not so perfect. You were mean and conniving . . . Diane said . . . and I know . . ." Openly as well as behind my back, Norma ridiculed me—and others. She complained about my cooking, my friends, my life, my feelings, my inabilities, and even (assumed by her) my thoughts and intentions. She'd often snicker along with the cutting remarks she tried to make sound like ongoing jokes. "Yeah, Sophia might not know who or where she is . . . but I love her so much!"

One apparently scissor-happy day I cut Mark's hair way too short. Norma convinced everyone, including Mark, I did it because I was mad at him. "That haircut was to punish him," she claimed. Of course, not one single word I said to the contrary mattered. If Norma said I was mad, I was. She knew how to twist each tiny flaw, simple mistake, thought, action, good intention, misunderstanding, or decision I made so it could become Mark's battering ram. And each one served to bolster his reasons to continually break his promises to me.

❧

I finished my early childhood class assignments and my student teaching. I went through several interviews and kept on with my life. Within a few weeks, a secretary in the Jordan School District office, called to ask if I would take on a long-term substitute position for a kindergarten teacher who was having pregnancy problems. I excitedly agreed.

While I was filling out forms, I asked why they hired me over the phone out of 250 applicants, especially without requiring an interview with the principal. The receptionist told me, "We looked through all the applications to find someone with a lot of early childhood experience. You had the most by far. We were also impressed with your high interview and test scores, but mostly because the kindergarten teacher liked your teaching philosophy."

I took all of that as some of the nicest compliments I'd ever received, as well as a gift from my higher power. I was ecstatic about my first job as a certified elementary schoolteacher.

In June, I proudly walked across the stage with all those young women and men I'd attended college with. At the very young age of forty-nine, I could finally lay claim to a Bachelor of Science degree in early childhood development and elementary education. Even better, I maintained my 4.0 GPA and graduated Summa Cum Laude!

Near the end of June, I was offered two teaching jobs within a fifteen-minute period. I was purple and pink all over to have been hired by one of my children's previous principals, who worked at a school close to home.

CHAPTER 48

Enough Is Enough
July–August 2002

Though there was little evidence Mark and I would be able to work things out, I clung on to one single strand of hope as if my very life depended on it. But even with coaxing and pleading, he could no longer convince me Norma wasn't leading and behind his every word and action.

I was elated when I was filling out health insurance forms and realized my two youngest children and Mark could be covered as well. Along with my teaching job came health security; one my children and I had hardly ever known.

"No!" Mark said. "You know I've already got good coverage under Diane's insurance and she is generous enough under the circumstances to keep it that way. I can't go off of her insurance without her wanting to know why."

"Of course she is happy with it like this," I told him. "Norma says she will do anything plausible, hoping when I'm completely out of the picture you'll return to her and live happily ever after! Nearly once a month you promise me after one of our knock-down drag-out fights you desperately want our love and marriage. You tell me there's no reason we can't work things out if I'll be patient with you in letting Diane down easily—the right way. It's been nearly a year since you said you divorced her, and you've been working so hard to let her down easy. It's been eight months since you asked me to come back to you. Still I have absolutely nothing to go on. Now is your chance to be honest with me, to do just one thing to show me you are serious about you and me, more than just a bunch of words and promises you haven't kept. Diane doesn't have to know if you don't want her to. You and Norma have that down pat. Or you can be honest with her, which I'd prefer. You can explain Sophia's insurance coverage will be better, so you're going to give it a try. Come on, Mark. After all, you can be insured with me, your divorced, still legal wife, or with your divorced common-law wife. You'll have to let me know while the district has open enrollment. I think we only have one month. I'll find out and let you know for sure."

Mark said he'd think it over. He said he didn't see why it couldn't work. I was very excited but had my reservations. Of course he'd mull it over with his best friend, Norma. Even so, I got my hopes up. I wanted us to be together like he said we would be. I asked him for a favor because it was the only solid, tangible move on his part that would prove any loyalty to me.

I had one teachers' meeting after another. In all the years I raised my seven children, I was intimidated by most of their teachers. It was always my intention to thank them for all their hard work and for their abilities to teach a million differing personalities. I thought I knew, being a teacher involved way more than educating students, but I found, actually making that happen was a completely different world. There was no end in sight: trying to acquire materials; make what I couldn't afford; set up my classroom; label books, desks, scissors, play equipment; decide routines, lessons, transitions; make charts, copies, bulletin boards; plan lessons… Indeed, I had no idea what teachers had to go through! I felt bad when I began to understand the appreciation my children's teachers surely deserved from me and never received. Teaching younger grades and the preparation time was (and is) much like planning and setting up for a huge conference every day for years with no end in sight. My time crunch and mega stress level were literally eating me alive.

In addition to all the pressure, Rosamond Elementary School was being remodeled, so we had to move all of our supplies and things to Riverton High School where the children would attend classes for three weeks before we got the privilege and joy of moving everything back to the elementary school to start again.

A few weeks before school started near the end of July, my guts started violently convulsing. The nausea was so intense I couldn't eat but a tiny bit at a time or it wouldn't stay down. It felt like the worst case of flu I'd ever had. Still, I couldn't stop working, and I practically couldn't stop crying. I was afraid I might have a nervous breakdown if I slowed down at all. Besides all the school meetings and preparations, I unwisely volunteered to sew my soon-to-be daughter-in-law's wedding dress, and there were still a million more things to do. Without any emotional or physical support, my body was rebelling.

From the sidewalk, I watched hundreds of children exit the buses and cars in front of the high school on their first day of school. I didn't see how I could possibly stay, but I couldn't leave my first-graders with a substitute on their first day of school, either. Yet I knew it would also be a true miracle if the pain in my guts didn't cause me to faint right there in front of everyone. I'd be so embarrassed. I forced the tears to stay behind my eyes and my body to endure until I could go home.

When I could no longer bear the pain, I rushed to the nearest bathroom. My blood-covered panties let me know my bowels were in worse condition than I ever imagined. Throughout the day I continued to layer paper towels between my slacks, panties, and me. Miraculously, with remarkable patience and kindness to my first-grade children, I finished a day that literally felt like ten.

Mark was lying on the bed when I got home. He wasn't feeling well either. I wanted to crash next to him and have him wrap his arms around me and make everything all right for both of us while we slept for three solid days and nights.

I changed, put a pad on my underwear, and slid underneath the sheet next to Mark. He turned over on one elbow and asked me how my first day went. My heart raced while I wondered where to begin, when even talking was cumbersome. As I started to tell him about the months of overwhelming stress and of my day of physical agony, the tears I'd forced inside poured from my eyes. "My stomach and abdomen hurt so bad, I think something isn't right inside of me. I'd better go to a doctor to find out what's wrong."

"What's the matter now?" Mark griped.

I tried to ignore his cold, frustrated tone and began to explain, I was bleeding from my bowels and thought my body was paying me back for pushing it so long and hard.

Mark jolted back and sat up on his the side of the bed. "What in the hell are you talking about, Sophia? You've got life easy right now! You've got a house, a good job and friends—you've got about every fucking thing you ever wished for, and now you're bitching and complaining! What in the hell is this about? What didn't I do now?"

He stood up, leaned his torso over me, and shouted some more. "You know what, So-ph-ia? You're just throwing another pouting tantrum to get your own way! This is about the insurance, huh? I didn't get back to you, so now you're throwing yourself a pity party! Norma warned me if you didn't get your way, you'd pout and sulk about it! Well, I'm fucking tired of placating you and giving in to your demands and your shit!"

Mark stormed out of our room. I found my way through blinding tears to the door. Behind the steering wheel, I sat and sobbed a billion more tears. When I could breathe and see again, I drove myself to the Sandy City Instacare.

In our entire marriage, it had never been so clear Mark and I were a lost cause. The man on my bed next to me—the man who was raging at me—certainly wasn't the man who claimed to love, adore, and honor me. Nor was he the man who kept saying he wanted us to live happily ever after. He wasn't the man I'd fallen so deeply in love with nearly twelve years previously, and he certainly wasn't the man I'd honeymooned with a few years later. That man no longer existed.

The doctor wanted me to go right to the hospital. He said there was way too much blood for this to be a minor situation. I assured him, aside from the pain, most of my uncontrollable tears were emotional trauma.

"That's the reason you need to get some bed rest," he said. "Get away from home and life's stresses for a while. Go to the hospital. They'll do the appropriate tests and make you have peace and quiet for a few days."

"There's no way I can take time now." I told him. "I've got two more days of teaching—then I can take a break over the weekend."

The doctor grudgingly handed me a few prescriptions to fill, along with orders for bed rest and a colonoscopy, then he warned. "You really should check yourself in to the hospital. I'm really worried about you."

I still couldn't understand or justify Mark's violent and atrocious conduct. His cruelty cut me to the core. In my codeine stupor, I sobbed and worried. *How could I make it through two more days of teaching before the weekend? At least I have some pain meditation. I can't possibly take time to rest. I have a million things to get done. Will my new insurance cover all the doctor bills and tests? Where is Lyle? I wish he could come and take me away for a while. He might if I called him—if he doesn't have someone else in his life by now. Why didn't I listen to him in the first place?*

As usual, there was no communication between Mark and me, only avoidance and sorrow. Why, I wondered, couldn't he see what was going on in his mind? Treating me with such hostility should bring him to his senses. But Norma had changed his mind again. He believed and touted her maxim: "You have to let Sophia go so she can spread her butterfly wings and fly away. If she returns to you, she will truly be yours. If not, she was never yours in the first place." What happened to her previous assertion; Mark and I were "twin rays" and belonged together forever? By then, it was obvious Norma's proclaimed friendship from God was the catalyst of his pushing Diane and me out of the nest and replacing us with her. With all of Norma's manipulation going on, Mark must have felt the need to literally shove me out of his life, off a virtual cliff, and hope my "butterfly wings" would carry me away, before I crashed in despair.

You know, don't you, Kristyn? You know the real meaning of in-

sanity? I heard my soul say to me. *Do I have to spell it out for you? Yes, I do know, I said. I just don't understand how Mark can treat me so horribly and not see what's going on. What did I ever do to deserve this kind of treatment?*

You don't, Kristyn! That's just it. You don't deserve any of this, my soul maintained. Can't you see what you are doing? You are begging and fighting for a nonexistent cause—for your children, for your posterity, and for dreams that aren't meant to be.

You are right! I concede, I said firmly to my soul. *I've done everything I can possibly do to make this marriage work. I've kept every promise I made to him before I came home from Cedar City last December. I've trusted in him and his godforsaken promises way beyond reason.*

I'd gone back to him at least seven times after his insidious behaviors toward me. Yes, that was totally crazy. Doing the same things over and over again and expecting different results was truly the definition of *my* insanity.

I'm sorry. I'm so sorry I haven't listened and honored you, I told my soul, my heart, and my aching guts. I've got to let go and move on with my life. I will. I'll do the best I can to leave.

From the previous December to August my "runaway train" had taken off many times. When things were tough, it beckoned me to jump on board and head for sanity and serenity somewhere far away from Mark's cabal of influence. Sometimes it moved tauntingly slow, and sometimes faster, depending on the journey. But at the "waiting station," when it was at a complete stop, I'd given my all.

❧

The doctor handed me a few pictures of my colon. There were several caved-in pockets full of tiny, bright red and white pustules.

"It's no wonder you've been bleeding so profusely," she said. "You'll have diverticulitis forever, Kristyn. All we can do is treat the symptoms. Watch what you eat and take your medication. Read this pamphlet. It will tell you what foods to eat and what foods to avoid.

Oh, yeah, and avoid stress! It triggers these little blastulas to act up all over again."

"No, I won't have it the rest of my life," I said under my breath. "I'll take care of me. I'll move on. I'll be happy and healthy. I know I can heal this too."

I took my doctor's advice and began hiking and playing more. A friend and I started taking line-dance lessons on Wednesday and Friday nights at a club in Salt Lake. No matter how busy and crazy life became, I could count on those fun times as exercise and healthy outlets away from stress.

Another big stress relief was my son Jake's change of heart. He was going through a divorce and wanted to talk. He said he never did really understand why he was so angry with me. He just was. It meant more than the whole world to have him back in my life again!

Mark sensed my change of heart. I was keeping busy, breathing and rapidly letting go. When he became himself for a few minutes, he asked me to forgive the stupid things he'd said and done. Another time, he promised to make things right. He'd get off Diane's insurance and get on mine as soon as possible. He said he was sure it was the best thing for both of us—it made sense we should be partners in everything.

I wanted to be shot to the moon! I was proud I didn't fall back in his line again. I made a pact with myself to be kind no matter what. I continued to move in my own space and direction and didn't expect for one minute he'd keep that promise either.

Aside from the feelings flying around everyone, I enjoyed our son Jack's marriage to Norma and Jared's daughter. At the wedding, I was single. I took off my shoes, danced up a storm, laughed and visited with friends and loved ones. While Diane was busy lining up her children, Mark, and herself for family pictures, I listened to my friends' dismayed comments. Through the whole evening Mark never said one word to me. It was as if we didn't exist to each other. It seemed everyone with even the slightest negative emotion covered them well, for our kid's joyous occasion.

444

Near the end of August, during a Friday-night line-dancing lesson, my friend and I sat with a few ladies we were getting acquainted with between dances.

"Would any of you ladies like a rose?" We looked up to see a beautiful, dark-complexioned young woman holding a bucket full of long-stemmed red roses.

"How much are they?" my friends and I asked in unison.

"Just three dollars each," she replied.

All of us told her no thanks.

"Here, I'd like to buy four of them," a man said as he approached her, holding out some cash.

While we continued to gab, the young woman pulled out four roses and handed one to each of us. "That man over there said to tell you" —she shifted her shoulder in the man's direction— "that these are for you beautiful ladies."

We turned and mouthed a thank you to the man, who was by then sitting across the room, watching us as we made our way back to the dance floor. His wink aimed in my direction made me blush a little, but I ignored him.

I had met Tom once before. About three weeks earlier he asked me to dance. "Only once," I told him. "I'm married, and we girls have a rule of thumb—'If you don't want anything going on, you won't dance more than once with the same man.'" He and I visited a little while, as I fumbled around a two-step I barely knew how to do. On the way back to my table, Sam told me to let him know if I were to ever be single.

Even before Mark's attack about the rose sitting on my windowsill, I wondered why he even came to our house any more. All it did was stir things up inside us, until both of us felt like we might gag. He looked at me like a forlorn puppy begging to be loved. I wouldn't talk to Mark about anything. I knew it wouldn't do any good.

Enough is enough! I reminded myself every time I wanted him to understand how he'd messed us up—how he should fix things and love me more than Diane's feelings and Norma's "friendship from God."

Ever conditioned to live with heartache and ill treatment, my ego would implore—*for hell sakes, Kristyn, you have seven kids together and a bunch of beautiful grandchildren! You two practically grew up together and have been through the pits of hell and in the realms of heaven with each other.* With all the insanity, a tiny thread of the unraveling umbilical cord still remained.

❧

I looked in the rearview mirror at the lines left on my face by the past few years. *Why in the world did I tell Tom after dance lessons I'd meet him for dinner? This is really stupid!*

I blotted my tears with a tissue. *Can I really go home with him just to, once and for all sever the cord binding me to Mark? What a mistake that would be. How sleazy I would feel! And what if Mark did decide to make everything right?*

My word, Kristyn, you are thinking crazy thoughts again! My head shouted. *You know things won't change. Just sleep with the guy! Then you won't ever be able to go back for more crap from Mark!*

My cell phone rang. It was Mark's number. My heart began to leap out of my chest.

"Can we talk right now?" he asked in his deep, kind voice.

"I'm in West Valley at the mall," I told him. "What do you want to talk about?"

"Will you come home right now? I need to talk to you."

"Okay, I'll be there in half an hour."

Elation filled my mind when I called Tom to cancel my dinner date with him. On my way home, I had to jerk my lead foot off the gas pedal a few times. I hoped beyond hope Mark would tell me he was sorry for getting so freaked out about the single red rose, for calling me a cheat and a liar. In total lunacy I pictured another romantic reunion. I imagined he'd be telling me he now realized Norma was controlling him. He'd promise to completely end his relationship with her so we could at last work things out without her interference. The itty-bitty thread of umbilical cord was pathetically tuned in and hopeful. By the time I pulled into our driveway, I'd already created a "happily ever after" scenario in my head.

The glum look on Mark's face sliced my crazy hopes in two. I plopped myself down on the opposite end of our sofa and faced him. "What's up?" I asked pleasantly.

"I need to know why you lied to me about the rose," he said.

"We've already been through this, Mark. Is this really what you called me home for?"

"I know you lied to me about it, and I want to know why!" he demanded.

"I told you a young lady who was selling roses gave one to four of us women. I didn't tell you a guy paid for them because there was no reason to. It had no meaning other than it was a beautiful rose!"

"You brought it home. You put it in a vase in our window. So it must have meant something to you!"

"Oh my gosh Mark! It's just a rose. Is this really what you called me all the way home to talk about, again? Why? So you can beat me up for not throwing it in the stranger's face or in the garbage can? I should have known you wanted to shout at me some more. I shouldn't have driven all the way home to subject myself to your madness again."

"I'm sorry, Sophia. I can't deal with the idea of another man giving you flowers. That's been my joy, my way of showing you love and appreciation."

I didn't say anything. How long had it been since Mark brought me flowers or showed me any love and appreciation, other than as a conflict resolution? I wanted to be the one to run out, slam the door, and fuck him off like he'd done to me so many times that year. I never wanted to speak to him again! But I just sat there and wondered why. What on earth was I waiting for—to be physically beat up this time?

Mark moved across the couch, closer to me, and started his apologies yet again, for not being there for me, for yelling so much, for saying such terrible things—things he never really meant at all.

"Norma told me not to ever yell at you again," he said. "I promise no matter how pissed off or angry I feel. I won't take it out on you or yell at you ever again."

With that insolent proclamation, he again declared to whom his heart and loyalties belonged. His pledge of willpower hadn't come from his own desires and determination. Neither had his affront come from my endless appeals, of begging him to stop raging because he loved and cared enough to quit hurting me so damn much. After all this time, with all he'd done, and said in Norma language; this promised had also been requisitioned by her!

I just sat there, waiting.

This is the insanity we were talking about, my soul interjected.

I know, I said, but maybe, just maybe this time?

My ego's words to my soul made me feel embarrassed and noxious. I'd listened to those same words from women in abusive relationships who went back again and again, hoping and dreaming, "If only he would . . . If only I could make him understand . . . Maybe this time . . ." And there I was waiting—waiting for what?

You do know how to end this marriage, and stop this insanity. My soul directed. I listened and obeyed.

"Mark," I finally said after a few minutes of dead silence. "It's been nearly two months since you told me you'd take yourself off of Diane's insurance and get on mine. You swore you would do something to help solidify our marriage." I could see his anger rising in the color of his cheeks. "Then you said you would be sure to tell me when you did, so you wouldn't accuse me again of being a nag if I asked. But you didn't keep that commitment, either. You didn't even have enough respect to tell me you didn't keep—"

He cut me off. "That's because I knew you wouldn't put me on your insurance! And after you did you'd divorce me and cut me off of it anyway. That's why I didn't take myself off Diane's fucking insurance plan in the first place! At least I can trust *her!*"

YOU finally did it! My soul applauded, just as my whole being literally felt the last strand of addiction snap in two.

"It's alright, Mark," I calmly said. "I knew clear back then, you would dismiss me, and another promise you made. And it's all okay, because *you* are the one who chose not to love *me* enough to make *us* work. I've done the best I could possibly do to keep my promises to you. I have no more hope and nothing more to give to *us*." I got up on one knee, leaned in close to his face, and proclaimed, "Enough is enough. I am through waiting!"

I calmly walked out our back door and drove away. I—Sophia, me, Kristyn—didn't even cry! I started to cross the railroad tracks going farther up our foothills but stopped right on top of them. I looked in both directions. The runaway train had egged me off and on from my birth and throughout fifty years in polygamy had finally derailed! It could no longer haul me off to hell or run over me while I tried to jump it. Nor could its toxic exhaust stifle me in that waiting station. I finally got enough courage to pull the switch and end the insanity. It no longer frightened or tempted me. I no longer needed to run away from anything or anyone. I drove straight across—another gigantic step toward a new life.

At one of Mother Earth's hallowed spaces, I dropped to the warmth of her ground and basked in her glorious sunshine. There I contemplated my fifty years in polygamy—my fifty years full of sorrow and joy.

With all my heart and soul, I used to sing the LDS hymn "How Firm the Foundation." Yet in all I had written and so much more, I knew the foundation I was raised on never was firm from the very beginning. It started with too many cracks and flaws. With each newly discovered truth, the few fragmented and remaining pieces were also turning into dust.

I thought of the many women who confided their torments while living polygamy—women young and old, who still believe and live that lifestyle because they have to—otherwise they surely wouldn't. There are far too many so-called happy women who've been abandoned in more ways than one, living in loneliness, poverty, seclusion, fear, and torment. Most "happy," sacrificing women pray every day of their lives to the God I grew up with, to make them more tolerant, submissive, sweet martyrs for His gospel. Like me, those Stepford Wives put on their smiley faces and exude happy looking righteousness all over the world.

Like most polygamists, I really believed I was happy in trying to live God's commandments. However, the tiniest glimpses of genuine truth and love I'd begun to see, after I wanted to die, let me know I wasn't happy. Happiness certainly wasn't the hell playing out all around me in the name of sacrifice, in exchange for a "someday," an "if," or a "when."

I was born into a religious belief, with oppressive rituals. The beliefs of seven generations held me fast. As time went forward the imps who used to chase, torment, and threaten Mom and me with guilt and shame just up and quit coming around anymore. My soul told me they never did exist. They were only there because I was told, and then believed they were there. They were created by a religion that dominates and buries souls with fear; threats of demise and bribes of eternity.

In truth my deep, dark depressions were there to get my attention because I was too busy wallowing in the upbringing of my ego to honor my soul, who was screaming, *Wake, up Kristyn—Sophia girl— and all you other beautiful women out there who believe you have to live that delusional, crazy-making, male-ego-devised scheme!*

We were told to ignore our soul's whisperings, our heartaches, moods, and warnings. We were told those promptings were evil. We should fast and pray those feelings away! We were to pray more, for love, understanding and the courage to be happy in our "blinded bliss"!

As I gradually dismissed each demeaning dogma of my old religion, I embraced more genuine love for myself and others. Every day since, I have found more divine happiness than I ever dreamed possible! With my awakening I am better able to deal with the sorrows and trials of this life as well. I know I am out of the hell I'd chosen to experience. And I will carry those life lessons with me in my eternal progress.

CHAPTER 49

What Happened Next
2002–2013

I wish I could say the next several years of my life went smoothly. Though I was happier and more content in many ways, my soul knew I had a few more arduous years before the calm.

A few dates with a few guys for a few months, and then I reluctantly had a steady. Happy was a gentle, round-faced, professional dancer. We started dancing (or tried to) a few times in November. By January we found ourselves, as well as others, considering us "partners."

I always loved dancing. The Allred Group stomps were the highlight of my life. So when I started dancing twice a week in the summer of 2002, it became my sanity. In line dancing, I could add my own spins, twists, and turns. Besides, I'd never been very good at following anyone's lead. But once Happy taught me several partner dances, I wanted to dance more and more.

Unfortunately, the time I spent dancing with him, as well as teaching and being with my family and friends didn't entirely squelch my feelings for Mark. On January 6, 2003, I wrote in my journal: "I've been having a tough time the last five or six days. I keep thinking of Mark. I miss him and wish we could have made things work. I dreamed of him twice in the past few days. The energy between us was warm and fuzzy." But as always, one has to give up on wishes that aren't meant to be.

In the spring I took my son Keith, who was nearly sixteen, and moved into a tiny, two-bedroom apartment in Draper, leaving our big, finally finished house fully occupied with eighteen-year-old Anne, our oldest son Jake, his two children, and several of our kids' friends. Mark moved back in as well.

Sure enough, Norma received another "vision" to spiritually nullify her marriage to Jared. According to him, her spirit guide told her she'd been married to her "teacher" long enough. Now it was her turn to be *his* teacher. In Jared's eyes, Norma was a true saint and goddess, because no matter how devastated she said she was to have to leave him, she had the courage to honor her convictions. He claimed she would take upon herself a "cloak" of celibacy, and moved forward without him.

To afford my apartment, I returned my leased car and started driving an ancient Toyota Tercell. It had no heat, no air conditioning, and no working windows. It was a rusty dull gray, just like a tin can. I thought I'd gone so far backwards in life, I cried for nearly three days. But as I put my things away and made the small apartment a home for Keith and me, I rejoiced in my quiet serenity.

From there, Mark and I had a semi-cordial relationship, unless his do-good friends egged him on again. In another one of those bizarre moods of his, he swore he'd never give me "one single penny of alimony." He'd quit work and sue me for support if he had to.

I said, "You don't have to worry, Mark. I don't want one single penny from you ever again. You know I've already been and will continue to be fair with you, no matter how you treat me."

In July 2003, right before our legal divorce was final, an old friend asked me to stay with her in California so I could meet her brother, Bart. After a few long visits at their parents' home where he was living again, and after a dancing date, Bart and I decided we wanted to see each other again.

Happy was a good man with good intentions. He cared deeply for me, but I always felt like his consolation prize rather than the number-ten gals he was always checking out, and the one he still seemed to be waiting for. He was also embarrassed by my newfound joy for life—what I called my wild natural highs. He didn't want me to discuss my polygamous past with him or his friends either. With those issues and his lack of interest in my family and grandchildren, our Friday dance dates and sleepovers came to an end after eight months.

In September, Mark and I drove to the Salt Lake County courthouse to see our appointed judge. He asked if we were in agreement with me in a tiny apartment and him in the huge house, and within a few minutes he proclaimed our thirty-three-and-a-half-year legal marriage was over.

Mark and I couldn't speak most of the way home for fear we might break down. In so many ways, it seemed like such an unnecessary divorce. The only thing he said was, "Two people who love each other as much as we do should have been able to make it through hell and all the way back."

All I could say was "It's obvious *our* love was not enough."

❧

Bart rolled out the red carpet. We talked a million hours on the phone. He drove all night to surprise me. We spent the night and the next morning together before he drove all the way back to the Bay Area to get to work in time. In October he surprised me with a five-day trip to Hawaii, after we'd already spent a few days and nights at the luxurious Benbo Inn, in Northern California. He lavished me with love, laughter, and gifts.

In a few months, he quit his steady job as a butcher, filed for unemployment, and moved to Utah. Though I never wanted to marry again, we married in January so he could have the medical insurance he needed. We had a quiet, simple wedding. The only two guests were my sisters, Amy and Jolie, who served as our witnesses.

About three weeks later, Bart's other personality revealed its ugliness. One night he turned his back to me and refused to talk. When I asked, "What's wrong? Please talk to me," one too many times, Bart exploded. He leaned his large, intimidating body over me and yelled, "Don't ask me what's wrong ever again!" He snatched the comforter off the bed and slammed himself down on my old couch, where he brooded and seethed for five days and nights.

I knew Bart's anger was conjured—I'd done nothing to justify his behavior. My brother and I had been laughing on the phone about the cute things our grandchildren say and do. A whole week later, Bart finally confessed that he'd determined an old boyfriend was on the other end of the line.

Nearly a month later, Bart went on another tangent. I went bonkers. My anger wasn't directed at him as much as it was at me. I despised myself for being with him. I should have known better! Outside of my apartment I sprinted, walked, and then jogged in a four-hour reckless craze. In another temporary state of insanity, I didn't give a rat's ass if a madman hauled me off to the desert and killed me. *I must truly be a despicable, worthless piece of cow dung to have fallen into another abusive situation, I thought. How stupid could I be? Where did I go wrong? I must have been completely blind to my soul's warning signs.*

At some point, after several unrestrained break-away hours, I stopped in the middle of a parking lot and called Mark. I screamed out my sorrows—about his betrayal and disloyalty to Diane and me, and to our children; about his absence in our lives and his choices to keep Norma in his life at our expense; about his neglect of the bills, child support, and house payments; about his, Jared's, and Norma's ongoing lies to Diane and our children. All of my purging gave me the strength to turn around and face life; and I didn't hear Mark say one word.

My legs could barely move. I had no idea why I married Bart. The only assurance I had from my soul that day, on my humble, four-hour journey back, was my relationship with him was also part of my soul's plan of progression—it was meant to be. I knew my marriage wouldn't last long, but I was to give it my very best, and I'd know exactly when I was through.

Those were the first of Bart's relentless bipolar behaviors. While in his manic highs, he treated me and others well. In his once-a-month-or-more depressive lows, he'd conjure up something I'd supposedly done or not done, and then spend the next four to seven days treating me like refuse.

Sure enough, as more time passed, I was slowly but surely taking back my power. Bart delighted in his irrational outbursts and long bouts of passive-aggressive cruelty; the ones he used to make me cry or fight with him. He was so miserable that he insisted I should be also. The stronger I got, the worse he behaved. His idiotic, drunken attempts to seduce women, his attempt to kill both of us while driving in a winter storm, his constant delusions of injustices, and his complete refusal to take responsibility for his outlandish behaviors—all in all, I was becoming even more calm and secure. His self-destruct modes could no longer bring me down, and he couldn't manipulate me into joining his battlefield. I refused to let him guilt me into not dancing anymore, or into neglecting my friends and family to hold his hand while he took pleasure in his never-ending bouts of depression.

From the beginning to the end, I separated myself from Bart at least six times. In August 2006, two and a half years after we were married, I moved away from him for the last time.

In the evenings after teaching school all day, or on weekends, I'd hang out with friends or family until I wanted or needed to go home. In my small office/bedroom space at the other end of the house, I'd write, read, plan lessons, and create. The powerful energy in my quiet cave was exhilarating. My mind and soul were reconciling. My insatiable need to be heard, believed, right, adored, and to help or fix him or others was coming to a close. The war within me was ending. Once again, I was honoring and loving Kristyn. Tranquility began to replace the tornados in my life, and self-respect started to fill the empty places in my heart.

I'd been teaching for two years at Rosamond Elementary and still wasn't sure of our lunch cooks' names. A few months after school started again, a loud voice (my soul) clearly told me I needed to "get to know Jody this year." In the early morning, I started taking time to have coffee and visit with her team in the kitchen, before I went to my classroom. In January 2007, she said she'd like me to meet her dad. I stretched my arms straight out in front of me, crossed my two index fingers in an X, and exclaimed, "No way! I don't ever want or need another man in my life. But thank you anyway."

Jody wouldn't take no for an answer. For five months she tried to persuade me. I later learned she was working on her dad as well. "All I'm asking you to do is have coffee together," she said to me. "You don't have to get married!" One night my soul adamantly told me twice, "You need to meet this man."

One morning when her dad called her, Jody asked him to deliver her Mother's Day card to her at school at the same time she knew I'd be there. When I stepped into the kitchen, I watched and waited. Soon, Jody interrupted her father to introduce us. LeRoy gently shook my hand, smiled, said, "Nice to meet you," and then went right back to his conversation with his daughter. I witnessed his uncensored verbosity about a frustrating family situation back in Illinois, where he'd just been. All of us gabbed some more about life and such and then I excused myself and went to work.

LeRoy's long, gray beard and mustache covered all of his face but his deep blue eyes and bald forehead. Other than his beard and mustache reminding me a little too much of my ex-husband's, I felt comfortable around him—especially with his complete lack of trying to impress me.

At lunchtime, Jody asked if her dad could call me. "Sure," I told her. "I will have *coffee* with him after my divorce is final. He seems like a down-to-earth, genuine man."

Near the end of May, Bart's contract as a bus driver for Jordan School District finally ended. He piled most of his things in his car and drove back to California, never to be seen again. I exuberantly rushed home, anticipating the lack of his presence. I opened all the curtains and windows he'd kept closed. The sun glistened through my crystals, transforming the darkness into a zillion multifaceted rainbows shimmering across the rooms. I barred the negative energy still hovering around, which would soon be cleared. My new life had already beckoned me thus far. Gratitude permeated my whole being. In those awakening moments, I knew what I'd deemed a totally senseless marriage had in fact been a favorable one. In two and a half years, I'd dropped three times Bart's and Mark's weight in baggage, and gained three times their weight in wisdom, love, and confidence.

The timing in our lives was perfect. The papers were mailed. I'd been a single woman for a whole week before I knew it. LeRoy and I talked on the phone for hours on end. More than anything, I appreciated he was his own person. He had a life without me! He didn't need or want me to quit living my life to keep him company or to take care of him. He'd been alone for three and a half years, since his wife of twenty-seven years had passed away. LeRoy was already a secure, very busy, stable man.

It took us nearly two full months to get together. We finally went on our first date at Wheeler Farm, where he exhibited his 1981 Firebird at the car show. We talked while we checked out hundreds of antique beauties. Then he asked me to dinner. A couple weeks later, between our busy lives, we went to a movie and then on another date. Before long, I didn't want to go home or let him go home. I was with the most amazing man on earth.

Talk about divine direction in our lives! Once LeRoy and I made time for our first date, we became nearly inseparable. Amid our developing, non-giddy love, I had both feet planted firmly on the ground.

The whole time Bart and I lived in Sandy, the house payments and utility bills were my responsibility. It turned out he had maxed out several credit cards to pay for the "red carpet." He was in debt up the yin-yang. With my wonderful boys', nephews', their friends', and LeRoy's help, we revamped the whole yard and house, and by selling it I made enough money to pay Bart off, give the boys some for helping and to carry me through the next year.

Jordan School District granted me a year's leave of absence to write my book. Before LeRoy, my plans were to rent a two-bedroom apartment and write. However, he offered me a bedroom in his home in Riverton. I could stay or leave at will.

Between our travels, families, and each other, he forever encouraged me to "hold still and write." I procrastinated with one excuse after another. How could I possibly write fifty years of life into one book? Which stories would be the most important, and which would have to be left out?

I was nearly two-thirds of the way through writing the rough draft of my book by April, 2008, when Texas authorities took the children from the FYZ ranch, to San Angelo. I was sick at heart and yet full of hope. My sweetheart man bought me a ticket to fly out there to find my sixty-eight-year-old sister Lucinda. Our family hadn't heard from her in over six years. We didn't know if she was even alive after he expelled her husband and requisitioned her to Texas to be a "House Mother" to those children he'd stolen from supposed unworthy mothers.

In February 2004, her prophet, Warren Jeffs, married her to Alan Woodruff Steed. By November, he'd re-assigned her to Merril Jessop, her daughter's new husband and the ex-husband of Carolyn Jessop, author of *Escape*. I hoped she'd dare talk to me away from his influence and while away from the YFZ compound.

I never did find Lucinda; in fact, I never saw her again. One evening in 2011, a cousin called to tell me she'd passed away.

The events filling those two weeks I spent in Texas and on the FYZ compound could have filled four or five chapters alone. As my amazing hostess and I sat in front of the San Angelo Coliseum and watched the FYZ children playing, I felt heartsick for them. How many times had they already been torn from their biological parents and "assigned" to other "worthy" parents? Warren Jeffs took delight in his manipulative, completely uncensored power to ruin lives and tear families apart. Many FLDS children had been shuffled from one parent to another several times already—not knowing for sure who their "real" mothers were. For many, this was another of those disruptions. Many believed, if those 401 children were sent back to the same horrendous system they'd been rescued from, they'd continue to be bartered, swapped, raped and abused. What little was left of their lives would be stolen, just as their parents had been trained to do by way of Warren's immoral, brainwashing sermons, and his elicit examples.

When the Division of Family Services was ordered to return the children to their parents, I wept for days. In foster care, life surely had been tough for some. But in most situations, the children were adjusting in the homes of normal families who genuinely cared about their welfare and stability. Even with initial strangers the children could have had at least an eighty-five percent less chance of being abused than in living with their polygamist parents, who as faithful followers, would (and still do) carry out any of Warren's blasphemous and perverted commands.

By the end of 2007, *Fifty Years in Polygamy* was pretty much scratched out, all but the last few chapters. Those were tough to write. By then, my desire to give the world and everyone else a piece of my mind had totally faded. I didn't want to hurt others with what I wrote, especially Diane, her children, and my children. But I also knew I had to speak my truth, while realizing others had their own perspectives. Then I turned my book over to the universe. If it was meant to be published, it would be. If not, that would be okay as well.

Mark and Norma are still together. Other than her ongoing battle with cancer, they seem quite content. I'm grateful Mark kept his promise to work things out with Diane "the right way." Though she is no longer his wife; she remains good friends with him and Norma.

I believe even though we don't always understand our circumstances, things most often happen as they are meant to be. I wrote a letter to Norma telling her I'd forgiven her for the control she had in my family's life. I asked her to forgive me for the resentment and anger I felt toward her, which only held me back anyway. These past seven years, I've been so grateful for her strong influence in Mark's life back then. It served to speed up our ending process; giving LeRoy and I more years together than we may have had otherwise.

I used to say, "The year I met LeRoy was the happiest year of my life," but that happiest year turned into another one and then more. Each year I'm with him is yet another of the happiest years in my life.

In November 2008, we bought a modest home on just over an acre of land in southern Utah, near Zion National Park. On weekends and vacation times, we painted and replaced the flooring. We bought our own furniture, including the first brand-new bed I've ever owned. After teaching my last year in Riverton, I rushed south to my sweetheart and our paradise, where we are surrounded by trees and love.

Here, I talk to my plants, the wildflowers, dragonflies, snakes, squirrels, lizards, and cottontail rabbits.

I was honored and grateful to be hired by Washington County School District. There were hundreds of applicants and a handful of teaching positions available.

In October 2010, when Linda Prince (the woman who encouraged me to get my book ready to be published) asked if she could read my book, I felt compelled to rewrite my life's stories without my former agenda. When I read what I'd written three years previous, it seemed like I was reading about another person's life.

Between teaching and family, I spent the next year in our sunroom, writing and rewriting. I'd give up, and then push forward some more. In May of 2012, I published portions of some of my stories, and nearly half of the rest of them. And just over one year later, my unabridged version of *Fifty Years in Polygamy* is hopefully in thousands of hands across the world as well as yours.

Afterword

Between our glorious and self-imposed busy lives, my husband LeRoy and I have read nearly every autobiography and book written about polygamy. We have tremendous admiration for people who were able to awaken and move forward. LeRoy and I continue to volunteer whenever and wherever we can to help people who are leaving polygamy and trying to repair their lives.

I resigned from teaching in May 2012, after twenty-eight-plus years in the Allred Group's private school, in Head Start, and in the public school system. My plan was to speak about my life in polygamy and advocate for those who were leaving. However, while publicizing my first book and speaking with media sources and a variety of audiences, as well as with hundreds of individuals, I learned of even more horrific experiences with polygamy. Armed with that information, I began doing more research about polygamy. With my dysfunctional past and the pasts of hundreds of former polygamists, and with human rights violations against thousands of women and children of polygamy, I became appalled that a few public families are pushing for polygamy to be decriminalized. While these families are anomalies, they'd have us believe they represent normal, average polygamous families, and that there is nothing morally or legally wrong with polygamy.

Before long, I found myself as an activist, promoting the extinction of generational patriarchal abuses. My book sales became second to the importance of getting these messages out. I resigned as president of the HOPE organization so I could have more time. Then, I founded the Sound Choices Coalition, a partnership of organizations and individuals uniting in an effort to end human-rights violations due to polygamy and other forms of patriarchal abuse.

After a magazine article I wrote about being and having a "sister-wife," I was invited to be a co-producer with RIVR Media. We are working toward a project we hope A&E will debut sometime next year.

In hopes the producers of *Sister Wives* would show the other side of patriarchal polygamy, not just the pro-polygamy attitudes of the Brown family, (who belong to the same Apostolic United Brethren) three other ex-polygamists and I participated in a filmed panel discussion at the University of Las Vegas in May 2013. What a trip! I hadn't seen Christine, Kody's third "wife," my second cousin and niece, in person in about fifteen years. Her smiles, nervous giggles, and dedication to plural marriage reminded me of when I tenaciously clung to the encoding of too many years; and just like her, believed it was all about choice. But then again, maybe I'd have been tempted to stay if we'd have had a lot of media money to travel, go on luxury dates, build new homes and buy furniture . . .

More recently, I'm hosting my own Internet radio talk show called *Polygamy Uncensored*, where most of my guests have polygamist backgrounds and are brave enough to inform the world about what polygamy is really about.

There are two sides to the stories you hear about polygamy. There are stories from those who live inside of the fence, and stories from those who have lived on both sides. Of course, when we lived and believed in polygamy, there was no way you'd have heard us speak the truth. First of all, we had no idea what the truth was. For heaven's sakes, anyone who is brainwashed certainly doesn't know it. Secondly, you definitely don't dare wake up and listen to your soul. (They call it the devil's temptations.) That could mean losing everything, everyone, and all you've ever known. Like those now living polygamy, we also had to preserve our beliefs, our families, and our clan at all costs, even if that meant throwing certain children, teens, and wayward people under the bus with lies, cover-ups, and feigned ignorance. More often than not, it meant having to keep your blinders on, deny, justify, and lie to yourself and others so you could "endure to the end" as you had been programmed and commanded to do. From ex-polygamous voices we hear numerous firsthand accounts of abuse, heartache, control, prejudice, suicidal depression and further explicit information.

Members of the AUB clan who are granted the gift of the temple ordinances are required to wear long, old-fashioned garments like my parents wore. They are not to be taken off during sex or for any other reason other than to bathe. In another part of the same ritual, valiant adherents agree to slit their throats or disembowel themselves if they divulge anything done or said during the long ceremony. I've always wondered, what in God's name is so darn secretive, He'd order His children kill themselves for?

Elite women and men in the AUB Group get to attend separate classes where they are taught more "special" rules and laws. They are told it is wrong to enjoy sex; it is for procreation only, and men are to "get it done—don't linger." No wonder many women say they felt raped by their polygamist husbands.

In addition to those "superb values," a woman who can't become impregnated by her husband has the right to have a brother-in-law do the deed. If that doesn't take after a few liaisons, she may ask a council member for his seed.

There's a constant desire and drive for Fundamentalists to draw closer to likeminded people by isolating themselves, and their children from the "outside world," where they believe God will safeguard their righteous little spots on earth while He destroys the rest of us. Many children of polygamy live in constant fear of the never-ending doomsday prophecies they hear—of the earth being destroyed, and of God killing their wicked mothers, sisters, and brothers who have apostatized. Most Fundamentalist's attitudes and beliefs are still racist and bigoted when it comes to blacks and same-sex partnerships; yet many use the plight of these groups to promote their own so-called religious freedom.

More simple directives are not to have dogs in the house. They can bring an evil spirit into the home. Women are still being told not to cut or color their hair, pierce their ears, or wear earrings and makeup. Such activities are deemed sources of pride and vanity, and they must be expelled.

The Pinesdale Montana Township is also a monopoly unto itself. It is run by AUB adherents to Fundamental Mormonism, polygamy, and the rule "God's laws supersede the laws of the land." Several ex-members of that group have confided, (as in Adam's case), that innumerable crimes and abuses have been and are being concealed or ignored to protect devout followers and their families.

I've tried very hard not to be known as an anti-polygamist. I can honestly say I'm not. Many of the people I personally know who are still "in" are precious, misguided, dear hearts. Since I have experienced the inner workings of polygamy, I'm familiar with the spiritual blackmail that is utilized to control and to create the miserable happiness that accompanies the righteous endeavors of those who really believe. Sadly, I also recognize the fear and resentment toward those of us who have left and dare speak out—as we are considered the "devil's advocates" and "sons (or daughters) of perdition."

This past year, I've done a great deal of research on the supposed pros of polygamy, as well as the cons. Hundreds of thousands of people admire Canada (one of the most liberal countries in the world) for not just adding polygamous marriages into the freedoms granted to same-sex partners, and for taking on the huge responsibility of extensive research about polygamy across the world. After the Supreme Court in British Columbia listened to the testimonies for and against polygamy, they realized polygamy doesn't begin to correlate with sexual freedom and same-sex marriages. After exhaustive investigations by the court, Chief Justice Baumann stated, "Based on the most comprehensive judicial record on the subject ever produced, I have concluded that the Attorney General and their allied Interested Persons have demonstrated a very strong basis for a reasoned apprehension of harm to many in our society inherent in the practice of polygamy as I have defined it in these reasons (http://stoppolygamyincanada.wordpress.com/court-documents/decision-polygamy-harms-are-endemic-polygamy-remains-illegal/).

According to Merriam Webster, the word *patriarchy* means "a social organization marked by the supremacy of the father in the clan or family, the legal dependence of wives and children, and the reckoning of descent and inheritance in the male line; *broadly*: control by men of a disproportionately large share of power." With Webster's definition of patriarchy, you can realize polygamy in itself is a human-rights violation. How can polygamy be based on equality when it is completely patriarchal?

Polygamist parents teach their children it isn't the gospel of plural marriage that's wrong or evil; it is evil people who make it look wrong. Yet in simple terms, polygamy is a human-rights violation. It is demeaning and suppressive. It demands that women sacrifice, ignore, and bury their desires, feelings, jealousies, and heartaches, and submit to their husbands, who will determine if they're worthy enough to help populate his world. It requires women to produce numerous children, whether they or their husbands have the capacity to adequately provide for those children's emotional, physical, and spiritual needs.

In short, to allow or decriminalize polygamy is to justify psychological torture and modern-day slavery.

Imagine all the people living in total peace...*it's easy if you try...*
Impart enough love to surrender equality for everyone under the sky...

"I no longer hold to any religion or ideology where belief systems require and assume that our highest aspirations—happiness, fulfillment and liberations lie in the future, and therefore justify present enslavement, dominance, suppression and suffering."

Eckhart Tolle

Namaste —

I honor the place in you in which the entire universe dwells. I honor the place in you that is of love, of truth, of light and of peace. When you are in that place in you, and I am in that place in me, we are one.

About the Author

With five kids still at home, Kristyn Decker began taking college courses and working as an assistant teacher in the Head Start program. After earning an associate's degree, she was a lead teacher for four years. Then Kristyn taught child development classes for Children First and volunteered with several projects relating to quality Child Care. In 2002, she received a bachelor's degree in elementary education and early childhood development from Southern Utah University. She ended her nearly thirty-three-year marriage in 2002. Seven years later, Kristyn married LeRoy Decker. She founded the Sound Choices Coalition in June 2012 after publishing her first book, *Fifty Years in Polygamy: Big Secrets and Little White Lies.* Kristyn spends most of her days volunteering with the Sound Choices Coalition and other organizations, in her quest to end human-rights violations due to polygamy and other forms of patriarchal abuse.

Since the publication of her first book, Kristyn has been a guest on many television and radio shows and stations across the country, including but not limited to *The Today Show; CNN Weekend News;* Good Morning, Arizona; NPR Community Voices; Jay Lawrence;

The Fawn Rigan Show (WCCO Minneapolis); KTAR Talk Radio; and KSL AM News. Kristyn also enjoys speaking at book clubs, churches, and libraries.

To learn more about Kristyn and her books, please visit www.kristyndecker.com. She loves to hear from her readers and may be contacted at kristyndeckerbooks@gmail.com.

For information about the Sound Choices Coalition, visit http://sound-choices.com or email Kristyn at soundchoicescoalition@gmail.com. Listen to her radio show, *Polygamy Uncensored*, each Wednesday at 10:00 AM Mountain Standard Time at www.blogtalkradio.com. Archived shows are available at: www.kristyn.srbroadcasting.com.